Pluralism and the Pragmatic Turn

Pluralism and the Pragmatic Turn

The Transformation of Critical Theory

Essays in honor of Thomas McCarthy

edited by William Rehg and James Bohman

The MIT Press   Cambridge, Massachusetts   London, England

This book was set in New Baskerville by Northeastern Graphic Services, Inc. and printed and bound in the United States of America.

Library of Congress Cataloging-in-Publication Data

Pluralism and the pragmatic turn : the transformation of critical theory : essays in honor of Thomas McCarthy / edited by William Rehg and James Bohman.
    p.   cm.
Includes bibliographical references and index.
  ISBN 0-262-18216-5 (HC : alk. paper) — ISBN 0-262-68132-3 (PB : alk. paper)
  1. McCarthy, Thomas A. 2. Frankfurt school of sociology. 3. Critical theory.
4. Pluralism (Social sciences) 5. Pragmatism. I. McCarthy, Thomas A. II. Rehg, William. III. Bohman, James.
HM467 .P58 2001
301—dc21
                                 2001018686

Contents

Acknowledgments

The editors gratefully acknowledge permission to reprint the following essays in this book:

"Critical Theory Today: An Interview with Thomas McCarthy," conducted by Shane O'Neill and Nick Smith, *Imprints* 2/1 (1997): 3–18.

Richard Rorty, "The Ambiguity of 'Rationality,'" *Constellations* 3 (1996): 73–82.

Introduction

A wide range of current theoretical approaches might plausibly claim the title of "critical social theory": not only Marxist analysis and its offshoots but also certain strands of poststructuralism, feminist thought, and liberal and communitarian political theory, to name the most obvious. The essays in this festschrift volume dedicated to Thomas McCarthy are all related in some way to the style of critical theory stemming from the Frankfurt School. The Institute of Social Research in Frankfurt was originally founded in 1924 with the goal of developing a new theoretical basis for emancipatory social theories such as Marxist historical materialism. Moreover, the project was an interdisciplinary one: the research program sketched by Max Horkheimer in his 1931 Inaugural Address was committed to an interdisciplinary approach that would involve philosophy, the human sciences, and economics.[1] The postwar reformulation of this program at the hands of Karl-Otto Apel, Jürgen Habermas, and others issued in a transformed critical theory—one more indebted to Kant and American pragmatism than to Marx, open to the entire range of humanistic social sciences, and increasingly attuned to the challenges of social complexity and cultural pluralism.[2] The title of this anthology reflects this transformation, to which Thomas McCarthy has been a major contributor.

As a critical theorist, as a translator of Habermas, and as general editor of the MIT Press Studies in Contemporary German Social Thought, Thomas McCarthy has played a key role in the transformation and dissemination of the new Frankfurt School tradition.[3] As translator and editor, he has perhaps done more than any other American scholar to introduce English-speaking audiences to German critical theory. As an original thinker in his own right, he has furthered the pragmatic approach to critical theory and the engagement with social pluralism. Indeed, in his work in social and political theory McCarthy has returned again and again to the themes of American pragmatism, insisting not only on the practical significance of rationality but also on plurality and unity in both methodology and politics. In his dialogues with postmodernists such as Derrida and Foucault and analytic and post-analytic philosophers such as John Rawls and Richard Rorty; in his critical appropriation of ethnomethodology, genealogies of impure reason, and interpretive social science; in his engagements with post-colonialist, feminist and critical race theory, Thomas McCarthy has always sought to expand the practical and theoretical basis of critical theory.[4] Thus an anthology organized around these themes provides an appropriate tribute.

The contributors to the anthology—comprising both colleagues and students of McCarthy—are only a sampling of those indebted to his generosity as interlocutor and mentor. Their essays fall into three broad categories, and we have arranged the book accordingly: part I includes essays dealing with social theory and the rational basis of communication, part II contains papers examining conceptions of the self, and the essays in part III focus above all on political theory. The reader should note at the outset that just as "critical theory" is understood in a broad sense, the "pragmatic turn" has a wider extension than American pragmatism. In their various interpretations of this turn and its implications, the contributors draw not only on authors such as Dewey and Mead but also on analytic pragmatists such as Robert Brandom, liberal-democratic theorists such as John Rawls, and various empirical approaches in the human sciences that reflect an emphasis on social practices and interaction. Given such variety, it should come as no surprise that the contributors do not always agree upon either the exact character of the pragmatic turn or even its importance for critical theory.

A number of the essays in the first part deal with more basic issues raised by the pragmatic turn in critical social theory. In his attempt to render critical theory more pragmatic, McCarthy has devoted his attention in particular to the idealizations that theorists such as Habermas and Apel have used to explicate the rational basis of social communication and discourse. Hoping to avoid both the excesses of Kantian idealism as well as the various skeptical and relativist alternatives, McCarthy has argued along the lines of George Herbert Mead and Harold Garfinkel for a more pragmatic interpretation of the "ideas of reason" than we find with Habermas.[5] Thus Habermas's contribution provides an apt starting point: a clarification of his own understanding of communicative idealizations as a detranscendentalized version of Kantian ideas. To this end, Habermas provides a genealogical account of the links joining the older Kantian motifs to four pragmatic presuppositions of communicative action: a common objective world, the accountability of subjects, the unconditional validity of truth and rightness claims, and the implicit orientation to discursive justification. The chapter that follows by Richard Rorty sets, as it were, the other end of the spectrum. In Rorty's view, McCarthy has awkwardly stopped halfway in executing the pragmatic turn: a "fully pragmatic view" dispenses altogether with context-transcending ideas of truth, objectivity, and universal agreement. All the complete pragmatist needs, rather, are the concrete moral values of a liberal democracy.

The essay by Kenneth Baynes defends a consensualist conception of rationality that lies close to Habermas's view. Extending Christine Korsgaard's analysis of the normativity of reasons, Baynes argues that anyone who acts "for a reason" is tacitly committed to the discourse principle, namely the principle that an action is justified only if it could be rationally agreed to by those who are affected. He goes on to argue that the capacity to act for reasons constitutes the substantive moral idea behind both Habermas's and Rawls's conceptions of public reason and toleration. In contrast to Baynes's contribution, the essays by James Bohman and William Rehg attempt to move somewhat further than McCarthy along the pragmatic spectrum while retaining his insistence on the normative categories needed for social criticism. Rejecting the last overly cognitivist residue in McCarthy's understanding of political discourse, Bohman argues that under conditions of social and theoretical pluralism, critical theorists should see their goal primarily in practical terms, namely to stimulate dialogue with and among citizens about the appropriate conditions for social cooperation. Critical theory does this by making explicit and extending the practical knowledge implicit in reflective participants' capacities for perspective taking. By informing examples of social scientific explanations, such knowledge becomes critical when it is able to cross between and employ various perspectives at the same time. Rehg picks up on McCarthy's appropriation of ethnomethodology and attempts to push it a step further by confronting the more radical contextualist implications of ethnomethodology. Focusing on the "ideas of reason" in contexts of scientific argumentation, Rehg maintains that a more contextualist understanding of such ideas need not lead to relativism or positivism, but rather can inform a more effective social critique of epistemic practices.

The final two selections in Part One address topics in critical social theory. Barbara Fultner deals with a fundamental issue, the relation between social theory and the philosophy of language. Insofar as social theories consider meaningful interaction as the keystone of social order, they must rely on a theory of meaning and, especially after the linguistic turn, a philosophy of language. But, contrary to the standard view, Fultner argues that the dependence must now be bidirectional: after the pragmatic turn, philosophers of language cannot link language with social practice without tacitly referring to a complementary social theory. Although more specific than Fultner's, Joseph Heath's target lies at the core of the prewar critical theory of Horkheimer and Marcuse: the "new" concept of ideology as an explanation for the reproduction of oppressive practices. This concept has the disadvantage of treating the critical theorist's addressees as irrational. To remedy this problem, Heath proposes in lieu of ideology some specific social mechanisms—for example, the forms of everyday trust described by ethnomethodologists—that lead to the reproduction of oppressive practices precisely because agents are rational.

Joel Anderson's contribution critically examines the kind of reflective autonomy required of participants in moral discourse; thus his essay provides a suitable transition into the second group of essays. Specifically, Anderson focuses on the idealization that participants should enjoy "need-interpretive competence." He argues that this particular idealization is so improbably strong as to engender a trilemma for Habermas: he must either relax the level of mutual intelligibility it assumes, limit the scope of consensus to people sharing an evaluative language, or relax the competence requirement itself. In the spirit of McCarthy's pragmatic approach to discursive idealizations, Anderson shows how a more pragmatic, contextualized interpretation of such competence renders the third horn benign. The remaining two essays in part II address problems in the pragmatic conception of the self. Such conceptions typically emphasize the intersubjective constitution of personal identity.[6] Johanna Meehan argues that Habermas's pragmatic account does not sufficiently attend to the constitution of *gendered* identity. To help remedy this deficit, she sketches an empirically informed, pragmatic model of gendered identity-formation that accounts for the embodied, psychic, and culturally mediated sense of self. Joel Whitebook, on the other hand, expresses general reservations regarding the "paradigm shift" in critical theory to an intersubjectivist framework, which in his view has lost sight of important truths contained in more pessimistic, conflict-oriented conceptions of the person, such as those of Hobbes and Freud. Because Axel Honneth's reading of Hegel and Mead represents one of the most developed attempts to integrate aspects of the pessimistic view into an intersubjectivist program, Whitebook closely criticizes Honneth's analysis in an effort to undermine a central category of all pragmatic conceptions of the self from Dewey and Mead onward, their shared emphasis on intersubjectivity over subjectivity.[7]

Finally, part III consists of those essays that treat issues in political theory—in particular, the various problems stemming from sociocultural pluralism. McCarthy has dedicated considerable effort to this area, grappling in particular with the problems connected with multiculturalism and globalization.[8] Thus in his efforts to further pragmatize Habermas's discourse theory, McCarthy has argued for a conception of political discourse more attuned to the obstacles that the contemporary value pluralism poses for the ideal of rational consensus.[9] Georgia Warnke's essay extends this initiative by drawing on McCarthy's account of multifaceted political discourse and majority rule to strengthen an ethical-hermeneutical approach to current moral-political disputes (such as abortion) in which values and principles are interwoven and conflict. When moral disputes involve conflicting interpretations based in different worldviews, then majority rule should be understood, not as a resting point on the way to a counterfactually anticipated consensus, but as a means of provisional closure in an ongoing process in which citizens learn from one another's interpretations without necessarily agreeing on shared principles or a single right answer.

As the disputes over how to make ideas of reason serviceable for today's world show, critical theorists find the Kantian heritage, with its sharp dichotomies and strong idealizations, not only a resource for ideas but also a source of problems, which indicates its need for a transformation that nonetheless preserves its normative core. Taking up the troubled side of this relation, Axel Honneth's essay reminds us that Dewey's pragmatism led to a surprisingly sharp critique of Kant, given the historical circumstances of the twentieth century. Specifically, Honneth analyzes Dewey's thesis that twentieth-century German aggression was the result of a cultural mentality shaped more by Kant's dichotomous idealism than by a Nietzschean will to power. Andrew Buchwalter is also less than enthusiastic about the Kantian heritage, specifically as it appears in the work of John Rawls. Rawls's lasting achievement was to provide a more pragmatic rendition of Kant's idea of public reason, a version specifically designed to accommodate sociocultural pluralism.[10] Buchwalter argues that, appearances to the contrary, Hegel provides a more robust solution to the problems associated with pluralism than does Rawlsian neo-Kantianism.

The last two essays in part III tackle issues connected with globalization and international politics. Seyla Benhabib addresses a weakness in liberal democratic theory in the face of the new cosmopolitan dimensions of pluralism: its failure to conceive political membership in relation to the "stranger," that is, foreigners, immigrants, temporary workers, refugees, and the like. Arguing that an adequate conception must start with the "constitutive tension" between universal human rights and democratic self-determination, Benhabib attempts to avoid an overly permissive, "open borders" approach and a civic-republican overemphasis on the self-determination of a culturally distinctive people. David Rasmussen turns his attention to difficulties in Rawls's *Law of Peoples*.[11] Here Rawls attempts to extend his conception of public reason to the international sphere. Rasmussen examines the unresolved tensions that Rawls's move into the international arena engenders in his system. Specifically, Rawls develops a concept of toleration that is sufficiently broad to accommodate non-liberal peoples who lack a commitment to individual rights. In doing so, however, he surrenders any potential for criticism that can be motivated in terms of the very moral-political ideals that are central to liberal democracy.

We include in an appendix a 1997 interview with McCarthy, in which he discusses his own intellectual biography and assesses the state of critical theory today, as well as a bibliography of his own writings and translations. We believe that these essays, taken as a whole, provide a good overview of the current state of critical theory in the Frankfurt School tradition. As the diversity of approaches exhibited here shows, Frankfurt School critical theory after the pragmatic turn encompasses a much broader range of perspectives than it did in the days of Horkheimer and Adorno. But it has thereby become a much richer source of critical analysis that is at the same time socially and politically more effective. These essays intend to show the ways in which the work of Thomas McCarthy has not only contributed greatly to that enterprise, but has also inspired many others to do so as well. For that, the editors, contributors, and many others are extremely grateful.

Notes

1. Max Horkheimer, "The Present Situation of Social Philosophy and the Tasks of an Institute for Social Research," *Between Philosophy and Social Science*, trans. G. F. Hunter, M. S. Kramer, and J. Torpey (Cambridge: MIT Press, 1993), 1–14. On the history of the Frankfurt School, see Rolf Wiggerhaus, *The Frankfurt School*, trans. M. Robertson (Cambridge: MIT Press, 1994).

2. The engagement with American pragmatism is evident in Karl-Otto Apel, *Charles S. Peirce*, trans. J. M. Krois (Amherst: University of Massachusetts Press, 1981); *Towards a Transformation of Philosophy*, trans. G. Adey and D. Frisby (London: Routledge, 1980); Jürgen Habermas, *Toward a Rational Society*, trans. J. J. Shapiro (Boston: Beacon, 1970), chap. 5; *Knowledge and Human Interests*, trans. J. J. Shapiro (Boston: Beacon, 1971); *The Theory of Communicative Action*, 2 vols., trans. T. McCarthy (Boston: Beacon, 1984; 1987), chap. 5; "Peirce on Communication" and "Individuation through Socialization: On George Herbert Mead's Theory of Subjectivity," *Postmetaphysical Thinking*, trans. W. M. Hohengarten (Cambridge: MIT Press, 1992), 88–112

and 149–204, respectively. Habermas's interdisciplinary commitment is evident not only in *The Theory of Communicative Action* but also, for example, in his *On the Logic of the Social Sciences*, trans. S. W. Nicholsen (Cambridge: MIT Press, 1988). Habermas has also engaged with neo-Kantians such as John Rawls; see esp. his *Between Facts and Norms*, trans. W. Rehg (Cambridge: MIT Press, 1996), chap. 2; and the exchange with Rawls: Habermas, "Reconciliation through the Public Use of Reason: Remarks on John Rawls's Political Liberalism," *Journal of Philosophy* 92 (1995): 109–131, followed by Rawls's "Reply to Habermas," 132–180.

3. For a list of McCarthy's translations, see the bibliography in the appendix; significant early treatments of Habermas include his "A Theory of Communicative Competence," *Philosophy of the Social Sciences* 3 (1973): 135–156; and *The Critical Theory of Jürgen Habermas* (Cambridge: MIT Press, 1978).

4. Many of these broader themes appear in David Couzens Hoy and Thomas Mc-Carthy, *Critical Theory* (Oxford: Blackwell, 1994); Thomas McCarthy, *Ideals and Illusions* (Cambridge: MIT Press, 1991); for an example of his engagement with Rawls, see "Kantian Constructivism and Reconstructivism: Rawls and Habermas in Dialogue," *Ethics* 105 (1994): 44–63. We cite other relevant essays below.

5. See especially Hoy and McCarthy, *Critical Theory*, chaps. 2–3.

6. See Habermas, "Individualization through Socialization."

7. See Axel Honneth, *The Struggle for Recognition*, trans. J. Anderson (Cambridge: MIT Press, 1992).

8. See, e.g., Thomas McCarthy, "On the Idea of a Reasonable Law of Peoples," in *Perpetual Peace: Essays on Kant's Cosmopolitan Ideal*, ed. J. Bohman and M. Lutz-Bachmann (Cambridge: MIT Press, 1997), 201–218; see also his "On Reconciling Cosmopolitan Unity and National Diversity," *Public Culture* 11/1 (1999): 175–210.

9. See Thomas McCarthy, "Practical Discourse: On the Relation of Morality to Politics," *Ideals and Illusions*, 181–199; "Legitimacy and Diversity: Dialectical Reflections on Analytical Distinctions," in *Habermas on Law and Democracy: Critical Exchanges*, ed. M. Rosenfeld and A. Arato (Berkeley: University of California Press, 1998), 115–153.

10. John Rawls, *A Theory of Justice* (Cambridge: Harvard University Press, 1971); *Political Liberalism* (New York: Columbia University Press, 1993).

11. John Rawls, *The Law of Peoples* (Cambridge: Harvard University Press, 1999).

I

Reason and the Pragmatic Turn in Critical Social Theory

1

From Kant's "Ideas" of Pure Reason to the "Idealizing" Presuppositions of Communicative Action: Reflections on the Detranscendentalized "Use of Reason"

Jürgen Habermas

In his preface to *Ideals and Illusions,* Thomas McCarthy characterizes the two directions that critics of Kantian conceptions of reason have taken since Hegel: "on one side are those who, in the wakes of Nietzsche and Heidegger, attack Kantian conceptions of reason and the rational subject at their very roots; on the other side are those who, in the wakes of Hegel and Marx, recast them in sociohistorical molds."[1] Even in their desublimated pragmatic forms, the Kantian "ideas" retain their original dual role. They are used to guide critique and, at the same time, are exposed as the fertile ground of a transcendental illusion: ideals and illusions. McCarthy opposes not only an iconoclastic deconstructionism that throws out the baby with the bathwater, but also an overly normative reading of Kant that leaves the illusion of pure reason intact. Even after the pragmatic turn, he keeps both functions of reason in view: the norm-setting function that enables critique and the concealing function that calls for self-criticism: "If we take a pragmatic turn, we can appreciate both aspects of the social-practical ideas of reason: their irreplaceable function in cooperative interaction and their potential for misuse."[2]

Elsewhere, McCarthy speaks of the "social-practical *analogues* of Kant's ideas of reason."[3] He is referring specifically to three formal-pragmatic presuppositions of communicative action, namely, the common supposition of an objective world, the rationality that acting subjects mutually attribute to one another, and the unconditional validity they claim for their statements with speech acts. These presuppositions refer to one another and form aspects of a desubli-mated reason embodied in everyday communicative practice: "the idealizations of rational accountability and real world objectivity both figure in our idealized notion of truth, for objectivity is the other side of the intersubjective validity of certain types of truth claims."[4] Thus the transcendental tension between the ideal and the real, between the realm of the intelligible and the realm of appear-ances, enters into the social reality of situated interactions and insti-tutions. It is this transformation of "pure" into "situated" reason that McCarthy masterfully brings to bear against the critiques that liqui-date reason through its abstract negation, such as Foucault's objec-tivating analysis or Derrida's use of paradox. Yet he does so without ignoring the insights gained by deconstructing those illusions of rea-son that seep into the very capillaries of everyday discourses.

Both the historicist tradition from Dilthey to Heidegger and the pragmatist tradition from Peirce to Dewey (and, in a sense, Wittgen-stein), understand the task of "situating reason" as one of detranscen-dentalizing the knowing subject. The finite subject is to be situated "in the world" without entirely losing its "world-constituting" spontaneity. To that extent, the encounter between McCarthy and the followers of Heidegger, Dewey, and Wittgenstein is a domestic dispute over which side accomplishes the detranscendentalization in the right way: whether the traces of a transcending reason vanish in the sands of his-toricism and contextualism or whether a reason embodied in histori-cal contexts preserves the power for immanent transcendence.[5] If cooperating subjects intelligently cope with what they encounter in the world, do their learning processes empower them to make ration-ally motivated revisions in their pre-understanding of the world as a whole? Is reason simply at the mercy of the "world-disclosive" hap-pening of language, or is it also a "world-transforming" power?[6]

In the debate with the deconstructionists, at least the *question itself* is not under dispute. However, for the heirs of Hume—and thus for a large segment of analytic philosophy—the dialectic between world-disclosing language and innerworldly learning processes does not even pose a meaningful question. Unless one subscribes to Kant's idea of a "world-formative" reason and the conception of an under-standing that "constitutes" the objects of possible experience, there can be no grounds for detranscendentalizing the "consciousness" of knowing and acting subjects, let alone for a controversy regarding the problems that arise from such a corrective. McCarthy defends a pragmatic explication of the "situatedness of reason" against *deconstructionist* objections. I shall try to address the *lack of understanding* for the very *question* of the detranscendentalized use of reason.

I do not, however, wish to lobby directly for a formal-pragmatic theory of meaning and repeat the familiar arguments.[7] The difficulty in understanding lies not in the details but in the point of departure. Unless I am mistaken, the transformation of Kant's "ideas" of pure reason into "idealizing" presuppositions of communicative action raises difficulties especially for understanding the *factual* role of performatively presupposed *counterfactual* assumptions. For they are actually effective in structuring processes of mutual understanding and in organizing contexts of interaction: "This (move) has the effect of relocating the Kantian opposition between the real and the ideal *within* the domain of social practice. Cooperative interaction is seen to be structured around ideas of reason which are neither fully constitutive in the Platonic sense nor merely regulative in the Kantian sense. As *idealizing suppositions* we cannot avoid making while engaged in processes of mutual understanding, they are *actually effective* in ways that point beyond the limits of actual situations. As a result, social-practical ideas of reason are both 'immanent' and 'transcendent' to practices constitutive of forms of life."[8]

In accordance with formal pragmatics, the rational structure of action oriented toward reaching understanding is reflected in the presuppositions that actors *must* make if they are to engage in this practice at all. The necessity of this "must" has a Wittgensteinian rather than a Kantian sense. That is, it does not have the transcendental sense of universal, necessary, and noumenal [*intelligiblen*] conditions of possible experience, but has the grammatical sense of an "inevitability" stemming from the conceptual connections of a system of learned—but for us inescapable [*nicht hintergehbar*]—rule-governed behavior. After the pragmatic deflation of the Kantian approach, "transcendental analysis" means the search for presumably universal, but only de facto inescapable conditions that must be met for certain fundamental practices or achievements. All practices for which we cannot imagine functional equivalents in our sociocultural forms of life are "fundamental" in this sense. One natural language can be replaced by another. But propositionally differentiated language as such (as a "species endowment") has no imaginable replacement that could fulfill the same functions. I want to clarify this basic idea genealogically, by tracing it back to Kant.

For present purposes, I am not concerned with the systematic task of explicating the concept of "communicative reason,"[9] but with the genealogical examination of the context in which this conception originated. I shall focus on the idealizing performative presuppositions of communicative action: the shared presupposition of a world of independently existing objects, the reciprocal presupposition of rationality or "accountability," the unconditionality of context-transcending validity claims such as truth and moral rightness, and the demanding presuppositions of argumentation that force participants to decenter their own interpretive perspectives. I speak of "presuppositions" because these are conditions that must be fulfilled so that that which is conditioned can take on one of two values: acts of referring can neither succeed nor fail unless there is a referential system; participants in communication can neither understand nor misunderstand one another unless there is a presupposition of rationality; truth claims can be called into question in any given context only if the corresponding propositions that are "true" in one context cannot lose that property in another; finally, neither pro nor con arguments can have any weight unless there are communicative situations that can bring out the unforced force of the better argument. The respects in which these presuppositions have an "ideal" content shall occupy us shortly.

Certainly there is a family resemblance between these presuppositions and Kantian concepts. One may presume there is a genealogical connection between the following:

(1) the "cosmological idea" of the unity of the world (or the totality of conditions in the sensory world) and the pragmatic presupposition of a common objective world;

(2) the "idea of freedom" as a postulate of practical reason and the pragmatic presupposition of the rationality of accountable agents;

(3) the totalizing movement of reason that, as a "faculty of ideas," transcends all that is conditioned toward an unconditioned and the unconditionality of the validity claims raised in communicative action; and

(4) finally, reason as the "faculty of principles," which takes on the role of the highest court of appeal for all rights and claims, and rational discourse as the unavoidable forum of possible justification.

In what follows I lay out these four genealogical connections in sequence. To be sure, the ideas of pure reason cannot be translated seamlessly from the idiom of transcendental philosophy into that of formal pragmatics. Establishing "analogies" is not the end of the matter. In the course of their transformation, the sharp clarity of Kant's oppositions (constitutive vs. regulative, transcendental vs. empirical, immanent vs. transcendent, etc.) diminishes because detranscendentalization signifies a profoundly invasive intervention into his basic architectonic.

The common objective world
In addition to the idea of the unity of the thinking subject and the idea of God as the unitary origin of the conditions of all objects of thought, Kant includes the cosmological *idea of a unitary world* among the ideas of theoretical reason. In speaking of a "hypothetical" use of reason, Kant has in view the heuristic function of this idea for the progress of empirical research. The totalizing anticipation of the entirety of the objects of possible experience does not make cognition possible but rather guides it. Whereas empirical cognition is "the touchstone of truth," the cosmological idea plays the role of a methodological principle of completeness; it points to the goal of a systematic unity of all knowledge.[10] In contrast to the constitutive categories of the understanding and the forms of intuition, the "unity of the world" is a regulative idea.

Metaphysical thinking falls victim to the dialectical illusion of a hypostatized world order because it uses this regulative idea constitutively. The reifying use of theoretical reason confuses the constructive projection of a *focus imaginarius* for ongoing research with the constitution of an object that is accessible to experience. This "apodictic"—hence excessive—use of reason corresponds to the "transcendent" use of the categories of the understanding beyond the realm of possible experience. Transgressing this boundary results in an undue assimilation of the concept of the "world"—as the entirety of all objects that can be experienced—to the concept of an object writ large that represents the world as such. The differentiation between the world and the innerworldly that Kant defends must be preserved even if the transcendental subject loses its position outside time and space and is transformed into a multitude of subjects capable of speech and action.

Detranscendentalization leads, on the one hand, to the embedding of knowing subjects into the socializing context of a lifeworld and, on the other hand, to the entwinement of cognition with speech and action. The concept of the "world" is altered along with the theoretical architectonic. I first explain what I mean by the "formal-pragmatic presupposition of the world" (a), in order to draw attention to important consequences that follow from it, namely: the replacement of transcendental idealism by internal realism (b), the regulative function of the concept of truth (c), and the embeddedness of references [*Weltbezüge*] in contexts of the lifeworld (d).

(a) As subjects capable of speech and action, language-users must be able to "refer" [*sich beziehen*] "to something" in the objective world from within the horizon of their shared lifeworld if they are to reach an understanding "about something" in communicating with one another or if they are to succeed "with something" in their practical dealings. Whether in communicating about states of affairs or in practical dealings with people and things, subjects can refer to something only if they start—each on her own, yet in agreement with everyone else—with a pragmatic presupposition. They presuppose "the world" as the totality of independently existing objects that can be judged or dealt with. All objects about which it is possible to state facts can be "judged." But only spatio-temporally identifiable objects can be "dealt with" in the sense of being purposefully manipulated.

To say that the world is "objective" means that it is "given" to us as "the same for everyone." It is linguistic practice—especially the use of singular terms—that forces us to pragmatically presuppose such a world shared by all. The referential system built into natural languages ensures that any given speaker can formally anticipate possible objects of reference. Through this formal presupposition of the world, communication about something in the world is intertwined with practical interventions in the world. Speakers and actors reach an understanding about and intervene in one and the same objective world. To achieve secure semantic references, it is important that speakers are, as agents, in contact with the objects of everyday life and that they can put themselves in contact with them repeatedly.[11]

Like Kant's cosmological idea of reason, the conception of a presupposed world rests on the transcendental difference between the world and the innerworldly, which reappears in Heidegger as the ontological difference between "Being" and "beings." According to this supposition, the objective world that we posit is not the same kind of thing as what can occur in it as object (i.e., state of affairs, thing, event). But otherwise this conception no longer fits within the Kantian framework of oppositions. Once the a priori categories of the understanding and forms of intuition have been detranscendentalized and thus disarmed, the classic distinction between reason and understanding is blurred. Obviously, the pragmatic presupposition of the world is not a regulative idea, but is "constitutive" for referring to anything about which it is possible to establish facts. At the same time, the concept of the world remains formal in such a way that the system of possible references does not fix in advance any specific properties of objects in general. All attempts to reconstruct a material a priori of meaning [*Sinn-Apriori*] for possible objects of reference—that is, to predetermine the descriptions under which it is possible to refer to objects—have failed.[12]

(b) From this perspective, the distinction between appearance and "thing-in-itself" also becomes meaningless. Experiences and judgments are now coupled with a practice that copes with reality. They remain in contact with a surprising reality through problem-solving activities that are evaluated by their success. This reality either resists our grasp, or it "plays along." Viewed ontologically, transcendental idealism, which conceives the totality of objects of possible experience as a world "for us," as a world of appearances, is replaced by an internal realism. Accordingly, everything is "real" that can be represented in true statements, although facts are interpreted in a

Jürgen Habermas

language that is always "ours." The world itself does not impose "its" language on us; it does not itself speak; and it "responds" only in a figurative sense.[13] In asserting a state of affairs, we say it "obtains." However, this "veridical being" of facts is mistakenly assimilated to the "existence" of objects once we conceive of the representation of facts as a kind of picturing of reality.

What we state as facts results from learning processes and remains embedded in the semantic network of possible justifications. It is therefore advisable to distinguish, with C. S. Peirce, between a "reality" that can be represented in true statements and the "world" of objects these statements are about—between "what is the case" and the "existing constraints" of what we "come up against" and have to "cope with" in our practical dealings. The "accommodation" or "resistance" of the objects being talked about is already assimilated in true statements. To that extent, the "being the case" or obtaining [*Bestehen*] of states of affairs indirectly expresses the "existence" [*"Existenz"*] of recalcitrant objects (or the facticity of constraining circumstances). The "world" that we presuppose as the totality of objects, not of facts, must not be confused with the "reality" that consists of facts, that is everything that can be represented in true statements.

(c) Both concepts, "world" and "reality," express totalities, but only the concept of reality can, in virtue of its internal connection with the concept of truth, be placed alongside the regulative ideas of reason. The Peircean concept of reality (as the totality of statable facts) is a regulative idea in Kant's sense because it commits the practice of fact-stating to an orientation toward truth, which in turn has a regulative function. For Kant, "truth" is not an idea, nor is it connected with the ideas of reason since the transcendental conditions of objective experience are also supposed to explain the truth of judgments of experience: "For Kant, the question . . . of the conditions of possibility of constituting objects, i.e., of constituting the meaning of objectivity, was the same as the question . . . of the conditions of possibility of the intersubjective validity of true knowledge."[14] Contrary to this, Karl-Otto Apel defends the distinction between the pragmatically interpreted a priori of experience [*Erfahrungsapriori*], which determines the meaning of the objects of possible experience, and the conditions of the argumentative justification of statements about such objects.

Peirce wanted to explain "truth" itself epistemically, in terms of progress toward truth. He defined the meaning of truth by anticipating a consensus that all participants in a self-correcting process of inquiry under ideal epistemic conditions would have to attain.[15] The unlimited ideal "community of investigators" constitutes the forum for the "highest court" of reason. There are good reasons against epistemologizing the concept of truth in this way, which assimilates "truth" to "idealized justification" or "ideal warranted assertibility."[16] Nonetheless, the *orientation* toward truth—as a property that a proposition "cannot lose"—acquires an indispensable regulative function for fallible processes of justification precisely if such processes can at best lead to decisions about the rational acceptability of propositions and not their truth.[17]

Even after objective knowledge is detranscendentalized and tied to discursive justification as the "touchstone of truth," the point of Kant's injunction against the apodictic use of reason and the transcendent use of the understanding is preserved. Only now the boundary separating the transcendental from the transcendent use of our cognitive capacity is not defined by sensibility and understanding, but by the forum of rational discourse in which the convincing power of good reasons must flourish.

(d) In a certain way, the distinction between truth and rational acceptability replaces the difference between "things in themselves" and appearances. Kant was not able to bridge this transcendental-empirical gap even by means of the regulative idea of the unity of the world. The reason is that the heuristic of completing all conditioned cognitions does not lead the understanding *beyond* the realm of phenomena. Even after the knowing subject is detranscendentalized, there remains a gap between what is true and what is warranted or rationally acceptable to us. Although this gap cannot be definitively closed within discourse, it can be pragmatically closed by a rationally motivated transition from discourse to action. Because discourses *remain* rooted in the lifeworld, there is an internal connection between the two roles taken on by the idea of an orientation toward truth—in the form of practical certainties in action [*Handlungsgewissheiten*] on the one hand and as hypothetical validity claims in discourse on the other.[18]

The regulative function of the orientation toward truth, supported by the supposition of an objective world, directs processes of justification toward a goal that mobilizes the highest court of reason. That is, in the course of detranscendentalization, the theoretical ideas of reason step out of the static "intelligible world" and unleash their dynamics *within* the lifeworld. Kant says that we have only an "idea" but no "knowledge" of the intelligible realm. After the cosmological idea has been transformed into the presupposition of a shared objective world, however, the orientation to unconditional validity claims makes the resources of Kant's intelligible world available for the acquisition of empirical knowledge. Giving up the background assumptions of Kant's transcendental philosophy turns ideas of reason into idealizations that orient subjects capable of speech and action. The rigid "ideal" that was elevated to an otherworldly realm is set aflow in this-worldly operations; it is transposed from a transcendent state into a process of "immanent transcendence." For in the discursive struggle over the correct interpretation of what we encounter in the world, lifeworld contexts that are drifting apart must be transcended "from within."

Language-users can only direct themselves *toward* something innerworldly *from within* the horizon of their lifeworld. There are no strictly context-independent references to something in the world [*Weltbezüge*]. Heidegger and Wittgenstein each in his own way showed that Kant's transcendental consciousness of objects feeds on false abstractions.[19] The lifeworld contexts and the linguistic practices in which socialized subjects "always already" find themselves disclose the world from the perspective of traditions and habits that generate meaning. Everything that members of a local linguistic community encounter in the world they experience not as neutral objects, but in the light of an inhabited and habituated "grammatical" pre-understanding. The linguistic mediation of our relations to the world [*Weltbezuges*] explains why the objectivity of the world that we presuppose in acting and speaking refers back to a communicative intersubjectivity among interlocutors. A fact about some object must be stated and, if necessary, *justified* before others who can object to my assertion. The particular demand for interpretation arises because even when we use language descriptively, we cannot disregard its world-disclosive character.

These translation problems shed light on the thicket of lifeworld contexts, but they are not grounds for subscribing to any incommensurability thesis.[20] Interlocutors can reach mutual understanding across the boundaries of diverging lifeworlds because in presupposing a shared objective world, they orient themselves toward the claim to truth, that is, to the unconditional validity they claim when they make a statement. I shall return to this orientation to truth below.

The accountability of subjects

The cosmological idea of the unity of the world branches into the pragmatic presupposition of an objective world as the totality of objects, on the one hand, and the orientation toward a reality conceived as the totality of facts, on the other. We encounter a different kind of idealization in the interpersonal relationships of language-users who take one another "at their word" and hold one another to "be answerable." In their cooperative dealings with one another, they must mutually expect one another to be rational, at least provisionally. In certain circumstances, it may *turn out* that such a presupposition was unwarranted. Contrary to expectations, it might *happen* that the other person cannot account for her actions and utterances and that we cannot see how she could justify her behavior. In contexts of action oriented toward reaching understanding, this kind of frustration can occur only against the background supposition of rationality that anyone engaged in communicative action must assume. This supposition purports that a subject who is acting intentionally is capable, in the right circumstances, of providing a more or less plausible reason for *why* she did or did not behave or express herself this way rather than some other way. Unintelligible and odd, bizarre and enigmatic expressions prompt follow-up questions because they implicitly contradict an unavoidable presupposition of communication and therefore trigger puzzled or irritated reactions.

Someone who cannot account for her actions and utterances to others becomes suspect of not having acted reasonably or "accountably" [*zurechnungsfähig*]. Even a criminal judge must first determine whether the accused could be held responsible for her alleged crime. Furthermore, the judge examines whether there are exculpatory grounds. In order to judge an offense fairly, we have to know whether the perpetrator was accountable and whether the offense should be attributed more to the circumstances or to the agent herself. Exculpatory grounds confirm the supposition of rationality that we make about other agents not only in judicial proceedings, but also in everyday life. But the example of legal discourse is a good one for comparing the pragmatic presupposition of accountability with Kant's idea of freedom.

Until now, we have considered reason "in its theoretical use" as "the capacity to judge according to principles." Reason becomes "practical" insofar as it determines will and action according to principles. Through the moral law expressed in the categorical imperative, the idea of freedom acquires its own "special kind of causality," namely, the rationally motivating force of good reasons.[21] Unlike the ideas of theoretical reason, which merely regulate the use of the understanding, freedom is constitutive for action because it is an irrefutable demand of practical reason. Of course we can always consider actions under the description of observable behavior as processes determined by natural laws. However, from a practical point of view, we have to relate actions to reasons for why a rational subject might have done them. The "practical point of view" signifies a shift in perspective to the kind of normative judgment in which we also engage when acting communicatively by presupposing rationality.

Of course the reasons that are relevant to "freedom" (in the Kantian sense) form but a fraction of the spectrum of reasons for assessing the accountability of subjects acting communicatively. Kant characterizes freedom in general as an agent's capacity to subordinate her will to maxims, that is, to orient her actions by rules whose concept she has mastered. Thus freedom of choice [*Willkürfreiheit*] enables one to adopt rules of prudence or skill depending on one's inclinations and subjectively selected ends, whereas "free will" [*freie Wille*] obeys universally valid laws that it has imposed on itself from a moral point of view. Freedom of choice precedes free will, but the former remains subordinate to the latter when it comes to the moral evaluation of ends. Kant thus confines himself to technical-practical and moral-practical reasons. Communicative action draws on a broader spectrum of reasons: epistemic reasons for the truth of statements, ethical orientations and modes of action as indicators for the authenticity of life choices or the sincerity of confessions, and, depending on the issue, aesthetic experiences, narrative declarations, cultural standards of value, legal claims, conventions, and so on. Accountability is not assessed simply by the standards of morality and purposive rationality—indeed, it involves more than just practical reason. Accountability consists, rather, in an agent's *general* ability to orient her action by validity claims.[22]

According to Kant, among the practical ideas of reason freedom is the only one whose possible realization we can *conceive* [*einsehen*] a priori. Hence this idea acquires legislative force for every rational being. It receives concrete expression in the ideal of a "kingdom of ends" in which all rational beings join together under common laws so that they never treat one another merely as means, but as ends in themselves. Every member of this kingdom "legislates universal laws, while also being himself subject to these laws."[23] We have an a priori understanding [*Einsicht*] of this model of self-legislation, which signifies two things. On the one hand, it has the categorical sense of an obligation (namely of realizing the kingdom of ends by one's own actions and omissions). On the other hand, it has the transcendental sense of a certainty (that this kingdom *can* be advanced by our moral actions and omissions). We can know a priori that it *is possible* to actualize this practical idea.

Considered under the first aspect, the comparison of the idea of freedom with the supposition of rationality in communicative action is not very fruitful. Rationality is not an obligation. Even with regard to moral or legal behavior, the supposition of rationality does not mean that the other feels obligated to obey norms; she is merely imputed to have knowledge of what it means to act autonomously. The second aspect is more promising: the idea of freedom provides the certainty that autonomous action (and the realization of the kingdom of ends) *is possible*—and not merely counterfactually demanded of us. According to Kant, rational beings think of themselves as agents acting on the basis of good reasons. With regard to moral action, they have an a priori knowledge of the possibility of actualizing the idea of freedom. In communicative action we also tacitly start with the assumption that all participants *are* accountable agents. It is simply part of the self-understanding of subjects acting communicatively that they take rationally motivated positions on claims to validity; agents mutually presuppose that they *indeed do* act on the basis of rationally warrantable reasons.

Of course we need not wait for social-scientific or psychological studies of behavior to show us that this performative "knowledge" is problematic. In everyday practice we are both participant and observer, and we discover that many expressions are motivated by things other than good reasons. From this empirical point of view, the accountability of communicative actors is no less a counterfactual presupposition than Kant's idea of freedom. Yet oddly enough, for the acting subjects *themselves* this empirical knowledge loses its contradictory character as they carry out their actions. The contrast between the objective knowledge of an observer and the performatively engaged knowledge of an actor is of no consequence *in actu*. First-year sociology students learn that all norms are valid counterfactually, even if they are obeyed on average: for the sociologist-observer, statistically likely cases of deviant behavior go hand-in-hand with any prevailing norm.[24] Knowing this, however, will generally not prevent addressees from accepting as binding any norm that the community recognizes.

Someone who is acting morally does not credit herself with "more or less" autonomy; and participants in communicative action do not sometimes attribute "a little more" and sometimes "a little less" rationality to one another. From the perspective of the participants, these concepts are binarily coded. As soon as we act out of "respect for the law" or "with an orientation to reaching mutual understanding," we cannot at the same time act from the objectivating perspective of an observer. While carrying out our actions, we bracket empirical self-descriptions in favor of the agents' rational self-understanding. Nevertheless, the supposition of rationality is a *defeasible* assumption and not a priori knowledge. It "functions" as a multiply corroborated pragmatic presupposition that is constitutive of communicative action. But in any given instance, it can be falsified. This difference in the status of practical knowledge cannot be explained solely in terms of the detranscendentalization of the acting subject who has been dislodged from the kingdom of intelligible beings into the linguistically articulated lifeworld of socialized subjects. This paradigm shift alters the whole outlook of the analysis.

Within his mentalistic conceptual framework, Kant conceives an agent's rational self-understanding as a person's knowledge of herself, and he abstractly opposes this first-person knowledge to an observer's third-person knowledge. The transcendental gap between these two forms of knowledge is such that the self-understanding of subjects as members of the intelligible realm cannot be corrected in principle by empirical knowledge. As speakers and addressees, however, communicatively acting subjects encounter one another literally at eye level by taking on first- and *second-person* roles. By reaching an understanding about something in the objective world and adopting the same relation to the world, they enter into an interpersonal relationship. In this performative attitude *toward* one another, they share communicative experiences *with* one another against the background of an intersubjectively shared—that is, sufficiently overlapping—lifeworld. Each can understand what the other says or means. They learn from the information and objections that their interlocutor conveys and draw their own conclusions from irony, silence, paradoxical expressions, allusions, and so on. Cases in which opaque behavior becomes unintelligible or communication breaks down represent a reflective mode of communicative experience. At this level, the presupposition of rationality cannot be refuted as such, but it is indirectly defeasible.

This kind of defeasibility does not seem to apply to idealizations in the domain of cognition, even if they also take the form of pragmatic presuppositions. The supposition of a shared objective world projects a system of possible references to the world and hence makes interventions in the world and interpretations of something in the world possible in the first place. The supposition of a shared objective world is "transcendentally" necessary in the sense that it cannot be corrected by experiences that would not be possible without it. The content of our descriptions is of course subject to revision, but the formal projection [*Entwurf*] of the totality of identifiable objects in general is not—at least not as long as our form of life is characterized by natural languages that have the kind of propositional structure with which we are familiar. At best, we may find out a posteriori that the projection was insufficiently formal. But "unavoidable" presuppositions are apparently "constitutive" for *practices* in a different sense than they are for *object domains*.

For rule-governed behavior, constitutive rules always open up the possibility of following or violating them. Beyond that, there is the possibility in principle of being able to do something and not being able to do it. Someone who has not mastered the rules of a game and is not even capable of making mistakes is not a player. This becomes clear *in* the course of the practice. Thus only during communicative action does it become clear who is frustrating the pragmatic presupposition of accountability and is not even "in the game." Whereas the supposition of a shared objective world is not subject to being checked against the kinds of experiences that it makes possible, the necessary supposition of rationality in communicative action holds only provisionally. The latter is open to being contradicted by experiences that participants have precisely through engaging in this practice.

The unconditionality of validity claims
Until now, we have examined the detranscendentalized use of reason in terms of the supposition of a shared objective world and the mutual supposition of rationality that agents must make when they engage in communicative action. We have touched in a preliminary way on another sense of "idealization," which appears in the regulative function of the orientation to truth that complements reference to the world. The practice of action oriented to mutual understanding forces on its participants certain totalizing anticipations, abstractions, and transgressions of boundaries. Certainly the genealogical connection with Kant's "ideas" suggests the term "idealization" in these cases. But what do the various kinds of idealizations really have in common?

Language-users must rely on a shared system of independently existing objects of reference about which they can form beliefs and which they can intentionally influence. The formal-pragmatic supposition of the world creates place-holders for objects to which speaking and acting subjects can refer. However, grammar cannot "impose" any laws on nature. A "transcendental projection" in the weak sense depends on nature "meeting us halfway." Thus in the "vertical" dimension of relating to the world, idealization consists in the anticipation of the totality of possible references. In the horizontal dimension of intersubjective relationships, the mutual supposition of rationality indicates what subjects in principle expect of one another. If reaching understanding, and thereby coordinating action, is to be possible at all, then agents must be capable of taking a warranted stance on criticizable validity claims and of orienting themselves by such claims in their own actions.

Here idealization consists in the preliminary abstraction from deviations, individual differences, and limiting contexts. Communicative disturbances and, in extreme cases, breakdowns of communication occur only when these deviations exceed the limits of tolerance. In contrast to the Kantian projection of totalities, there is a Platonic sense of idealization that makes itself felt here. As long as they maintain a performative attitude, actors are immune to acknowledging empirically observable imperfections until these reach a threshold at which the discrepancy between the ideal and its incomplete realization in a given instance becomes intolerable. The totalizing anticipation is not what is decisive in this dimension. Decisive rather is the neutralization *in actu* of negligible deviations from the ideal, toward which even objectively deviant action is oriented.

Finally, the orientation toward truth in the critical testing of unconditional claims to validity mobilizes still another kind of idealization. This kind seems excessive, for it combines the Kantian and the Platonic senses of "idealization" into an apparent hybrid. Because our contact with the world is linguistically mediated, the world eludes the direct grasp of the senses and immediate constitution through the forms of intuition and the concepts of the understanding. The presupposed objectivity of the world is so deeply entwined with the intersubjectivity of reaching an understanding about something in the world that we cannot transcend this connection and escape the linguistically disclosed horizon of our intersubjectively shared lifeworld. This of course does not rule out communication across the boundaries of particular lifeworlds. We are able reflectively to transcend whatever our given initial hermeneutic situations are and attain intersubjectively shared views on disputed matters. Gadamer describes this as a "fusion of horizons."[25]

The supposition of a common world of independently existing objects about which we can state facts is complemented by the idea of truth as a property that assertoric sentences cannot "lose." However, if fallible sentences cannot immediately confront the world, but can only be justified or denied by means of further propositions, and if there is no basis of self-warranting, self-evident propositions, then claims to truth can only be tested discursively. Thus the two-place relation of the validity [*Gültigkeit*] of propositions is extended into the three-place relation of a validity [*Geltung*] that valid propositions have "for us." Their truth must be recognizable to an audience. But then claims to *unconditional* truth unleash, under the prevailing epistemic *conditions* for their possible justification, an explosive power *within* the existing communicative relationships. The epistemic reflection of unconditionality is the ideal inflation of the critical audience into a "final" court of appeal. Peirce uses the image of the socially and historically unlimited ideal community of inquirers that continues to pursue the process of inquiry—until they reach the ideal limit of a "final opinion."

This image is misleading in two respects: to begin with, it suggests that truth can be conceived as idealized warranted assertibility, which in turn is assessed in terms of a consensus attained under ideal conditions. But a proposition is agreed to by all rational subjects because it is true; it is not true because it could be the content of a consensus attained under ideal conditions. Moreover, Peirce's image does not direct our attention to the *process* of justification in the course of which true propositions have to stand up to objections, but to the *final state* of an agreement not subject to revision. This is contrary to a fallibilist self-understanding that expresses itself in the "cautionary use" of the truth-predicate. As finite minds, we have no way of foreseeing changes in epistemic conditions; hence we cannot rule out that a proposition, no matter how ideally justified, will turn out to be false.[26] Despite these objections to an epistemic conception of truth and even after abandoning foundationalist justifications, the idea of a process of argumentation that is as inclusive as possible and that can be continued at any time has an important role in explaining "rational acceptability," if not "truth." As fallible, situated beings, we have no other way to *ascertain* truth than through discourses that are both rational and open-ended.

No matter how misleading the image of an ideally extended communication community (Apel) that reaches a warranted mutual agreement [*Einverständnis*] under ideal epistemic conditions (Putnam), before an ideal audience (Perelman), or in an ideal speech situation (Habermas), we can in no way forego making some such idealizations. For the rift opened up in everyday practice by a truth claim that has become problematic must be healed in a discourse that cannot be terminated "once and for all," either by "decisive" evidence or by "compelling" arguments. Though truth claims cannot be definitively redeemed in discourses, it is through arguments alone that we let ourselves be *convinced* of the truth of problematic propositions. What is convincing is what we can accept as rational. Rational acceptability depends on a procedure that does not shield "our" arguments from anyone or anything. The process of argumentation as such must remain open to any relevant objections and any improvements of our epistemic condition. This kind of argumentative practice that is as inclusive and continuous as possible is subsumed by the idea of continually going beyond the limitations of current forms of communication with respect to social spaces, historical times, and substantive competencies. The discursive process thereby increases the responsive potential by which rationally accepted claims to validity prove their worth.

With their intuitive understanding of the meaning of argumentation in general, proponents and opponents force one another into decentering their interpretive perspectives. Thus Kant's idealizing anticipation of the whole is carried over from the *objective* to the *social* world. In the performative attitude of participants in argumentation, this "totalization" is connected with a "neutralization": they prescind from the obvious gap between, on the one hand, the ideal model of an "endless conversation" that is completely inclusive both socially and thematically and, on the other hand, the finite, spatio-temporally limited discourses that we actually engage in. Because the participants are oriented toward truth, the concept of an absolutely valid truth is reflected at the level of the discursive ascertainment of truth in performative idealizations that make this argumentative practice so demanding. Before I can enter into the details of these pragmatic presuppositions of rational discourse, I must briefly sketch the spectrum of validity claims beyond "truth." According to the Kantian concept of practical reason, we claim unconditional validity not only for true assertoric propositions but also for correct moral—and with some reservations, legal—propositions.

Discourse as the forum of justification

Until now, whenever I have spoken about communicatively acting subjects reaching an understanding about something in "the" world, I had in mind the reference to a common objective world. The claims to truth raised for assertoric sentences have served as the paradigm for claims to validity in general. In regulative speech acts such as recommendations, requests, and commands, agents refer to actions that (they believe) their interlocutors are obliged to perform. As members of a social group, they share certain practices and value orientations, they jointly recognize certain norms, are used to certain conventions, and so forth. In the regulative use of language, speakers rely on an intersubjectively recognized or habituated constellation of habits, institutions, or rules that regulate interpersonal relations in the group so that its members know what kind of behavior they may legitimately expect of one another. (With commissive speech acts, a speaker produces a legitimate relationship by entering into an obligation; in doing so, participants assume that communicatively acting subjects bind their will to maxims and are able to take responsibility for what they promise to do.)

In such normative language games, agents also refer to something in the objective world via the propositional contents of their utterances, but they do so only incidentally. They mention the circumstances and success conditions of the actions they demand, request, recommend, accuse someone of, excuse, promise, and so on. But they refer directly to actions and norms as "something in the social world." Of course they do not conceive of norm-governed actions as social facts that form a segment of the objective world, as it were. To be sure, from the objectivating point of view of the sociologist-observer there "really" are normative expectations, practices, habits, institutions, and regulations of all sorts "in the world" in addition to physical things and mental states. However, agents who are immediately involved have a different attitude toward the network of their normatively regulated interactions, namely, the performative attitude of actors who can "violate" norms only because they recognize them to be binding. They use a reference system that complements that of the objective world from the point of view of a second person whose "good will" is subject to normative expectations. This reference system lifts the relevant segment for their norm-governed action out of the encompassing context of their lifeworld for purposes of thematization. Thus members comprehend their "social world" as the totality of possible legitimately regulated interpersonal relationships. Like the "objective world," this system of reference is also a necessary supposition that is grammatically coupled to regulative (as opposed to constative) language use.

(The expressive use of first-person sentences completes this architechtonic of "worlds." Based on a speaker's epistemic authority for sincerely expressing her own "experiences," we delimit an "inner world" from the objective and social worlds. The discussion of first-person perceptual and experiential reports, which arose in connection with Wittgenstein's private language argument and Wilfrid Sellars's critique of mentalism, shows that the totality of experiences to which a subject has privileged access cannot simply be understood as one more system of reference analogous to the objective and social worlds. "My" experiences are subjectively certain; unlike objective data or normative expectations, they do not have to be identified, nor can they be. Rather, the subjective "world" is determined negatively as the totality of that which neither occurs in the objective world nor is taken to be valid or intersubjectively recognized in the social world. The subjective world complements these two publicly accessible worlds by encompassing all experiences that a speaker can turn into the content of first-person sentences when she wants to reveal something about herself to an audience in the expressive mode of self-presentation.)

The claim to rightness of normative statements relies on the presumed validity of an underlying norm. Unlike the truth of descriptive statements, the validity domain of a rightness claim varies according to the legitimating background, that is, according to the boundaries of a social world in general. Only *moral* imperatives (and legal norms such as human rights that can only be justified morally) claim absolute validity, that is, universal recognition, in the way that assertions do. This explains Kant's demand that valid moral laws must be "universalizable." Moral norms must be able to command the rationally motivated recognition of *all* subjects capable of speech and action, beyond the historical and cultural confines of any particular social world. Thus the idea of a thoroughly morally ordered community implies the counterfactual extension of the social world in which we find ourselves to a completely inclusive world of well-ordered interpersonal relationships: *all* human beings become brothers and sisters.

Of course it would equally be a mistake to hypostatize such a universal community of persons capable of moral judgment and action in the sense of a spatio-temporally unlimited community. The image of the self-determined "kingdom of ends" suggests the existence of a republic of rational beings, although it is a construct that, as Kant notes, "does not exist but can be made actual by our conduct."[27] It ought to and can be brought about in accordance with the practical idea of freedom. The kingdom of ends "exists" in a certain sense, yet it is more a task we are charged with [*aufgegeben*] than something that is given to us [*gegeben*]. This ambiguity was not the least of Kant's motives for dividing human practices into the intelligible realm and the realm of appearances. As soon as we no longer subscribe to this transcendental bipartition, we have to bring out the *constructive meaning* of morality in some other way.

We can represent moral learning processes as an intelligent expansion and reciprocal interpenetration of social worlds that in a given case of conflict do not yet sufficiently overlap. The disputing parties learn to *include* one another in a world they construct together so as to be able to judge and consensually resolve controversial actions in the light of the same [*übereinstimmender*] standards of evaluation. G. H. Mead described this as the expansion of a reversible exchange of interpretive perspectives. At first rooted in their own particular lifeworlds, the participants' perspectives become increasingly "decentered" (as Piaget puts it) as the mutual process of perspectival interpenetration approaches the ideal limit of complete inclusiveness. Interestingly, this is precisely what the practice of argumentation aims at by its very structure. Rational discourse is a process that ensures the inclusion of all those affected and the equal consideration of all the interests at play. Thus in view of the idea that only those norms equally good for all merit recognition from the moral point of view, such discourse presents itself as the appropriate method of conflict resolution.

"Impartiality" in the sense of justice converges with "impartiality" in the sense of the discursive ascertainment of cognitive claims to validity.[28] This convergence makes sense if we compare the orientation of moral learning processes with the conditions for participating in argumentation at all. Conflicts are triggered by contradictions among social opponents with dissonant value orientations. Moral learning processes resolve such conflicts through each participant's reciprocal inclusion of the other(s). As it turns out, however, argumentation as a form of communication is already tailored to such an interpenetration of perspectives and enriching expansion of world horizons. Lest the discussion of disputed validity claims forfeit its cognitive purpose, participants in argumentation must subscribe to an egalitarian universalism that is structurally mandated and that at first has only a formal-pragmatic, rather than a moral, meaning.

The cooperative nature of the competition for better arguments is explained by the goal or function constitutive for the language game of argumentation: participants want to convince one another. In continuing everyday communicative action at the reflective level of thematized claims to validity, they are still guided by the goal of mutual understanding inasmuch as a proponent can win the game only if she *convinces* her opponents that her validity claim is warranted. The rational acceptability of the corresponding statement is based on the convincing force of the better arguments. Which argument does convince is not decided by private insight, but by the stances that, bundled together in a rationally motivated agreement, are adopted by everyone who participates in the public practice of exchanging reasons.

Now, standards for whether something counts as a good or a bad argument may themselves become controversial. Anything can come under the pressure of opposing reasons. Hence the rational acceptability of validity claims is *ultimately* based only on reasons that withstand objections under certain demanding conditions of communication. If the process of argumentation is to live up to its meaning, communication in the form of rational discourse must, if possible, allow all relevant information and explanations to be brought up and weighed so that the stance participants take can be intrinsically motivated solely by the revisionary power of free-floating reasons. However, if this is the intuitive meaning that we associate with argumentation in general, then we also know that a practice may not seriously count as argumentation unless it meets certain pragmatic presuppositions.[29]

The four most important presuppositions are: (a) publicity and inclusiveness: no one who could make a relevant contribution with regard to a controversial validity claim must be excluded; (b) equal rights to engage in communication: everyone must have the same opportunity to speak to the matter at hand; (c) exclusion of deception and illusion: participants have to mean what they say; and (d) absence of coercion: communication must be free of restrictions that prevent the better argument from being raised or from determining the outcome of the discussion. Presuppositions (a), (b), and (d) subject one's behavior in argumentation to the rules of an egalitarian universalism. *With regard to moral-practical issues,* it follows from these rules that the interests and value orientations of every affected person are equally taken into consideration. And since the participants in practical discourses are simultaneously the ones who are affected, presupposition (c)—which *in theoretical-empirical disputes* requires only a sincere and unconstrained weighing of the arguments—takes on the further significance that one remain critically alert to self-deception as well as hermeneutically open and sensitive to how others understand themselves and the world.

These argumentative presuppositions obviously contain such strong idealizations that they raise the suspicion of a rather tendentious description of argumentation. How should it be at all possible for participants in argumentation performatively to proceed from such obviously counterfactual assumptions? After all, people engaged in discourse are aware, for example, that the circle of participants is highly selective, that one side of their communicative space is privileged over the other, that one person or another remains caught in prejudices about this topic or that, that many people sometimes behave strategically, or that yes- and no-positions are often determined by motives other than a better understanding of the issue. To be sure, an observer analyzing a discourse could more accurately spot such deviations from an "ideal speech situation" than could the engaged participants, who presume they have approximated the ideal. But even when taking a performative attitude, participants do not allow themselves to be fully consumed lock, stock, and barrel by their engagement to the point of not being aware—at least intuitively—of much that they could know thematically by taking an observer's objectivating attitude.

At the same time, these unavoidable presuppositions of argumentative practice, no matter how counterfactual, are by no means mere constructs. Rather they are *actually efficacious* in the behavior of the participants themselves. Someone who seriously takes part in an argument de facto proceeds from such presuppositions. This is evident from the inferences participants will draw, if necessary, from perceived inconsistencies. The process of argumentation is self-correcting in the sense that in the course of an unsatisfactory discussion, for example, reasons spontaneously arise for an "overdue" liberalization of the rules of procedure and discussion, for changing an insufficiently representative circle of participants, for expanding the agenda or improving the information base. One *can tell* when new arguments have to be taken into account or when marginalized voices have to be taken seriously. On the other hand, perceived inconsistencies are not *in every case* the motive for such or similar repairs. This is explained by the fact that participants in argumentation are convinced by the substance of the reasons rather than by the communicative design for exchanging reasons. The procedural properties of the process of argumentation warrant the rational expectation that the relevant information and reasons get "put on the table" and have an influence on the outcome. As long as participants in argumentation proceed from the assumption that this is the case, from their perspective there is no reason to be worried about inadequate procedural properties of the process of communication.

The formal properties of argumentation bear on the difference between rational assertibility and truth. Because no evidence is decisive and no arguments are compelling "in the final instance," because no assertions however well justified are infallible, it is only the quality of the discursive truth-seeking procedure that warrants the reasonable expectation that the best attainable information and reasons are indeed available and do "count" in the end. Perceived inconsistencies that provoke doubts about the genuineness of an argumentative exchange do not arise until obviously *relevant participants* are excluded, *relevant contributions* suppressed, and yes/no stances are manipulated or conditioned by other kinds of influences. The idealizing anticipation associated with argumentative presuppositions displays its operative efficacy in its critical function: an absolute claim to validity has to be justifiable in ever wider forums before an ever more competent and larger audience against ever new objections. This intrinsic dynamic of argumentation, the progressive decentering of one's own interpretive perspective, in particular drives practical discourses, which aim not to assess truth claims but insightfully to construct and apply moral (and legal) norms.[30]

The validity of such norms "consists" [*bestehen*] in the universal recognition that they merit. Because moral claims to validity lack the ontological connotations that are characteristic of claims to truth, reference to the objective world is replaced by an orientation toward an expansion of the social world, that is, toward the progressive inclusion of strangers and their claims. The validity of a moral statement has the epistemic significance that it would be accepted under ideal conditions of justification. However, if the meaning of "moral rightness," unlike that of "truth," is *exhausted* by rational acceptability, then our moral convictions must ultimately rely on the critical potential of self-transcendence and decentering that—as the "restlessness" of idealizing anticipations—is built into the practice of argumentation and the self-understanding of its participants.

I have attempted to trace what Thomas McCarthy calls a "relocation" of the Kantian opposition between the real and the ideal. To the extent that we transform the "ideas of reason" into idealizations performed by speaking and acting subjects, the ideal no longer depends on the assumption of a noumenal sphere beyond the phenomena we can describe. Rather, with idealizations we explain from a participant's perspective the operations that actors must accomplish in their actual performance of certain everyday practices, namely those we describe as communicative action and rational discourse.

Translated by Barbara Fultner

Notes

1. Thomas McCarthy, *Ideals and Illusions* (Cambridge: MIT Press, 1991), 2.

2. McCarthy, *Ideals and Illusions*, 4.

3. David Couzens Hoy and Thomas McCarthy, *Critical Theory* (Oxford: Blackwell, 1994), 38. [Note that references to this work hereafter refer to the chapters written by McCarthy.—Trans.]

4. Hoy and McCarthy, *Critical Theory*, 39.

5. Here I need not revisit the domestic dispute within the domestic dispute. Cf. Thomas McCarthy, "Practical Discourse: On the Relation of Morality to Politics," *Ideals*, 181–199; "Legitimacy and Diversity: Dialectical Reflections on Analytical Distinctions," in *Habermas on Law and Democracy*, ed. M. Rosenfeld and A. Arato (Berkeley: University of California Press, 1998), 115–153; for my reply see "Reply to Symposium Participants," in *Habermas on Law and Democracy*, 391–404.

6. Jürgen Habermas, *Wahrheit und Rechtfertigung* (Frankfurt am Main: Suhrkamp, 1999).

7. Jürgen Habermas, *On the Pragmatics of Communication*, ed. and trans. M. Cook (Cambridge: MIT Press, 1998).

8. Hoy and McCarthy, *Critical Theory*, 38.

9. Jürgen Habermas, "Some Further Clarifications of the Concept of Communicative Rationality," *Pragmatics of Communication*, chap. 7.

10. See Immanuel Kant, *Critique of Pure Reason*, trans. N. K. Smith (New York: St. Martin's, 1929), 98, 118–119, 384ff.

11. On Putnam's theory of reference, which is relevant here, see A. Mueller, "Referenz und Fallibilkismus" (Ph.D. diss., University of Frankfurt, 1999).

12. For a discussion of Peter Strawson's investigations on this topic, see M. Niquet, *Transzendentale Argumente* (Frankfurt am Main: Suhrkamp, 1991), chaps. 4 and 5.

13. On Putnam's "internal realism," cf. Jürgen Habermas, "Werte und Normen: Ein Kommentar zu Hilary Putnams kantischen Pragmatismus," *Deutsche Zeitshrift für Philosophie* 48 (2000): 547–564.

14. Karl-Otto Apel, "Sinnkonstitution und Geltungsrechtfertigung," in *Martin Heidegger: Innen- und Außenansichten,* ed. Forum für Philosophie (Frankfurt am Main: Suhrkamp, 1989), 134.

15. C. S. Peirce, *Collected Papers,* vols. 5 and 6 (1934), 268: "The opinion which is fated to be ultimately agreed to by all who investigate, is what we mean by the truth, and the object represented in this opinion is the real" (5.407). See also Karl-Otto Apel, *Charles S. Peirce: From Pragmatism to Pragmaticism,* trans. J. M. Krois (Amherst: University of Massachusetts Press, 1981).

16. See the critique of the discursive conception of truth in Albrecht Wellmer, "Ethics and Dialogue: Elements of Moral Judgement in Kant and Discourse Ethics," *The Persistence of Modernity,* trans. D. Midgley (Cambridge: MIT Press, 1991), 145ff.; Cristina Lafont, *The Linguistic Turn in Hermeneutic Philosophy* (Cambridge: MIT Press, 1999), pp. 283ff.

17. Jürgen Habermas, "Richard Rorty's Pragmatic Turn," *Pragmatics of Communication,* chap. 8.

18. Habermas, *Wahrheit und Rechtfertigung,* 48ff., 261ff., 291ff; "Rorty's Pragmatic Turn."

19. On the "hermeneutics of an always already linguistically interpreted being-in-the-world," see Karl-Otto Apel, "Wittgenstein und Heidegger," in B. McGuinness et al., *Der Löwe spricht . . . und wir können ihn nicht verstehen* (Frankfurt am Main: Suhrkamp, 1991), pp. 27–68.

20. Richard F. Bernstein, *Beyond Objectivism and Relativism* (Philadelphia: University of Pennsylvania Press, 1983).

21. The quoted phrase is found in Kant's *Grounding for the Metaphysics of Morals,* 2nd ed., trans. J. W. Ellington (Indianapolis: Hackett, 1981), 59 (Ak. 460).

22. Jürgen Habermas, *Between Facts and Norms,* trans. W. Rehg (Cambridge: MIT Press, 1996), 5.

23. Kant, *Grounding,* 40 (Ak. 433).

24. This insight can already be found in Emile Durkheim, *The Rules of Sociological Method,* 8th ed., trans. S. A. Soloray and J. H. Mueller, ed. G. E. G. Catlin (New York: Free Press, 1966).

25. Hans-Georg Gadamer, *Truth and Method,* 2nd ed., trans. J. Weinsheimer and D. Marshall (New York: Crossroad, 1990). Because he has in mind the appropriation of classical works, however, Gadamer is misled to aestheticize the problem of truth; cf. Jürgen Habermas, "Wie ist nach dem Historismus noch Metaphysik möglich?" *Neue Zürcher Zeitung,* 12/13 (February 2000).

26. See Wellmer's critique in "Ethics and Dialogue," 160ff.

27. Kant, *Grounding*, 42 note 28 (Ak. 436).

28. William Rehg, *Insight and Solidarity* (Berkeley: University of California Press, 1994).

29. On the following, cf. Jürgen Habermas, "A Genealogical Analysis of the Cognitive Content of Morality," in *The Inclusion of the Other*, ed. C. Cronin and P. DeGreiff (Cambridge: MIT Press, 1998), 3–46, here 43f.

30. On the following, cf. Habermas, "Richtigkeit versus Wahrheit," *Wahrheit und Rechtfertigung*, 271–318.

2

The Ambiguity of "Rationality"

Richard Rorty

In 1994 David Couzens Hoy and Thomas McCarthy engaged in a debate published under the title *Critical Theory*.[1] It is tempting to describe *Critical Theory* as an American version of the Habermas-versus-Foucault debate, a debate that has agitated Europe in the ten years since the publication of Habermas's *Philosophical Discourse of Modernity*. It is also tempting to read it as a contribution to the debate over postmodernism that is presently agitating the American academy. But neither description is quite right.

Although McCarthy is a reasonably orthodox Habermasian, Hoy's allegiance is more to Gadamer than to Foucault. Nobody has, as far as I know, described Gadamer as a postmodern. Further, Hoy has no wish to defend Foucault against the most important criticism that Habermas made of him: namely that nobody would guess from Foucault's books that human freedom, and the chances of human happiness, increased considerably as a result of the Enlightenment. Hoy's defense of Foucault against Habermas is largely a defense of Foucault's refusal to offer a general theory of rationality, something Gadamer too refuses to do. As Hoy says, "The question . . . is whether [Foucault's] substantive genealogical histories need to be supplemented by an abstract, universal and procedural conception of reason that is validated solely by philosophical arguments (for instance, transcendental ones) instead of by historiographical and sociological data" (148).

In his rejoinder to Hoy, Thomas McCarthy agrees that we need Foucauldian "critical histories of contingent regimes of rationality." But he disagrees with Hoy on the question of "whether there is *anything universal at all* to say about reason, truth, objectivity, and the like, or rather anything that would not be too 'thin' to be of any use" (223). McCarthy thus lays out what I take to be the central issue of the book: namely, whether these traditional topics of philosophical debate are relevant to sociopolitical deliberation.

I doubt that they are. So I am on Hoy's side of the argument. I agree with him when he says that McCarthy's ideal of a "validity that could be rationally acknowledged by all competent judges under ideal epistemic conditions" (268) is too thin to help us change our minds about anything, too thin to do anybody any good. Most of what I will be saying will be devoted to pressing this charge of thinness against McCarthy. I agree with Foucault, Gadamer, and Hoy that rationality is not as fruitful a topic as Habermas and McCarthy think it.

Habermas and McCarthy are not inclined to resurrect a correspondence theory of truth. But their ideal of universal validity is an awkward halfway house between the old idea that Truth is correspondence to the One Way the World Is and Hoy's fully pragmatic view. More generally, the Habermasian idea of "communicative reason" is an unsatisfactory compromise between what Habermas calls "subject-centered reason" and the pragmatists' suggestion that if we pursue freedom, tolerance, and equality we need not worry about either rationality or universal validity. On the version of pragmatism that I favor, we should just let the notions of reason and rationality wither away. For we can use such concrete, explicitly political, notions as freedom of speech, democratic government, international law, and universal literacy to do the inspirational work that these notions have done in the past.

Getting rid of the notion of rationality would at least have the merit of eliminating an ambiguity. Rationality is the name of both a cognitive and a moral virtue. The epistemological notion of rationality is that the human subject can surmount appearance and reach reality—a feat lesser animals cannot perform. The brutes, so this story goes, can only have useful habits, whereas we, thanks to rationality, can strive for universal validity. The moral notion of rationality is just a preference for persuasion over force: you are rational insofar as you would rather argue than fight, rather use words than blows. The epistemological notion of rationality concerns our relation to something nonhuman, whereas the moral notion is concerned entirely with our relations to our fellow human beings. I should like to drop the epistemological notion of rationality altogether by dropping the subject-object model of knowing. I should also like to use less ambiguous and more concrete terms when commending persuasion over force.

Habermas dislikes the subject-object model as much as pragmatists do. He describes the contrast between subject-centered reason and communicative reason by saying that "the paradigm of knowledge of objects has to be replaced by the paradigm of mutual understanding between subjects."[2] This way of putting the contrast suggests that he might be willing to disengage the notion of rationality from that of truth-tracking. If he did so, he could say that we no longer need the word "Truth" as the name of the goal of inquiry, since we have another term to describe that goal—namely, "increased mutual understanding—agreement about what to believe and do among ever larger and more various sorts of people." If he took this tack, Habermas could have said that although we can continue to use the word "true" as an adjective, in all the familiar ways, getting rid of the useless notion of corresponding to the One Way the World Is also gets rid of the useless nominalization of an irreplaceable adjective. By taking this tack, Habermas could avoid one more temptation to do what he says he does not want to do, namely "resurrect the purism of pure reason" within communicative reason.[3]

But, of course, this is not the tack he takes. By insisting that communicative rationality incorporates the notion of universal validity Habermas accomplishes precisely the resurrection he hopes to avoid. For this insistence resurrects the idea of unconditionality. As Habermas says, "The validity claimed for propositions and norms transcends spaces and times, 'blots out' space and time."[4] Like Truth, and unlike "increased mutual understanding among ever more various persons and groups," the "agreement of all competent judges operating under ideal epistemic conditions" is something we can never know whether we have attained. Unknowability and unconditionality go hand in hand. Both expressions name a goal which we could never know ourselves to have reached, and which we can never know we are closing in on rather than veering off from.

The skeptic has always been there to remind us that the One Way the World Is might have nothing to do with any of the ways in which human beings find it useful to describe their environment. Analogously, these ideally competent judges might be people whose existence we have no reason to encourage. There will always be a Foucault or a Feyerabend around to suggest that the very procedures we think of as increasing communicative rationality are the ones that prevent the emergence of those competent judges and of those ideal epistemic conditions. You have to accept the bitters as well as the sweets of unconditionality. The more unconditional, the more unknowable. The more unknowable, the thinner.

McCarthy, however, thinks that reference to the unconditional "opens up assertions to one's discursive examination" (74). He says that

While we have no standards of truth wholly independent of particular languages and practices, it remains that "truth" serves as an idea of reason with respect to which we can criticize the standards we inherit and learn to see things in a different way. Neither the particularity of context-immanence nor the universality of context-transcendence of truth claims can be ignored without doing violence to our actual practices of truth. We can, and typically do, make contextually conditioned and fallible claims to objective truth. (39)

I think that Hoy is right in saying that the thought that there is context-independent validity to be had is "not pragmatically relevant enough to be the motivation of challenging our assertions"(268). I agree with him when he goes on to suggest that any work done by envisaging such validity can be done equally well by reminding ourselves that our present consensus about what to believe and to do is a function of the needs of those who have reached agreement, and that other people may have different needs. Only concrete suggestions about what these other needs are or might be can do the job that McCarthy describes as "criticiz[ing] the standards we inherit and learn[ing] to see things in a different way."

On the other hand, I think that McCarthy has a point when he says, in the passage I just quoted, that we cannot give up unconditionality and universal validity "without doing violence to our actual practices of truth"—at least if "actual practices" means "the way we have been brought up to describe what we are doing." Our common sense does in fact encourage us to nominalize the adjective "true." It tells us that the love of Truth is a virtue, that the search for Truth takes precedence over the search for happiness, and so on. So pragmatists are being consciously counterintuitive when they say that the true is simply what is good in the way of belief, and that the search for truth is merely one species of the generic search for happiness.

As McCarthy says earlier in *Critical Theory,* we are heirs to "centuries of distinguishing between appearance and reality, doxa and episteme, prejudice and reason, custom and morality, convention and justice, and so on" (32). So if we are to drop not only the idea that there is One Way the World Is and One Truth that corresponds to that Way, but also the Habermasian idea of truth as something universal and context-transcendent, we shall have to change our ways of speaking considerably. We shall have to stop exalting the stable over the transitory. We shall have to stop thinking that it is a good idea to "blot out space and time."

McCarthy thinks that anybody who criticizes a theory of rationality must do so on the basis of an alternative theory of rationality. Similarly for theories of truth and objectivity. He thinks that these are inescapable topics, and that people like Hoy and myself who eschew theories about them are evading their intellectual responsibilities. Hoy, however, who uses "pluralism" as the antithesis of universalism, says that "pluralism is . . . a negative meta-position, and is not setting itself up as offering positive claims to replace the universalist's axioms" (201). Hoy thus hopes to escape McCarthy's charge that any radical historicism will entail "familiar self-referential contradictions" (32).

I think that Hoy adopts the right strategy here, but that his strategy can be reinforced by granting McCarthy's point that the universalistic ideas to which Habermas appeals are so "deeply embedded in our culture" that "dislodging them is less a matter of frank self-acceptance than of radical self-transformation" (33). People like Hoy and me should admit that the only way to escape the sort of charge of self-referential contradiction that McCarthy brings against us is to replace the vocabulary in which he brings it. We have to answer McCarthy's rhetorical question "How can one deconstruct all ideas of reason without at the same time relying on them, at least tacitly?" (35) by saying "We aren't so much deconstructing ideas of reason as suggesting replacements for them—replacements that will do the inspirational job just as well, without some of the unfortunate side-effects of universalism." We are not saying that we have objective, universalizable, rationally defensible ideas about rationality and truth. We are saying instead that we think that human happiness might be better served by turning objectivity and truth over to philosophers of language like Brandom and Davidson and sociologists of science like Latour, and by turning rationality over to students of what McCarthy calls "contingent regimes of rationality"—historians-of-disciplines like Foucault and Hacking. This would amount to saying that our use of adjectives like "true" and "objective" can be semantically explicated without making either Truth or Objectivity a goal of inquiry. Again, our use of the adjective "rational" can be understood sociohistorically without developing a theory about the nature of Rationality.

Charges of self-referential absurdity such as those McCarthy brings against Hoy assume an unchanging heuristic vocabulary—one that includes reference to Truth and Rationality as the names of universally agreed-upon goals. Such charges assume that we are all working within a single terminological horizon, and that we have agreed to use the terminology in question. But the Gadamerian line of thought that Hoy is developing suggests that our job is to keep the color of the sky changing by continually merging old horizons with new ones. As Gadamer has said, "Changing the established forms is no less a kind of connection with the tradition than defending the established forms" (quoted by Hoy at p. 127). Encouraging old topics to shuffle off stage is a traditional form of intellectual progress. Hoy's position should, I think, be that Truth, Objectivity, and Rationality are topics that we can safely let go of once we let go of the philosophy of consciousness.

I agree with Habermas that the philosophy of consciousness produced a pendulum movement between scientism and romanticism. The pendulum has swung between insisting that the important thing is to get something out there right, thus glorifying the object, and insisting that the most important thing is to make something new, thus glorifying the subject. This "found or made?" "discovered or constructed?" question is the one currently being debated in American academic circles under the rubric "common sense versus postmodernism." The triteness and sterility of the latter debate is further evidence that Habermas is right in thinking that the philosophy of consciousness has outlived its usefulness. But Habermas is wrong in thinking that you can keep universalism without setting the same old pendulum swinging again. That pendulum will keep swinging as long as the search for truth is thought to be distinct from the search for happiness. That is the separation that pragmatism hopes to end.

Habermas and McCarthy think it enough to unite the search for truth with the search for consensus and freedom by making rationality communicative rather than subject-centered, thereby dropping correspondence to reality in favor of intersubjectivity. Taking that step does rule out what Putnam calls metaphysical realism: the suggestion that what everybody agrees to believe may have nothing to do with the Way the World Is. But it does not eliminate the contrast between what makes beliefs true and what makes them conducive to human happiness, the contrast that pragmatists hope to blur. As long as rational inquiry is thought to converge to a single point, and as long as we think that there are many different ways for human beings to be happy, pragmatism will seem counterintuitive.

Hoy makes the repudiation of the notion of convergence central to his formulation of what he calls "Critical Theory as Genealogical Hermeneutics" (201ff). I think that this is just the right strategy for him to pursue. The idea of convergence to something context-independent should be sharply distinguished from the idea of ever-broader agreement. If one retains the idea of convergence one will see Truth as a goal of inquiry, and then look around for some definition of "Truth" which chimes with the idea that reason is essentially communicative. The agreement of competent judges in ideal epistemic conditions will fill the bill—empty, thin, and uninstructive as such a definition is. But if one drops the idea of convergence, and of context-independence, one will see agreement between communities that have different needs and concerns not as a closer approach to a *focus imaginarius* but simply as a way of attaining more happiness by cooperation than either community could have attained on its own.

Richard Rorty

On the pragmatist view, there will always be new contexts, produced by the fusion of horizons that inevitably occurs when two rather different individuals or communities meet and create a new context by formulating a cooperative project. But none of these new contexts produces beliefs that are more context-independent than their predecessors. Just as no spatio-temporal position is closer than any other to a region in which space and time are blotted out, so no recontextualization of disputed issues gets you closer to context-independence and universal validity than any other recontextualization. If, with Bain, Peirce, and James, you take beliefs to be habits of action, you will think of attaining agreement in belief as just a way of arranging for cooperative action. Then you will not see the point of asking whether the beliefs agreed upon have some further advantage, such as universal validity. You will be content to see them as tools for producing increased human happiness. Convergence will have dropped out of consideration.

To put this point another way, pragmatists do not assume that the same beliefs will form the right habits of action for everybody. So they find it implausible that "all competent judges" will reach the same conclusion on all disputed matters. Nor can they make sense of the notion of these judges working in "ideal epistemic conditions," since they do not think of knowing as an activity for which there are ideal conditions—as there are, for example, for raising mushrooms. Unlike mushrooms, knowings—as Michael Williams's book *Unnatural Doubts* has recently argued—do not form a natural kind.[5]

The pragmatists' principal reason for being suspicious of convergence and context-independence is that you cannot make much sense of the notion of convergence of descriptive or deliberative *vocabularies,* even though, once such a vocabulary is isolated, you can make sense of the notion of convergence on one or another of the statements which that vocabulary provides as options for belief. Once the usual Kuhnian and Gadamerian points about changes of such vocabularies in the course of history are granted, the only way to make sense of convergence is to suggest that vocabularies are adopted and discarded depending upon how well they are found to fit something that is not a vocabulary. This something is usually called "reality" or "the facts." But Habermasians have to give up this notion of "fit" once they admit that the correspondence theory of truth is a relic of sub-ject-centered reason. Once we drop knowledge as a relation between subjects and objects and start thinking of it as a product of consen-sus, the notion of "fit" is no longer available.

McCarthy, in his rejoinder to Hoy toward the end of *Critical Theory,* suggests that we can use ideas of "completeness and unity or coher-ence" as ways of judging progress toward universal validity. These ideas, he says, "seem anything but empty." Without such ideas, Mc-Carthy goes on, "we would likely drift into an uncritical pluralism of 'whatever serves your purposes, whatever they may be'" (233). "Can we write history—in contrast . . . to fiction, propaganda, or rational-ization," McCarthy asks, "without being oriented to the idea of truth?" This, he continues, is "the sort of question for which Hoy will have to find convincing answers if he is to persuade us to deempha-size the idea of truth in favor of that of usefulness, and the idea of unity in favor of that of proliferation" (234).

In this rejoinder, McCarthy is taking for granted that there are in-terest-free and context-free criteria of unity, coherence, and com-pleteness. I do not think that there are. A complete, coherent, unified, nonfictionalized, and nonpropagandist historical account is one that is able to answer all questions of the form "What about this document?" and "How do you fit the following facts into your ac-count?" to the satisfaction of competent judges. What these judges take to be a satisfying answer is a matter of the context in which they themselves are working. So are their ideas about what documents are relevant and which citations are to the point. All the usual Kuhnian and Gadamerian arguments can be marshaled here to show how these contexts have changed in the course of history, and why they may be expected to keep right on changing.

The only way we could make the regulative ideals of truth, com-pleteness, and coherent unity relevant to the practice of historians would be to do what Kuhn and Gadamer tell us we cannot do: lay down context-free criteria of relevance that are thick and rigid enough to exert some pressure. Words like "truth" and "complete-ness" and "coherence" seem to me no better able to provide such cri-teria than the word "good." Gadamer seems to me quite right in saying that one context's domination is another context's liberation, and that the ideas of complete freedom from domination and complete independence of context are empty. Foucault seems to me right in suggesting that history will always reveal domination hiding behind enlightenment, and wrong only in not mentioning that it will often reveal enlightenment riding in on the coattails of tyranny. Foucault's notion of resisting power and Habermas's notion of resisting domination seem to me fine as long as they are explained by reference to concrete instances: Nazis, Communists, or religious fundamentalists, for example. But I think that any attempt to give them context-free significance will drive us right back into the arms of the philosophy of consciousness, the problematic of subject and object, and the correspondence theory of truth.

Hoy, McCarthy, Gadamer, and Habermas all agree that the more different sorts of people we talk to about what ought to be believed and done the better off we shall be. They are all good democrats, good listeners, good conversationalists. All are equally eager to tolerate and encourage difference, novelty, and freedom. The only thing that divides them is whether such tolerance and encouragement is all one can do for the human future, or whether there is more to do. Hoy and Gadamer think that there is nothing much more to do. In particular, they think that specifically philosophical reflection cannot do much to help realize, or even to clarify, our sociopolitical hopes. McCarthy and Habermas, however, are inclined to protest that there must be something more to political idealism than "our preferences." So we find Habermas blaming Castoriadis for being a mere romantic decisionist[6] and McCarthy telling Hoy that his liberal political outlook must be more than the expression of "an aesthetics of personal existence" (234). McCarthy won't let up on Hoy until Hoy gives him good, nonaesthetic, rationally defensible reasons for wanting social justice, and Habermas won't let up on Castoriadis until Castoriadis admits that the politics both men share is a result of rational reflection rather than mere decision.

Let me conclude by trying to say something general about the very idea of "critical theory." In the first chapter of *Critical Theory*, McCarthy approvingly quotes Marcuse as saying that "reason is the fundamental category of philosophical thought" (22). He approvingly paraphrases Horkheimer as saying that "the turn to the psychological, social, and historical roots of thought did not herald the end of reason; it was the latest and most radical phase of its radical self-critique" (12). The biggest difference I have with McCarthy, perhaps, is that he thinks the word "reason" still useful in describing philosophy's nature and function. I do not find the word useful for either purpose. I have never seen any way to bring together what Kant was doing in the *Critique of Pure Reason* with what Marcuse and Horkheimer wanted to do. I am baffled by the Germans' ability to use the word *Kritik* to encompass both Kant's criticism of Wolff and Marx's criticism of capitalism.

If I had to define "critical theory" I should say that it is the attempt of philosophy professors to make the study of Kant, Hegel, and various other books intelligible only to philosophy professors, relevant to the struggle for social justice. I do not think that this attempt has been very successful. Although I agree with McCarthy that Horkheimer and Foucault both gave useful warnings against taking the social scientists as seriously as they often take themselves, I do not think that these warnings suffice to show the relevance of philosophy to (in McCarthy's words) "an investigation of the social, economic, political, and cultural conditions that perpetuate misery and injustice" (234). These investigations are, I think, best carried out by journalists who can report their findings to the rest of us without using either the jargon of the social sciences or that of philosophy.

McCarthy says that in order to investigate the conditions that perpetuate misery and injustice we "need a critical theory of contemporary society at the level of Marx's *Capital* or Habermas's *Theory of Communicative Action*" (234). I think that what we need, in addition to the journalists and their academic allies, are imaginative and well-read trend-spotters. That is how I should describe Marx, Habermas, and Foucault. Marx warned us against such trends as the tendency of the modern state to become the executive committee of the bourgeoisie, and the increasing ability of capitalists to immiserate the proletariat by maintaining a reserve army of the unemployed. When Habermas invented the term "colonization of the life-world" and Foucault the term "medicalization of sexual life," they too spotted dangerous trends. I do not see that any of these three men were much assisted in their trend-spotting work by having read the *Critique of Pure Reason*.

Richard Rorty

Discussion in such areas as epistemology, philosophy of language, philosophy of mind, and philosophy of science is not easily made relevant to spotting sociopolitical trends, nor to the construction of safeguards against the dangers these trends foretell. But we philosophy professors still like to think that the various things we learn in graduate school somehow make up a natural kind. One quick way to tie them all together is to say that, as philosophers, we are professionally concerned with rationality. But this seems to me an empty verbal flourish. As I have already said, I think that this slogan conceals the fact that "rationality" can mean either a cognitive faculty or a political virtue. The popularity of the term "critical theory" seems to me a result of this ambiguity.

I agree with Hoy when he writes that "the wrestling over how best to 'inherit' the tradition of critical theory may be the most pressing controversy in the recent decade of European philosophy" (144). But I regret this fact. Not all politically engaged art has been bad art, but a lot of it has. Not all politically engaged philosophy has been bad philosophy, but a lot of it has been boringly programmatic and tiresomely self-righteous. I think that we philosophy professors should think of our discipline as no more, and no less, involved with the struggle for human freedom than any other academic discipline. It is true that Kant was both the institutor of philosophy as an autonomous academic discipline and a hero of the Enlightenment. But as far as I can see, that was just a coincidence. We should not infer from this coincidence that our choice of discipline helps us play an important sociopolitical role.

Notes

1. David Couzens Hoy and Thomas McCarthy, *Critical Theory* (New York: Blackwell, 1994); intralinear numbers refer to pages in this book.

2. Jürgen Habermas, *The Philosophical Discourse of Modernity,* trans. F. Lawrence (Cambridge: MIT Press, 1987), 295–296.

3. Ibid., 301.

4. Ibid., 323.

5. Michael Williams, *Unnatural Doubts* (Cambridge, Mass.: Blackwell, 1991).

6. Habermas, *Philosophical Discourse of Modernity,* 318ff.

Practical Reason, the "Space of Reasons," and Public Reason

Kenneth Baynes

The concept of reasons for action faces us with a question about their content that it is very difficult to answer in a consistently egoistic or agent-relative style.
—*Thomas Nagel,* The Last Word

In several of his writings Thomas McCarthy pursues, with great effect, a strategy of interpreting Habermas's philosophical project as the development of some Kantian themes with the beneficial hindsight of other Hegelian reflections.[1] I consider this to be an extremely promising strategy and would like to pursue it further with respect to a central Kantian thesis: the claim that we can act only under the idea of freedom.[2] McCarthy has also appealed to this thesis in developing his own interpretation of Habermas: "As practical reasoners we must suppose (Habermas would say: make the idealizing supposition) that we are free to respond to the rational force of evidence and argument. Even when examining just how culturally and historically situated our reasoned responses inevitably are, we cannot avoid presupposing *in actu* the capacity for autonomous reasoning."[3] I believe the thesis is correct but that, in connection with Habermas's overall project, its significance has not been fully appreciated. In particular, I think it can be used not only in connection with Habermas's conception of communicative freedom but also to help ground Habermas's discourse principle—that is, his claim that a norm of action is justified only if it could be agreed to by all those affected as participants in a discourse.[4] To anticipate my argument, we can act for reasons at all only if we assume (as an idealizing supposition) not only that we are free but also that our actions are in general subject to the expectation that the considerations for them could meet with the agreement of others in the relevant discourse.[5] This would in effect amount to a kind of transcendental (or "regressive") argument for the basic principle of Habermas's discourse theory—at least if the idea that a person often acts for reasons is widely accepted, as I believe it is. At the same time, however—and this is now one example of a subsequent Hegelian reflection—this transcendental argument for the discourse principle does not provide a full account of the necessary conditions for rational action. Rather, for Habermas (as also for Hegel) successful rational willing (or practical deliberation) also requires a set of social institutions and a liberal political "ethos" that, in Habermas's phrase, "meets it halfway".[6] McCarthy has also developed Habermas's project along this path; I believe that it parallels in many interesting ways a reading of Hegel developed by both Robert Pippin and Terry Pinkard.[7] On this general approach, the capacity for practical reason also requires the presence of certain social practices and institutions, and within these, forms of mutual recognition that outrun more traditional Kantian accounts of the necessary conditions for rational action. In my own discussion below I will draw upon the work of Christine Korsgaard and Robert Brandom in defending a version of this thesis (I). I will then defend Habermas's strong or "consensualist" notion of public reason against some recent criticisms by McCarthy and others (II) and indicate, at least in rough outline, its relevance for some more directly political concerns (III).

I From Practical Reason to the Discourse Principle

A theory of practical reason (or deliberation) should offer, *inter alia*, an account of how it is that a person can be obligated to pursue a particular course of action as well as an account of how a person can act for a reason.[8] It ought, that is, to explain both what it means for a person to have a reason *to* act (where a reason to act is seen as somehow necessitating or obligating that person) and what it means for a person to act *for* a reason.9 Initially, such an account may be quite general; that is, it need not assume that the different types of practical reason (e.g., instrumental, prudential, and moral) will imply different accounts of how a person can be obligated—although this may turn out to be the case. However, what a theory of practical reason should minimally provide is an account of the normativity (i.e., the capacity to obligate) of reasons and how these reasons *to* act can (at least on some occasions) be the reasons *for* which a person acts. Yet a persuasive account of practical reason on either of these scores is hard to find and, in my opinion, even one of the most successful attempts so far (e.g., Christine Korsgaard's) still comes up short.10 Drawing on her important work, I will sketch the basis for a reading of Habermas's project that does provide such an account. To anticipate, the normativity of reason is due, in the last analysis, to the attitudes—or to what Philip Pettit and Michael Smith have recently called the "conversational stance"—of those actors who ascribe to one another the capacity to take a "yes/no" position on the validity of claims raised in their speech-acts.11 Or, to express the same point differently, the normativity of reason is due to the mutual expectations actors impose on one another in the context of certain social practices. Further, a person's reason *to* act can be the real or "primary" reason *for* which he or she acts only if it figures in the best interpretive explanation of the person's conduct.12 However, unlike some other recent approaches, the capacity to act *for* a reason must not be too directly or exclusively tied to her ability to "reflectively endorse" (Korsgaard), "incorporate" (O'Neill; Allison) or "decisively identify" (Frankfurt) with it, at least not if this ability is conceived as the unique achievement of a solitary individual agent. Rather, as I shall argue, the individual capacity to act for a reason must equally be seen as a function of a wider social practice of "recognition" or ascription of status in which the aspect of individual reflection or awareness is not unduly privileged.13 In other words, the capacity is an interpretively ascribed status as much as it is an individual disposition. This, at least, is how I propose the following remark by Habermas, in response to Herbert Schnädelbach's critique of his "discursive" concept of rationality, should be read: "Reflection [or

Kenneth Baynes

"reflective endorsement," etc.—KB], too, is due to a prior dialogical relation and does not float in the vacuum of an inwardness constituted free from communication. The discursive thematization of validity claims . . . and the reflexive character of these expressions stand in a complementary relation: they refer to one another."[14] (This in fact is yet another instance of a Hegelian variation on a Kantian theme—to which I will return below—that underscores what has been called the "sociality of reason" [Pinkard].)

It is sometimes assumed that there is no particular problem or special difficulty with explaining the normativity of instrumental reason (in contrast, for example, to moral reason) and, indeed, many efforts to account for the normativity of moral reasons do so by attempting to show how it can be derived from considerations of instrumental reason (e.g., Gauthier). Instrumental reasons in turn are thought to acquire their binding force or normativity from the fact that they are rooted in (or can be deliberatively reached from) the desires or "pro-attitudes" within an agent's actual "subjective motivational set."[15] Thus, one "ought" (or has reason) to do X, given the agent's desire for Y and the agent's belief that X is the best means to Y. However, as both Korsgaard and Jean Hampton have argued, even explaining the normativity of instrumental reason is more problematic and, in fact, seems to require a conception of agency that outruns the more standard Humean (or neo-Humean) accounts.[16] That a person "ought" to do X does not simply follow from the (descriptive) fact that she has certain beliefs and desires (or pro-attitudes) unless it is also assumed that the agent accepts (at least if she is rational) the principle that one ought to pursue means toward one's ends or that "he who wills the ends wills the means." This, of course, is Kant's hypothetical imperative and an account of the normativity of instrumental reason must show how it is that an agent (at least insofar as she is rational) stands under this principle. Hume, however, consistently (if notoriously) argued that reason was indifferent toward the ends agents set and thus that it would not be against reason for a person to prefer the destruction of the whole world over the scratching of his finger. And, he continues, "Tis as little contrary to reason to prefer even my own acknowledged lesser good to my greater, and have a more ardent affection for the former than the latter."[17] This suggests that for

Hume it is not irrational to ignore Kant's hypothetical imperative and that it is not the case that a person (whatever her desires or pro-attitudes) necessarily has a reason to pursue means toward their realization. It appears, then, that within Hume's own account of practical reason one cannot account for the normativity of even instrumental reason.[18]

Bernard Williams's account of practical reason (like other 'neo-Humean' accounts), however, supposes that agents are obligated by the desires or pro-attitudes in their actual subjective motivational set. The question then is: how can he account for that normativity?[19] How does the mere fact that I desire something (or have a particular pro-attitude) obligate me or give me a reason to act? The general neo-Humean strategy seems to be one that responds to the question of *practical* necessitation by drawing on the idea of *causal* necessitation: if he wants X and believes doing Y will bring about X then *ceteris paribus*, he does Y. And, so the argument goes, he thus ought to do Y in much the same sense that if X is copper and X is heated then X ought to expand.[20] To have a reason to act (just like acting for a reason) is, on this neo-Humean account, seen within the framework of a causal explanation of action, where having the relevant belief and desire, other things being equal, causes one to act and in this sense, gives one reason to act.

Korsgaard argues, convincingly I think, that the standard Humean (or rather neo-Humean) accounts are inadequate in that they do not show how or why an agent can be "guided" by reasons (rather than merely caused by them) in their action. An alternative account must address this question by explaining not only how a person can have a reason *to* act, as I suggested above, but also how that reason can be the reason *for* her action.[21] Korsgaard's own account of the "sources of normativity" goes a long way toward answering this question for instrumental, prudential, and moral reasons.

Korsgaard begins with an alternative concept of the person or agency in which the capacity for a reflective distance on our "first-order" desires figures prominently. To have a practical *identity* at all, she claims, requires that a person not be simply a "location" of desires that move her but rather that she endorse or "take up" the desire as a reason for action and this in turn requires that she has the capacity for a reflective distance with respect to them.[22] As agents who at least sometimes deliberate, we must view ourselves not simply as caused to act by our strongest desire but as deciding whether a particular desire or pro-attitude fits in with some conception we have of ourselves. Williams's own theory of practical reason might be able to concede this much, so long as one's practical identity remains dependent on an individual's "subjective motivational set." However Korsgaard's further claim is that the capacity for reflection also entails a "moral identity" that, so to speak, "stands behind" (121) any particular practical identity and this "moral identity" (or conception of ourselves as human agents *simpliciter*) requires that at least some of our reasons must be "agent-neutral" (that is, not dependent on any particular subjective motivational set). The claim then is that to act for a reason (to be obligated or necessitated) requires a conception of ourselves as capable of reflective endorsement and that the capacity for reflective endorsement, when properly thought through, entails that at least some of our reasons for acting be ones that are "agent-neutral." Both of these revisions need further clarification and, at least at first glance, might even seem to stand somewhat in tension with one another. The first step emphasizes a certain reflective capacity that must be exercised by the individual agent if something is to count as a reason. The second step, which modifies Nagel's discussion of "agent-neutral reasons" with Wittgensteinian insights about language-use, would seem to trace the authority of reasons to a wider social practice. However, I believe that the argument Korsgaard presents is an important one and that, with perhaps just a bit of revision of my own, it parallels and fills in the Habermasian thesis that acting for a reason requires a conception of ourselves as standing under the expectation that we can justify the reasons for our action to others. I will thus attempt to clarify and elaborate an interpretation of these two steps in Korsgaard's own account.

Korsgaard's first revision to the standard neo-Humean account of practical reason is to claim that in order to see ourselves as acting for reasons (rather than as simply caused by motives or desires) we must view ourselves as agents with the capacity for reflection. Further, the capacity for reflection as she understands it entails more than discerning which among our desires is most compelling or what is the best means for realizing them. It involves as well asking whether we want to be moved by certain desires or, in other words, whether we can *endorse* a particular impulse or desire as a *reason* for action. But, it might be asked, just what does this further capacity consist in and how does this sort of "reflective endorsement" transform a desire into a reason or, in her terms, grant it normativity or obligatoriness (252)? How does an individual's endorsement of a desire generate the kind of normativity she thinks must be explained?[23]

Korsgaard's response to this question points to the special features the appropriate sort of reflective endorsement possesses. To "endorse" a desire as a reason for action—or, to use Kant's language, to incorporate it into a maxim of the will—is to treat the considerations as stemming from, or as fitting into, a practical conception of oneself as an agent. For Korsgaard this means that even with respect to one's particular practical (as opposed to moral) identity, a certain level of generality or universality is introduced and that these considerations in turn serve to shape or "constitute" the person that I am (or my practical self-conception). To "endorse" a desire—say, to have your child placed with a particular classroom teacher—as a reason to act is (at least implicitly) to acknowledge that anyone similarly situated would also have a reason to act. As such it is not simply my reason in the sense that it is relative to *my* (contingent) subjective motivational set; rather, the reflective endorsement of the desire means treating the desire as a reason any similarly situated agent would have. So far, though, we do not have a notion of "agent-neutral" reasons (as Korsgaard following Nagel employs this term) but rather of universal or general agent-relative reasons (that is, reasons that are still dependent upon the content of a particular kind of subjective motivational set). Yet both Korsgaard and Nagel want to claim more: each wants to claim that there are also reasons to act that obligate the agent even if they are not dependent in some way on the agent's subjective motivational set. Nagel's strategy is found in an appeal to objective realism that is not available to Korsgaard (see 40–42).

Korsgaard's constructivist approach, by contrast, appeals to an argument about the conditions of possibility for both self-identity and autonomy: if I am to conceive of myself as a (unified) mind or self at all and if this mind or self is to be conceived as autonomous or legislating its own laws—if, in other words, the self is to be anything more than the locus of impulses that move me—then, Korsgaard argues, I must be capable of acting from rules or principles that have a general or universal character (that bind, in other words, because of my identity as a reflective agent *per se* rather than (solely) my more determinate practical identity (see 228f). Curiously, however, Korsgaard concedes that this notion of universality or generality of reason is still extremely formal and does not lead to the conclusion that we are bound by moral reasons (or that we must see ourselves as subject to moral laws and not just to a categorical imperative).[24] To achieve this further end she appeals to well-known (if obscure) Wittgensteinian considerations about the impossibility of a private language.

Before turning to this second revision to the neo-Humean account of practical reason, I would like to point to a similarity between Korsgaard's account of reflective endorsement and some other accounts of autonomy (or responsibility) influenced by P. F. Strawson.[25] To claim that a person acts for a reason or that she "endorses" a particular motive as her reason is also to claim that she is responsible or accountable for the action under that description. Further, on the view I wish to defend, to claim that a person *is* responsible or accountable (in general as well as for a particular action under a description) is to claim that she is *held or taken to be* responsible or accountable by others.[26] The order of explanation here is the opposite of what we are apt more commonly to suppose is the case: namely, a person is responsible *because* others hold her responsible. Of course, this status may be (at least temporarily) withdrawn from a person to the extent that we think her conduct was subject to one or another "excusing conditions." But, there is no further natural or non-normative ("causal") fact to be discovered about a person that could settle the question (in general) of whether she is responsible; rather, her status as a responsible agent is a function of a stance or attitude others adopt toward her.

Strawson accounted for this practice of holding one another responsible in terms of the various "reactive attitudes" (praise, blame, indignation, etc.) that constitute that practice. His account is clearly an improvement upon earlier "influence" theories (that is, the view

that we hold them accountable because we want to shape their behavior). Others have sought to further amend Strawson's account to
provide a more explicitly *cognitive* account of moral responsibility
that ties our reactive attitudes to judgments we would make about the
character of a person's will.[27] However, what is important in all these
accounts, despite their further differences, is that a person's being responsible is a function of a stance others take toward her or a status
ascribed to her by others. The normativity that Korsgaard locates in
our capacity for reflection (and hence in the notion of responsibility) can thus be further traced to the "stance" taken toward an individual or status ascribed to an individual. The main point I wish to
make here is that the capacity for reflection (or reflective endorsement) that creates normativity must itself be seen in connection to a
wider social practice of holding people accountable. The capacity to
act for a reason requires, in general, that one be considered part of
a practice—a co-participant, if you will—in which the participants
hold one another responsible. I would even say that to act for a reason just is to be answerable in principle to others or to be under the
expectation that you could give an account to them for that action.[28]
Someone who does not stand under such a general expectation simply cannot be said to act for a reason.

This reading of Korsgaard's account of acting for a reason may
seem too "interpretationist," too Davidsonian for her liking—though
I do not see anything in her text that counts against such a reading.[29]
Like the model of rational action-explanations in general, it assumes
that in holding a person responsible for an action (or claiming she
has acted for a reason) we must employ (as a matter of interpretive necessity) our own norms of rationality and evaluative standards or, in
Sellarsian language, we must locate her within the space of reasons. In
fact, I think this *is* one of the more promising ways to understand
Kant's notion that we must act "under the idea of freedom."[30] In holding others responsible for their action, we take them to be (at least
capable of) acting for reasons, that is, capable of acting on considerations they are (or should be) prepared to justify to others. For reasons
that Korsgaard herself emphasizes, such an interpretation plays an
important part in our view of what unifies an agent—a person, so to
speak, by the normative force of the reasons that govern her conduct

(see 229). To claim that an agent must "endorse" a consideration for it to be a reason for her action is just to claim that her action must be interpretable by us as supremely (subjectively) reasonable for her, given what we know (and otherwise assume) about her situation. If she has not endorsed the considerations then, though they may still "rationalize" her action in some sense, they will not "explain" her action—that is, they will not constitute the "primary reason" (Davidson) for the action.[31]

Korsgaard's second revision to the neo-Humean account of practical reason is set out particularly in the fourth lecture of *The Sources of Normativity*. There she argues that reasons are not essentially or fundamentally "private mental entities," but rather are inherently public and shareable (131f.). At least part of her goal at this point is to resist those strategies that, in her words, try to "bridge the gap" between public and private reasons by arguing that we have private reasons to acknowledge public ones. She shares the conviction with many others, including Rawls, Scanlon, and Habermas, that that conception of morality rests on a mistake. But Korsgaard also offers a positive argument to show that reasons are essentially public or shareable (again in the sense that they are agent-neutral or are reasons that all have regardless of their more determinate subjective motivational set). She appeals in this context to Wittgenstein's arguments against the possibility of a private language and suggests that a "parallel argument" can be developed for the public character of reasons (137). However, the specific structure of the argument is not clearly laid out and, it seems to me, she does not sufficiently pursue certain Wittgensteinian insights. In fact, at this point her account of public reasons seems to me to suffer from an unsuccessful attempt to blend two different traditions of discourse: the discussion centering around Nagel's notion of agent-neutral reasons (which looks for reasons that all share in the sense that they are from an "impersonal viewpoint") and the discussion deriving from Wittgenstein (and Hegel) (which looks for reasons all can share as participants in a common community of language-users). Though her sympathies are clearly with the Wittgenstein tradition and opposed to what she describes as Nagel's "objective realism," her discussion of "agent-neutral reasons" (and her repetition of Nagel's argument in her "Reply")[32] tends to obscure this fact.

Further, the conflation of these two traditions also obscures the fact that not all reasons are "agent-neutral" (as Nagel eventually came to see) even though all reasons are "public" in a Wittgensteinian sense.[33] However, in pursuing her claim about the "sources of normativity" what Korsgaard really wants and needs to show is that to have any reason to act (that is, to be practically obligated or necessitated at all) we must grant that there are some (agent-neutral and indeed moral) reasons that all share. As I understand it, the work of Robert Brandom is, by contrast, particularly well suited to the second, Wittgensteinian, line of argument because Brandom understands reasons in terms of the statuses (entitlements and commitments) that actors ascribe to one another in certain social practices. Reasons, on this view, will be public or shareable among competent participants in that social practice.

A central feature of Brandom's (semantic) pragmatism is the thesis that both propositional content (or meaning) and propositional attitudes (beliefs, desires, etc.) are ultimately to be explained in terms of the social practice of reason giving that must be taken as primitive (that is, cannot be cashed in for non-normative, naturalistic currency).[34] To adopt a complex intentional stance toward someone, that is, to treat them not only as having beliefs and desires but also as equally capable of ascribing beliefs and desires to another—or in Brandom's phrase, to adopt a "discursive scorekeeping stance" toward them—is just to assign them a status in the social practice of reason-giving. This can be done either from the external perspective of one who is interpreting another linguistic community or from the internal perspective of one who is him- or herself a participant in the social practice in question. In both cases, it seems to me, this activity must proceed in accordance with Davidson's principle of charity, or an approximation of it, in which the interpreter must make certain general assumptions about the intentional states or propositional attitudes of others.

This is not the place to consider the details of Brandom's account. What is relevant for our purposes is the fact that Brandom's theory offers an instructive way to understand what Korsgaard calls the inherently public character of reasons. To *be* a reason-giver (and thus capable of complex intentional states), for Brandom, is fundamentally

Kenneth Baynes

to be *taken as* or treated as a reason-giver by the relevant social community. (This claim, to my mind, parallels the claim made above that to be a responsible agent is fundamentally to be held responsible by others.) It means that the individual is assigned a status as a competent member of the community in the sense that she is considered a competent participant in the relevant community and thus as capable of responding to the range of entitlements and commitments recognized as appropriate to that community. In an important sense, then, one cannot reason privately—or more precisely, reasoning or deliberating *in foro interno* must be seen as importantly dependent upon a prior social practice. Further, in the case of a particular individual action, to claim that an individual has acted for a reason (and not simply been caused to act) is to say, with respect to that action, that it is appropriate to hold the individual accountable for the action under at least that description. Finally, Brandom sees the normative character of practical reason not simply in terms of individual's reflective endorsement alone, but also in connection with the attitudes of members of a wider community. To act for a reason on this account, then, is to act under a norm, where acting under a norm itself means that you are treated by the community to be appropriately responsive to—and (in general, though often implicitly) aware of—the particular set of entitlements and commitments relevant to the action in question. This account, of course, is Brandom's development of the Sellarsian idea of a "space of reasons" as a fundamentally normative and social space that cannot be replaced by a non-normative description of causal relations and interactions. It is equally an interpretation of Kant's notion that we can act only under the idea of freedom, but one that, to use Strawson's phrase, does not entail a "panicky metaphysics" of freedom. I believe Brandom's account also provides, as Rorty remarks, "just the sort of philosophy of language that Habermas has been asking for."[35] For, to be ascribed a status in the "space of reasons" is to be viewed as someone able to give reasons for one's actions; to claim (of oneself or another) in a particular case that one has acted for a reason is to claim that one is responsible for that action—that is, answerable to others for the action under a given description.

This reworking of Korsgaard's own two revisions to the neo-Humean account of practical reason helps to lessen the tension between them. On the one hand, the act of reflective endorsement is not viewed solely as the solitary undertaking of an individual actor (though this undertaking must be presupposed). On the other hand, the idea of the inherent publicity or shareability of reasons can be given a plausible (broadly Davidsonian type) rendering that is more attractive than the objectivistic model proposed by Nagel. Furthermore, the two revisions complement one another in that they fit within a broadly interpretivist approach to action and the general constraints provided by such an approach. This reading of Korsgaard also helps to make sense of the passage from Habermas with which I began: namely, his claim that a reflective model of rationality (such as Schnädelbach's and, I would add, Frankfurt's) and his own (and, I would add, Brandom's) "discursive" model of rationality " . . . stand in a complementary relation: they *refer to one another.*"

In concluding this first section, I would like to address briefly some problems or objections that might be raised in connection with the position I have outlined above. I have tried to show that for a person to act for a reason entails as well that she acts under the expectation that the reasons for her action could meet with the agreement of others in a discourse. But, one might object, I have not yet shown that Habermas's principle of discourse specifies a criterion of (rational) validity for any norm of action. Clearly there are many other details that still need to be provided. However, if whenever a person acts for a reason she is under the expectation that the reasons can be justified to others, then I think one can say that a person stands under a general principle that one's actions (which is to say one's relevant act-descriptions or "maxims") are justified (i.e., rationally valid) only if they could meet with the agreement of others. And that is just what the discourse principle asserts.

Another objection to the claim that in acting for a reason a person is committed to accepting something like the discourse principle would be to claim that in the end the principle as I have formulated it doesn't carry any real bite, that it is mere "window-dressing" where all the normative work is done by the (independently identifiable) good reasons themselves.[36] Again an adequate response would require more detail than I can give at this time. A first observation is simply to note that the discourse principle (like the rival principle of utility) should not be understood primarily as a practical method for decision making, but as standard or criterion of deontic (including moral) rightness.[37] However, I believe that this objection also rests on the mistaken assumption that something like good reasons exist or can be identified apart from discourses themselves.[38] While it is true that in a discourse individuals must be convinced on the basis of insight that their considerations are indeed "good reasons," their status as good reasons for acting depends on the mutual supposition of the possible agreement of others. Thus, to give but one (provocatively counterintuitive) example, in the final analysis the judgment that it is morally wrong to needlessly inflict harm on innocent persons—and thus the belief that we have "good reasons" not to do it—does not depend on any property to be discovered in the action per se (whatever that might mean) nor even on a determination of the overall consequences that would predictably follow from it, but on the fact that such action could not be justified to others in a moral discourse. At any rate, for better or worse, the discourse-ethical position on this metaphysical question is not unique but finds itself in company with other contractualist and constructivist moral theories.[39]

Finally, to consider an important objection from a quite different perspective, it might be claimed that the account of acting for reasons outlined above conflates the distinction between justifying reasons and motivating reasons.[40] In fact, the objection might continue, it only considers the question of the (justifying) reasons a person might have *to* act and fails to address the explanatory question of a person's (motivating) reasons *for* action. Consequently, the attempt to ground the discourse principle would fail because I have not shown that it must be presupposed by a person's motivating reasons. Echoing again Hegel's earlier critique of Kant, the discourse principle (and indeed any justifying reasons that are not also shown to actually be motivating ones) would remain "impotent." This objection is, I think, partially correct because I am suspicious of some of the uses to which the distinction between motivating and justifying reasons has been put and of the ways in which it seems to presuppose a neo-Humean account of practical reasons.[41] On the view defended here the strategy is just the reverse: any motivating reason must be at least a *subjectively* justifying reason—that is, for a person to act for a reason she must believe (at least implicitly, or, perhaps better put, we must at least implicitly suppose her to believe) that she can justify that action to others. To suppose that a person can have a motivating reason that is not equally or at the same time at least a subjectively justifying reason would be to lapse again into just the sort of causal theory of action and action-explanation that I have resisted—it would be to step outside the "space of reasons" for an explanation of human action.

II   The Sources and Limits of Public Reason

In this section I would like to turn to a related concern about Habermas's account of public reason. Public reason for Habermas refers not only to the sense in which in acting communicatively (or indeed, as I have argued, in acting for a reason at all) a person must suppose that she can justify her action to others. The idea of public reason also plays a crucial role in Habermas's account of political legitimacy. Basic political norms (e.g., what Rawls calls the "constitutional essentials" and matters of basic justice) are legitimate only if they conform to a demanding ideal of public reason, that is, only if they could be agreed to by all citizens as participants in a practical discourse for the same (publicly available) reasons. McCarthy and others have argued that Habermas's conception of political legitimacy, together with this idea of public reason, is too strongly oriented to the idea of consensus or "rational agreement" and that he should move more in the direction of Rawls's notion of an overlapping consensus that allows for "reasonable disagreement" and "reasonable pluralism" within a public culture.[42] Political legitimacy neither can nor should depend on such a demanding idea of rational agreement but rather should draw upon the idea of a "mutual accommodation" among diverse worldviews and corresponding forms of life. This revision also entails a more thoroughly "proceduralist" interpretation of political legitimacy.

On the other hand, in an extended engagement with Rawls's work, Habermas has argued that Rawls's notion of an overlapping consensus cannot serve the purpose to which Rawls puts it and that Rawls himself requires a stronger, more consensualist notion of practical reason to support his own liberal principle of legitimacy.[43] This principle, it will be recalled, reads as follows: "Our exercise of political power is fully proper only when it is exercised in accordance with a constitution the essentials of which all citizens as free and equal may reasonably be expected to endorse in the light of principles and ideals acceptable to their common human reason"[44] or, as he has expressed it in more recently: "Our exercise of political power is proper only when we sincerely believe that the reasons we would offer for our political actions—were we to state them as government officials —are sufficient, and we also reasonably think that other citizens might also reasonably accept those reasons."[45] According to Habermas, however, Rawls (at least in *Political Liberalism*) interprets this principle of legitimacy in connection with the *de facto* emergence of an overlapping consensus rather than, as one should, in terms of a more abstract (communication-theoretical) idea of rational agreement or acceptability.

In the following I would like not only to defend Habermas's own position, as I understand it, against McCarthy's "friendly amendment" but also argue that Habermas has misunderstood Rawls's position, which, rightly understood, is in fact much closer to Habermas's own. Even (or precisely) a *liberal* principle of political legitimacy requires a substantive (and not merely "indirect" or procedural) agreement on a "core morality" (Larmore) that can be the focus of, or specify the content for, a *reasonable* overlapping consensus.[46] However, in contrast to Habermas's reading, this overlapping consensus is not simply a "lucky convergence" that just "happens" to come about.[47] Rather it can only play an appropriate role in justification if it contributes to social stability, as Rawls puts it, "for the right reason."[48] I thus agree with Larmore when he writes, "[Rawls] seems clearly not to believe, contrary to some of his recent critics, that the commitments on which his political liberalism rests are simply those that people in modern Western societies share as a matter of fact. What he holds is that these commitments would be the object of consensus to the extent that people view themselves, as they should, as free and equal citizens."[49] These considerations suggest that the notion of the reasonable (together with his account of public reason) functions for Rawls in a different manner than Habermas has suggested. It also suggests that the procedural/substantive contrast may be overdrawn by several of the participants in this debate.

To begin, then, I will briefly review McCarthy's criticisms of Habermas that, in this context, I assume are quite familiar. According to McCarthy, Habermas has not yet articulated a conception of public reason (and, hence, political legitimacy) that can adequately respond to the value pluralism that characterizes liberal-democratic societies. On the one hand, there typically is no homogeneous ethico-political culture that could provide the necessary background for an agreement on "constitutional essentials and matters of basic justice." On the other hand, the model of discourse that Habermas proposes does not make sufficient allowance for "reasonable disagreements" about moral/ethical questions. Rather, cases supporting the idea of a reasonable value pluralism are either interpreted as "interim reports" on an ongoing moral disagreement, where it is claimed there is only one right answer, or they are too quickly treated as a matter of negotiation and compromise, in just the way that conflicts of "interest" are to be handled.[50] The result is a certain inadequacy within Habermas's theory in responding to the value pluralism characteristic of modern societies. McCarthy's suggestion is that, to accommodate the fact of reasonable pluralism, Habermas must relinquish the strong claims concerning rational agreement [*Einverständnis*], make room for a notion of mutual accommodation (152) and, consequently, give his theory a still more "procedural twist" (151). By making greater use of his own distinction between direct and indirect justification of a norm, for example, Habermas could allow for the idea of a "reasonable disagreement" on values, while nonetheless still providing citizens with a strong procedural reason for accepting as legitimate those norms and decisions they oppose at a substantive level (128).

An initial interpretive question that should be raised concerning this proposed revision, a question of which McCarthy is aware, concerns the nature of the proceduralism he has in mind. What, for instance, is the relation between the procedural and substantive elements of the theory and how, after this "proceduralist twist," is Habermas's position to be distinguished from the more common varieties of proceduralism in which the "fairness" of the procedure is secured by a much more minimal notion of equal consideration of interests than either Habermas or Rawls would be comfortable with?[51] I have discussed this question elsewhere and will not dwell on it here except to note that—despite Habermas's own frequent use of the term procedural—neither Habermas (nor Rawls) are proceduralists "all the way down."[52] Rather, both attempt to mirror in a set of procedures a prior substantive value or set of values—autonomy, in the case of Habermas, and the idea of citizens as free and equal persons, in the case of Rawls. It is these values or ideals that then confer a presumption of reasonableness or fairness on the proposed procedures.[53]

I would like instead to focus here on another general question concerning the use of the term "reasonable" in McCarthy's reference to a "reasonable disagreement" and a "reasonable pluralism." I assume that McCarthy takes over these terms relatively unmodified from Rawls, but I want to suggest that Rawls's own use of them, along with their relation to the idea of an overlapping consensus, has not always been well understood. A correct interpretation, I believe, puts Rawls and Habermas much closer together than either McCarthy or Habermas suppose, since both are committed to the view that there must be a prior agreement on a "core morality" that each citizen can affirm for the same (publicly available) reasons.

The idea of the reasonable is invoked at many levels within Rawls's theory, but its most basic use is with respect to persons: a citizen is reasonable if she is willing to accept and abide by fair terms of cooperation and willing to accept the "burdens of judgment," that is, to acknowledge and abide by the limits of reason.[54] These two basic virtues of the citizen are themselves understood in connection with what Rawls calls the basic moral powers of the person: the capacity for a sense of justice and the capacity for a conception of the good. These moral powers (or basic human capacities) are part of a moral psychology or conception of the person that, along with the idea of social cooperation, form one of the "fundamental intuitive ideas" found in a liberal political culture and from which his political conception is drawn. Though this idea is according to Rawls not itself part of a comprehensive doctrine or theory of human nature, it is nonetheless part of a general set of normative reflections, informed as well by moral and social-scientific theory, on the basic capacities of human agency.[55] Like Korsgaard's conception of practical agency outlined above, this "fundamental intuitive idea" of the person is (I believe) a conception of the agent that "stands behind" our other, more determinate practical identities and is more or less implicitly assumed by many different religious and secular traditions. It refers to the general human capacity to respond to and act for reasons. The appeal to this capacity gives normative content to Rawls's idea of the reasonable and ultimately shapes his notion of a (rational) justification (e.g., what is acceptable to "common human reason").

The further notions of a "reasonable comprehensive doctrine," a "reasonable overlapping consensus," and "reasonable pluralism" all draw upon this prior notion of reasonable persons: a doctrine, for example, is reasonable if its more specific elements fall within the "burdens of judgment" of reasonable citizens and an overlapping consensus is reasonable just in case it is a consensus among reasonable comprehensive doctrines. Finally, a reasonable disagreement is a disagreement that persists even after reasonable people, exercising good faith and recognizing the "burdens of judgment," nonetheless fail to agree on a particular matter. According to Rawls, in a liberal polity such disagreements are to be expected.

It is important to note, however, even in this brief outline, that what Rawls describes as the reasonable is *not* the conclusion or outcome of an agreement or overlapping consensus that just happens to exist. Rather, the prior idea of the reasonable *informs* what can count as a reasonable comprehensive doctrine and thus what could finally be part of a (reasonable) overlapping consensus. The idea of the reasonable, in other words, is something that must in this sense be given in advance of any existing overlapping consensus, rather than something that results from it. It might be objected, in response, that this reading does not follow Rawls's own recent distinction between "moral autonomy" and "political autonomy" (or, relatedly, between "persons" and "citizens") and thus still gives Rawls's position a too Kantian interpretation—one his "freestanding" political conception is meant to avoid.[56] However, though Rawls's own formulations sometimes lend support to such a reading, I think this cannot be his considered position. He is himself explicit that a "political" conception is still a "moral conception" and, in introducing his "criterion of reciprocity" (in which citizens must reasonably think that others can reasonably accept the terms of cooperation proposed), he states that this criterion bars slavery and other violations of basic liberties.[57] In short, even his conception of the political autonomy of citizens, along with the terms of social cooperation they could "reasonably" undertake, presupposes the two moral powers or "basic human capacities" Rawls earlier introduced in *A Theory of Justice*.[58]

A related question often posed in connection with Rawls's political liberalism—and one that Habermas himself raises—concerns the role that the idea of an overlapping consensus plays in its justification (in contrast to its stability or likelihood to endure over time).[59] According to Rawls, the idea of an overlapping consensus is first introduced at a second stage, in connection with the question of social stability, not at the first stage when the initial justification of the principles of justice is at issue. This does not mean, however, that the overlapping consensus is not at all relevant to the process of justification. Rawls's considered view seems to be that if it turns out that the political conception justified at the first stage is not stable—that is, could not become the object of a reasonable overlapping consensus—then this would somehow call into question its earlier claim to being justified.[60]

In his own interpretation of Rawls, however, Habermas seems to take a different tack. That is, he attributes a *more* significant justificatory role to the idea of an overlapping consensus than, I believe, Rawls has in mind. Habermas apparently does not consider that the idea of the reasonable must already be presupposed prior to the identification of those comprehensive doctrines that might be eligible candidates for a reasonable overlapping consensus, but rather regards the notion of the reasonable as itself the outcome of a contingent or "lucky" convergence: "Only the lucky convergence of the differently motivated nonpublic reasons can generate the public validity or 'reasonableness' of the content of this 'overlapping consensus' that everyone accepts. Agreement in conclusions *results* from premises rooted in different outlooks."[61] Now, while it is true that each citizen may and even should look to his or her own comprehensive doctrine to see whether he or she has reason to affirm the content of the overlapping consensus, it is not the case either that the justification of the content rests upon these "nonpublic" reasons or that a contingent overlapping consensus produces or defines the "reasonableness" of that content.

This repositioning of the reasonable within Rawls's conception of political liberalism also then suggests how Rawls may in fact be closer to Habermas's own position. It is the basic idea of the citizen as reasonable and rational and, behind this, the idea of the basic moral powers of the person that importantly shapes the subsequent employment of the reasonable in Rawls's work. In ways that closely resemble Habermas's basic assumptions about communicative freedom—the capacity to take a position on a speech act offer, Rawls's idea of the reasonable acquires at least some of its normative authority from the fundamental human capacity to respond to and act from reasons: the legitimacy of a political order depends on what citizens can endorse in view of their "common human reason" (though a lot of further philosophical argument—contained in *A Theory of Justice* and *Political Liberalism*—is required to show what kind of political order might possibly satisfy this requirement).

Given McCarthy's reservations about Habermas's model of public reason sketched above, his response to this reading of Rawls might simply be, "Well, so much the worse for him!" If the best reading of Rawls is one that also commits him to a stronger, more consensualist model of political legitimacy, then perhaps he too should be urged to move more in the direction of McCarthy's proceduralism and idea of "mutual accommodation." However, I do not believe this is an option for McCarthy because I do not think he is able to make a convincing case that his proposed revision constitutes a real alternative to Habermas. It only *seems* to be a real alternative because McCarthy does not clarify what he means by a *reasonable* pluralism and a *reasonable* disagreement. How are these to be distinguished from their unreasonable counterparts? I see no alternative to the view that a disagreement is reasonable only if there exists at another level an agreement on core values that all can accept for the same publicly available reasons—in the last analysis, values based on our conception of ourselves as free and equal persons. We could think a disagreement arose from the "burdens of judgment" rather than willful ignorance or prejudice only if there were a further agreement on other basic values. Similarly, we can "(reasonably) agree to disagree

Kenneth Baynes

(reasonably)" (McCarthy) only if we believe other procedures that are available for regulating our coexistence at a more abstract level reflect norms and values that all could accept for the same (publicly available) reasons. In short, it would not be a reasonable pluralism or a reasonable disagreement if there were not (or could not be) this deeper agreement. McCarthy rightly notes that Habermas's discussion of practical rationality does not adequately address ways to handle cases of reasonable disagreement, but I do not think a more adequate or nuanced account can finally break with Habermas's criterion of rational acceptability.[62] As Habermas points out in his reply to McCarthy, even McCarthy's treatment of tolerance and mutual accommodation seem to presuppose the ideal of a rationally motivated agreement.[63]

III   The Practice of Public Reason

In concluding I will briefly consider some implications this more abstract debate regarding the idea of public reason might have for more concrete political practice. In particular, I want to suggest some ways that it might inform both the practice of toleration and the practice of *political* public reasoning.

(a) As many commentators have pointed out, toleration is an important yet elusive liberal virtue.[64] It asks that we live with what we might find deeply repugnant from a personal point of view. In this respect, it is an attitude that, despite its almost banal ring, is both extremely demanding and indispensable to a liberal political culture: on the one hand, we may personally (and justifiably) feel quite opposed to the practice or way of life we are asked to tolerate yet, on the other hand, we are asked actively to affirm the right of others to engage in that practice or way of life (even though we need not have any regret should that practice or way of life cease to exist).[65] How is it possible to cultivate such an attitude, particularly in a pluralist society where we are likely to frequently encounter attitudes and ways of life with which we disagree? And, second, what are the appropriate limits of such an attitude: is it necessary to tolerate the intolerable? Is not this paradoxical virtue simply one more symptom of an impoverished liberalism that finds itself obliged to defend practices it finds morally offensive? These are not easy questions to answer but several brief observations can be made. Habermas's distinction between a political culture and the larger societal culture, as well as Rawls's parallel distinction between what he calls the "politically public" and the larger background culture, is important here inasmuch as the first term in these pairs helps to set the basic frame and limits of the tolerable. In this respect it defines the minimal "core morality" the violation of which need not be tolerated, either from a legal or a moral point of view.[66] (I do not mean that, as a matter of policy, questions such as the legal regulation of hate speech or violent pornography are now immediately settled; but rather that this core morality provides the general framework within which a political community is first properly bound to address those topics.) At the same time, however, matters that do not concern the "core morality" of the political culture are ones that all citizens have an obligation to tolerate as a matter of public morality. It may also be that, as part of an attitude of toleration, citizens also have an obligation to try to reach a greater mutual understanding of one another's perspective. The exercise of toleration thus may (*but need not*) develop into stronger forms of appreciation and "civic friendship."

(b) In the context of his exchange with Rawls, Habermas has defended a conception of public reason and corresponding conception of "reasonableness" as an important political virtue and one that is probably as demanding as the virtue of toleration. In connection with his version of "political liberalism" based on the idea of an "overlapping consensus" among divergent comprehensive moral or religious worldviews, Rawls has argued that, as a duty of civility, citizens have a moral obligation, when they consider how to cast their vote, to regard themselves as "ideal legislators" and ask whether the reasons in support of the proposed legislation or policy are ones that it is reasonable to think other citizens could also endorse. In response to criticisms of his initial formulation, he now endorses what he calls an "inclusive" model of public reason that allows citizens to act from reasons drawn from their comprehensive moral or religious convictions so long as they believe the positions they support could "in due course" also be supported on the basis of public reasons that all affected could acknowledge on the basis of their shared conception of themselves as

Kenneth Baynes

free and equal persons.[67] Rawls goes on to indicate that this "duty" applies only to political discussions within the "public political forum" and not to discussion within the larger "background culture" of civil society.[68] Thus, while it is permissible for a person to advocate laws, say, prohibiting same-sex marriages in various associations and fora of civil society, it would be inappropriate for that same person to make such an argument in a political forum where it is not reasonable for him or her to assume that the coparticipants (and cocitizens) could share the same grounds of the argument.[69] Nonetheless, it is clear that this still represents a quite demanding requirement for public reason.

In his own reflections Habermas is led to a similar conception of public reason and, if anything, gives it an even stronger interpretation.[70] He writes: "Anything valid should also be capable of a public justification. Valid statements deserve the acceptance of everyone *for the same reasons.*"[71] Thus, for Habermas, though it may indeed be possible for individuals to embed their shared political ideals within their own comprehensive moral or religious worldviews, this connection between private moralities and public reason does not provide a sufficiently stable or normatively appropriate basis for the legitimate exercise of coercive political authority. Rather, citizens must simultaneously both presuppose and strive to articulate a basic political consensus (focused on the idea of a "core morality" mentioned above) that all citizens can endorse as valid for the same (publicly available) reasons. The legitimate exercise of political power requires that the reasons that justify at least the basic principles of justice and "constitutional essentials" be ones that all citizens can endorse for the same reasons—that is, in view of their shared conception of themselves as free and equal persons. Moreover, the political virtue of reasonableness requires that citizens, in regarding themselves as "ideal legislators," seek to find for the policies and legislation they support reasons that they reasonably believe others could reasonably endorse.

Two important objections to this account of the civic virtues need to be addressed: First, are they themselves exclusionary and/or sectarian in conception? And, second, is it at all plausible to think that they can be effectively promoted and sustained within the two-track model of deliberative democracy advocated by Habermas?

Practical Reason, the "Space of Reasons," and Public Reason

(1) The first objection, which has been raised from some quite diverse perspectives, is that the virtues of toleration (and reasonableness) are not innocent but rather function in ways that are both exclusionary and sectarian. Although this objection raises a number of extremely complex issues, I want to claim in response that, when properly understood, these virtues do not have to have the exclusionary consequences its critics have claimed. While Kirstie McClure, for example, may be right that the practice of toleration asks, say, religious believers to regard the truth claims of their faith as matters of private belief, it does not follow that it constitutes an unjustifiable or unacceptable harm against them.[72] There is no guarantee that within a liberal polity matters of religious faith and practice or, for that matter, other individual or collective ways of life will remain unchanged. The question must be whether or not individuals have their equal rights and liberties denied them in their treatment by the state. It does not seem to constitute a harm or violation of a right to, say, freedom of speech, if one is told that he or she is not morally entitled, in certain political fora, to press claims against others that others do not (and cannot reasonably be expected to) acknowledge. Similarly, the claim that citizens act unreasonably if they promote policies and legislation on the basis of nonpublic reasons does not per se imply that they themselves are the victims of exclusionary or sectarian politics. On the one hand, to claim that it is a violation of a moral duty to pursue positions on the basis of nonpublic reasons within the more narrowly circumscribed political public sphere does not mean that there are not many other fora available within civil society in which those views can be aired and discussed. Second, I have again not broached the difficult topic of when (or whether) it is permissible to respond to such moral infractions with legal remedies (e.g., the legal regulation of hate speech).[73] Rather, my more general and limited point has been to claim that the civil duty of toleration does not necessarily imply an (unjustifiable) exclusion of others or their points of view.

(2) The second objection is equally challenging: is it in fact reasonable to assume that in a civil society characterized as "wild" and "anarchic" the social and cultural conditions will exist that would be required for the promotion and maintenance of the civic virtues of toleration and reasonableness? Habermas is himself quite aware of

this challenge: "On account of its anarchic structure, the general public sphere is . . . more vulnerable to the repressive and exclusionary effects of unequally distributed social power, structural violence, and systematically distorted communication than are the institutionalized public spheres of parliamentary bodies."[74] There can thus be, it seems, no guarantee that the associations arising within civil society will not be "tribalistic," inegalitarian, or ones that contribute to a culture of group bias and discrimination. Can a liberal political culture be fashioned and sustained under such conditions? It is unlikely that a definitive answer can be given to this question one way or the other. However, at least until we have more evidence to the contrary perhaps we should not be overly pessimistic about the possibilities for wider civility even in the face of a civil society that is deeply pluralistic and even "anarchic." On the one hand, the form of civility that is required for a democratic polity may not need to be as "thick" as some communitarians and others have supposed. What is required, it would seem, is a liberal political culture that is based on, and incorporates in its own norms of civility, the "core morality" mentioned above. The bonds of civility may not have to reach so deeply into particular and often sectarian worldviews that it threatens their (at any rate always fluid) identities, and it may be possible to embrace the central elements of a core morality from the perspective of otherwise very different worldviews. (This, I take it, is the important lesson to be learned from Rawls's idea of an overlapping consensus.)[75]

On the other hand, it is perhaps also the case that we have not sufficiently explored the ways in which government, through its regulatory policy, can help to promote the minimal bonds of civility. This indeed may be one of the major differences between the liberal egalitarianism of the welfare state and Habermas's "two-track" model of a deliberative politics.[76] The largely interventionist and regulatory practices of the liberal welfare state, some have argued, may be counterproductive to their own intended effects.[77] What is required—though it is by no means an easy task—is a focus on the (limited) ways in which the state, in cooperation with institutions of civil society, can help to foster the virtues necessary for a liberal political culture.[78]

Notes

1. See especially several of the essays in Thomas McCarthy, *Ideals and Illusions* (Cambridge: MIT Press, 1991); "Legitimacy and Diversity: Dialectical Reflections on Analytical Distinctions," in *Habermas on Law and Democracy*, ed. M. Rosenfeld and A. Arato (Berkeley: University of California Press, 1998), 115–153, and David Couzens Hoy and Thomas McCarthy, *Critical Theory* (New York: Blackwell, 1994), chap. 3.

2. Kant, *Grounding for the Metaphysics of Morals*, trans. J. Ellington (Indianapolis: Hackett, 1993), 50 [GMM, 448].

3. *Critical Theory*, 43.

4. For Habermas's most recent discussion of this principle, see *Between Facts and Norms*, trans. W. Rehg (Cambridge: MIT Press, 1996), 107–109, where he introduces it at a more abstract level, prior to the distinction between its role as a moral principle (principle-U or the principle of universalizability) and its role as a principle of political legitimacy (the "principle of democracy").

5. In fact, I think these two ideas—the idea of freedom of action and the idea that our actions are subject to the expectation that the reasons for them could meet with the agreement of others—are, as Henry Allison has put it in a related context, "reciprocal"; see Allison's "Morality and Freedom: Kant's Reciprocity Thesis," *The Philosophical Review* 95 (1986): 393–425.

6. Habermas, "Morality and Ethical Life: Does Hegel's Critique of Kant Apply to Discourse Ethics?" *Moral Consciousness and Communicative Action*, trans. C. Lenhardt and S. W. Nicholsen (Cambridge: MIT Press, 1990), 207–208; this is also part of Habermas's response to Hegel's "emptiness" charge against Kantian morality.

7. I have in mind particularly several essays in Robert Pippin's *Idealism as Modernism* (New York: Cambridge University Press, 1997) and Terry Pinkard's *Hegel's Phenomenology: The Sociality of Reason* (New York: Cambridge University Press, 1994).

8. This task has not always been recognized as an important feature of a theory of practical reason; compare, for example, the list of tasks in Robert Audi, "A Theory of Practical Reason," *American Philosophical Quarterly* 19 (1982): 25–39. For some recent accounts that do recognize the importance of this task see, in addition to the central work of Korsgaard discussed here, Jean Hampton, *The Authority of Reason* (New York: Cambridge University Press, 1998), and Warren Quinn, "Putting Rationality in Its Place," *Morality and Action* (New York: Cambridge University Press, 1993), 228–255.

9. The distinction I draw here between a reason *to* act and a reason *for* action partly follows the distinction, found in the literature, between a justifying (or normative) reason and a motivating reason; see, for example, Michael Smith, "The Humean Theory of Motivation," *Mind* 96 (1987): 36–61. However, for reasons that I consider below, I have some reservations about the way in which that distinction is drawn.

10. See especially Christine M. Korsgaard et al., *The Sources of Normativity*, ed. O. O'Neill (New York: Cambridge University Press, 1996) and Korsgaard, "The Normativity of Instrumental Reason" in *Ethics and Practical Reason*, ed. G. Cullity and B. Gaut (New York: Clarendon Press, 1997), 215–244.

Kenneth Baynes

11. See especially Jürgen Habermas, *The Theory of Communicative Action*, 2 vols., trans. T. McCarthy (Boston: Beacon Press, 1984), v. 1, chap. 3; Philip Pettit and Michael Smith, "Freedom in Belief and Desire," in *Human Action, Deliberation and Causation*, ed. J. Bransen and W. Cuypers (Boston: Kluwer, 1998), 89; Robert Brandom also employs Dennett's notion of the intentional stance in his own related account of the "discursive score-keeping stance" that I discuss below; see *Making It Explicit* (Cambridge: Harvard University Press, 1994), 639f.

12. I leave open for now the difficult question of whether the best interpretation of a person's reason for action must also be her interpretation (or in what sense it must be hers). In some sense this surely must be the case (for how else could it explain her action?); on the other hand, clearly the reason for a person's action is often not one of which she is directly or immediately aware and, it seems, the reason of which she may be aware is often not the reason for which she acted. This problem, of course, is what motivates Davidson's causal theory. Nonetheless the account of action and action-explanation developed here is a broadly "intentionalist" or "interpretivist" one to be contrasted with a causal account such as Davidson's for reasons that I hope will become clear. For important criticisms of currently more popular causal accounts, see especially Julia Tanney, "Why Reasons May Not Be Causes," *Mind and Language* 10 (1995): 105–128, Grant Gillet, "Actions, Causes and Mental Ascriptions," in *Objections to Physicalism*, ed. H. Robinson (Oxford, 1993), 81–100, and Frederick Stoutland, "The Real Reasons," in *Human Action, Deliberation and Causation*, 43–46. Stoutland has recently argued that a broadly interpretivist approach to reasons for action (in which the reason explains the action by "rationalizing" it) may in the end not be so far from Davidson's causal theory (once Davidson's theory has been properly understood); see Stoutland's "Intentionalists and Davidson on Rational Explanations" in *Actions, Norms and Values*, ed. G. Meggle (New York: de Gruyter, 1998), 191–208.

13. To say that self-reflection or self-awareness must not be unduly privileged is not, however, to deny that it must be present. For an important corrective to at least some "community views" of rule-following, see Denis McManus, "The Epistemology of Self-Knowledge and the Presuppositions of Rule-Following," *The Monist* 78 (1995): 496–515.

14. Habermas, "Some Further Clarifications of the Concept of Communicative Rationality," *On the Pragmatics of Communication*, ed. M. Cooke (Cambridge: MIT Press, 1998), 308. Schnädelbach criticizes Habermas's discursive model of rationality from the perspective of a reflective model close in detail, I believe, to Harry Frankfurt's hierarchical account.

15. See Bernard Williams, "Internal and External Reasons," *Moral Luck* (New York: Cambridge University Press, 1981), 102.

16. Korsgaard, "The Normativity of Instrumental Reason," 220f.; see also Hampton, *Authority of Reason*, chap. 4.

17. *A Treatise of Human Nature* (Oxford: Clarendon, 1978), Book II, Part iii, chap. 3, p. 416.

18. See again both Korsgaard, "The Normativity of Instrumental Reason" and Hampton, *Authority of Reason*; see also Cullity and Gaut, "Introduction," *Ethics and Practical Reason*, 7: ["On [Hume's] view, there are no normative practical reasons, hypotheti-

Practical Reason, the "Space of Reasons," and Public Reason

cal or categorical"] and Simon Blackburn, *Ruling Passions* (New York: Oxford, 1998), chap. 8.

19. Williams, "Internal and External Reasons," and Michael Smith, "The Humean Theory of Motivation," *Mind* 96 (1987): 36–61.

20. The argument I make here, I believe, parallels the suggestion made by John Mc-Dowell that the Humean model of practical reason works with " . . . a quasi-hydraulic conception of how reason explanations account for action."; see his "Non-cognitivism and Rule Following" in *Wittgenstein: To Follow a Rule*, ed. S. Holtzman and C. Leich (Boston: Routledge, 1981), 154; see also Hampton, *Authority of Reason*, 140: "For Hume, acting on a hypothetical imperative does not involve accepting (or being motivated by) the authority of such a norm, but instead involves being caused to act in this way by a process that is affected by both one's desires and the information about how to satisfy them supplied by reason."

21. This point can also be expressed by saying that the account must show how a "justifying reason" can also be a "motivating reason" as this distinction is sometimes drawn in the literature. I take up a possible objection to my account on the basis of this distinction below.

22. Korsgaard, *Sources of Normativity*, 93ff. Intralinear numbers in this section refer to this book.

23. In her Introduction to *The Sources of Normativity*, Onora O'Neill asks, "How can reflective responses, and in particular endorsement, provide or constitute norms?" (xii).

24. See 233; for Korsgaard's novel distinction between the categorical imperative and the moral law—a distinction Kant does not make—see 98–100.

25. See Strawson's "Freedom and Resentment" in *Free Will*, ed. G. Watson (Oxford, 1983), 59–80, as well as my own discussion of Strawson's position in "Public Reason and Personal Autonomy," in *A Handbook of Critical Theory*, ed. D. Rasmussen (Oxford: Blackwell, 1996), 243–254.

26. This approach has been especially pursued in R. Jay Wallace, *Responsibility and the Moral Sentiments* (Cambridge: Harvard University Press, 1994); see also the discussion of Wallace's position in John Martin Fischer, "Recent Work on Moral Responsibility," *Ethics* 110 (1999): 93–139.

27. See esp. T. M. Scanlon, "The Significance of Choice," *The Tanner Lectures on Human Values*, vol. 8, ed. S. McMurrin (Salt Lake City: University of Utah Press, 1988), 149–216.

28. Of course, to say that a person who acts for a reason is answerable to others does not mean that he is as a matter of fact required to justify his conduct to anyone who asks. As Habermas points out in *Between Facts and Norms*, 120, it is an important function of the so-called "subjective liberties" that they relieve us of this obligation in many situations; see also Habermas, "Reply" in Arato, 391.

29. By invoking Davidson at this point I do not mean to embrace his causal theory of action-explanation, but rather his broadly interpretivist and holist account of how rational explanations must be developed; see note 31 below.

Kenneth Baynes

30. It also supports a compatibilist interpretation of Kant, such as that found in Ralf Meerbote, "Kant on the Nondeterminate Character of Human Actions" in *Kant on Causality, Freedom and Objectivity*, ed. W. A. Harper and R. Meerbote (Minneapolis: University of Minnesota Press, 1984), chap. 8.

31. By invoking Davidson's notion of a "primary reason" to distinguish between a "mere" rationalization and an explanation of an action, I do not mean to endorse the particular (causal) account he gives for this distinction. On the contrary, I think Korsgaard's position is much closer to interpretivist or intentionalist accounts, to which Davidson's theory is often contrasted. For an important criticism of Davidson that also suggests a model of action-explanation closer to the position advocated here, see, in addition to the essay by Stoutland above (note 12), Julia Tanney, "Why Reasons May Not be Causes," *Mind and Language* 10 (1995): 105–128, and Grant Gillet, "Actions, Causes, and Mental Ascriptions," in *Objections to Physicalism*, 81–100.

32. Korsgaard, *Sources of Normativity*, chap. 9.

33. In "The Reasons We Can Share" [*in Creating the Kingdom of Ends* (CUP, 1996, chap. 10)] Korsgaard offers a similar attempt to show that all reasons have a public, shareable aspect; yet Nagel's claim which she criticizes was to show that there might be agent-relative reasons for which there are not also corresponding agent-neutral reasons.

34. See Brandom's *Making It Explicit*, chap. 1, and "Knowledge and the Social Articulation of the Space of Reasons," *Philosophy and Phenomenological Research* 55 (1995): 895–908.

35. Richard Rorty, "What Do You Do When They Call You A 'Relativist'?" *Philosophy and Phenomenological Research* 57 (1997): 173–177, here 176; Rorty's remark is, of course, a bit tendentious since Habermas has himself taken many steps toward the elaboration of such a philosophy of language.

36. Versions of this argument can be found in G. Sayre-McCord, "Contractarianism" in *The Blackwell Guide to Ethical Theory*, ed. Hugh LaFollette (New York: Blackwell, 2000), 247–267, and, relatedly, Philip Pettit, "Two Construals of Scanlon's Contractualism," *Journal of Philosophy* 97 (2000): 148–164. As I understand it, this is also at least part of Christopher McMahon's complaint against Habermas's discourse ethics in "Discourse and Morality," *Ethics* 110 (2000): 514–536, esp. 524–525. I believe that McMahon's reading also rests on some deep misunderstandings of Habermas's position, especially the claim that Habermas must be committed to an extremely strong rendering of an agent's first-person authority with respect to his need-interpretations. In fact, his reading runs directly counter to the interpretation of reasons for action that I have given here in apparently supposing that reasons are private mental states to which an individual has a nondefeasible privileged access (see 525).

37. David Brink makes this distinction in connection with his interpretation of utilitarianism in *Moral Realism and the Foundation of Ethics* (New York: Cambridge University Press, 1989), 265.

38. See the similar remarks by Habermas on this question in his "Reply to Symposium Participants," in *Habermas on Law and Democracy*, 408–409.

39. See T. M. Scanlon, *What We Owe To Each Other* (Cambridge: Harvard University Press, 1998), 5; and Habermas, "Reply," 408.

40. This distinction, introduced by Nagel in *The Possibility of Altruism* (Oxford: Clarendon, 1970), is now widely found in the literature on action-explanations; see, for example, Smith, "Humean Theory of Motivation."

41. For similar suspicions, see Jonathan Dancy, "Why There Is Really No Such Thing as The Theory of Motivation," *Proceedings of the Aristotelian Society* 95 (1995): 1–18.

42. McCarthy, "Legitimacy and Diversity"; see also James Bohman and William Rehg, "Discourse and Democracy: The Formal and Informal Bases of Legitimacy in *Between Facts and Norms*," in *Democracy and Discourse: Essays on Habermas's 'Between Facts and Norms,'* ed. R. von Schomberg and K. Baynes (Albany: SUNY Press, 2001).

43. See *The Inclusion of the Other* (Cambridge: MIT Press, 1998), chaps. 2 and 3.

44. Rawls, *Political Liberalism* (New York: Columbia University Press, 1993), 137.

45. "The Idea of Public Reason Revisited," *The University of Chicago Law Review* 64 (1997): 771.

46. Joshua Cohen also questions attempts to distinguish sharply between "procedure" and "substance" with respect to political values in "Pluralism and Proceduralism," *Chicago-Kent Law Review* 69 (1994): 589–618. For Charles Larmore's notion of a "core morality," see his *The Morals of Modernity* (New York: Cambridge University Press, 1996), where he argues it includes, among other elements, a "norm of rational dialogue" and a "norm of equal respect." Larmore, it should be noted, does not think this "core morality" can be derived from a concept of practical reason alone (see 56–57); but he also assumes a conception of practical reason that is more restrictive than Habermas's and one that is too sharply contrasted with tradition.

47. Habermas, *Inclusion of the Other*, 84.

48. "Reply to Habermas," *Journal of Philosophy* 92 (1995): 132–180, here 142.

49. Larmore, *Morals of Modernity*, 149; for a similar interpretation of Rawls's later writings, with their focus on "stability for the right reasons," see also Thomas E. Hill, "The Problem of Stability in Political Liberalism," *Respect, Pluralism, and Justice* (New York: Oxford University Press, 2000), chap. 9.

50. McCarthy, "Legitimacy and Diversity," 150. Intralinear numbers in this section refer to this essay.

51. I have in mind, for example, the views of Brian Barry in "Is Democracy Special?" in *Philosophy, Politics and Society*, ed. P. Laslett (Oxford: Blackwell, 1979), 155–156, or Peter Singer, *Democracy and Disobedience* (New York: Oxford University Press, 1974).

52. See my "Deliberative Democracy and the Regress Problem: Response to Michelman," *The Modern Schoolman* 74 (1997): 333f., and "Democracy and the *Rechtsstaat:* Habermas's *Faktizität und Geltung*," in *The Cambridge Companion to Habermas*, ed. S. K. White (New York: Cambridge University Press, 1995), chap. 9; see also the important discussion by Cohen, "Pluralism and Proceduralism."

53. See Habermas, *Between Facts and Norms*, 266 and 295; "Reply," 406.

54. *Political Liberalism*, 49 note 1.

55. *Political Liberalism*, pp. 86–87.

56. See, for example, Rainer Forst, "Die Rechfertigung der Gerechtigkeit" in *Das Recht der Republik*, ed. H. Brunkhorst and P. Niesen (Frankfurt: Suhrkamp, 1999), 105–168.

57. Compare *Political Liberalism*, p. xliv and li.

58. The distinction between "moral autonomy" and "political autonomy" is thus not a claim that political autonomy does not presuppose the (Kantian) moral powers of the person, but rather a claim that these moral powers do not entail the more comprehensive (Kantian) ethic of personal autonomy (see *Political Liberalism*, p. xlv; and also the helpful discussion in Larmore, "Political Liberalism" [*The Morals of Modernity* (Cambridge University Press, 1996), 134–141].

59. *Inclusion of the Other*, 61, 89f.

60. See "Reply to Habermas," 142f.

61. *Inclusion of the Other*, 84.

62. For some important suggestions on this topic, see James Bohman, *Public Deliberation* (Cambridge: MIT Press, 1996).

63. Habermas, "Reply," 402.

64. See *Toleration: An Elusive Virtue*, ed. David Heyd (Princeton: Princeton University Press, 1996).

65. See T. M. Scanlon, "The Difficulty of Tolerance" in *Toleration*, ed. David Heyd, and Habermas's remarks in his "Reply," *Habermas on Law and Democracy*, 393.

66. I draw this idea of a shared "core morality" from Larmore, *Morals of Modernity*, 12–13.

67. Rawls, "The Idea of Public Reason Revisited," 776, 784.

68. Rawls, "The Idea of Public Reason Revisited," 768, 775 note 28.

69. Rawls, it seems to me, is in fact unclear as to whether this constraint applies to all citizens or only to legislators and candidates for public office (see 767–768 and 769, where he suggests that all citizens are to think of themselves *as if* they were legislators).

70. Habermas, "'Reasonable' versus 'True,' or the Morality of Worldviews," *Inclusion of the Other*, chap. 3. Though, as I will argue, this is not the most charitable way to read Rawls, it is one that is widely shared; see for example Joseph Raz, "Facing Diversity: The Case for Epistemic Abstinence," *Philosophy and Public Affairs* 19 (1990): 3–46.

71. Habermas, "'Reasonable' versus 'True,'" 86; see also his "Some Further Clarifications of the Concept of Communicative Rationality," *Pragmatics of Communi-*

cation, 321, where he writes: *"Agreement [Einverständnis]* in the strict sense is achieved only if the participants are able to accept a validity claim for the *same* reasons."

72. Kirstie McClure, "Difference, Diversity and the Limits of Toleration," *Political Theory* 18 (1990): 366.

73. See, however, the cautious defense of a regulation of hate speech by Joshua Cohen, "Freedom, Equality and Pornography " in *Justice and Injustice in Law and Legal Theory,* ed. by A. Sarat and T. Kearns (Ann Arbor: University of Michigan Press, 1996), 99–137, and the very interesting critique of liberal arguments against the regulation of hate speech by Susan Brison, "The Autonomy Defense of Free Speech," *Ethics* 108 (1998): 312–339.

74. *Between Facts and Norms,* 307–308.

75. See Rawls's *Political Liberalism* as well as the argument for mutual respect based on a principle of reciprocity despite deep moral disagreement, found in Amy Gutmann and Dennis Thompson, *Democracy and Disagreement* (Cambridge: Harvard University Press, 1996).

76. See Habermas's discussion of a new legal paradigm, in contrast to both the classical liberal and the welfare state paradigms, in *Between Facts and Norms,* chap. 9.

77. See, among others, Avishai Margalit, *The Decent Society* (Cambridge: Harvard University Press, 1996).

78. See on this the interesting proposal concerning the use of the "intangible hand" of the state for such a purpose in Philip Pettit, *Republicanism* (Oxford: Clarendon, 1997).

4

Participants, Observers, and Critics: Practical Knowledge, Social Perspectives, and Critical Pluralism

James Bohman

Perhaps one of the best ways to characterize much of Thomas McCarthy's work is to see how persistently he attempts to reconcile opposing sides of various philosophical dualisms. This is indeed the guiding impulse common to the two traditions of philosophy that he draws upon most heavily: the critical theory of the Frankfurt School represented by the work of Habermas and Horkheimer and the pragmatism of American philosophers such as Mead and Dewey. In *Ideals and Illusions,* he attempts to overcome the opposition between deconstruction and reconstruction through a "critique of impure reason" that affirms both the transcendence and situatedness of reason, in its "ideals and illusions." In his debate with David Hoy in *Critical Theory,* he argues for this claim in more detail, developing a "pragmatics of communicative reason" and a "general history of the present" in which its potentials and dangers could be located. In both cases, McCarthy finds the common thread uniting critical theory and pragmatism: while truth is "deabsolutized" and reason "detranscendentalized," the same practical turn retains their emphatically normative meaning for regulating and criticizing social practices.

The key to such a pragmatic turn, McCarthy argues, is to avoid both "a pure 'insider's' or participant's standpoint and a pure 'outsider's' or observer's standpoint," but instead to adopt the "perspective of a critical-reflective participant." Once we give up on the God's-eye point of view, "we can do no better than move back and forth between the different standpoints, playing one off against the other"

(McCarthy 1994, 81). My goal here is to elaborate this insight further and to argue that such a description of the role of perspective taking in situated criticism correctly characterizes the methodological and social pluralism that is distinctive of critical social inquiry. As one of the practical abilities of communicatively rational actors, these perspectives are not those of various theories but rather are based in inherently perspectival, yet potentially critical knowledge of the social world. The full implications of such an account, however, are at odds with some of McCarthy's strong cognitivist commitments, especially when the plurality of social perspectives further complicates the political role of the critic in pluralist societies. The fact of pluralism complicates the pragmatic turn in critical theory, a turn that McCarthy rightly sees as a turn to a "sociologic" of rationality. Its critical force is based in the logic of perspective taking.

Two Forms of Critical Theory: The Pragmatic Turn

In the tradition of critical theory, there have been two possible answers to the question of what is distinctive about critical inquiry: one practical and one theoretical. The first is that they employ a distinctive theory that unifies such diverse approaches and explanations. Long a goal of both Marxian and Frankfurt School social science, this approach demands a comprehensive theory that will unify the social sciences and underwrite the epistemic superiority of the critical standpoint. The second is practical. According to this view, such theories are distinguished by the form of politics in which they are embedded and the method of verification that this politics entails. In this essay I want to defend a version of the second approach, grounded in the pragmatic conception of democracy as a mode of inquiry. Although not reducible to democratic politics, critical social science is the moment of inquiry for such reflective practices from the perspectives of their participants. I say "perspectives" here because critical social inquiry (like democracy itself) capitalizes on the perspectival character of agents' own practical social knowledge for its justification and verification. I argue that, despite his insistence on the place of general theories, McCarthy is committed to just such a practical account to the extent that he takes the plurality of methodological and cultural perspectives as seriously as he does. McCarthy's perspectival pluralism raises a number of unanswered questions: how does one reconcile the potential conflicts and disagreements among the various possible perspectives that reflective participants may adopt? Is such a plurality of perspectives consistent with the strong pragmatic assumption of "a single correct answer" that McCarthy makes central to reflective practices? Or do critics implicitly adopt a different idealization to underwrite the cognitive component of criticism more directly related to perspective taking?

The problem of the plurality of social perspectives is not only central to the methodology of critical inquiry. It is also a fundamental political issue, especially if, like the pragmatists, we see critical social inquiry as the distinctive mode of inquiry of practices of democratic deliberation. Given the moral and ethical pluralism that McCarthy also shows to be endemic to any modern, complex society, such a reconciliation of perspectives becomes the central issue for critical social theory. Given the possibility of conflicts between various social perspectives, the acceptance of pluralism at least indicates that no one perspective or no one theory may lay claim to epistemic, moral, or rational superiority in advance. What does each perspective provide to criticism? How do critics adjudicate between the various nonexclusive standpoints that they may adopt? How might critical social inquiry contribute to the reconciliation of such conflicting perspectives in democratic practices?

Whatever the achievements of social science in garnering theoretical knowledge of the features of human society in general, critical theory sees social science as a distinctive form of reflective practical knowledge from a specific point of view. Thus, in the interpretation I develop here, critical social science is distinctive, not because of the type of knowledge it employs as such, but because it does something with social scientific knowledge. It is reflexive social inquiry into the practical knowledge (i.e., the knowledge of practical knowledge) that is needed for effective social agency and freedom in the social world. This sort of practical knowledge, I argue, is tied up with the capacities of agents to adopt and to relate a variety of social perspectives. Such a practical account of social inquiry has much in common with pragmatism, old and new (Bohman 1999a, 1999b). The requisite practical knowledge, I argue, is pluralistic and diverse in structure and content, combining not only different methods and theories but also relating various possible social perspectives in establishing the normative status and epistemic basis for the activity of criticism itself. Theories, methods, and modes of inquiry are all formulated from within some particular perspective of the first, second, or third person; thus the same pretheoretical knowledge of agents' abilities to take up and to relate such perspectives to each other is precisely the practical basis for the act of successfully communicating criticisms to their intended audience. Critical theories articulate explicit knowledge of the social world from within such perspectives, making it the job of the critic to relate various perspectives to each other in acts of criticism within reflective practices that articulate and adjudicate such conflicts.

I argue for such a practical approach to critical social inquiry in three steps. First, I compare the practical and the theoretical conceptions of critical theory. Each is guided by its own conception of practical knowledge: in one case, as the instrumental application of independent theoretical knowledge, in the other case, as continuous with the reflective abilities and practices of knowledgeable social actors being criticized. In establishing the latter form of practical inquiry, critical social theory rejects the dominant first-person and third-person accounts of practical knowledge such as those of hermeneutics or naturalism. Rather, it demands a methodological and theoretical pluralism that is not tied to any single distinctive theory, method, or perspective of inquiry. Second, I argue that various types of explanations and interpretations embody various social perspectives; consequently, identifying any particular type of explanation as distinctively critical would only limit the scope and possibilities of criticism. This is true of interpretation of general theories or histories of the sort McCarthy makes central to critical theory. Theories instead have a more direct role in reconstructing the nature and scope of actors' pretheoretical knowledge of the social world. Third, and finally, I argue that the conflicts between such perspectives and between the standpoints of social actors are not resolved theoretically by the critic, but practically in ongoing and reflective practices such as democracy and science. Like public reason more generally, critical inquiry is the attempt to unite various perspectives by engaging in a form of reflective inquiry that crosses among them.

This practical turn is the only way to avoid what Rorty calls "the ambiguity of rationality," between its status as "a cognitive faculty and a moral virtue." Rorty wants to keep them distinct. "The epistemological notion of rationality concerns our relation to something nonhuman, whereas the moral notion concerns our relations to our fellow human beings" (Rorty 1996, 74). The practical account that I propose here reconciles this ambiguity as McCarthy does by putting the epistemological component in the social world, in our various cognitive perspectives toward it. Rather than privileging the pragmatic presupposition of "the single correct answer," I argue that the cognitive act typical of social criticism is the joining and crossing of social perspectives. The ambiguity is then between plurality and unity and its resolution is their ongoing tension in reflective and self-critical practices. The role of critical social science is to keep reflective practices open to the variety of possible perspectives and thus to maintain the productive tensions among them that make them vital and self-critical. They can do this only through establishing a particular social relationship in which the validity of acts of criticism is practically verified by fellow participants in reflective practices.

Social Inquiry as Practical Knowledge

Rather than look for something epistemically and theoretically distinctive in the universal and necessary features of social scientific knowledge, critical theory has instead focused on the social relationships between inquirers and other actors in the social sciences. Such relationships can be specified epistemically in terms of the perspective taken by the inquirer on the actors who figure in their explanations or interpretations. The two dominant and opposed approaches adopt very different perspectives. On the one hand, naturalism gives priority to the third-person perspective on reductionist grounds; on the other hand, the antireductionism of interpretive social science argues for an irreducible methodological dualism. As McCarthy suggests, critical theory has long offered an alternative to both views.

James Bohman

Social inquiry that only develops optimal problem-solving strategies in light of purely third-person knowledge of the impersonal
consequences of all available courses of action is rightly called "tech-
nocratic" by Habermas and other critical theorists and is rejected by
pragmatists from Mead to Dewey (Habermas 1971, 1973; Dewey
1988). It models the social scientist on the engineer, who masterfully
chooses the optimal solution to a problem of design. For the social
scientist as an ideally rational and informed actor, "the range of permissible solutions is clearly delimited, the relevant probabilities and
utilities precisely specified, and even the criteria of rationality to be
employed (e.g., maximization of expected utilities) is clearly stated"
(Hempel 1965, 481). This abstract model of the social scientist as ob-
serving agent (rather than reflective participant) always needs to be
contextualized in the social relationships it constitutes as a form of
socially distributed practical knowledge.

By contrast with the engineering model, interpretive social science
takes up the first-person perspective in making explicit the mean-
ingfulness of an action or expression. Interpretations as practical
knowledge are not based on some general theory (no matter how
helpful or explanatory these may be when interpretation is difficult),
but reconstruct agent's own reasons, or at least how these reasons
might seem to be good ones from the first-person perspective. This
leaves the interpreter in a peculiar epistemic predicament: what
started as the enterprise of seeing things from others' points of view
can at best approximate that point of view only by providing the best
interpretation for us of how things are for them. As a matter of interpretive responsibility, there is no getting around the fact that
ethnography or history is our attempt "to see another form of life in
the categories of our own" (Geertz 1971, 16–17; Bohman 1991, 132).
Given both "our" and "their" cognitive limitations, such knowledge
remains within the first-person plural perspective of a good practi-
tioner rather than that of a critic. The only way out of this problem
is to see that there is more than one form of practical knowledge.

Naturalist and hermeneutic approaches see the relationship of the
subject and object of inquiry as forcing the social scientist to take either the third-person or first- person perspective. Even when justified
in dualistic and antinaturalist terms by Habermas and others, critical

social science necessarily requires complex perspective taking and the coordination of various points of view, minimally that of the social scientists and the subjects under study. The second-person perspective differs from both the third-person observer and the first-person participant perspectives in its specific form of practical knowledge; it employs the know-how of a participant in dialogue or communication. It is an alternative to the weaknesses of the other, opposing perspectives especially when they get it wrong. It is indeed often the case that we are wrong in our first-person knowledge (whether singular or plural), so that lack of transparency is an unavoidable problem. When faced with interpreting others' behavior we quickly run into the limits of first-person knowledge simpliciter. From a third-person perspective, it is indeterminate whether behavior follows some common rule or merely some regular idiosyncrasy. Third-person accounts face the same "gerrymandering problem" as made clear in the private language argument (Brandom 1994, 28ff). That is, it is always possible to interpret some behavior as related to many different and even incompatible contextual factors. Neither the interpreter's nor the observer's perspectives are sufficient to specify these opaque intentional contexts for others. Since actions therefore underdetermine the interpretations that may be assigned to them by third-person or first-person interpreters, there is no alternative besides interpretations of agents' self-interpretations that can be settled only practically in ongoing dialogue and interaction. For social scientists as well as participants in practices more generally, the adjudication of such conflicts requires mutual perspective taking, which is its own mode of practical reasoning.

Theories of many different sorts locate interpretation practically in acts and processes of ongoing communication. Communication in turn is seen as the exercise of a distinctive form of practical rationality. Like other such accounts of the practical knowledge put to use in interpretation, the theory of communicative action offers its own distinctive definition. In good pragmatist fashion, critical theorists offer a definition that is epistemic, practical, and intersubjective. For Habermas, for example, rationality consists not so much in the possession of knowledge as such, but rather in "how speaking and acting subjects acquire and use knowledge" (Habermas 1984, 11). I call any

James Bohman

such account "pragmatic" because it shares a number of distinctive features with other views that see interpreters as competent and knowledgeable agents. Most important, a pragmatic approach develops an account of practical knowledge in the "performative attitude." It is pragmatic not only because it sees "saying something" as a performative act and thus a kind of doing (and also interpreting as itself a kind of doing in establishing and maintaining social relationships); it also takes up a position that classical pragmatism develops in different contexts, such as James's theory of truth as successful action or Peirce's account of inquiry and habits of action. Robert Brandom has developed the central features of such a pragmatic and hence performative account of truth, at least two of which apply by analogy to the pragmatic theory of interpretation as practical knowledge (Brandom 1988, 79). The first is that interpreting is not merely describing something and hence does not provide some true description from the observer's point of view but establishes commitments and entitlements between the interpreter and the one interpreted. Second, interpreting is performative in the sense that the interpreter takes up particular normative attitudes. These "normative attitudes" must be those of the interpreter. In interpreting one is expressing and establishing one's attitude toward a claim, such as when the interpreter takes it to be true, appropriate according to social norms, or correct or incorrect in its performance. Some such attitudes are essentially two-person attitudes: the interpreter does not just express an attitude in the first-person perspective alone, but rather incurs a commitment or obligation to others by interpreting what others are doing. To offer an interpretation is thus to establish the terms of a social relationship.

The critical attitude shares with interpretation a structure derived from the second-person perspective. In this attitude agents' beliefs, attitudes, and practices cannot only be interpreted as meaningful or not, but must also be assessed as correct, incorrect, or inconclusive. Nonetheless, the second-person perspective is not yet sufficient for criticism, since the criticism must often resort to first- and third-person perspectives as well. Like the third-person perspective, the second-person perspective holds out the possibility of employing normative standards of rationality. However, unlike the third-person critic who must claim epistemic superiority over other participants, the second-person perspective is not yet transperspectival. Because the reflective participant must take up all stances, it is the proper attitude of critical inquiry. Only such an interperspectival stance is fully dialogical, giving inquirer and agent equal standing as agents in a shared practice (whatever the goals of that practice may be). It is this political relationship of equal agency that critical inquirers seek to establish. They address those they criticize as fellow reflective participants in practices, including practices of inquiry. The critic engages in the inquiry into the basis of the cooperative character of the practices that the first-person interpreter simply presupposes, as prejudgments or prejudices in the hermeneutic sense. If all cooperative activity "involves a moment of inquiry" (Putnam 1994, 174), then they also need a moment of self-reflection on the prejudgments of such inquiry itself and this type of reflection calls for a distinctively practical form of critical perspective taking.

If critical social inquiry is inquiry into the basis of cooperative practices as such, it takes practical inquiry one reflective step further. The inquirer does not carry out this step, but rather the public whom the inquirer addresses does. As in Kuhn's distinction between normal and revolutionary science, second-order critical reflection considers whether or not the framework for cooperation itself needs to be changed. Such criticism is directed at current institutions as well as toward formulating new terms of cooperation under which problems are solved. When participants hold norms constant, then instrumental and strategic modes of inquiry are useful in determining the objective and social consequences of policies and practices. In this case, critical reflection is not confined to the limits of first-person knowledge, nor does it suffer from the gerrymandering problem of independent standards of rationality. In order to occupy the normative realm between the two perspectives, detailed social science as cooperative inquiry into cooperative practices is necessary. Such analysis must be both methodologically and theoretically pluralistic, if it is to identify all the problems with cooperative practices of inquiry. It must also be able to occupy a variety of perspectives if it is to enable public reflection among free and equal participants.

Consider the problem of the availability of experimental drugs for the treatment of AIDS. It is clear that the development and testing of drugs is a matter for scientific experts who learn more and more about the virus and its development in the body. So long as experts unproblematically engage in first-order problem solving, AIDS patients are willing to grant these experts a certain authority in this domain. Nonetheless, the continued spread of the epidemic and lack of effective treatments brought about a crisis in expert authority, an "existential problematic situation" in Dewey's sense (Dewey 1986, 492). By defining expert activity through its social consequences and by making explicit the terms of social cooperation between researchers and patients, lay participants reshape the practices of gaining medical knowledge and authority. Indeed, as Stephen Epstein points out, the effects of AIDS activism did not just concern extra-scientific problems such as research funding, but rather challenged the very standards of statistical validity employed in experimental trials (Epstein 1996, Part 2). The affected public changed the normative terms of cooperation and inquiry in this area in order that institutions could engage in acceptable first-order problem solving. This required reflective inquiry into scientific practices and their operative norms.

This public challenge to the norms on which expert authority is based may be generalized to all forms of research in cooperative activity. It suggests the transformation of some of the epistemological problems of the social sciences into the practical question of how to make their forms of inquiry and research open to public testing and public accountability. This demand also means that some sort of "practical verification" of critical social inquiry is necessary. How do we judge its practical consequences, especially if it is second-order rather than first-order problem solving? If such second-order reflection involves testing existing norms, then it also must test norms of social inquiry, including norms of public justification.

If we examine the writings of critical social theorists on their own activity, we find neither any clear answer to the problem of verification, nor any clear way to think about the social organization of critical inquiry itself. Two problems stand in the way, both having to do with the epistemic status of the social sciences. The first has to do with the way in which the epistemological problems of critical social inquiry have traditionally been dealt with. Instead of searching for practical transformations of epistemological problems, critical theorists (such as Habermas) have sought to ground their form of social inquiry in a comprehensive social theory. The failure of this attempt leads to a second problem. The main reason to abandon the search for the best comprehensive social theory as providing the warrant for good social criticism is that there are many different theories and methods that provide critical insight into the normative organization of society. While Habermas's earlier philosophy of social science comes remarkably close to the pragmatic solution to the problem of pluralism in inquiry (Habermas 1971), he draws back from its implications for fear of the loss of critical force. In many respects, McCarthy's emphasis on critical theories as a kind of "practical history of the present" returns to this earlier conception, where the emphasis is on practical orientation rather than theoretical unification. Such an account faces the problem of the fact of social pluralism within critical inquiry itself.

Pluralism and Critical Inquiry

McCarthy responds to the situation of pluralism in critical social inquiry in two ways, once again embracing and reconciling both sides of the traditional opposition between epistemic and nonepistemic approaches to normative claims. On the one hand, he affirms the need for general theories, while weakening the strong epistemic claims made for them in underwriting criticism. On the other hand, he situates the critical inquirer in the pragmatic situation of communication, seeing the critic as making a strong claim for the truth or rightness of his critical analysis. This is a presupposition of the critic's discourse, without which it would make no sense to engage in criticism of others. But once again this strong cognitivism is offset by an equally strong acceptance of the situated character of such claims, particularly in light of the fundamental cultural pluralism that makes it more likely that such political discourse "would normally be shot through with ethical disputes that could not be resolved consensually at the level at which they arose" (McCarthy 1998, 152). In good pragmatist fashion McCarthy shows that the issue is practical rather than theoretical. In light of these facts of complex and pluralistic modern

James Bohman

societies, it is hard to see how critics as reflective participants would not face the same epistemic constraints regardless of how they employ theoretical knowledge. Such knowledge is not only interpretive in the application, but the theories themselves embody various social perspectives.

Like Dewey, McCarthy rejects the straightforward application of "the apparatus of general theories" to the social sciences, even if causal and functional explanations still play a role in correcting participants' perspectives. Failing such general theories, the most fruitful approach to social scientific knowledge is to bring all the various methods and theories into relation to each other. Whatever the merits of large-scale theories favored by critical theorists since Marx, their practical role is to identify recurrent problems of social coordination in large-scale market societies. They are tools for cross-perspectival, second-order reflection.

Such a form of inquiry does not deny that there is an important role for general theories. When they are successful and complete, they aim at possible explanations of large-scale social and historical processes and relate different phenomena together. As such they may also provide "general interpretive frameworks" on which it is possible to construct "critical histories of the present" (McCarthy 1994, 229–230). But this more modest account of critical theories no longer sees general theories as comprehensive. Rather, they are interpretations that are validated by the extent to which they open up new possibilities of action that are themselves to be verified in democratic inquiry. Not only that, every such theory, I argue later, is itself formulated from within a particular perspective. General theories are then best seen as practical proposals whose critical purchase is not moral and epistemic independence but practical and public testing according to criteria of interpretive adequacy. They are not just indeterminate as social scientific interpretations; their practical, critical role also remains indeterminate, insofar as they do nothing more than offer a general interpretive framework which agents may for good reasons sometimes reject as inadequate. Indeed, such reasons may be formulated from another social perspective that the theory fails to adequately consider or take into account. This means that it is not the theoretical or interpretive framework that is decisive, but the practical ability that critics employ in using such frameworks to cross various perspectives in acts of social criticism.

Why is this practical dimension decisive? There seems to be an indefinite number of perspectives from which to formulate possible general histories of the present. Merely to identify a number of different methods and a number of different theories connected with a variety of different purposes and interests leaves the social scientist in a rather hopeless epistemological dilemma. Either the choice among theories, methods, and interests seems utterly arbitrary, or the critical theorist has some special epistemic claim to survey the domain and make the proper choice for the right reason. While the former, more skeptical horn of the dilemma is one endorsed by "new pragmatists" like Richard Rorty (1991) who sees all knowledge as purpose-relative and by Weber in more decisionistic moments in his methodological writings, the latter demands objectivist claims for social science generally and for the epistemic superiority of the critical theorist in particular—claims that Habermas and other critical theorists have been at pains to reject (Weber 1949; Habermas 1973, 38). Is there any way out of the epistemic dilemma of pluralism? The way out, it seems to me, has already been indicated by a reflexive emphasis on the social context of critical inquiry and the practical character of social knowledge it employs. Both are necessarily perspectival.

The problems of pluralism cannot be avoided simply by shifting the debate to practical criteria or general interpretive frameworks. Not only are there many distinct practical interests or purposes, the social sciences may also be practical in many different senses. To the extent that we can identify the epistemological basis of the social sciences in forms of practical knowledge, the dilemma of pluralism becomes more tractable as a problem: identifying the type of knowledge required by the specific social context of inquiry. The analysis of interests takes us some of the way toward a solution. Technical knowledge does not only represent a particular interest, say the interest in controlling outcomes; but in the case of the social sciences, it also presupposes a particular practical relation between the social scientists and the subjects of their inquiry. In order to control certain social outcomes or processes, a particular context of inquiry must be created: the regulative control of institutions over certain kinds of practices or processes. As second-order reflection, critical social inquiry presupposes and sometimes attempts to create a different social context of inquiry. It addresses the subjects of inquiry as equal reflective participants, as knowledgeable social agents. In this way, the asymmetries of the context of technical control are suspended; this means that critical social inquiry must be judged by a different set of practical consequences, appealing to increasing the "reflective knowledge" that agents already possess to a greater or lesser degree. As themselves agents in the social world, social scientists participate in the creation of the contexts in which their theories are publicly verified.

Given this appeal to practical knowledge, what sort of claim do critics make? Here McCarthy wants to save the cognitivist dimension that he finds in Habermas, locating criticism in critical, reflective, and argumentative dialogue about questions of truth and justice. According to McCarthy, such critical reflective discourse "rests on the pragmatic presupposition of a single right answer, to which any reasonable, well-informed person could agree to under ideal conditions" (McCarthy 1994, 239). Such a presupposition is pragmatic, in the sense that people will not necessarily agree, but deliberate and discuss with each other as if such agreement were possible. To use Kant's vocabulary this assumption is regulative rather than constitutive, since it changes the way dialogue occurs in practice (McCarthy 1991, 33–34; McCarthy 1994, 73). But is this strong assumption a necessary presupposition of critical reflection? That depends on the goal of criticism: whether it is for agents to see their circumstances correctly or whether it is for them to see them more reflectively and thus differently. The question is whether there is a fact of the matter about the human world, a single right answer independent of agent's needs, interests, and self-interpretations that would underwrite the pragmatic presupposition. Even if there is nothing of the sort, the critic is not left without communicative resources. Instead of seeking to engage others directly in argumentation about the single correct answer, critics can aim at something else: to change participants' perspectives and thus to begin processes of reflection anew.

The goal of critical inquiry is then not to control social processes or even to influence the sorts of decisions that agents might make in any determinate sort of way. Instead, its goal is to initiate public processes of self-reflection (Bohman 1996, chapter 5). Thus, critical social science can measure its success against the standard of attaining such a practical goal. In its context of inquiry, critical social science treats social actors as knowledgeable social agents to whom its claims are publicly addressed. In this way, critics do not employ reflexive theories in an "objectivating fashion" (Habermas 1971). "Objectivating" here refers not to the third-person perspective, but to a way of treating agents as objects of manipulation rather than as the audience of criticism or practical proposals. By contrast, critical inquiry does not seek to achieve specific ends, but rather to bring about those social conditions in which its insights and proposals could be validated or falsified by agents themselves. The fact that agents do not now accept some proffered interpretation of their practices does not refute such a criticism; the practical conception of verification allows that agents could be mistaken about the character of their practices. Rather than being based on "the fact of the matter," a criticism is verified if it is acceptable to those to whom it is addressed under the appropriate reflective conditions in a public process of judgment and validation. If it is not accepted, this criticism may still be valid, in that it supposes a future audience for whom the appropriate conditions of judgment apply.

In such an ongoing and socially organized process, the critic's role is practical in a variety of ways. The regulation of means and ends has more to do with determining what is acceptable to those participating in this large collective and cooperative enterprise than with approximating some ideal state of full causal knowledge of society. The epistemic features of democracy make it the location not only for specific acts of social criticism, but also for ongoing and institutionalized critical social inquiry. In it, we create a self-reflective practice that seeks to constantly create and recreate the conditions for the practical verification of judgments and interpretations. When understood as solely dependent upon the superiority of theoretical knowledge, the critic has no foothold in the social world and no way to choose among the many competing approaches and methods. But such a conception is based on the wrong model of verification for critical social inquiry. On the pragmatic account that I have been defending, we can see why it is that critical inquiry aims at creating the reflective conditions necessary for its own practical verification. In practical verification, agents may not in the end find these insights acceptable and thus may not change their second-order self-understandings. The publicity of such a process of practical verification entails its own particular standards of critical success or failure that are related to social criticism as an act of interpretation addressed to those who are being criticized.

An account of such standards has to be developed in terms of the sort of abilities and competences that successful critics exhibit in their criticism. Once more this reveals a dimension of pluralism in the social sciences: the pluralism of social perspectives. As addressed to others in a public by a speaker as a reflective participant in a practice, criticism certainly entails the ability to take up the normative attitudes of the second-person perspective. But this is not what is distinctive about critical social inquiry. Once again, it is doubly distinctive. It is criticism addressed in the normative attitude of the second-person perspective, but in relation to other perspectives: the first-person, second-person, and third-person perspectives are all interrelated in different ways in different forms of criticism. Indeed, I argue in the next section that criticism requires relating two or more perspectives in the communication addressed to others in the normative attitude of the second person. Even if actual consensus is not a necessary and sufficient condition for the validity of such criticism, the public process of testing for agreement or disagreement by those addressed is the ultimate practical verification; this testing process requires self-reflectively employing multiple pragmatic perspectives in communication and in acquiring reflexive knowledge of the limits of available reflective practices in which acts of criticism are embedded. Such limits are various and can only be revealed in a variety of explanations, each of which allows agents to take a critical perspective on their own practices.

Reflexivity, Perspective Taking, and Practical Verification

If the argument of the last section is correct, a pragmatic account is inevitably methodologically, theoretically, and perspectivally pluralistic: any kind of social scientific method or explanation-producing theory can be potentially critical. There are no specific or definitive social scientific methods of criticism or theories that uniquely justify the critical perspective. One reason for this is that there is no unique critical perspective, even for a reflexive theory that provides a social scientific account of acts of social criticism and their conditions of pragmatic success. Looking at what critics do rather than at their theories suggests that the more typical feature of socially situated acts of criticism is their cross-perspectival character: criticisms cross over from the third-person to the first-person, the second-person to the first-person plural perspective, and so on. Such interperspectival criticism allows for the reflexive distance necessary for criticism, even in the case of a single person reflecting upon the possibility of self-deception. The second-person perspective does have justificatory priority, but no priority as the source of criticism. It has justificatory priority because of what a critic does in acts of criticism: C (the critic) communicates CC (the critical claim) to S (the audience of the criticism). Such a claim must be such that S could accept CC given the proper changes in the normative attitudes of S. The critic then is successful in the act of criticism only by adopting the attitude of S as the second person, that is, the normative attitude of the second person to whom CC is directed.

Those critical theorists who have favored the view that there are specific and comprehensive critical theories have tended also to argue that criticism ultimately must be given from an objective, third-person perspective. Standard theories of ideology see agents' social beliefs as systematically false in ways that require the independent standpoint of a theory to untangle. Such a theory in turn requires that criticism be objective in the sense that it has no perspective: it is non-perspectival in the sense that it has no point of view; it is a view from nowhere. Instead, third-person, explanatory criticisms of ideology are *trans*perspectival; they show the limits of participants' first-person perspectives from the point of view of a theoretical explanation grounded in their own experience of the social world (as did Marx in discussing the exploitation of workers). Rejecting such nonperspectival theories for *inter*perspectival critical explanations provides the basis for going beyond a "mere" pluralism and to a "critical" pluralism that is able to adjudicate among the often contradictory claims of theories and explanations in the social sciences and among often conflicting perspectives in reflective practices. But the indeterminacy of the third-person perspective (its inadequacy for nonarbitrarily selecting among competing interpretations) suggests that the normative attitude of the critic cannot be confined to a single social perspective or the supposed correctness of the particular content of any theory. Rather, whatever objectivity a theory can achieve for criticism is "a matter of perspectival form and not of nonperspectival or cross-perspectival content" (Brandom 1994, 600). The limitations of perspectival form as opposed to nonperspectival content suggest the need for epistemic modesty for all criticisms based on theoretical justifications. Theories themselves are formulated from within various social perspectives.

Rather than being objective in a transperspectival sense, critical theorists have always insisted that their form of social inquiry takes a "dual perspective" (Habermas 1996, chapter 2; Bohman 1991, chapter 4). This dual perspective has been expressed in many different ways. Critical theorists have always insisted that critical approaches have dual methods and aims: they are both explanatory and normative at the same time, adequate both as empirical descriptions and as practical proposals for social change. This dual perspective has been consistently maintained by critical theorists in their debates about social scientific knowledge, whether it is with regard to the positivism dispute, universal hermeneutics, or micro- or macrosociological explanations. In the dispute about positivism, critical theorists rejected all forms of reductionism and insisted on the explanatory role of practical reason. In disputes about interpretation, critical theorists have insisted that social science not make a forced choice between explanation and understanding. Even if social scientists can only gain epistemic access to social reality through interpretation, they cannot merely repeat what agents know practically in their "explanatory understanding." Here we might think of explanations that create micro- and macrolinkages. Such dual perspective explanations and criticism both allow the reflective distance of criticism and the possibility of mediating the epistemic gap between the participants' more internal and the critics' more external point of view. Given the rich diversity of possible explanations and stances, here I can only indicate some of the more salient possibilities in contemporary social science. They are not limited to general theories or general interpretive frameworks.

Such a dual perspective provides a more modest conception of objectivity: it is neither transperspectival objectivity nor a theoretical metaperspective, but always operates across the range of possible practical perspectives that knowledgeable and reflective social agents are capable of taking up and employing practically in their social activity. It is achieved in various combinations of available explanations and interpretive stances. At various times with respect to various social phenomena, critical social inquiry has employed various explanations and explanatory strategies. Marx's historical social theory permitted him to relate functional explanations of the instability of profit-maximizing capitalism to the first-person experiences of workers. In detailed historical analyses, feminist and ethnomethodological studies of the history of science have been able to show the contingency of normative practices (Epstein 1996; Longino 1990). They have also adopted various interpretive stances. Feminists have shown how supposedly neutral or impartial norms have built-in biases that limit their putatively universal character (Mills 1997; Minnow 1990). Such explanations take up the stance of those who suffer the exclusions that cultural analysis reveals.

More modest forms of third-person criticism need not be so narrowly interpreted. The third-person perspective identifies nonintentional processes, feedback mechanisms, byproducts and other features of complex social structures not under fully voluntary control. Here we might think of unintended consequences of profit maximization, self-defeating strategies or policies, the macroconsequences of microbehavior, and other social scientific mechanisms that operate through agents' intentional actions but produce aggregate and unintended effects that agents do not anticipate. An example is Thomas Schelling's analysis of tipping points in nonintended residential segregation or of various perverse consequences of state regulatory schemes (Schelling 1971). The theory of ideology provides a more directly instructive example within traditional critical social inquiry. As the target of dual- or cross-perspective criticism, ideology might be rethought in terms of restrictions of communication that give rise to

James Bohman

justification under conditions that undermine successful communication, or in terms of limits of the experiences of agents due to social positions (Kelly and Bohman 2000). Such restrictions and biases may also present general impediments to collective goals, such as the achievement of a democratic form of life (Bohman 1995).

Theories are not the only means by which social scientists are able to expose such normative biases and cognitive limitations. Agents can adopt the first-person singular perspective to criticize the limitations of various other perspectives as well as by employing acts of criticisms that go across the limits of various perspectives. In this way excluded actors can point out the biases and limitations of traditions that have collective authority, showing how the contours of their experiences do not fit the self-understanding of an institution as fulfilling standards of justice (Young 1991; Mansbridge 1991). Such criticism requires holding both one's own experience and the normative self-understanding of the tradition or institution together at the same time, to expose bias or cognitive dissonance. Such criticism uses expressions of vivid first-person experiences to bring about cross-perspectival insights in actors who do not otherwise see the limits of their cognitive and communicative activities. They initiate an act of communication in which the critic takes the role of the representative second person to whom such normative justifications can be addressed and then whose testimony shows them to fail. For example, offering testimony is an act of social criticism, not simply as an act of self-expression but as embedded in a complex form of communication that exhibits how such true testimony can help agents cross various perspectives and achieve reflective distance from the unreflective and often implicit assumptions of their practices.

At this point, an answer must be provided for the following question: what is it to cross perspectives? Here the second-person perspective has a special and self-reflexive status in criticism. It is within this perspective that the social relationship of critic and audience is established in acts of interpretation and criticism. Such dialogical relations employ practical knowledge in the normative attitude, that is, knowledge about norms and the normative dimensions of actions and conditions of success. It is knowledge of the normative from within the normative attitude. As the attitude of the second-person interpreter, such practical knowledge is manifested in interaction and in dialogue and proves itself in terms of the success of dialogue and communication: in the ability of the interpreter to offer interpretations of the normative attitudes of others that they could in principle accept. This requires that we view interpretation very differently as a second-person form of knowledge. The question for critics is not "what evidence makes one interpretation better than the other?" It is rather "what are better and more self-reflective interpretations able to do?" If accepted, critical interpretations can establish and potentially transform the norms that govern social relations of obligation and commitment.

The normative attitudes of the second person are neither true descriptions nor self-expressive claims. Rather, they are assessments that become explicit only in actual dialogue. By treating what others are saying as true or taking them to be correct or incorrect in their performance, the interpreter establishes nothing more than the possibility of more and perhaps better interpretations and thus the possibility of future dialogue or interpretive exchange. Gadamer puts this in a practical way: "Every interpretation establishes the possibility of a relationship with others" (Gadamer 1992, 397). Such a relationship could only be established in the normative attitude. Gadamer goes on to say that these relationships institute obligations, since "there can be no speaking that does not bind the speaker and the person spoken to" (Gadamer 1992, 397). It is to this binding power of interpretations and the implicit know-how of establishing normative relations that critics appeal, to the ability to open up or close off various practical possibilities with others with whom we are engaged in the process of mutual interpretation or of reaching understanding.

McCarthy discusses precisely the contestability of all interpretations as a way to distinguish subject-subject from subject-object domains of inquiry. In discussing the interpretive character of subject-subject relations, McCarthy argues that "the objectivity and adequacy of participant observers' 'third-person' accounts of beliefs and practices that are already informed by 'first-' and 'second-person' accounts cannot, in the end, be warranted independently of the latter" (McCarthy 1994, 87). This lack of independence holds for the practical situation of the critic as well, even when the critic is using theoretical knowledge or broad interpretive frameworks. Criticisms can only have their transformative effects if their addressees are able to shift perspectives and see themselves from the critic's perspective. Given that the goal of the critic is not merely to describe a state of affairs but to address an audience it is hard to see how the presupposition of the single right answer in critical-reflective discourses can be warranted independently of agents' acceptance. Thus this lack of transperspectival independence means that what is at stake is not a belief or "the right answer" but rather the employment of different perspectives in evaluating and criticizing a practice.

This practical and second-person account of understanding suggests that certain debates about the relationship between criticism and interpretation need to be reformulated. If my argument about the cross-perspectival nature of criticism is correct, then it is a mistake to see such debates as about tradition and its authority on the one hand and social scientific and critical explanations such as the critique of ideology on the other. The plurality of perspectives suggests that there is no inherent conflict between a first-person plural (or the "we" perspective of the internal participant) and a third-person perspective of the external critic. It is rather about correctives needed to expand the normative attitudes of interaction within the second-person perspective. Certainly, it is sometimes necessary to invoke the standards of the community in order to make them explicit enough to judge them; at other times it is necessary to refer to features of the situation of interpretation that may limit its practical possibilities. The real problem is the role of reflection in the context of interpretation. Reflection establishes the possibility of epistemic improvement even when know-how cannot be transformed into theoretical knowledge, since it is the means by which we make explicit and thus come to accept or reject the practical consequences of the interpretations that we offer to others.

Once we view critical social inquiry as fundamentally practical and employing practical knowledge from a variety of perspectives, then we can see the limits of hermeneutic and instrumental accounts of practical knowledge. The third-person perspective shifts the superiority of the expert in means/ends reasoning to the interpersonal domain; the hermeneutic perspective limits reflection by granting final authority to the community over its norms. Both suggest particular political relations of authority that the social scientists would borrow. The account of critical social inquiry that I have been developing here abandons such claims of authority and thus unlinks social scientific objectivity from such demands for epistemic superiority. Instead, the critics are only participants in the public sphere and establish social relations of obligation and authority only by addressing their audience as a public, even when there is no existing audience for whom such criticisms could be accepted. This idealization of the future audience that can appropriately verify a critical claim captures McCarthy's cognitivist concern with the context-transcendence of critical reason. This sort of pragmatic assumption is all that pluralism requires. While it falls short of the requirement of convergence on a single right answer, it still suggests a way to judge critical success consistent with the regulative role of ideals of reason.

Conclusion: The Politics of Critical Social Inquiry

My argument here develops a contrast between two interpretations of critical social science: the one is theoretical and dependent on the heritage of German idealism, and the other is practical and pluralistic in the spirit of pragmatism. Thomas McCarthy's work has often shown why the pragmatic interpretation is superior. The main epistemic weakness of the first interpretation is that it depends on the overly ambitious goal of a comprehensive social theory that unifies all the diverse methods and practical purposes of social inquiry. The practical alternative offers a solution to this problem by taking critical social theory in a pragmatic direction. In this respect, I have argued in McCarthy's spirit that a pragmatic reinterpretation of the verification of critical inquiry changes seemingly intractable epistemic problems into practical ones. The role of critical social science is to supply methods for making explicit just the sort of self-examination necessary for ongoing democratic regulation of social life. This practical regulation includes the governing norms of critical social science itself. Here the relation of theory to practice differs from that found in the original pragmatists: more than simply clarifying the relation of means and ends for decisions on particular issues, these social sciences institutionalize reflection upon institutionalized practices and their norms of cooperation. Critical social science is also reflexive in the sense that among such practices is included the examination of practices and modes of inquiry itself, including their underlying social norms and relationships.

What does this discussion of practical verification say about the general political consequences of a practical and perspectival account of critical inquiry? It might be possible to see pragmatism as a procedural form of politics that is concerned only with second-order issues of open procedures and agenda setting. On this reading, the democratic commitments of pragmatists leave them with no substantive political point of view, only the cooperative and second-order testing of a variety of alternative procedures, goals, and frameworks. However, the substantive commitments of such democratic and egalitarian practices are not politically neutral and inform the social scientist about what norms and consequences are relevant and important. Nor does a practice such as science remain neutral among competing claims, seeking some de facto consensus. Instead of neutrality, critical theory and pragmatism both offer a distinct sort of politics of cooperative inclusion that aims at resolving social conflicts in ways that include all perspectives and interests. What critical social inquiry can add to reformist democratic politics is second-order reflection, especially by taking the operations of power within democracy and science more seriously than did its pragmatist predecessors. To the extent that modern power depends on the cooperation of many social actors, such cooperation may be publicly scrutinized and challenged in order to transform relations of power and authority into contexts of democratic accountability (Bohman 1999a).

On his pluralist side McCarthy is sensitive to the permanent possibility of disagreement, indeed that many issues put up for democratic deliberation will not be resolved consensually (McCarthy 1998, 127–128). This is because our pragmatic presuppositions are not constitutive of our practices, but regulative; they are not guarantees that the problems we face will be resolved in ways that would be independently acceptable to all as the best solution. But McCarthy is true to his pragmatic insights by arguing consistently that we ought not abandon such presuppositions, simply because they remain in tension with the facts of pluralism. This leads critics like Rorty to point out the ambiguity of McCarthy and Habermas's conception of rationality (Rorty 1996). My response is to take up the pragmatist challenge. As the role of ongoing challenge and disagreement in criticizing and improving practices shows, accepting tensions that cannot be resolved theoretically may improve rather than diminish the rationality of a reflective practice. Indeed, McCarthy agrees that the "sociologic" of communicative rationality is the effort "to understand how such ideas of reason work in practice, for it is only in practice that the aporetic tensions between the ideal and the real, the transcendent and the immanent, the first and the third person points of view can be, not dissolved, but put into play and rendered productive" (McCarthy 1994, 73). Even if the theoretical/practical debate in critical theory turns out to be another false dualism, such arguments make the pragmatist point that this opposition can only be overcome from the practical side of the debate. Far from being an inconsistency, McCarthy's commitments to the cognitivist emphasis on the ideal of agreement and the pluralist insight into the equal importance of disagreement are best seen as two sides of the same practical coin. Reflective practices cannot remain so without critical social inquiry, and critical social inquiry can only be tested in such practices.

References

Bohman, James. 1991. *New Philosophy of Social Science: Problems of Indeterminacy.* Cambridge: MIT Press.

Bohman, James. 1995. "Modernization and Impediments to Democracy: Hypercomplexity and Hyperrationality." *Theoria* 86: 1–20.

Bohman, James. 1996. *Public Deliberation: Pluralism, Complexity and Democracy.* Cambridge: MIT Press.

Bohman, James. 1999a. "Democracy as Inquiry, Inquiry as Democratic: Pragmatism, Social Science, and the Cognitive Division of Labor," *American Journal of Political Science* 43: 590–607.

Bohman, James. 1999b. "Theories, Practices, and Pluralism: A Pragmatic Interpretation of Critical Social Science." *Philosophy of the Social Sciences* 29: 459–480.

Bohman, James. 2000. "The Importance of the Second Person: Normative Attitudes, Practical Knowledge, and Interpretation." Pp. 222–242 in *Empathy and Agency: The*

James Bohman

Problem of Understanding in the Human Sciences, ed. K. Stueber and H. Koegler. Boulder: Westview Press.

Brandom, Robert. 1988. "Pragmatism, Phenomenalism and Truth Talk." Pp. 75–93 in *Midwest Studies in Philosophy* 12, ed. P French, T. Uehling and H. Wettstein. Notre Dame: University of Notre Dame Press.

Brandom, Robert. 1994. *Making It Explicit.* Cambridge: Harvard University Press.

Dewey, John. 1986. *Logic: The Theory of Inquiry*, in *The Later* Works. Volume 12. Carbondale: Southern Illinois University Press.

Dewey, John. 1988. *The Public and Its Problems*, in *The Later Works*. Volume 2. Carbondale: Southern Illinois University Press.

Epstein, Stephen. 1996. *Impure Science: AIDS, Activism and the Politics of Knowledge.* Berkeley: University of California Press.

Gadamer, Hans-Georg. 1992. *Truth and Method.* New York: Seabury.

Geertz, Clifford. 1971. *The Interpretation of Cultures.* New York: Basic Books.

Habermas, Jürgen. 1971. *Knowledge and Human Interests.* Boston: Beacon Press.

Habermas, Jürgen. 1973. *Theory and Practice.* Boston: Beacon Press.

Habermas, Jürgen. 1984. *The Theory of Communicative Action.* Volume 1. Boston: Beacon Press.

Habermas, Jürgen. 1987. *The Theory of Communicative Action.* Volume 2. Boston: Beacon Press.

Habermas, Jürgen. 1988. *The Logic of the Social Sciences.* Cambridge: MIT Press.

Habermas, Jürgen. 1996. *Between Facts and Norms.* Cambridge: MIT Press.

Hempel, Carl. 1965. *Aspects of Scientific Explanation.* New York: Free Press.

Horkheimer, Max. 1982. *Critical Theory.* New York: Seabury Press.

Horkheimer, Max. 1993. *Between Philosophy and Social Science.* Cambridge: MIT Press.

Kelly, Terrence, and James Bohman, eds. 2000. *Theories of Ideology.* Special issue of *Constellations* 7:3.

Kögler, Hans-Herbert, and Karsten Stueber, eds. 2000. *Empathy and Agency: The Problem of Understanding in the Human Sciences.* Boulder: Westview Press.

Longino, Helen. 1990. *Science as Social Knowledge.* Princeton: Princeton University Press.

Mansbridge, Jane. 1991. "Feminism and Democratic Community," Pp. 339–396 in *Democratic Community*, ed. J. Chapman and I. Shapiro. New York: New York University Press.

McCarthy, Thomas. 1991. *Ideals and Illusions*. Cambridge: MIT Press.

McCarthy, Thomas, and David Hoy. 1994. *Critical Theory*. London: Basil Blackwell.

McCarthy, Thomas. 1998. "Legitimacy and Diversity." Pp. 115–153 in *Habermas on Law and Democracy*, ed. M. Rosenfeld and A. Arato. Berkeley: University of California Press.

Mills, Charles. 1997. *The Racial Contract*. Ithaca: Cornell University Press.

Minnow, Martha. 1990. *Making All the Difference*. Ithaca: Cornell University Press.

Putnam, Hillary. 1994. *Words and Life*. Cambridge: Harvard University Press.

Rorty, Richard. 1991. "Inquiry as Recontextualization." In *The Interpretive Turn*, ed. D. Hiley, J. Bohman, and R. Shusterman. Ithaca: Cornell University Press.

Rorty, Richard. 1996. "The Ambiguity of 'Rationality.'" *Constellations* 3: 74–82.

Schelling, Thomas. 1971. *Micromotives and Macrobehavior*. New York: Norton.

Weber, Max. 1949. *The Methodology of the Social Sciences*. New York: Free Press.

Wiggershaus, Rolf. 1994. *The Frankfurt School*. Cambridge: MIT Press.

Young, Iris. 1991. *Justice and the Politics of Difference*. Princeton: Princeton University Press.

5

Adjusting the Pragmatic Turn: Ethnomethodology and Critical Argumentation Theory[1]

William Rehg

Introduction

In recent decades, a number of critical theorists in the Frankfurt School tradition have attempted to base their critical analyses on a pragmatic theory of argumentation or "discourse theory." A range of positions on the "pragmatic turn" has emerged, distinguished by the level of contingency and context they admit into the structures of argumentation. Despite their apparent differences, Karl-Otto Apel and Jürgen Habermas both invest the "pragmatic presuppositions" of discourse with a significant level of transcultural universality, in marked contrast to the postmodern pragmatism espoused by Richard Rorty. In this context, Thomas McCarthy's attempt to develop a more thoroughly "pragmatized" but nonrelativistic approach deserves attention—especially in light of the many criticisms leveled against the highly idealized approaches taken by Apel and Habermas.

In the course of his pragmatizing effort, McCarthy drew on the ethnomethodology developed by Harold Garfinkel and his coworkers. But he hesitated to follow out the more radical implications of ethnomethodology. In this paper I take McCarthy's efforts a step further by examining these implications for our understanding of argumentation. In line with McCarthy's emphasis on the ideas of truth and objectivity, I focus especially on scientific argumentation, which is playing a growing role in social policymaking. My analysis emerges through a series of "passes" at ethnomethodology that generate increasingly stringent contextualist challenges for a critical argumentation theory. In a first pass, I examine the ethnomethodological critique of Habermas's formal pragmatics, a critique that applies by extension to the associated discourse theory. McCarthy's revisions of Habermasian discourse theory meet a moderate version of the contextualist challenge and provide the occasion for a second pass at ethnomethodology. I then make a third pass, in which I engage the more radical challenge and consider the possibility of a critical argumentation theory that incorporates such challenges without losing its critical potential.

First Pass: The Contextualist Critique of Formal Pragmatics

The pragmatic turn, for present purposes, can be understood negatively as a *turn away from* both the premoderns' metaphysical concerns with the structures of being and the moderns' epistemological focus on the possibility of a subject's access to an objective world; positively, the turn consists of a *turn toward* the conditions and presuppositions of language use as the unavoidable context and medium for philosophical inquiry. In this context, it is not surprising that critical theorists committed to making this turn have looked to argumentation theory as a way into the normative issues connected with social critique, enlightenment, and emancipation. Besides being eminently relevant to critique, processes of argumentation presumably depend on rational structures built into language use. Argumentation theories with normative intent typically elaborate such structures as rules for good, or cogent, argumentation. Going beyond a system of formal logic, such rules often extend to dialectical analysis, rhetoric, and so on.

For the moment I am less concerned with the particular rules of argumentation than with their status, which varies according to the particular theorist's understanding of the pragmatic turn. At one end of the spectrum we have positions like that of Karl-Otto Apel, who considers the rules, or "pragmatic presuppositions," of argumentation to be capable of an inescapable, ultimate justification impervious to cultural and historical contingencies. Although Habermas rejects Apel's foundationalist claims, he holds onto the cross-cultural validity of these presuppositions. Not surprisingly, this transcendental, decontextualized account of argumentation has drawn critical fire from postmodern pragmatists at the other end of the spectrum—for example, Rorty, whose "frankly ethnocentric" approach rejects such universalistic arguments.[2] More telling, however, is the fact that even sympathetic theorists working in the Frankfurt School tradition have found problems with Habermas's emphasis on idealized consensus.[3]

We might gloss these various criticisms as a *contextualist challenge* to critical argumentation theory. Some versions of this challenge are more radical than others. In this section I construe the ethnomethodological version of this challenge in fairly moderate terms, as a challenge to the a priori theorizing that, at least in the eyes of the critics, characterizes aspects of Habermas's formal pragmatics. I do not intend to settle this particular debate, but to use it as an occasion for an initial understanding of ethnomethodology. The select contrasts with formal pragmatics should, I hope, prepare us better to understand the critical implications of ethnomethodology for argumentation theory—the more radical contextualist challenge that I reserve for the second and third passes.

Ethnomethodologists and their close cousins, conversation analysts, present a moderate contextualist challenge insofar as they reject formal, decontextualized analyses of language use. Drawing on Wittgenstein, Jeff Coulter argues that language does not have an "intrinsic" logical structure identifiable a priori, apart from actual practices of use. Concrete contexts are always built into linguistic meanings: "No expression in a natural language can have *any* intelligibility *without* a context" that is at least tacitly assumed.[4] The doctrine of indexicality behind this claim I take up in the next section. The important point for the moderate challenge is this: Coulter calls on language theorists to proceed more empirically, to examine "*actual*, and not exclusively hypothetical, cases of *praxis*."[5]

David Bogen has turned this policy into a critique of Habermas's theory of communicative action. Habermas fears that a critical analysis of actual communication will go astray without the guidance provided by a formal pragmatics, with its idealized system of validity claims, and the corresponding argumentation theory. One must then link these abstractions with "empirical pragmatics" through a rather tortuous program of contextualization.[6] Bogen challenges the central assumption behind Habermas's program: that one can accurately capture the rationality basis of speech only by starting with a set of formal structures free of the complexities in which empirical studies are mired. In Bogen's view, Habermas assumes but does not adequately demonstrate the situated relevance of his ideal-typical categories for actual speech; indeed, his formal approach misses the concrete "rationalities" or "endogenous logic" of actual social practices—the "rationality basis" that ethnomethodology and conversation analysis (CA) are at pains to elucidate.[7] The moderate challenge boils down to the objection that a contextualization program starting from above will do a poor job of illuminating linguistic interaction.[8]

This objection implies that CA and ethnomethodology cannot be equated with "empirical pragmatics" in Habermas's sense. To be sure, some conversation analysts maintain that the investigator should use only those "resources intrinsic to the data themselves" in striving to explicate the methods that members themselves use in their situated achievement of social order.[9] Descriptive adequacy is achieved insofar as the investigator has described members' methods in such a way that "anyone" can "replicate the observations described."[10] However, such demands hold up only when they are freed of their logical-positivist overtones. As Coulter has argued, CA is not a presuppositionless "pure empiricism" that relies solely on inductive generalizations. Conversation analysts and ethnomethodologists must also formulate the a priori's or "rational intuitions" they share with their subjects of study as competent language users.[11] For example: without a grasp of the adjacency-pair structure, the conversation analyst would be at a loss to follow a conversation in which answers count as answers precisely because they follow questions as a matter of convention. At the same time, the formulation of such structures results, not from armchair speculation, but from "a great deal of study of actual transcribed materials."[12]

By way of illustration, consider Harvey Sacks's treatment of statements employing such universal expressions as "everyone" (e.g., "everyone has to lie"). Sacks does not assume such utterances are truth claims with a literal sense under standard conditions. Rather, he first establishes that truth-oriented assessment of such utterances can be "sequentially relevant" in actual conversation. And rather than taking "everyone" simply in a "summative sense," as an easily falsifiable universal quantifier, he also attends to its "programmatic" use, as referring to what someone ought to do in a certain type of conversational situation. In contrast to a crude inductivism, Sacks adduces empirical evidence here in the service of a close, perspicuous attention to, and understanding of, the details of actual practice. His approach assumes his own and the readers' linguistic competence.[13]

Again, my aim is not so much to defend formal pragmatics as to understand ethnomethodology and its implications for argumentation theory, in particular scientific argumentation. In the next section I draw some of those implications and then turn to McCarthy's position, which offers us one way to meet the moderate contextualist challenge.

Second Pass: Ethnomethodology à la McCarthy

Although the foregoing criticisms of Habermas focused primarily on his theory of communicative action, they clearly apply to his argumentation theory as well. That theory Habermas has formulated as a system of pragmatically unavoidable presuppositions or rules of cogent argumentation. He derives these through transcendental arguments that demonstrate performative self-contradictions in skeptical attempts to reject them.[14] However, difficulties arise as soon as one attempts to link these idealized rules to actual processes of controversy and argument. Contextualizing adjustments become necessary that are not themselves directly based on the rules. To be sure, Habermas is quite aware of this: these rules should not be confused with the limited procedures that structure actual discourses.[15] Rather one must presume that actual discursive procedures either sufficiently approximate such rules or that they could be justified in approximately ideal discourses.

Consider, for example, two such rules in relation to scientific argumentation: (1) Every subject with the competence to speak and act is allowed to take part in a discourse, and (2) Everyone is allowed to question any assertion whatever (provided one gives grounds for the questioning). If we understand the first rule to open up scientific discourse to nonexperts, that is, any reasonable person,[16] then it hardly describes the norms that legitimately organize actual scientific argumentation and the entry points available to nonexperts. Rule (2) is likewise problematic: even with justifications one cannot plausibly question just any assertion in science; rather, a sense of what claims are open to contest partly defines disciplinary competence. On Habermas's approach, the criticism and defense of such contextual restrictions tacitly presuppose the idealized court of appeal in which rules (1) and (2) apply. But given the impossibility of an ideal discourse, such rules are too vague to help us understand and criticize actual cases of scientific argumentation. Such criticism, to be effective, must be appropriately contextualized. But on what basis?

In this context, we can understand McCarthy's efforts to further pragmatize Habermas's formal pragmatics. Two of McCarthy's moves deserve mention here. First, he does not account for the rationality of discourse in terms of a formal system of rules but in relation to broader idealizations or "ideas of reason"—above all, "the accountability of subjects, the objectivity of the world, and the truth of statements." As we shall see, McCarthy elucidates these ideas not as metaphysical definitions but in relation to the pragmatics of communication and action.[17] Second, his analyses have a contextually situated character insofar as he draws on ethnomethodological studies of everyday interaction. McCarthy can thereby demonstrate the *situated relevance* of the ideas of reason for members' own production of social order. McCarthy's analysis thus provides the occasion for a second pass at ethnomethodology. I start with some general remarks.

In contrast to Parsonian sociology, which accounted for social order in terms of norms internalized and applied by compliant members, the ethnomethodology initiated by Harold Garfinkel emphasizes the agency that members exercise in actively constructing orderly social interaction in concrete situations.[18] Social order arises not from the mechanical application of rules to situations whose intelligibility is given ahead of time, but as an ongoing, occasioned accomplishment in which members actively constitute—and ongoingly transform—the sense of their situations. Shared normative expectations and general interpretive schemas certainly play a role here, but members employ these creatively, engaging a vast array of ad hoc mechanisms for weaving them together in an orderly interaction that continually adjusts to and reconstitutes changing circumstances. As providing a shared "grid" in relation to which actions "become visible and assessable," general norms and situation-definitions are employed reflexively either to reassert business as usual or to make some further point, as when a person deliberately refuses to return a greeting to indicate indignation over a previous slight.[19]

The first idea of reason, the *mutual imputation of rational agency, or accountability,* lies at the heart of this process of orderly interaction. Although McCarthy considers this presupposition an idealization that might always be counterfactual,[20] the various mechanisms for producing order require its constant exhibition. Accountability is displayed, that is, by the various moves that members use for continuing intelligible interaction. Our situated use of this repertoire of interactive competences involves normatively laden expectations—which Garfinkel once glossed as "trust"—that others will appropriately contextualize, and thereby give a definite sense to, actions or utterances that by themselves are indefinite and vague. Garfinkel famously demonstrated the reality of these expectations precisely by challenging them in "breaching experiments" in which the experimenter demanded full explicitness.[21] The moral indignation[22] provoked by such noncooperation reveals, as the flip side of the accountability displayed in the active mastery of behavioral moves, a corresponding receptive accountability for taking those moves in the appropriate way. Actors hold one another accountable not only for their words and deeds but also for the situationally appropriate interpretation of words and deeds.

The second idealization is the presupposition that *actors share the same objective world accessible to all.* Note that this presupposition is a further mode of accountability: "We are held accountable, and in turn hold our interaction partners accountable, for the transcendent objectivity of the world as invariant to discrepant reports."[23] Drawing on the work of Melvin Pollner, McCarthy points out that this presupposition underlies the use of "error accounts." In order to maintain the world's objectivity in the face of conflicting reports, we must account for differences by revoking one or another ceteris paribus assumption about the "community of observers" and the conditions of reliable observation.[24] The objectivity of the world, in the sense of its intersubjective accessibility, is thus an unfalsifiable presupposition by virtue of which actors anticipate that, "all other things being equal," competent observers should be able to reach unanimity in their factual reports.[25] Without this presupposition, neither the problem of discrepancy nor the means used to resolve it are intelligible.[26]

Finally, there is the *idea of truth.* Here McCarthy draws not so much on ethnomethodology as on the intuitive awareness that what we consider factually true at one point, we might later recognize as false in the light of new information.[27] This awareness of fallibility points to the context-transcending force of the truth we claim in making factual assertions: truth cannot simply reduce to what is true-for-us-now, but should hold for everyone. Thus the idea of truth "keeps us from being locked into what we happen to agree on at any particular time and place," it "opens us up to the alternative possibilities lodged in otherness and difference."[28]

The idealization of truth simply appears to draw the implications of the idea of objectivity for assertions about the world: if the unitary objective world is intersubjectively accessible, then true reports and assertions should be intersubjectively acceptable. Thus the idea of truth, like that of objectivity, is a specific mode of accountability. Because of its context-transcending force, a truth claim involves a tacit commitment on the part of the speaker to be accountable beyond the particular situation in which the claim was made. In making a truth claim in a particular forum, we "implicitly assume responsibility . . . for demonstrating its rational acceptability in other relevant forums as well."[29] Thus objectivity and truth constitute presuppositions that structure some *specific ways* in which mutual accountability is organized and exhibited. Though they are especially important for science, one need not take them as the privileged mode of accountability for all contexts.

In his presentation of these idealizations, McCarthy acknowledges the notion of indexicality. He agrees with ethnomethodologists that all language, and not just the standard indexical expressions such as "this," "I," "you," "now," and so on, acquire a definite sense only in the concrete situation. This holds even for attempts to translate indexical expressions into fully explicit, context-free "objective" statements. Not only do such explications always contain further ambiguities, in some cases they actually *lose* the situated meaning of the original utterance by eliminating elisions that hearers depend on and expect as ordinary. For example, making a child's cry "Mommy!" more explicit as "My mommy!" changes its situated sense. Garfinkel considers the irremediable indexicality of language to be empirically demonstrated by a number of studies.[30]

McCarthy also agrees with ethnomethodologists in seeing such indexicality more as a *virtue* than as a problem. General rules have to be vague inasmuch as they "are *supposed* to cover an indefinite range of specific instances, and those instances are not marked out as such in advance of any interpretive work."[31] That is, precisely because of their vagueness, general rules and ideals have a "local particularization potential" that makes them relevant across different contexts.[32]

The foregoing exposition shows that McCarthy can meet the moderate version of the contextualist challenge. More specifically, if we recall the ethnomethodological critique of formal pragmatics, we can see that McCarthy meets the central demand described in the first pass above. He does not start with a formal system of rules that must be subsequently contextualized, but rather he develops the universals of rational discourse from the ground up by drawing on ethnomethodological studies of actual practices. As a result, his bottom-up approach shows how such idealizations are relevant in actual discourse. At the same time, by holding on to context-transcending idealizations, his contextualist revisions retain the potential for social critique: ideas of reason inform a *situated* critical consciousness evident in members' own practices. However, as we shall see, McCarthy's moderate contextualism contains ambiguities that call for an exploration of the more radical ethnomethodology that he consciously avoided.[33]

Critical Ambiguities: Truth and the "Universal Audience"

In McCarthy's view, indexicality extends not simply to general terms and social norms but also to "standards, criteria, principles, schemes, ideals, and so forth" inasmuch as these "allow for an indefinite number of possible contextualizations . . . determined through participants' on-the-spot interpretations."[34] This suggests that idealized rules of argument and even the ideas of reason are indexical. On the one hand, argumentative standards can vary in light of our search for truth: "Appealing to the idea of truth, we can criticize . . . the very standards we have inherited." This point might help explain the variety of rules and methods that have actually informed argumentation in science.[35] On the other hand, McCarthy also seems to endorse an indexical account of truth itself, in the pragmatic sense of "making truth claims and offering warrants for them."[36] This suggests that scientific assertions of truth boil down to claims of "true enough for (our current, contingent) practical purposes."

However, McCarthy's strong notion of the universal audience stands in some tension with the indexicality of truth:

Scientists have reflexively to anticipate the scrutiny of their work by others who share the cognitive, normative, and evaluative presuppositions marking them as members of the same scientific subcommunity. If they can convince that particular audience, they have reason to expect they could convince other relevant audiences as well. That is to say, in virtue of its presumed competence, that audience can plausibly stand in for the "universal audience" of all rational beings able to judge the matter.[37]

McCarthy's process-oriented supposition of universal inclusiveness clearly excludes such reifications as Peirce's "end of inquiry." But the unqualified idea that one group can stand in for all contexts seems to suggest that indexicality can finally be overcome. Moreover, this idea tacitly privileges experts in public policy-making arenas—a problem that pragmatists have long recognized in democratic theory.[38] Behind these concerns lay three ambiguities, which turn on the interrelated conceptions of rationality, audience, and truth.

(1) On one reading, the orientation to a universal audience ensures singleness of meaning and objectivity across contexts: if a claim is true, then the claim in its original sense should be confirmable across an indefinitely extended series of further contexts. Insofar as subsequent inquiry alters or refines such claims, it constitutes an ongoing purification of science from local distortions and inadequacies. Not only does this idea suggest a problematic notion of verisimilitude,[39] it also involves a dubious conception of universal cogency that will not stand up to close ethnomethodological descriptions of the diverse,

concrete rationalities that characterize scientific practices. The idea of a universal audience must be abandoned or revised insofar as it points asymptotically toward an idealized way of assessing arguments that is unaffected by contingent and variable contextual rationalities, for such contingencies make up an essential dimension of human reason.

(2) Moreover, one might ask whether the invocation of a nonexistent universal audience accurately captures the force of scientific claims. Even if scientists sometimes say that "anyone" can see how evident a given belief is, studies of scientists' actual discourse reveal that, on closer inspection, such assertions come with indexical qualifiers.[40] That is, anyone with the requisite disciplinary competence and not led astray by prejudice should see the force of the assertedly true claim. The relevant audience, in other words, is quite specific. (If one objects that disciplinary definitions of competence should be open to broader criticism, then one has shifted the topic of argument.) If this observation is not to lead us into a relativistic view of science, then we require a more sophisticated conception of scientific truth, a problem I take up in a later section.

(3) The implications of McCarthy's conception of truth for the status of experts are somewhat unclear. On the one hand, he holds that truth claims are "never divorced from social practices of justification," even though they "cannot be reduced to any particular set thereof."[41] Such a view should undermine scientists' claims to epistemic privilege, inasmuch as their modes of justification are not free of context-specific determinations. On the other hand, the idea that scientists stand in for the universal audience suggests that their justifications are somehow intrinsically superior, are less distorted by context—hence scientists' privileged position. On that reading, the idea that a truth claim "carries beyond the particular circumstances of utterance" in virtue of its "regulative 'surplus' of meaning"[42] could mean that truth somehow *stands above* the circumstances and particular practices of argument. That is, validity as such is unconditioned by circumstantial contingencies; truth per se is not indexical.

I doubt that McCarthy intends such a reading. An alternative lies in the idea that a truth claim "carries beyond" local contexts in the sense of being *potentially relevant and defensible* for other contexts and audiences. To work out this idea requires us to examine the indexical status of formulations or accounts, both those generated by engaged members (e.g., scientists) and those produced by argumentation theorists who talk about a "universal audience." To address these issues—and to spell out an alternative that goes beyond and, I hope, strengthens McCarthy's analysis—requires yet a third pass at ethnomethodology. This time we let the radical ethnomethodologists speak for themselves.

Third Pass: Radical Ethnomethodology

The "central recommendation" of ethnomethodology, in Garfinkel's own terms, "is that the activities whereby members produce and manage settings of organized everyday affairs are identical with members' procedures for making those settings 'account-able.'"[43] That is, in everyday practices members do and say things that they can observe, and they continually contextualize and update these sayings and doings so that their interaction makes sense. Just these ongoing contextualizing activities or "procedures" make their sayings and doings "reportable" in formulations, and thus "account-able." It follows that formulated accounts are indexically tied to the concrete occasion of their production, and have a rational character only in the concrete context:

[R]ecognizable sense, or fact, or methodic character, or impersonality, or objectivity of accounts are not independent of the socially organized occasions of their use. Their rational features *consist* of what members do with, what they "make of" the accounts in the socially organized actual occasions of their use. Members' accounts are reflexively and essentially tied for their rational features to the socially organized occasions of their use for they are *features* of the socially organized occasions of their use.[44]

This text could serve as a summary for any number of ethnomethodological studies. For example, Kathleen Jordan and Michael Lynch have shown how even highly standardized, "cookbook" techniques in molecular biology cannot be used simply by following written accounts, but rather require a tricky personal appropriation.[45]

Particularly interesting in this regard are Eric Livingston's studies of mathematical arguments. Livingston does not deny that mathematical proofs appear most universal, objective, and anonymous.[46] Rather, he insists that the ability of a proof to travel beyond the context of origin does not reside in the formulated proof alone, the written or diagrammatic "proof-account." Such accounts are partial descriptions that have their intelligibility only in relation to the practices of a particular culture of proving and the actual "lived work" of proving. An effective proof-account supplies just those relevant concrete details that allow other members of the mathematical culture to contextualize the account and "do" the work of proving. In analogy to one's grasp of a gestalt figure in a set of lines and shapes, appropriately contextualized material cues allow members to make just those embodied, spatio-temporal moves required to "see" the "gestalt of reasoning"—and thus grasp the ideal object and its properties—that the proof-account describes.

However, the appropriate contextualizing methods are so ordinary —for example, knowing the sequence of physical actions involved in the construction of a diagram—that competent members take them for granted as "essentially uninteresting."[47] Concrete methods do not deserve explicit comment, indeed such commentary would only distract, and might even mislead, competent practitioners. These practical moves are seen but unnoticed, they are "witnessed but ignored."[48]

Thus ethnomethodologists of mathematics and science do not deny the importance of abstract, general accounts in these disciplines. Rather, they strive to notice and describe the concrete, mundane details of practice *through which alone* these general accounts— as "glosses" that leave out the details[49]—acquire their local, definite sense and relevance for actual scientific practice.

However, it's one thing for mathematicians and natural scientists to ignore these mundane features of doing science, quite another for the sociologist or argumentation theorist to overlook them. Unlike scientists interested in natural order, sociologists and argumentation theorists presumably are interested in the rational production of social order, and so they miss their mark if they do not attend carefully to—take an interest in and thematize—the concrete, local, and unspoken details of social practice. Inasmuch as abstract rules of method and argumentation derive from, and only acquire their co-gency within, lived practice, theorists misunderstand their subject of investigation as long as they merely refine such abstractions.

Herein lies a more radical challenge, then: accepting the indexi-cality of rational accounts carries with it a rejection of generalizing theory, whether in the form of general sociological explanations or as traditional epistemology, with its attempt to formulate general defini-tions of such concepts as representation, truth, observation, and so on. Such theories are, after all, accounts, but accounts that either for-get or pretend to overcome the methodological obstacles posed by an irremediable indexicality.[50] Indeed, the radicalist critique does not spare its own offspring, conversation analysis, which eventually built for itself an abstract technical vocabulary that contrasted with, and was considered superior to, members' everyday knowledge.[51]

The honest alternative to grand theory, according to Lynch, is a deflationary descriptive approach that "respecifies" traditional con-cepts as "epistopics." The investigator simply notices and describes the variety of situated ways in which actors actually *do* such things as represent, observe, and so on—but resists "all efforts to build general models and to develop normative standards that hold across situa-tions."[52] Lynch's approach counts as theorizing only in a loose sense, inasmuch as its core theoretical contention—Garfinkel's "central rec-ommendation" quoted above—robs the ethnomethodologist of any methodical program or substantive general model of social order. The production of social order and the appropriate method of its study must be discovered anew for each local practice.[53]

At its core, the radical position involves an inversion of the tradi-tional view that human reason displays its power primarily in rising from the concrete to the universal. Radicalists insist on the opposite: that we display our reason precisely by plunging into the concrete. More precisely, rationality is exhibited, in the first instance, by an in-sight into the relevant situated practical moves in a local achievement of order. Universal formulas provide at best fragmentary clues for in-sight. If such insight grasps a more idealized "universal," it is a uni-versal that resides in the observed-and-reportable cogencies of a set of particular practical moves, what Lynch calls the "instructable" or "instructive reproducibility of a practice."[54]

Applying this point to argumentation, we should say that its rationality lies in the practical, local achievement of cogent arguments—as a situated grasp of reproducibility. As glosses, formulated rules of argument and idealizations acquire their intelligibility and relevance only in relation to the situated rationalities of local practice. Competent arguers must discover each time the concrete methods, the situated rhetorics, by which they can argue reasonably. Consequently, one cannot simply invoke formal structures or idealizations to account for the rationality of argumentation. Herein lies a demanding challenge that goes beyond the earlier noted demands for descriptive adequacy. Even if one has doubts about the alleged all-pervasiveness of an irremediable indexicality, one can hardly deny *its relevance for argumentation theory*, given the many contextualist objections to strong idealizations.

This poses a problem for a critical theory that has taken the pragmatic turn in the manner of Habermas and McCarthy. Although critical theory involves much more than argumentation theory, the nonarbitrariness of its critical analyses crucially depends on such a theory. That is, critical theorists must rely on a normative theory whose rules or idealizations they can invoke to criticize actual cases of controversy and consensus formation. But they can make this critical move, it seems, only if they believe these idealizations properly "account for the rationality of argumentation"—just what I said deflationary ethnomethodology prohibits, given its doctrine of indexicality. This poses a dilemma for critical theorists: On the one hand, the project of emancipatory critique seems to require a conceptual framework that, precisely because of its formality, provides a stable platform for critical assessment. On the other hand, if indexicality applies to such ideas, then no such platform exists that could set critical theorists above the social fray. One can, to be sure, formulate such ideas, to which engaged arguers might then appeal. Arguers can invoke these, however, only as glosses that they must contextualize in the much richer local rationalities of practice—whereupon the ideas of reason take on all the local interpretive contingencies the theorist hoped to avoid.

To recapitulate, our third pass at ethnomethodology was motivated by questions about the indexicality of truth and the status of "universal audience" formulations. What we found is yet a further challenge beyond that of relativism, a challenge that casts doubt on the very possibility of a pragmatically inflected critical theory that rests its claim to rationality on practices of argumentation.

Incorporating the Radical Challenge

The deflationary approach I have just described leads into the policy of "ethnomethodological indifference," that is, the policy of "abstaining from all judgments of [the] adequacy, value, importance, necessity, practicality, success, or consequentiality" of the argumentative practices.[55] According to Lynch, this policy does not "set up a disinterested social science" but rather "assigns epistemic privilege to no single version of social affairs, including sociology's own professionally authorized versions."[56] As a result, issues of sociological method are set aside in order to attend more closely to the situated "methods" that members themselves use to produce social order. Indifference thus forbids criticism based on the investigator's own moral, political, or epistemological beliefs.[57]

The policy of indifference suggests the following formulation of the radical contextualist challenge: is there any way that the critical theorist can coherently acknowledge the indexicality of such idealizations as accountability, truth, and objectivity without adopting the ethnomethodologist's full-blown policy of indifference? In this section I argue that there is.

To see how, consider the position of the critical argumentation theorist. Suppose, on the one hand, that such theorists were simply to become ethnomethodologists of controversy. If so, then indifference requires them to examine and describe the ordered and accountable activities by which arguers produce and resolve controversies. But such studies reveal that arguers regularly invoke various rules and ideals, precisely as part of the reportable accountability of their argumentative practices. This is evident, for example, in cases of scientific controversy, particularly interdisciplinary and interparadigmatic debates—a point that Thomas Kuhn made some time ago.[58] As both anecdotal evidence and systematic discourse analysis demonstrate, scientists explicitly invoke normative ideals of scientific method—

typically drawn from logical empiricism and Popperian philosophy of science—in order to recommend one position and criticize opponents. Moreover, scientists act like sociologists and psychologists inasmuch as they appeal to alleged "consensus positions," or charge opponents with bias, and so on.[59] Indifferent argumentation theorists would simply accept these various accounting procedures as participants employ them—an approach that clearly departs from that of Habermas or McCarthy.

If, on the other hand, argumentation theorists adopt the critically engaged position of participants, then like those participants they may invoke whatever rules and ideals they deem appropriate—without fearing any rebuke from indifferent ethnomethodologists. At the same time, an engaged, participant-level perspective does not prevent critical theorists from drawing upon ethnomethodological insights, any more than it prevents scientists from drawing upon logical empiricist models of justification or simplistic representations of "consensus." This synthetizing move, I propose, provides the answer to the radical contextualist challenge.

My claim is that critical theorists like McCarthy can accept the more radical aspects of indexicality in relation to truth—and still take sides as engaged participants. Just as participants can make their critical discussion accountable by talking like, but not becoming, epistemologists and sociologists, so too can argumentation theorists insofar as they occupy a participant position. They can invoke ideas of reason *in the manner* of participants even as they *fill out* those ideas with ethnomethodologically descriptive detail. As engaged arguers, critical theorists are not ethnomethodologists—but neither are they armchair epistemologists. In the remainder of this section I briefly sketch the two sides of the proposed synthesis: the indexicality of the ideas of reason, and the nature of the critical theorist's participation. How much critical purchase this synthesis allows I take up in the conclusion.

Idealizations as indexical
Although ethnomethodological science studies tend to focus on local interactions (e.g., laboratory shop talk), they have not entirely neglected the broader aspects of science.[60] To this extent, ethnomethodology is not completely at odds with other ethnographic approaches

that look beyond the laboratory.[61] In fact, one can see even at the local level that scientists frame their arguments and claims so that these will find acceptance not only by members of their particular subspecialty but also in broader contexts in which those claims have some relevance or applicability. On the one hand, then, scientists strive to make publishable, *locality*-transcendent claims that hold up among peers working in the same area of research.[62] In grasping the accountable cogencies of their lived work, scientists in a particular laboratory observe and grasp the reportability of their findings for other members of their subdiscipline—thus its objectivity or independence from the local laboratory. The published article formulates just this recognition for the broader community.

On the other hand, we can distinguish such locality-transcendence, which extends only to those further sites of reproduction that share the background assumptions of the particular subspecialty, from the broader *context*-transcendence exhibited insofar as local findings are taken up by scientists in other areas and by nonscientists. Context-transcendence is possible because scientists work in the awareness of numerous contexts and practices simultaneously—the broader science community, the immediate institutional setting (university, corporation, government lab), funding agencies, technologists, and numerous other interested lay publics.[63] Each of these contexts enters into the lived work of scientists and shapes their local practice and methods of accountability. Because these different contexts involve different practices of argumentation, with different notions of relevance and cogency—in a word, different practices of accountability—the context-*transcendence* of scientific findings first proves itself in these broader extra-disciplinary spheres. Consequently, any adequate attempt to formulate idealizations or rules of argumentation must first of all attend to the obvious and not-so-obvious differences in how members in different settings actually employ such idealizations in their production of order.

Indeed, core idealizations vary even inside science itself. The idealization of a unitary objective world appears in experimental physics, for example, primarily as a *uniformity supposition*, the idea that the basic laws and makeup of the universe are the same for all times and places. The locality-transcending truth of such claims is understood accordingly: anyone anywhere who reproduces the asserted conditions should arrive at the same observations, and if despite their best efforts they do not, then the truth of the claim is in doubt. These *inflected* suppositions of objectivity and truth in turn define accountability among physicists: if other laboratories repeatedly fail to replicate one's findings, then one's own competence eventually comes into question. In other areas of science, however, objectivity does not always imply uniformity. In geology, for example, objectivity involves the supposition of a single earth history. Whether an established finding at one site (e.g., anomalous iridium deposits at the K/T boundary layer in Italy) also holds in corresponding strata elsewhere is not a supposition but an open research question.

In sum, the supposition that the reality we apprehend and understand here and now, in a particular local practice, is the same reality for everyone has a different sense that varies with context and practice. The same goes for the ideas of truth and rational accountability: what counts as "true enough" for the purposes at hand, and what adequacy requirements one must meet before a claim is taken seriously, will vary according to context. If the above observations hold true *within* science, we should expect them to hold a fortiori for contexts in which scientists must interface with nonscientists. The conflict of background expectations and modes of accountability that can arise in such situations—for example, situations in which scientific experts appear in court, or participate in popular media presentations—have been well documented.[64] The context-transcendence of a truth claim assumes that such obstacles can be overcome. This assumption points in turn to a revision in McCarthy's approach: a scientific truth claim assumes, not the counterfactual assent of a "universal audience," but the potential relevance and contextualizability of that claim in a range of scientific and extra-scientific contexts.

Engaged participation

In calling for engaged participation, I do not mean that critical argumentation theorists must become scientists or public intellectuals and engage directly in this or that controversy. Although they may (and at least some should) do that, there is also a *vicarious* mode of engagement available to critical theorists working in academic settings.[65] This vicarious engagement is evident in those controversies in which participants explicitly invoke argumentative ideals as part of their advocacy. I have already noted this phenomenon among scientists engaged in interdisciplinary controversies. In such settings scientists appeal to ideal models of method and cogency in order to make sense of their discursive practices, to produce an orderliness in the controversy, and to persuade—in sum, as an accountability procedure.[66] Argumentation theorists are vicariously involved in these debates insofar as participants draw upon formulated ideals of argumentation. Scientists may acquire such ideas in a number of ways— in undergraduate philosophy or critical thinking courses, through contact with philosophers of science, from their reading of science textbooks, works by public intellectuals and science journalists, and so forth.

These observations suggest that the context for critical argumentation theory arises from a dialectic of indirect, more or less disengaged theorizing that characterizes academic practices, on the one hand, and the directly engaged uses of formulated argumentative ideals by participants in controversy, on the other. By formulating indexically sensitive idealizations that participants find relevant to their situated accounting procedures, academic theorists avoid a disconnected top-down approach. But they meet the more radical contextualist challenge only when they recognize formulations as no more than potential accounting procedures that acquire a definite sense only insofar as they inform members' situated assessments of cogency in actual controversies. One thereby avoids mistaking them for foundations or rules with free-standing jurisdictional force over actual argumentative practices.[67] Argumentatively effective ideals enjoy, not transcendental necessity, but a situated practical necessity that is defeasibly acknowledged by actual participants who are committed to the reasonable resolution of disputes.

Sufficient Leverage for Critique?

By way of conclusion I want to address the relativist worry that lies behind the critical theorist's insistence on such idealizations as the universal audience. I am not so concerned here with a relativism based on frank ethnocentrism. For engaged arguers such avowals are rhetorically self-defeating: it hardly makes sense for scientists of one laboratory, say, to reinforce the cogency of their claims by citing argumentative norms that hold only in their own laboratory. Rather, my question is this: can contextually indexed ideas of reason as described above provide *sufficient* critical leverage, or must they fall captive, finally, to the status quo precisely because they depend so heavily on participants' situated—and often ad hoc—methods?

Here I can only provide a preliminary reply by noting some of the possible modes of critique enabled by ethnomethodological studies—modes that ultimately point to a larger issue. Some of these modes of criticism hearken back to earlier days of critical theory, with its use of immanent critique, critique of technocracy, and the like. Thus ethnomethodology can help to reinvigorate older areas of critical theory.

The first possibility is one that Lynch considers compatible with indifference. By choosing to study a group whose practices are assigned a marginal status by the dominant culture, ethnomethodologists "alert us to possible alternative rationalities," thereby casting doubt on official versions of reason and valorizing the marginalized culture.[68] To be sure, for critical theorists, the choice of research topic is not an "indifferent" matter. It makes a critical difference, for example, whether one chooses to valorize the practices of Aryan supremacists or poor sharecroppers. Thus from the standpoint of a normative critical theory, the partisan commitment built into the research program calls for some justification, a sociopolitical "accounting." Therein lies the larger question, which I take up momentarily.

Two further possibilities exploit the indexicality of formal accounts and idealizations. The straightforward mode attempts dialectically to undermine or refute simplistic ideals of scientific method invoked in contexts of controversy.[69] The relevant critical moves should not be difficult to imagine, at least in broad outline: essentially the critic adduces more detailed descriptions of situated methods as a counterargument against justifications based on formal ideals. Exactly how such counterarguments work depends on the particular context. One can, for example, imagine science-based policy debates in which descriptively enriched critique undermines official policy justifications that assume positivistic models of scientific objectivity. The postcolonialist critique of Western science could, I suspect, be cast as a combination of this and the former types of critique.[70]

One can also employ this dialectic ironically. Here the critic challenges science-based justifications as failing to meet ideals of scientific method. I call this move ironic because the critic's real aim is to elicit justifications that elaborate the situated rationalities and local discretionary judgments that the justification did not at first attend to. The critique thus has the maieutic function of eliciting from the participants themselves (1) the recognition of the insufficiency of formal ideals and (2) a further articulation of the actual, concrete reasonableness of their practices. Of course, it may turn out that the articulation lacks plausibility—but then that too would constitute a critical advance in the controversy.[71]

Each of these first three types of criticism trades on the indexicality of the standards and ideals that inform our notions of the "reasonable." At the same time, these moves do not specify any particular critical agenda. Thus the larger question remains of how critical theorists justify their specific critical orientation—that is, their commitment to emancipatory democracy.

We can approach a possible answer to this question by noting a still further mode of critique, one that shows that a radical indexicality need not leave us entirely at the mercy of local rationality assumptions. Recall that the indexicality of the ideas of reason is constituted, even at the local level, as a complex social reality. The interleaving-and-nesting of contexts harbors the possibility of criticizing and revising local assumptions in light of broader social demands. This permeability of scientific practices makes possible the public scrutiny of scientific findings, goals, and institutional structures. Indeed, the Frankfurt School critique of science has traditionally been concerned primarily with this socially encompassing level of sociopolitical criticism. At this level, the context-transcending force of scientific truth claims must pass its severest test—not as acceptability before a universal audience but as contextualizability and relevance across a range of interested practical domains or "social worlds."

The possibility of critically scrutinizing the science used in legal and political decision making arises precisely from the indexicality of such ideas as truth and objectivity. In adducing scientific findings as justification for policy, one insists on the probable truth and practical relevance of the findings for settings beyond the artificial laboratory contexts of origin. Consequently, an adequate justification requires one to make the science plausible in extrascientific contexts. Here laboratory expertise alone cannot guarantee the expert's authoritative status *for legal decisions and policymaking*. Again, the context determines exactly how this issue is framed. The most straightforward example of this is the situation in which the extrascientific context involves various complicating factors not present in the laboratory. The public dispute over the methodology of AIDS research provides a further example.[72]

The justification of the critical theory project must be developed at this more complex level of political discourse and decision making. Although I cannot give the full argument here, its point of departure lies in the various kinds of social problems confronting pluralistic societies and the requirements such problems impose on legitimate solutions, which must be reached through processes of social argumentation and dialogue that participants consider reasonable and noncoercive. The justification of critical theory thus relies on (1) the practical political need to settle conflicts and resolve truth-based policy disputes in order to maintain social order, and (2) the claim that deliberative democratic models are best suited for this task. To be sure, terms such as "reasonable" and "noncoercive" are highly indexical and contestable. But notice that, by starting with specific problems in need of resolution, this approach builds context into the normative ideals from the outset.[73] To this extent, the critique is "grounded" in practice itself, so that formulated idealizations gain their effectiveness in virtue of *their local relations* to the exigencies of the specific contexts in which the critique is embedded. As a result, critical theory outperforms rival approaches insofar as it attends more carefully to practices and their realities, a task for which ethnomethodology can provide considerable assistance.

Notes

1. I thank David Bogen, Michael Barber, Scott Berman, and James Bohman for their feedback on earlier versions of this essay.

2. See Karl-Otto Apel, "The Problem of Philosophical Foundations in the Light of a Transcendental Pragmatics of Language," trans. J. Bohman, in *After Philosophy: End or*

Transformation? ed. K. Baynes, J. Bohman, and T. McCarthy (Cambridge: MIT Press, 1987), 272–283; also his "Normatively Grounding 'Critical Theory' through Recourse to the Lifeworld? A Transcendental-Pragmatic Attempt to Think with Habermas against Habermas," in *Philosophical Interventions in the Unfinished Project of Enlightenment,* ed. A. Honneth, T. McCarthy, C. Offe, and A. Wellmer, trans. W. Rehg (Cambridge: MIT Press, 1992), 125–170. Habermas's views are elucidated in his "Discourse Ethics: Notes on a Program of Philosophical Justification," *Moral Consciousness and Communicative Action,* trans. C. Lenhardt and S. W. Nicholsen (Cambridge: MIT Press, 1990), 43–115. For Rorty's view, see his "Pragmatism and Philosophy," in *After Philosophy,* ed. Baynes et al., 26–66; also *Objectivity, Relativism, and Truth* (Cambridge: Cambridge University Press, 1991).

3. See, for example, Thomas McCarthy, *Ideals and Illusions* (Cambridge: MIT Press, 1991), chap. 7; Seyla Benhabib, *Situating the Self* (New York: Routledge, 1992), esp. chap. 1.

4. Jeff Coulter, "Logic: Ethnomethodology and the Logic of Language," in *Ethnomethodology and the Human Sciences,* ed. G. Button (Cambridge: Cambridge University Press, 1991), 20–50, here 35; see also 32.

5. Coulter, "Logic," 49.

6. See Jürgen Habermas, *The Theory of Communicative Action,* vol. 1., trans. T. McCarthy (Boston: Beacon, 1984, 1987), 328–337; the implications for argumentation theory are drawn on 22ff.

7. See David Bogen, *Order without Rules* (Albany: SUNY Press, 1999), chap. 2; cf. Coulter, "Logic," 39ff, also 34: "arguments and propositions considered by logicians are rarely embedded in a discourse-context explicitly, so that their logical properties may come to have an unknown relationship to any actual or *situatedly assignable* processes or achievements of inference-making . . . or illocutionary force specification"; finally, see also Kathleen Jordan and Michael Lynch, "The Sociology of a Genetic Engineering Technique: Ritual and Rationality in the Performance of the 'Plasmid Prep,'" in *The Right Tools for the Job,* ed. A. Clarke and J. Fujimura (Princeton: Princeton University Press, 1992), 78, 108 note 3.

8. According to Bogen, *Order without Rules,* 46: were formal pragmatics "to become the touchstone for empirically guided analysis, it would serve more to attenuate our intuitions of natural language use than to illuminate them."

9. Harvey Sacks, Emanuel A. Schegloff, and Gail Jefferson, "A Simplest Systematics for the Organization of Turn Taking for Conversation," in *Studies in the Organization of Conversational Interaction,* ed. J. Schenkein (New York: Academic, 1978), 45.

10. Michael Lynch, *Scientific Practice and Ordinary Action* (Cambridge: Cambridge University Press, 1993), 208.

11. Jeff Coulter, "Contingent and *A Priori* Structures in Sequential Analysis," *Human Studies* 6 (1983): 361–376, esp. 370–371, 374; see also Michael Lynch's extended critique of CA: *Scientific Practice,* chap. 6.

12. Coulter, "Contingent and *A Priori,*" 366.

13. Harvey Sacks, "Everyone Has to Lie," in *Socio-Cultural Dimensions of Language Use,* ed. B. Blount and M. Sanchez (New York: Academic, 1975), 57–79; the last point is explicit in Harvey Sacks, "On the Analyzability of Stories by Children," in *Directions in Sociolinguistics,* ed. J. J. Gumperz and D. Hymes (New York: Holt, Reinhart and Winston, 1972), 329–345, esp. 330.

14. See Habermas, "Discourse Ethics," 86–94.

15. See Habermas, "Discourse Ethics," 91.

16. Habermas suggests this interpretation in his "Vorbereitende Bemerkungen zu einer Theorie der kommunikativen Kompetenz," in J. Habermas and N. Luhmann, *Theorie der Gesellschaft oder Sozialtechnologie—Was leistet die Systemforschung?* (Frankfurt: Suhrkamp, 1971), 123ff. For the rules themselves, see Habermas, "Discourse Ethics," 89; also Robert Alexy, "A Theory of Practical Discourse," in *The Communicative Ethics Controversy,* ed. S. Benhabib and F. Dallmayr (Cambridge: MIT Press, 1990), 151–190, here 167–169. Although Habermas and Alexy use these as presuppositions of practical discourse, they seem to regard them as applying quite generally to any language game of justification (Alexy, "Theory," 166) or to "the practice of argumentation as such"; Habermas, *The Inclusion of the Other,* ed. C. Cronin and P. DeGreiff (Cambridge: MIT Press, 1998), 43.

17. McCarthy, *Ideals,* 27; see also David Couzens Hoy and Thomas McCarthy, *Critical Theory* (Oxford: Blackwell, 1994), 38–40; for the pragmatic character of McCarthy's approach, see 73. Unless otherwise noted, my citations of this work refer to chapters written by McCarthy, which should not be attributed to Hoy.

18. For an introduction, see John Heritage, *Garfinkel and Ethnomethodology* (Cambridge: Polity, 1984); for McCarthy's treatment of this material, see Hoy and McCarthy, *Critical Theory,* chap. 3. For Garfinkel's program, see his *Studies in Ethnomethodology* (Englewood Cliffs, N.J.: Prentice-Hall, 1967).

19. See Heritage, *Garfinkel,* chap. 5; the quote is from 117. For the intricate norms associated with greetings, see Sacks, "Everyone Has to Lie," 64–72.

20. McCarthy, *Ideals,* 30.

21. Harold Garfinkel, "A Conception of, and Experiments with, 'Trust' as a Condition of Stable Concerted Actions," in *Motivation and Social Interaction,* ed. O. J. Harvey (New York: Ronald, 1963), 187–238; also Heritage, *Garfinkel,* 78–84. Terrance Kelly has argued for a more differentiated approach to trust that ranges over a spectrum including "thin," "institutional," and "thick" forms; see his "Rationality, Reflexivity, and Agency in the Critique of Everyday Life" (Ph.D. dissertation, Saint Louis University, 1998), chap. 4.

22. See Heritage, *Garfinkel,* chap. 4.

23. McCarthy, *Ideals,* 31–32.

24. Melvin Pollner, "Mundane Reasoning," *Philosophy of the Social Sciences* 4 (1974): 35–54; reprinted in *Ethnomethodological Sociology,* ed. Jeff Coulter (Brookfield, Vermont: Elgar, 1990), 138–157; citations refer to the reprinted version; here p. 153; see also Hoy and McCarthy, *Critical Theory,* 72. For scientists' use of error accounts, see

William Rehg

G. Nigel Gilbert and Michael Mulkay, *Opening Pandora's Box* (Cambridge: Cambridge University Press, 1984), chaps. 4–5.

25. Pollner, "Mundane Reasoning," 143, 150–151.

26. See Pollner, "Mundane Reasoning," 142, also 143: "competence as a mundane reasoner consists not only of the capacity to hear a puzzle on the occasion of a disjuncture, but to be able, as well, to formulate and recognize candidate correct solutions."

27. Hoy and McCarthy, *Critical Theory*, 39; *Ideals*, 33–34.

28. McCarthy, *Ideals*, 34.

29. Hoy and McCarthy, *Critical Theory*, 75.

30. Egon Bittner, "Must We Say What We Mean?" in *Communication and Social Interaction*, ed. P. F. Ostwald (New York: Grune and Stratton—Harcourt Brace, 1977), 83–97; for the example, see 87; see also Lynch, *Scientific Practice*, 17–22. For a discussion of Garfinkel's research, see Heritage, *Garfinkel*, 92–97, 144–157.

31. Hoy and McCarthy, *Critical Theory*, 66–67.

32. Hoy and McCarthy, *Critical Theory*, 68; the quoted term is taken from Sacks, Schegloff, and Jefferson, "A Simplest Systematics," 10.

33. Hoy and McCarthy, *Critical Theory*, 93 note 2.

34. Hoy and McCarthy, *Critical Theory*, 67.

35. Hoy and McCarthy, *Critical Theory*, 73; cf. Paul Feyerabend, *Against Method* (London: Verso, 1975; 1978), 23: "given any rule, however 'fundamental' or 'necessary' for science, there are always circumstances when it is advisable not only to ignore the rule, but to adopt its opposite."

36. Hoy and McCarthy, *Critical Theory*, 73.

37. Hoy and McCarthy, *Critical Theory*, 76.

38. For a recent treatment, see James Bohman, "Democracy as Inquiry, Inquiry as Democratic: Pragmatism, Social Science, and the Cognitive Division of Labor," *American Journal of Political Science* 43 (1999): 590–607.

39. See, for example, Laurens Laudan, "C. S. Peirce and the Trivialization of the Self-Corrective Thesis," in *Foundations of Scientific Method in the 19th Century*, ed. R. Giere and R. Westfall (Bloomington: Indiana University Press, 1973), 275–306.

40. Gilbert and Mulkay, *Opening Pandora's Box*.

41. Hoy and McCarthy, *Critical Theory*, 73–74.

42. Hoy and McCarthy, *Critical Theory*, 74.

43. Harold Garfinkel, "What Is Ethnomethodology?" *Studies in Ethnomethodology*, 1.

44. Garfinkel, "What Is Ethnomethodology?" *Studies in Ethnomethodology*, 3–4.

45. Jordan and Lynch, "Sociology of a Genetic Engineering Technique' (see note 7); also their "The Dissemination, Standardization and Routinization of a Molecular Biological Technique," *Social Studies of Science* 28 (1998): 773–800.

46. The following summarizes Eric Livingston, *Making Sense of Ethnomethodology* (London: Routledge, 1987), chaps. 14–18; and his "Cultures of Proving," *Social Studies of Science* 29 (1999): 867–888. Livingston has extended this kind of analysis to physics in "The Idiosyncratic Specificity of the Methods of Physical Experimentation," *Australian and New Zealand Journal of Sociology* 31, no. 3 (1995): 1–22.

47. Garfinkel, "What Is Ethnomethodology?" 7–9.

48. Livingston, *Making Sense*, 56.

49. See Garfinkel and Sacks, "On Formal Structures of Practical Actions," in *Theoretical Sociology*, ed. J. C. McKinney and E. A. Tiryakian (New York: Appleton-Century-Crofts/Meredith, 1970), 343–345, 362–366.

50. For Garfinkel's antitheoretical policy, see "What Is Ethnomethodology?" 32–34; for the critique of the sociology of science, see Lynch, *Scientific Practice*, chaps. 2–3, 5; for critiques of mainstream sociology, see Graham Button, ed., *Ethnomethodology and the Human Sciences* (Cambridge: Cambridge University Press, 1991), esp. Douglas Benson and John A. Hughes, "Method: Evidence and Inference—Evidence and Inference for Ethnomethodology," 109–136; cf. also Livingston, *Making Sense*, chaps. 8–9.

51. Lynch, *Scientific Practice*, chap. 5.

52. Lynch, *Scientific Practice*, 306, also 200–201; also 282, where Lynch distinguishes his view from that of nominalism.

53. See Michael Lynch, "Silence in Context: Ethnomethodology and Social Theory," *Human Studies* 22 (1999): 211–233, esp. 217–221.

54. Lynch, *Scientific Practice*, 15, 291 (emphasis removed).

55. Garfinkel and Sacks, "On Formal Structures," 345.

56. Michael Lynch, "Ethnomethodology without Indifference," *Human Studies* 20 (1997): 371–376, here pp. 371–372; see also his *Scientific Practice*, 141–147.

57. Lynch, "Ethnomethodology without Indifference," 375–376.

58. See Thomas Kuhn, *The Structure of Scientific Revolutions*, 3rd. ed. (Chicago: University of Chicago Press, 1996), 47–48.

59. For a discourse-analytic argument, see Gilbert and Mulkay, *Opening Pandora's Box*; for some anecdotal support, see Elizabeth S. Clemens, "Of Asteroids and Dinosaurs: The Role of the Press in Shaping Scientific Debate," in *The Mass Extinction Debates*, ed. W. Glen (Stanford: Stanford University Press, 1994), 438–440; for an actual example of this by participants in the impact-hypothesis debate, see Charles Officer and Jake

Page, *The Great Dinosaur Extinction Controversy* (Reading, Mass.: Helix Books/Addison-Wesley, 1996), "Afterword: Pathological Science," 178–187.

60. On laboratory shop talk, see Michael Lynch, *Art and Artifact in Laboratory Science* (London: Routledge, 1985); for translocal phenomena, see Jordan and Lynch, "Dissemination, Standardization and Routinization" (see note 45).

61. See, for example, Bruno Latour, *Science in Action* (Cambridge: Harvard University Press, 1987), which takes an "actor-network" approach; for a "social worlds" model stemming from symbolic interactionism, see Adele E. Clarke, "A Social Worlds Research Adventure: The Case of Reproductive Science," in *Theories of Science in Society*, ed. S. E. Cozzens and T. F. Gieryn (Bloomington: Indiana University Press, 1990), 15–42; Joan H. Fujimura draws on both the social worlds model and ethnomethodology in her *Crafting Science* (Cambridge: Harvard University Press, 1996). Jordan and Lynch seem to view these various ethnographies favorably, including Latour's: see their "Sociology of a Genetic Engineering Technique," 109–110, notes 9, 10, 16; "Dissemination," 795 note 3.

62. Besides Livingston's studies of mathematical proofs, see Harold Garfinkel, Michael Lynch, and Eric Livingston, "The Work of a Discovering Science Construed with Materials from the Optically Discovered Pulsar," *Philosophy of the Social Sciences* 11 (1981): 131–158, esp. 153–155; also Michael Lynch, "Extending Wittgenstein: The Pivotal Move from Epistemology to the Sociology of Science," in *Science as Practice and Culture*, ed. A. Pickering (Chicago: University of Chicago Press, 1992), 247–256.

63. See Peter Galison, *Image and Logic* (Chicago: University of Chicago Press, 1997), esp. chaps. 4–8, for a detailed account of these mutually interpenetrating contexts—even inside the laboratory—in particle physics.

64. See, for example, Jeffrey H. Goldstein, ed., *Reporting Science* (Hillsdale, N.J.: Erlbaum, 1986); Sheila Jasonoff, *Science at the Bar* (Cambridge: Harvard University Press, 1995), chap. 1.

65. A theorist's "vicarious" participation goes beyond virtual participation insofar as the former exists only when the theorist's formulations are actually picked up and used by actors. Argumentation theory involves virtual participation insofar as the theorist takes the attitude of a participant.

66. Cf. Heritage, *Garfinkel,* 198ff.

67. This latter metaphor I take from Lynch, *Scientific Practice,* 187: "Formulations have no independent jurisdiction over the activities they formulate, nor are the activities otherwise chaotic or senseless."

68. Lynch, "Ethnomethodology without Indifference," 375.

69. This possibility is also proposed by Lynch, "Silence in Context," 227–229.

70. Cf. Sandra Harding, *Is Science Multicultural?* (Bloomington: Indiana University Press, 1998).

71. Michael Lynch's study of the cross-examination of an expert witness in the O. J. Simpson trial provides an inadvertent use of this method on the part of the defense:

"The Discourse of Courtroom Science: An Ethnomethodological View," paper delivered at a Conference on Studies of Work, Technology, and Practice, Harvard University, Cambridge, Mass., May 5, 2000. Lynch also noted how courtroom experience in such trials led to a revision of the official scientific protocol for DNA sampling methods in forensic contexts.

72. Complications arise, for example, when laboratory techniques for testing DNA are used in forensic settings; see Jordan and Lynch, "Dissemination," 792–793. On the AIDS case, see Bohman, "Democracy as Inquiry," 599–603.

73. For a fuller justification in the context of moral-political disputes, see my "Intractable Conflicts and Moral Objectivity: A Dialogical, Problem-based Approach," *Inquiry* 42 (1999): 229–258.

6

Do Social Philosophers Need a Theory of Meaning? Social Theory and Semantics after the Pragmatic Turn

Barbara Fultner

The answer to the question in my title may appear obvious to critical theorists, and certainly to Habermasians. As Thomas McCarthy has argued, the normative ideals on which a postmetaphysical critical theory relies—truth, objectivity, and accountability—are to be understood as pragmatic presuppositions of communication.[1] By replacing the Kantian question of how experience is possible with the question of how mutual understanding among interlocutors and interacting agents is possible,[2] Jürgen Habermas has given critical theory its linguistic turn and placed the theory of meaning at the very heart of the theory of communicative action. This forges an obvious connection between the theory of communicative action and philosophy of language. For although a theory of *meaning* is not the same as a theory of *communication*, there could be no communication if there were no meaningful expressions: as Donald Davidson says, "language is an instrument of communication because of its semantic dimension."[3] In addition to giving the meaning of expressions in the language, it is the task of philosophy of language to explain how language works, and that means explaining how it contributes to successful communication. In what follows I shall not go into the details of Habermas's critique of analytic philosophy of language or of the alternative theory of meaning he has outlined in the form of a formal pragmatics. Rather, I want to reconsider the relationship between social theory and philosophy of language in light not only of Habermas's interventions in philosophy of language but also of other recent attempts to bridge the continental-analytic divide and to develop so-called social theories of meaning. I shall argue that there is a dialectical connection between social theory and philosophy of language and that they are in fact interdependent. This means that social philosophers need to pay heed to philosophers of language and vice versa, that they should take the mutual implications of their theories into account, and that collaboration between the two fields should be fostered. Finally, I shall argue that, while social philosophy ought to defend a social theory of meaning, it remains an open question to what extent the social theory is affected by the details of the semantic theory.

1 After the Linguistic Turn

One of the central issues that arises in connection with the relationship between philosophy of language and social philosophy concerns the direction of argument. How is it that the correctness or appropriateness or general merit of a given theory—be it semantic or social-political—is to be determined? Much of the literature in philosophy of language is devoted to determining the conditions of adequacy for a theory of meaning. It must assign a meaning or interpretation to every expression in a language; it must be learnable; it must be finitely statable and recursive, and so forth. Demanding as such conditions of adequacy may be, we can ask further whether broader implications should also be taken into account. Can we defend a given social theory on the basis of a given theory of meaning or vice versa? Should we accord primacy to one or the other or should (or can) they simply be assessed independently of one another? Is, say, philosophy of language somehow foundational, or can one start with a given social-political theory and then search out the epistemology, metaphysics, or philosophy of language that suits it best?

In the wake of the linguistic turn, analytic philosophy has asserted the primacy of philosophy of language over other domains of philosophy. According to Michael Dummett, for instance, the philosophy of language underlies metaphysics and epistemology.[4] But this primacy may of course also be extended to cover ethics, social-political philosophy, and aesthetics—that is, value theory in general. At the same time, however, in light of the work of Quine, Davidson, and others, philosophy of language, epistemology, philosophy of mind, and metaphysics have been widely recognized to be interdependent. (For the sake of brevity, I shall at times distinguish in what follows between meaning- and value-theories broadly construed.) As one thinker approvingly remarks, "philosophers increasingly are clear that questions about meaning are intimately bound up with questions of metaphysics, epistemology, mind, empirical science, and *even rationality and evaluation*" and this recognition has *deepened* rather than *flattened* philosophical inquiry.[5] A good model for how such interdependence might be exploited and taken in novel directions is the recent collection *Mind and Morals,* which represents a fledgling dialogue between moral philosophers and cognitive scientists.[6] As even the editors acknowledge, although the volume's introduction discusses the possible contributions of cognitive science to ethics and vice versa, the essays themselves tend to elaborate the former rather than the latter connection, indicating just how difficult it is to abandon the traditional thesis of the primacy of meaning theories. We shall see that there continues to be (at least implicit) resistance to including the evaluative component in this holistic perspective. Nonetheless, it is this kind of dialogue between disciplines, namely, philosophy of language and social theory, that the present paper advocates.

Analytic philosophers have not, as a rule, paid much attention to the connection between philosophy of language and political or social theory or, for that matter, politics. Philosophy of language and philosophy of mind have for the most part evolved independently of ethics and social-political thought. And analytic philosophers have not deemed it appropriate to evaluate a theory of meaning on the basis of its political merits or potential, let alone on the basis of the moral character of its proponent.[7] Whereas in the case of Nietzsche or Heidegger the connection between their philosophical position and their personal views and character arises immediately, Frege's anti-Semitism, though now occasionally mentioned, is generally taken to be irrelevant to his logic. By the same token, one is hard pressed to discern Davidson's or Dummett's political views from their writings— though there is arguably something ruggedly individualist about Davidson's insistence on the conceptual primacy of idiolects. On the other hand, some moral philosophers assert the autonomy of ethics by pointing out, for instance, that cognitive science is a *descriptive* discipline whereas ethics is *normative*.[8] Both of these approaches tend to compartmentalize the discipline of philosophy, thus supporting the twentieth-century rejection of grand theoretical narratives.

Whatever one's view of such narratives, rather than simply insisting on the autonomy (and consequent compartmentalization) of the various subdisciplines of philosophy, it is more common to assert the *primacy* of philosophy of language, which, following the linguistic turn, becomes the "successor discipline" to epistemology and metaphysics. Accordingly, ethical theories are derived from epistemologies, so that in order to determine the validity of the former, we must establish the validity of the latter. The worst examples of this attitude are social Darwinism or sociobiology. But the same conception of the primacy of epistemology or philosophy of language and mind over any kind of value theory underlies debates about moral realism. It constitutes a vestigial kind of post-linguistic-turn foundationalism. It is present even in the efforts of someone such as Owen Flanagan to develop a "naturalized ethics." To be sure, Flanagan and others work on the assumption that an epistemology or philosophy of mind that cannot account for ethics would have to be rejected. That is, they are aiming for a theory with maximal explanatory power. Moreover, Flanagan is a pragmatist committed to the view that ethical reflection is enriched by "everything we know . . . : data from the human sciences, history, literature and the other arts, from playing with possible worlds in imagination, and from everyday commentary on everyday events."[9] Nonetheless, his moral pluralism, on the one hand, and his rejection of the idea of moral progress and convergence, on the other, in the end turn out to be based on his acceptance of the "postmodern *mental* architecture" of moral network theory—which is to say that the normative part of ethics naturalized is based on the descriptive part.[10]

In contrast, the reverse relation, arguing from value- to meaning-theories, is frowned upon. It is generally held to be a shortcoming if a philosopher's views on meaning and knowledge are seen to derive from her politics or morals—or, presumably, from the theories of society and morality that she endorses. Thus feminist epistemologists or philosophers of science often face the criticism that either their critique is based on moral-political grounds—in which case it could not be a valid critique of epistemology. Or, it is simply a critique of "bad" epistemology or scientific practice—in which case it is unclear what is "feminist" about it.[11]

There are good reasons to endorse the argument for the primacy of philosophy of language that emerges after the linguistic turn. Moral theories or aesthetic theories invariably do presuppose certain ontologies, epistemologies, and theories of meaning. Consider debates over moral realism (ethical cognitivism). Peter Railton, for example, in providing an elaborate taxonomy of realism, maintains that "a chief cause of the changing character of the realism dispute over time has been changes in philosophical approaches to language and meaning."[12] Perhaps no philosopher exemplifies and, indeed, has fostered, this development better than Hilary Putnam, who has applied the insights of his internal realism to questions of moral as well as epistemological realism.[13] Another example, this time from aesthetics, are interactionist theories of metaphor according to which the meaning of metaphors are multiple and a function not just of authorial intention, but of interpreter responses. Underlying this view of metaphor is presumably some broader theory of meaning (lest of course we take the theory of metaphor to *provide us with* such a theory).[14] These presuppositions and connections are sure to be stronger still for a social theory that conceives societies as *meaningfully structured* systems. They suggest that semantics is somehow foundational for and independent of moral and aesthetic theory, that you have to "fix" it (or your epistemology or metaphysics) before you can fix your moral theory. This is the case if we allow for a plurality of realisms (i.e., realism about a given subject matter or within a given discourse rather than Realism *tout court*).

However, this primacy and autonomy does not necessarily follow from the linguistic turn. At least two arguments from within the philosophy of language challenge both the primacy and the autonomy of semantics. The first stems from the increasing prevalence of pragmatist semantics; the second from the irresolvability of certain debates within philosophy of language.

(i) First, the growing proliferation of pragmatist theories of meaning marks an important shift in philosophy of language (as well as in epistemology and metaphysics). Following Quine and Wittgenstein, philosophers like Donald Davidson, Hilary Putnam, Tyler Burge, and John McDowell have embraced the idea that language is a social practice, that meanings cannot be picked out individualistically, and that mental states are a function of an individual's natural and social environments. This has brought philosophy of language and mind, as well as epistemology, to a significant crossroads with social philosophy. For this position calls not only for a (social) account of propositional content, or reference, or intentionality; it calls for an account of social practices, for a *social theory*. In other words, this kind of philosophy of language directly refers to and demands social theory. Purported pragmatist philosophers of language have not always (or even often) acknowledged this need. Rather, the appeal to social practice has functioned as a kind of bedrock. That is, practice is, as it were, a primitive or basic term for the theory of meaning. Davidson, for example, influenced by the later Wittgenstein, opts for drawing the limits of theory at this point. His position is that semantics is limited to giving a truth-conditional theory of meaning for a language. Yet how we use such a theory (which is after all a theoretical reconstruction of our interpretive competence) can at most be explained by appeal to general maxims and methodological generalities[15]; it cannot be otherwise theoretically captured. This means, in effect, that there can be no theory of the pragmatics of language. Within the Davidsonian framework, the potential of the appeal to practices as the ground of meaning, as it were, remains theoretically untapped—and, indeed, untappable. In other words, when Davidson runs out of resources within the confines of his theory of interpretation, his spade is turned. But given that there *are* various accounts of social practices on offer in social theory, this is an ad hoc stopping point.

(ii) Not every philosopher of language is a pragmatist whose account of meaning is based on an account of social practice. Yet pragmatism can also appear at a different level of debate. There are certain disputes within philosophy of language that appear to be irresolvable, and this irresolvability suggests that one's stance in such debates is a function of external factors. It is not that further arguments don't continue to be produced by different camps. But such arguments constitute a further elaboration of the system endorsed by the camp; they don't seem to convince anyone from the other camp. Examples include the disputes over whether theories of meaning ought to be individualist or social, atomistic or holistic.[16] As philosophers take certain commitments to be basic, they struggle to develop a consistent theory of meaning that can explain all the relevant phenomena on their basis. Jerry Fodor, for instance, freely acknowledges that his biggest challenge is to demonstrate that his three fundamental commitments (a) to nomological and intentional explanation in psychology, (b) to a naturalistic and atomistic account of intentional content, and (c) to computational theory of mind can be made to cohere in a unified theory.[17] And he has been known to bite all sorts of bullets (particularly that of narrow content) in order to persevere in his theoretical approach. The apparent irresolvability of these debates and the intransigence of at least some participants suggest that ultimately one does not choose one view over another because it is *better*—or even more rational. At best, it better accounts for some aspect or other of semantics or epistemology. Or it does better justice to some of our intuitions—whether language is spoken in the first instance by individuals or by communities, whether meanings can be determined atomistically word by word or holistically in relation to other words, and so on. The trouble is that *any* theory of meaning seems to have problems accounting for some aspects (and runs the danger of resorting to ad hoc moves). The toughest problem for someone like Fred Dretske seeking to give a naturalized account of semantic content lies in accounting for linguistic normativity. If intentional content is causally determined, how can our mental or linguistic representations ever *misrepresent?* On the other hand, a thoroughly social inferentialist semanticist like Robert Brandom faces the challenge of explaining the representational function of language. If intentional content is determined by proprieties of inference that are socially adjudicated, in what sense are our representations *objective?* It seems that reliance on intuitions (or treating certain of our intuitions as more basic than others) is as difficult to justify as it is to avoid. Once we enter into a debate over which of these intuitions get at what are ultimately the basic features of language, it seems to become difficult to distinguish an author's intuitions from his or her theoretical commitments.[18]

Barbara Fultner

Nor are analytic theories of meaning alone in this predicament. On the continental side, we might contrast Derridian and Habermasian approaches. The former emphasizes differences of meaning from one occasion of use to another: since meaning is determined by context and every new utterance occurs in its own particular context, there can be no exact repetition of the same meaning. The latter, by contrast, emphasizes sameness: unless interlocutors can mean the same thing by their words, communication is impossible. Here, neither position denies that communication actually occurs nor that actual communication is rarely if ever perfect. In fact, both positions appeal to important features of language use that should arguably be regarded as *equally* important. The difficulty lies in showing how these aspects can be fit into a unified semantic theory without according primacy to one or the other.

The argument thus far allows for a number of possible, though not necessarily compatible, conclusions. First, one might conclude that there simply is no unified theory of language to be had (Wittgenstein). We might further conclude that such debates are, after all, just so many edifying conversations (Rorty). Perhaps the best we can do is to be "metapragmatists" picking and choosing whatever theory can best deal with the problems currently at hand. Yet this smorgasbord approach becomes less attractive in light of the mutual incompatibility of different semantic theories and the interconnectedness of problems in semantics. The problem of reference, for instance, is not independent of the problem of truth or of the question of semantic holism. In the end, therefore, the theoretician must show how, say, a causal theory of reference fits with a holistic (or atomistic) theory of meaning. Alternatively, one might conclude that linguistic and social theories ought to be viewed as interdependent. This would mean that in choosing between fundamentally different and competing theoretical frameworks within semantics, we may—indeed must—appeal to social theory and vice versa. As Railton puts it, "Owing to the multilayered, interconnected character of philosophical issues it is impossible to assess the merits of competing philosophical positions without looking at the whole view in which they are embedded."[19] This is reminiscent of Rudolf Carnap's distinction between framework-internal and framework-external choices, the former of which are governed by the logic of the given framework, whereas the latter are at best subject to pragmatic considerations.[20] However, emphasis on the *mutual interdependence* of semantics and social theory weakens the sharp distinction between what is internal and what is external to a theory.

We have seen that assuming the primacy of a theory of meaning over value theories and vice versa is problematic. What happens if meaning- and value-theories are interpreted as mutually interdependent or implicatory? Rather than taking philosophy of language to be autonomous in relation to moral theory or social-political philosophy, I'm suggesting we view them as complementary. We might say that the value theory *commits* us to a given meaning theory, which then of course remains to be worked out and justified in its own right. However, part of its justification must involve ensuring that it does not violate central tenets of our social or moral theory. Or if it does, we must acknowledge and assess this implication in turn. This latter step has been almost entirely absent from broadly analytic approaches to meaning and mind. (As always, there are exceptions to the rule. Louise Antony, for instance, embraces Quine's naturalized epistemology, at least in part, because it is compatible with and conducive to feminist sociopolitical goals.[21])

In contrast, continental approaches seem far more amenable to the kind of complementary relationship between meaning- and value-theories. From Nietzsche to Foucault and Derrida, we find strong connections between language and the workings of power and thus a thematization of the relationship between language and practice. Although Habermas regards language in the first instance not as a medium of power, but of freedom, he does appeal to the theory of meaning in order to undergird a particular ethics and social theory. Even though he maintains that this theory of meaning *grounds* the social theory, which is suggestive of postlinguistic-turn foundationalism, the primary goal is to shore up the social theory. As I will show in the next section, his preferred theory of meaning—and his critique of Robert Brandom's inferentialist semantics—is based on his vision of social theory and practice.

2 Implications and Limitations

Thus far I have argued that social theory and semantics are interdependent. I now want to pursue the idea that social theories and social theories of meaning are less intimately connected than one may think. Even if one acknowledges the complementarity or interdependence of semantics and social theory, the concept of meaning operative in one cannot be seamlessly transposed into the other. The fine-grained distinctions, for example, between different kinds of meaning that emerge in the philosophy of language ("sense," "reference," intension," "extension") have no immediately obvious application in social theory. Conversely, nonpropositional or noncognitive kinds of meaning that may play important roles in social theory have not as a rule figured prominently in philosophy of language.

With the increasing prevalence of pragmatist approaches to meaning, the question of the relationship between social theory and a theory of meaning is gaining renewed urgency. If this relationship is one of complementarity, then philosophers of language as well as social theorists surely have the responsibility to weigh the implications of semantics for social theory and vice versa. I want to mention at least briefly two points in this connection. The first concerns the grounding of social theory on formal pragmatics. If, as we have seen, a pragmatist theory of meaning *presupposes* a social theory much as a given aesthetic theory presupposes a particular semantics, this arguably has an effect on Habermas's project of grounding the theory of communicative action in a formal-pragmatic theory of meaning. For if the theory of meaning in turn rests on a theory of society (or of social practices), the status of such grounding becomes problematic. However, by taking a postmetaphysical stance that presents only "quasi-transcendental" arguments—arguments, in other words, that are at least in principle defeasible in the sense that they are open to be criticized at any time—Habermas can avoid serious difficulties. Indeed, he implicitly relies on the complementarity of social and semantic theory.

The second point concerns the kind(s) of meaning that social theory and semantics respectively deal with. I would like to use Brandom's inferentialist semantics, which I take to be the most promising pragmatic theory of meaning available today, to explore further the nagging suspicion that the kind of meaning Habermas (qua social theorist) is after and the kind that Brandom (qua philosopher of language) analyzes are not quite the same.

Brandom seeks to provide an account of intelligibility (understood as conceptual or propositional contentfulness). Habermas criticizes Brandom for providing a theory of meaning that has undesirable consequences for social and moral theory.[22] For it allegedly assimilates moral to empirical validity and objectifies relationships of interaction. Independently of whether this criticism is justified,[23] it is obviously driven by Habermas's understanding of and commitments within social and moral theory, specifically his commitment to an intersubjective conception of society, rather than an objectivist or subjectivist one. For Habermas, at least, both social theory and semantics must be consistent with the intersubjectivity of social interaction, paradigmatically in the form of action coordination and communication. To do justice to the performative attitude of agents in interaction, intersubjectivity must, so to speak, be conceived in terms of first-to-second person rather than third-person relationships. Interlocutors are not mutual observers but partners in dialogue. As James Bohman puts it, "The I who is an interpreter is a *you* as a participant in communication. . . . I do not simply adopt your point of view or even mine in offering an adequate interpretation. Instead I do something that is much more complicated and dialogical: when I offer an interpretation of your actions or practices, I adopt the point of view that you are an interpreter of me. This is a capacity or ability that can only be explicated as a form of practical knowledge from the second-person perspective."[24]

But what follows from this for the *form* of a theory of meaning? Habermas would argue that it means that a theory of meaning cannot take assertions to be basic on the grounds that this would privilege the objective, that is, the representational dimension of language (truth). Yet Brandom weakens the connection between assertions and representationalist objectivity by analyzing them in terms of deontic commitments and entitlements and only subsequently developing an account of representation on that basis.

Brandom's account presupposes that there are implicitly normative practices. Now it is hard to see how such practices are not always already intelligible or meaningful—in some sense—to their practitioners. However, this notion of "meaning" is not the one Brandom is after. He is interested in propositional contentfulness, in what specifically makes linguistic expressions meaningful. In fact, he is liable to maintain that we can only talk about meaning in this pragmatic sense (intelligibility$_1$) in a way that is derivative from the way we talk about meaning in the sense of propositional intelligibility (intelligibility$_2$). That is, unless we have intelligibility$_2$, intelligibility$_1$ is not conceptually accessible to us. Yet, paradoxically, unless we "have" intelligibility$_1$, we cannot have intelligibility$_2$.

Habermas does not distinguish clearly between these two kinds of intelligibility. Nor does he differentiate between sense and reference or intension and extension when drawing on the philosophy of language in defending a linguistic foundation of sociology; rather he speaks of meaning broadly conceived.[25] This is not in and of itself unreasonable or problematic within social theory. However, it does need to be acknowledged in the context of relating semantics and social theory since it is unclear how these differentiations of meaning that have emerged from analytic philosophy are to be mapped onto the broad notion of meaning or intelligibility$_1$. This mapping problem needs to be brought into relief and addressed if we are to fully appreciate the implications of contemporary semantics for social theory (and vice versa).

Within social theory, the concept of meaning tends—not surprisingly—to be used more loosely than in philosophy of language. David Bogen, for example, claims that social theorists and ethnomethodologists may argue that "the normative order of practical action is both the object and the medium for social scientific inquiries, and it is the ordinary concepts we use which, in the final analysis, provide us with what leverage we have on the problem of understanding meaning."[26] Yet note the slippage here from practical action to (everyday) concepts as the key to understanding meaning. While Bogen on the one hand claims practical action to be prior to linguistic form (and criticizes Habermas for privileging the latter), he on the other hand appeals to ordinary concepts. How are we to understand the notion of "concept" and "conceptual content" if not through linguistic analysis? (One sometimes encounters an objection to this line of argument from some pragmatists and Wittgensteinians. For they seem to argue both that *language* games are the paradigmatic clues to our understanding of social interaction as well as linguistic normativity *and* that nonlinguistic social games tell us just as much about meaning as linguistic ones. In other words, all social interactions, the argument goes, are language games. Yet this seems to deny any specificity at all, let alone any special status, to language.)

To say that it is unclear how semantic categories of meaning map onto social categories is not to say, of course, that it cannot be done or that there are not advantages to trying. For one, such a mapping—or an analysis of where and why it fails—would help to clarify the relationship between social theory and philosophy of language. Moreover, the notion of intension, for instance, introduced by Frege to resolve certain puzzles about reference, can be seen as capturing what might be called "subjective" meaning whereas extension can be seen as capturing "objective" meaning. A pragmatically conceived notion of intension and extension could be used to elucidate the relationship between idiosyncratic (subjective) and socially shared (objective) meanings and beliefs.[27] This in turn could be used to gain a better understanding of how interlocutors or social actors adjudicate the different ways they describe the world from their various interpretive perspectives.

There are *prima facie* reasons for defending a social theory of meaning for social theorists—provided, of course, that we accept a certain conception of social theory. For there is a parallel split within social theory parallel to the choice between holistic/social and atomistic/individualist theories of meaning. There are social theories that take a third-person perspective, such as systems theory, for example. Although meaning is admitted as a fundamental category of social-systems theory by, for example, Niklas Luhmann, it is presented as "a mode of reducing the complexity peculiar to social systems."[28] As such, this kind of social theory is likely to fit better with a more objectivist and individualist naturalized semantics. An example of such a theory might be Fred Dretske's naturalized account of representation and content, according to which communication is analyzed as flow of information.[29] It is unlikely that a nonsocial semantics of this sort would dovetail successfully with an intersubjective conception of social practices.

Nonsocial theories of meaning face difficulties liable to make them unsuitable partners for an intersubjectively conceived social theory. Some variants may appear at first glance to provide just as firm a basis for intersubjectivity, but on closer analysis, their commitment to methodological individualism resists integration with an intersubjectivist social theory. The kind of semantics proposed by Jerry Fodor, for example, is deeply committed to methodological individualism. To be sure, he holds that fundamental linguistic structures are *hardwired* and *universally distributed*. It is ultimately this hardwiring rather than engaging in social practices that allows us to mean the same thing by the same words. One might argue that this makes social relations none the less real; if anything, it makes them more solidly grounded, namely in biology. Why not simply agree that communicative, no less than linguistic, competence is hardwired?[30]

The kind of social theory that takes the linguistic turn is in the first place one that conceptualizes societies as *meaningfully structured* entities. Its insight is that social interactions are meaningful *to* the agents involved in them and guided by rules or normative expectations (conventions). It is prima facie highly implausible that social conventions are hardwired. Furthermore, nonsocial semantics invariably conceives the language learner as intrepid observer-investigator bent on hypothesis-formation. Yet the conception of language learners as hypothesis-forming and -testing observers that we find in Fodor or Chomsky is precisely the kind of model of the subject that intersubjectivist social theory rejects.

Nevertheless there remains a whiff of the tautological about the claim that social theory be paired with a social semantics. After all, from the perspective of philosophy of language, a social theory of meaning can be *defined* as a semantics that accords a fundamental role to social practices in the determination of meaning. What are the criteria that social theory provides for semantics? First, as I have sought to show above, semantics must take proper account of intersubjectivity. This means that it cannot be individualist or accord primacy to idiolects. But a social theory might also contribute other normative criteria in the form of sociopolitical values with which a semantics ought to accord. A theory of meaning could, for example, be evaluated by the extent to which it is consonant with fostering freedom, justice, and objectivity. Thus, one might argue, a semantics based on the social practice of giving and asking for reasons—and which thus builds in mutual criticizability from the outset—is preferable to a semantics that gives a purely causal account of content. Arguments along these lines have begun to emerge in feminist approaches to philosophy of language.[31] But beyond that, a social theory of meaning can take different forms, as the example of Habermas and Brandom illustrates. Perhaps social theorists simply need not worry about which form a theory of meaning should take (as long as it is social) inasmuch as they may not need as differentiated a theory of meaning as philosophers of language are seeking to provide. This would preserve a division of labor and a certain degree of autonomy of the two fields.

The difference between social theories of meaning and linguistic theories of society is that for the former, social practices are basic, whereas for the latter, meaning is taken to be a basic notion. This formulation shows that the relation between the two must be one of complementarity. Social theory and philosophy of language depend on one another. Working on their own, both social theorists and semanticists are bound to run out of resources. On the one hand, a social theory that conceives societies as meaningfully structured has a need to clarify the fundamental notion of *meaning*, and that is best done through philosophy of language. On the other hand, a semantics that does justice to intersubjectivity must appeal to some notion of social practice. By the same token, their complementarity is not straightforward. For what is understood by both meaning and practice is not always immediately transferable from one context to another. Philosophers of language do have a responsibility to consider the implications for social theory in developing their theories. Such implications should be included in the criteria of adequacy for theories of meaning. Conversely, social theorists should defend social theories of meaning. If one of the adequacy conditions for a theory of meaning is that it "work" with social theory, then an adequate theory of meaning must itself be social. However, it remains to be seen what form this theory ought to take. What is needed, therefore, is more collaborative work between these two disciplines in order to elucidate their interdependence.

Barbara Fultner

Notes

1. Thomas McCarthy, *Ideals and Illusions* (Cambridge: MIT Press, 1991), 4, 34, and passim.

2. Ibid., 130.

3. Donald Davidson, "The Method of Truth in Metaphysics," *Inquiries into Truth and Interpretation* (Oxford: Clarendon, 1984), 201.

4. See, for example, Michael Dummett, *The Logical Basis of Metaphysics* (Cambridge: Harvard University Press, 1991).

5. Peter Railton, "Moral Realism: Prospects and Problems," in *Moral Knowledge*, ed. W. Sinnott Armstrong and M. Timmons (Oxford: Oxford University Press, 1996), 50–51, italics mine. See also Geoffrey Sayre-McCord, *Essays on Moral Realism* (Ithaca: Cornell University Press, 1988).

6. Larry May, Marilyn Friedman, and Andy Clark, eds., *Mind and Morals* (Cambridge: MIT Press, 1996). It should also be pointed out that the contributions to this collection exemplify a range of conceptions of the relationship between philosophy of mind and moral theory.

7. In a sense, the logical positivists are a noteworthy exception, although their emphasis on the value-neutrality and objectivity of science as the route toward freedom and a better society led to objectivism in the human and social sciences on the one hand and, on the other hand, ironically contributed to widening the gap between science and moral theory.

8. See, for example, Virginia Held, "Whose Agenda? Ethics versus Cognitive Science," in *Mind and Morals*, 69–87. Held argues that "cognitive science has little to offer ethics, and that what it has should be subordinate to rather than determinative of the agenda of moral philosophy" (69).

9. Owen Flanagan, "Ethics Naturalized: Ethics as Human Ecology," in *Mind and Morals*, 19–43, here 35.

10. Ibid., 35, italics mine.

11. For examples of this kind of approach, see some of the essays in Sandra Harding, ed., *Feminism and Methodology* (Bloomington: Indiana University Press, 1987).

12. Railton, "Moral Realism," 50.

13. E.g., *Realism With a Human Face* (Cambridge: Harvard University Press, 1990).

14. Cf. Max Black, *Models and Metaphors* (Ithaca: Cornell University Press, 1962) and "More About Metaphor," in *Metaphor and Thought*, ed. Andrew Orony (Cambridge: Cambridge University Press, 1981). See also Mark Johnson and George Lakoff, *Metaphors We Live By* (Chicago: University of Chicago Press, 1980), and Eva Feder Kittay, *Metaphor: Its Cognitive Force and Linguistic Structure* (Oxford: Clarendon Press, 1987). Determining what that underlying theory of meaning ought to be is beyond

Do Social Philosophers Need a Theory of Meaning?

the scope of the present paper. The two most plausible candidates are some version of the description theory and some kind of inferential-role theory (cf. Kittay's defense of a relational theory of meaning). For a discussion of interactionist theories of metaphor, see Kirk Pillow, "Jupiter's Eagle and the Despot's Hand Mill: Two Views on Metaphor in Kant," forthcoming in *The Journal of Aesthetics and Art Criticism.*

15. "A Nice Derangement of Epitaphs," in *Truth and Interpretation,* ed. E. Lepore (Oxford: Blackwell, 1986), 433–446. We might say that this stance puts Davidson squarely in the postmodernist camp. For it amounts to a denial of the theoretical surveyability of rules and conventions of social life.

16. These are divisions operative even within the context of a shared framework of pragmatist approaches to meaning. Thus the mere designation of "pragmatist" does not yet determine a particular theory of meaning. The social/individualist debate is particularly well articulated by Davidson on the one hand and Dummett on the other. The issue here is whether a shared, communal language or an individual idiolect ought to be taken as theoretically primary. As I have argued elsewhere, this (rather than their disagreement over holism vs. molecularism) constitutes the watershed between them.

17. Cf. *The Elm and the Expert* (Cambridge: MIT Press, 1995), chap. 1. Fodor's willingness to reformulate his position in seemingly ever more implausible ways is laudable in that it serves the better articulation of thorny issues in the philosophy of mind. (Arguably this tells us a lot about what philosophy in general is or does; whether social philosophy can do more is another question.) However, it also calls into question the purported commitment on the part of philosophers to be convinced by the force of the better argument.

18. Arguably, these claims are already too theoretical to qualify as "ordinary" intuitions, certainly as phrased here. They seem to be somewhat akin to Wittgensteinian "hinge" propositions. More "basic" intuitions might be, e.g., that each word has its own meaning, that the purpose of language is communication or conveying thoughts, etc.

19. Railton, "Moral Realism," 51.

20. Cf. George Alexander, "On Washing the Fur without Wetting It: Quine, Carnap, and Analyticity," *Mind* 109 (2000): 1–24.

21. Louise Antony, "Quine as Feminist: The Radical Import of Naturalized Epistemology," in *A Mind of One's Own,* ed. L. Antony and C. Witt (Boulder: Westview Press, 1993), 185–225.

22. Jürgen Habermas, "Von Kant Zu Hegel: Zu Robert Brandoms Sprachpragmatik," in *Wahrheit und Rechtfertigung* (Frankfurt: Suhrkamp, 1999), 138–185.

23. I do not believe that it is. Brandom's account is not objectivist in the way that Habermas claims since the linguistic mechanisms he invokes (substitution, inference, and anaphora) rely on and foster intersubjective social relations among interlocutors. See Robert Brandom, *Making It Explicit* (Cambridge: Harvard University Press, 1994).

24. See James Bohman, "The Importance of the Second Person: Interpretation, Practical Knowledge, and Normative Attitudes," in *Empathy and Agency: The Problem of Un-*

derstanding in the Human Sciences, ed. H. H. Kögler and K. R. Stueber (Boulder: Westview, 2000), here 223–224.

25. "On the Linguistic Foundations of Sociology," *On the Pragmatics of Social Interaction*, trans. B. Fultner (Cambridge: MIT Press, 2000). For Habermas's most recent reflections on the problem of reference, see his *Wahrheit und Rechtfertigung* as well as his contribution to this volume.

26. David Bogen, *Order without Rules: Critical Theory and the Logic of Conversation* (Albany: SUNY Press, 1999), 7.

27. Cf. Brandom, *Making It Explicit*, 483ff.

28. McCarthy, *Ideals and Illusions*, 152–180, here 156.

29. Fred Dretske, *Explaining Behavior* (Cambridge: MIT Press, 1988).

30. Cf. Gerd Gigerenzer, "The Modularity of Social Intelligence," in *Machiavellian Intelligence II*, ed. A. Whiten and R. W. Byrne (Cambridge: Cambridge University Press, 1997), 264–288.

31. See, for instance, Alessandra Tanesini, "Whose Language?" in *Women, Knowledge, and Reality*, ed. A. Garry and M. Pearsall (New York: Routledge, 1996), 253–269.

7

Problems in the Theory of Ideology

Joseph Heath

One of the most persistent legacies of Karl Marx and the Young Hegelians has been the centrality of the concept of "ideology" in contemporary social criticism. The concept was introduced in order to account for a very specific phenomenon, namely, the fact that individuals often participate in maintaining and reproducing institutions under which they are oppressed or exploited. In the extreme, these individuals may even actively resist the efforts of anyone who tries to change these institutions on their behalf. Clearly, some explanation needs to be given of how individuals could systematically fail to see where their interests lie, or how they might fail to pursue these interests once they have been laid bare. This need is often felt with some urgency, since failure to provide such an explanation usually counts as prima facie evidence against the claim that these individuals are genuinely oppressed or exploited in the first place.

There is of course no question that this kind of phenomenon requires a special explanation. Unfortunately, Feuerbach, Marx, and their followers took the fateful turn of attempting to explain these "ideological" effects as a consequence of *irrationality* on the part of those under their sway.[1] While there are no doubt instances where practices are reproduced without good reason, the ascription of irrationality to agents is an explanatory device whose use carries with it considerable costs, both theoretical and practical. As a result, it should be used only in the last resort. In this paper, I will argue that many of the phenomena traditionally grouped together under the category of "ideological effects" can be explained without relinquishing the rationality postulate. I will try to show that agents *can* rationally engage in patterns of action that are ultimately contrary to their interests, and that they can rationally resist changing these patterns even when the deleterious or self-defeating character of their actions has been pointed out to them.

I think that an approach such as this, one that is sparing in its ascription of irrationality and error, has two principal advantages. First, it allows one to engage in social criticism while minimizing the tendency to insult the intelligence of the people one is trying to help—whether it be the working class, women, or the subaltern. This may reduce the tendency exhibited by some members of these groups to reassert their autonomy precisely by rejecting the critical theory that impugns their rationality. The second major advantage is also practical. The vast majority of oppressive practices are not reproduced because people have false or irrational beliefs. As a result, simply persuading people to change their beliefs will have no tendency to change the underlying mechanism through which the practices are reproduced. Even worse, the institutions in question may acquire the appearance of being impervious to social criticism, simply because people continually criticize them, and yet nothing changes. Correctly diagnosing the mechanism through which these institutions are reproduced has the potential to suggest new strategies for social change.

1 Ideology and Irrationality

One might begin by asking what the big problem is with the assumption that people are behaving irrationally. After all, everyone knows that people make mistakes, and do things without thinking. If people are acting in a way that is making their own lives miserable, it seems likely that they are making some kind of mistake. When the peasant rallies to the defense of his feudal lord, or the hostage begins to promote the goals of her kidnappers, we are likely to think that these people are behaving in a muddle-headed way. We may even come up with a name for what has muddled them up, calling it "Christianity," or "Helsinki syndrome." When they persist in this behavior, even after having been told that they are suffering from one of these ailments, we might start to think that the problem is even deeper, and that something has impaired their ability to assess the information they have been given. We begin to think that they are not just mistaken, but in the grip of some deeper form of irrationality. This diagnosis seems fairly intuitive—so what is the big problem?

The problem is the one raised by Donald Davidson in his famous critique of "conceptual schemes."[2] Davidson's argument is roughly as follows: there is no fact of the matter about what people mean by what they say. The meaning of their utterances is determined by the best interpretation that hearers confer upon them. However, the meaning that I ascribe to a person's utterances depends in a crucial way upon the set of beliefs that I take that person to hold true. For instance, when people talk about meeting on "Thursday," I can only figure out which day they are referring to by assuming that they share with me the belief that today is Tuesday. If I thought they believed that today was Monday, I would start to think that they meant Wednesday when they said "Thursday." But since we can only find out what peoples' beliefs are by asking them, and since they can only express their beliefs by putting them in the form of sentences that in turn require interpretation, any particular interpretation that we might confer upon a person's utterances is massively underdetermined by the evidence available to us. There are an infinite number of ways to interpret anyone's speech, each supported by the ascription of a different set of beliefs.

But then how do we ever understand one another? Davidson argues that all interpretations are constrained by a principle of charity. The best interpretation is the one that ascribes the most reasonable set of beliefs to that person, which is to say, the one that maximizes the number of true beliefs the person is thought to hold. From the standpoint of the hearer, this means that the best interpretation is the one that is consistent with the highest level of agreement between the speaker and the hearer. This requirement of charity is not a methodological assumption, it is a constitutive principle. To interpret someone is to interpret that person charitably—if you are not interpreting them charitably, then what you are doing simply does not count as interpretation.

Davidson's argument has the effect of eliminating a certain Cartesian form of skepticism. Imagine a person transported from the real world, in which she has true beliefs about the objects around her, into a dream world, in which she is fooled into retaining the same beliefs about her environment, despite the fact that the corporeal objects have all disappeared. Her beliefs, which were once predominantly true, are now predominantly false. But how could she ever know? This is the basic structure of the Cartesian thought-experiment. Davidson's argument exposes a crucial presupposition. It is simply assumed that the person's beliefs are *the same* in both the real world and the dream world, and in particular, that they have the same content. However, since beliefs are propositional attitudes, that is, interpreted sentences of a natural language, this amounts to the assumption that the meaning of linguistic expressions is determined by something that remains invariant in the transition from the real world to the dream world. But according to Davidson, the meaning of expressions is determined by the practices of interpretation of a linguistic community. As a result, the meaning of the person's beliefs would change in the transition from the real world to the dream world, in such a way that they remained predominantly true. Why is this? Interpretation governed by the principle of charity requires as much, for it requires a practice of interpretation that treats the speaker as having predominantly true beliefs. If a particular interpretation made someone come out as having too many false beliefs, all this would do is supply evidence against that interpretation.

To take a real-life example of this principle in action, consider the following episode from the history of ethnography. Lucien Lévy-Bruhl infamously suggested that he had discovered the existence of "prelogical" cultures.[3] He found that his subjects persistently made contradictory statements, incoherent observations, and generally believed ridiculous things. Later generations of ethnographers, of course, returned to these societies somewhat skeptical about this claim, and quickly discovered other ways of interpreting the kind of utterances that had stumped Lévy-Bruhl, interpretations that made the "natives" come out sounding a lot more reasonable. For example, by distinguishing between expressions that were meant literally and those that were meant metaphorically or figuratively, a substantial portion of the "contradictions" Lévy-Bruhl uncovered could be dismissed. The Davidsonian point is this: these later interpretations were better than Lévy-Bruhl's, not because they came closer to what the people "really" meant, but because they were more restrained in their ascription of error. They were right precisely *because* they made the natives sound reasonable. What other evidence could there be for the correctness of an interpretation? There is no "third thing" against which the two interpretations can be compared—only more interpretations.

The more general problem is this: suspending the assumption that people are by-and-large reasonable, and that their beliefs are predominantly true, removes the only constraint that prevents one from interpreting their utterances as meaning anything at all. The problem then is not that one can no longer construct a plausible explanation of their behavior, but that one can construct too many plausible explanations, and it is hard to rule any of them out. This means that the critical theorist can only go so far in ascribing irrationality and error to people. Once she crosses a certain threshold, this ascription of error stops being an exposé of their mistakes, and starts to count as evidence against the proposed interpretation of their behavior. It starts to suggest that, rather than having uncovered a massive, all-encompassing ideology, she has simply failed to understand what it is that people are doing. The interpretation that appeals less heavily to ideology then wins, for that very reason—it appeals less heavily to ideology.

This is a classic problem in the history of Frankfurt School critical theory. The "grandfathers" of critical theory, Marx and Freud, both developed theories that diagnosed very widespread error in popular belief.[4] In so doing, they ran the risk of undermining themselves. Attributing massive error to people significantly expands the range of motives and beliefs that *can* be ascribed to them. This makes it very hard to show that any one interpretation is better than another. For this reason, Marx and Freud both had to bring in some kind of an "external" theory—historical materialism, psychoanalysis—that could be used to assess the merits of their interpretations. The problem is that this standard then needed to be grounded in something "above" the fray of competing interpretations and theories. It had to be more than just the best interpretation of some data set, since it purported to provide the criterion of interpretive adequacy.

Marx and Freud tried to handle this problem by claiming that their metainterpretive theories were "scientific," and thus presumably justified in a foundational manner. Unfortunately, there was no particular merit in either claim; both merely traded on the prestige associated with "scientific" inquiry. As a result, critics were quick to turn the critical theories of Marx and Freud against the critics. Karl Mannheim argued that if classical economics was merely the ideology of the bourgeoisie, then historical materialism was nothing more than the ideology of the proletariat, and therefore no more true.[5] Similarly, psychoanalysts were quick to suggest that Freud's instinct theory, which was to serve as a guide for the construction of interpretations, was itself nothing but a manifestation of his own unconscious desires.[6] What these criticisms have in common is that they deny any privileged status to the metainterpretive theories, thereby drawing them down to an interpretive level. But once this is done, then the Davidsonian problematic begins to loom large—it becomes very unclear what is supposed to make one critical theory more plausible than the next.

Much of the history of critical theory in the twentieth century can be seen as an attempt to work around this problem. However, one of the things that is seldom questioned in this body of work is the very basic assumption that when people act in a way that is contrary to their interests, they must somehow be acting irrationally. I would like to suggest that this is often not the case. While people do sometimes makes mistakes and get confused, this is more the exception than the norm—especially when it comes to their core economic interests. I will try to show that individuals often get outcomes they don't want, not because they have chosen wrongly, but because their actions combine with those of others in undesirable ways. Thus greater attention to the structure of social interaction reduces the need for a theory of ideology. In the next three sections, I present three different ways in which agents can rationally choose to perform actions that are, in some sense, contrary to their interests.

2 Collective Action Problems

The most common error that critical theorists have made, in my view, is to mistake the outcome of a collective action problem for an effect of ideology. Collective action problems arise in situations where agents can best pursue their own goals and projects only by imposing some kind of a cost upon others. The prisoner's dilemma is the classic example: each suspect can reduce his own expected jail time by turning in his partner. Doing so, however, increases the amount of jail time that his partner must serve. As a result, both suspects turn each other in, and so both serve more jail time than either would have had they remained silent.

Many interactions involving large numbers of people have precisely the same structure. For example, telephone companies did not used to bill their customers for individual calls to directory assistance. Instead, customers paid for the directory assistance service as part of their basic monthly package. The problem with this arrangement is that it generates overuse of the service, since the cost of serving any individual caller is paid by *all* of the firm's customers. So individuals who were too lazy to look up a number could get someone else to do it for them, while effectively displacing the cost of this action onto others. But when everyone does this to each other, everyone winds up using more directory service, and paying more for it, than anyone actually wants to. As a result, when phone companies switched to charging individuals directly for calls to directory assistance, the volume of calls dropped dramatically. (In a trial run in Cincinnati, imposition of a $0.20 per call charge reduced the average number of directory assistance calls from 80,000 to 20,000 per month. As a result, average residential telephone rates dropped by $0.65 per month.[7])

In the case of directory assistance, people get into a collective action problem in part because the interaction is completely anonymous. The same dynamic, however, can show up in face-to-face interactions. For example, if a large group of people all know that a restaurant bill is going to be divided evenly among them, regardless of what they order, individuals will often order a more expensive meal than they would if they were eating alone. But if everyone does this, then everyone winds up spending more than they want to. If you are eating out in a party of six, then the $12 appetizer that you order only costs you $2 (and you are going to pay for part of your neighbor's appetizer, regardless of whether you order one for yourself, so you might as well indulge). For the same reason, individuals in large groups tend to shortchange the house staff on the tip. Everybody undertips on their portion of the bill, because instead of making you look *very* cheap, it just makes everyone in your party look a little cheap. Of course, when everyone does it, it just makes everyone look *very* cheap. (This is a common outcome, and is in fact the reason why most restaurants impose a mandatory minimum gratuity on large parties.)

The most significant thing about these collective action problems, from the standpoint of critical theory, is that agents often have a hard time getting out of them, even if they realize that they are engaging in collectively self-defeating behavior. The reason is that the mere recognition that the outcome is suboptimal does not change the incentives that each individual has to act in a way that contributes to it. Even if I realize that I shouldn't overuse directory assistance, it doesn't mean that my phone bill will get any lower if I stop. It is only if *everyone* stops that I will begin to see a difference. But I have no control over what everyone else does (and furthermore, if everyone else stops overusing the service, and I continue to do so, then I am even better off). Not only that, but even individuals who are not actively seeking to displace costs onto others may have to do so just to avoid being exploited by those who are. When I sit down with my friends in a restaurant, and they start out by ordering a round of expensive drinks, then I might as well have one too. That way instead of just paying for their drinks, at least I get to have one too.

The point is that collective action problems can be extremely hard to shake. (That's why they're called collective action problems—in order to change the interaction pattern, you need to get everyone to stop doing what they have been doing.) As a result, one good clue that people are stuck in one of these equilibria is that everyone knows what the problem is, but nothing ever changes. For example, it has been common these past years to hear complaints about the way a "media circus" develops around certain events or stories, such as the

Lewinsky-Clinton scandal, or the O.J. Simpson trial. One of the most commonly criticized characteristics of this pattern is the way that coverage achieves a "saturation" level—the clearest instance being when every major network is showing exactly the same thing. This is clearly a suboptimal outcome—if one channel is providing twenty-four-hour live coverage of a particular story, then there is no point in having the others do the same. It would be better if they showed something else, so that viewers not interested in that story would have something to watch. The same thing applies when every news program covers exactly the same five or six stories in their evening broadcast, to the neglect of other newsworthy subjects.

In any case, what is interesting about this criticism is that it is not just circulated in the broader public sphere. When the journalists who are actually providing the "saturation" coverage are asked for their views, they also often say that the situation is ridiculous, that there are interesting stories being ignored, and so forth. In other words, the people who are covering the news stories often think that they should be covering something else. Thus the problem is not that the members of "the media" have mistaken priorities, or a poor understanding of what should be on television. They can see perfectly well what is going on. The problem is that they are stuck in a suboptimal equilibrium. Stations compete with one another for viewers. Imagine a two-channel universe in which a big news story breaks. Suppose that 70 percent of television viewers will be interested in that story. If a station knows that its rival down the street will be covering it, then it has a choice of covering something else, and attracting 30 percent of the viewers, or providing exactly the same coverage, and attracting 35 percent of viewers. Both stations reason the same way, and so both provide exactly the same coverage. The result is simply a waste of one broadcast frequency.

As a result, if everyone knows what the problem is, but nothing ever changes, there is good reason to suspect the existence of a collective action problem. Similarly, if people know that a certain social change would be *in their interest* (broadly construed), this does not mean that they will have an incentive to do anything about it. I may know that it is in *our* interest, as telephone rate-payers, to use directory assistance in moderation, but that does not make it in *my* interest to do so. In the same way, journalists may recognize that their entire profession loses credibility when they pursue sensational or lurid stories—and so it is not in *their* interest—but it may still be in the interest of each individual reporter, each individual news organization, to do so (since it is possible to increase your *share* of viewers even when the total *number* drops—exactly the same logic underlies "negative" campaign ads).

From the outside, then, it may look as if people are simply confused about where their interests lie, that they are in the grip of some ideology. But upon closer examination, they turn out to be perfectly rational. They may even join the critical theorist in lamenting the sad consequences of their own actions.

This analysis invites us to look back on some of the classic cases of ideology to see if something similar might not be going on there as well. Take the working class, for instance. Once it was decided that the workers would be better off under communism than under capitalism, many theorists simply assumed that workers would go out and overthrow the system. The fact that they failed to show up at the barricades was felt to require some explanation. Ideology was the most popular candidate. So Marx suggested that they were the victims of commodity fetishism—they mistook the social relations between individuals for objective relations between things, and so became convinced that the existing economic order was immutable. However, after half a century of Marxist critique, the working class still failed to make a revolution. Theorists began to suspect that a deeper, more insidious form of ideology was at work. The most popular diagnosis was consumerism—workers had become seduced by the materialistic values of late capitalism, and so failed to support the revolution because of a mistaken belief that they enjoyed living in suburban houses, using labor-saving appliances, eating TV dinners, and so forth.

These social critics simply failed to see the more obvious explanation. Revolutions are risky business. Setting up picket lines, not to mention barricades, is tiresome, difficult, often cold, and sometimes dangerous. Even if it were in the interests of the working class to bring about a socialist revolution, this does not make it in the interest of each individual worker to help out. There is no point going to the barricades unless thousands of your comrades intend to join you, but if thousands of your comrades are going anyhow, no one will miss you if you stay home.[8] Revolutionary fervor can generate the solidarity needed to overcome this collective action problem in some instances. But in general there is no reason to think that workers will show any more solidarity with one another than phone company customers. And broad segments of the working class have consistently shown themselves willing to free-ride off each others' collective achievements—this is why unions usually seek legally enforced "closed-shop" arrangements.[9]

Now consider a more controversial example. We often hear the complaint that cosmetics companies, the diet industry, plastic surgeons, and so forth, exploit women. In the mid-nineties, women in the United States spent around $20 billion a year on cosmetics, a sum that could have been used to finance 400,000 day care centers, or 33,000 battered women's shelters, or 50 women's universities, and so on.[10] This is clearly a suboptimal outcome. Furthermore, the fact that men (who earn more on average) spend only a fraction of this amount maintaining their appearance, and do not suffer much anxiety over their physical condition, adds insult to injury. The difference is also widely felt to perpetuate a set of gender roles that are disadvantageous to women: it encourages the identification of male status with money, female status with beauty; it perpetuates the idea of the female sexual role as passive, and so on. Thus feminists have for a long time argued that women need to free themselves from the dependence upon beauty, and the beauty industry.

But what has become most striking about this critique is that even though the vast majority of women accept it, it has little bearing on their personal conduct. Plenty of schoolgirls can explain to you how the cosmetics industry exploits women, but this doesn't stop them from wanting to wear lipstick. Once they graduate from university, many can tell you all about the double standards of our culture, the evils of distorted body image and the objectifying male gaze, while still counting calories and drinking skinny lattes. (Companies like Kellogg's have even used the feminist critique to sell low-fat breakfast cereal to women, under the slogan "look good on your own terms." Their goal was to allow sophisticated female consumers to purchase diet products without having to worry that others would think that they were merely victims of the diet industry. It allowed them to be ironic victims.)

These observations have led many feminist theorists to suggest that there must be an even more insidious form of ideology at work. If women understand the structure of their oppression, and they can see how the cosmetics and fashion industry actively exploit them, then they must be out of their minds to drop a hundred dollars on the latest moisturizer. Naomi Wolf basically suggests as much, when she describes how, "to reach the cosmetics counter, [a woman] must pass a deliberately disorienting prism of mirrors, lights and scents that submit her to the 'sensory overload' used by hypnotists and cults to encourage suggestibility."[11] She claims that women experience an "unconscious hallucination," that female consciousness has been "colonized," that women have been "stunned and disoriented" by changing gender roles, and so forth.[12] In short, they are not acting rationally. Why are they acting so dumb? The answer is ideology: "Women are 'so dumb' because the establishment and its watchdogs share the cosmetics industry's determination that women are and must remain 'so dumb.'"[13]

However, the very fact that everyone has heard this critique a hundred times and yet nothing ever changes, suggests that what we are dealing with is a collective action problem, not a problem of ideology. This is often overlooked in the case of beauty, because the literature has a tendency to focus on the role of ideals, or archetypes, in setting the standards of beauty. As a result, it distracts from the fact that beauty has an inherently competitive structure. Although standards of beauty vary from culture to culture, every culture has *some* kind of beauty hierarchy. People derive very significant material and social advantages from their position in this hierarchy. There is a sense in which beautiful people live in a world that is very different from the one that ugly people live in (consider how different the high school experiences can be, and how much beauty has to do with that). Apart from the fact that in a traditional patriarchal marriage market, a woman can gain significant material advantages from her beauty, there is also the fact that, at the level of face-to-face interaction, beautiful people simply get treated better than not-so-beautiful people.

People can improve both their quality of life and their material position by moving up a few levels in the beauty hierarchy. This is where the "archetype" model of beauty proves misleading. The advantages of beauty do not flow to those who are beautiful in some absolute sense, but to those who are more beautiful than those around them. This is what generates the competitive structure—moving up the beauty hierarchy means bumping someone else down.

None of this would be a problem if people were unable to amplify their natural endowments. Unfortunately, cosmetics and plastic surgery make it possible to reproduce synthetically some of the characteristics that are considered beautiful. As a result, people have the ability to buy their way up the hierarchy. This generates a classic collective action problem. Consider the example of face-lifts. Many women seek to make themselves look younger through artificial means. Unfortunately, how old a person looks is entirely relative. If a woman "looks fifty," it is only because, when compared to other fifty-year-old women, she looks about the same. This means that when a fifty-year-old woman gets a face-lift that makes her look forty, the action can be described in one of two ways. In a sense, she has made herself look younger. But in another sense, all she has done is make all the *other* fifty-year-old women in the population look a little older. These women may then be motivated to get a face-lift *just to retain position.* If this leads all fifty-year-old women to go out and get face-lifts, then their behavior has become perfectly self-defeating. They will be right back where they started—all looking like fifty-year-old women—except that now they will be paying a lot of money to look that way.

This is clearly the dynamic at work in a number of different areas (as any resident of California can attest). Many women would be glad to stop wearing makeup—as long as every other woman stopped too. What they are not willing to do is stop unilaterally, because the *private* cost would outweigh the *private* benefits. It's like standing up to get a better view at a ballgame. You may be able to see better, but only by blocking the person behind you. As a result, once one person stands up, soon everyone else does too. Naturally they would all be more comfortable sitting, and they would be able to see just as well. But sitting down while everyone else stays standing is hardly an option.

Why do women get into this kind of collective action problem and not men? Every so often the cosmetics industry publishes hopeful news bulletins on the "new" body-consciousness among men. Clearly they are hoping that men will begin to engage in similar beauty competition. After all, every arms race is enormously profitable for those who supply the weapons. To date, however, such competition has not materialized. In my view, this is the result of social norms that prevent men from doing so. Use of cosmetics is stigmatized among men as a sign of effeminacy. Much of the power of this norm stems from male homophobia. This is reflected in the fact that beauty competition among gay men is much more intense than it is among heterosexuals, and that critics in the gay community routinely lament the cult of body image that has developed, not to mention the amount of time they have to waste in the gym just to stay in the game.

3 Trust

Collective action problems are an example of how individuals can do things that are against the interests of a group to which they belong because it is in their individual interest to do so. A more subtle class of problems involves the role of trust in stabilizing interpersonal relations. In a collective action problem, people get into trouble because they are acting instrumentally. This is the predominant mode of interaction whenever there is a very large group, so that individual actions are only partially observable, or else in an interaction that is anonymous, so that individuals have no opportunity to communicate or coordinate their actions. On the other hand, in smaller groups or in face-to-face interactions, people's behavior tends to be more sharply constrained by social norms, and so they are less likely to engage in purely instrumental deliberation. In such contexts, intractable collective action problems are unlikely to arise. The fact that the interaction is normatively constrained, however, creates the opportunity for a new type of "perverse" behavior pattern to emerge—individuals may choose to respect and even enforce norms that are clearly unfair to them. Thus they may actively participate in reproducing institutions that oppress them. The question then is why they would be willing to do so.

This question has become increasingly pressing in recent years, particularly because some of the most spectacularly offensive practices, such as female genital mutilation, are often reproduced by the victims of that same practice. Various accounts have suggested that, even though the practice is expressly designed to secure patriarchal authority, it is often perpetrated by mothers against their daughters. Again, it is tempting to think that there is some kind of ideology at work here—that these women have been brainwashed by men, and so on. This imputation has in turn generated the predictable backlash, in which people point out that the women who do this are perfectly intelligent and reflexive; that they can run off a whole list of reasons why they consider the practice to be justifiable, and so on. Some liberals have even adopted an apologetic stance toward the practice, merely because they don't like the paternalistic tone that Western critics have taken toward it.[14]

Closer attention to the way that stable cooperative practices are maintained helps to shed light on how unjust institutions can be reproduced. By directly prescribing particular patterns of action, social norms permit agents to achieve outcomes that would not be the equilibria of purely strategic interactions. Thus agents stuck in a collective action problem might agree to a rule that constrains their future conduct. The suspects in the prisoner's dilemma story, for instance, might promise not to turn each other in, or they might become members of a criminal syndicate with a code of silence, and so forth. Norms of this type give each suspect a reason not to perform the action that generates the suboptimal equilibrium.[15] However, even if this reason is one that each of them finds motivating, this is still not enough to secure cooperation. They must also each believe that the other will find the reason motivating, and so will cooperate. One might say that their norm-conformative dispositions must be common knowledge, or more plainly, that they must trust one another.

Unfortunately, a norm-conformative disposition is something that is difficult to just reveal. No matter how much you say you intend to keep your promise, you cannot prove that you intend to, short of actually doing it. This means that people often wind up in situations where they have an opportunity to engage in mutually beneficial cooperation, but where they are not sure they can trust one another.

This is especially problematic where the costs of being exploited are very high, and so the cooperative gains may not be worth the risk. One standard strategy in such a situation is to "build up" trust. People start out by engaging in joint projects in which there is an opportunity for defection, but where the costs associated with being exploited are very low. If neither one takes advantage of this situation, then they may try trusting each other with something more significant. Eventually they reach a point at which future defection would be inconsistent with past behavior (i.e., each can say, "If he was going to sell me out, he would have done it already").

As a result, small symbolic gestures often play an important role in establishing trust among individuals who do not know each other well. A good example of this is table manners. Although not terribly important in their own right, table manners allow individuals to demonstrate their capacity for self-restraint. Waiting until others are served before starting to eat, for example, shows that one is able to subordinate one's desires to the requirements of a more abstract social rule. This signals to those around you that you are capable of playing by the rules, and that you intend to do so. This has the effect of putting others at ease, by suggesting that you are unlikely to violate more significant social norms. It tells them that you are not going to do anything unexpected, anything that would make them feel uncomfortable, or take advantage of them.

The collection of these symbolic practices defines what it is to act "normally." As a result, "being normal," or "ordinary," is a normative achievement, one that individuals actively strive for. Someone who behaves abnormally is not only unpredictable, but also untrustworthy. Thus stable cooperation requires that agents, as Terrence Kelly puts it "do being ordinary."[16] The normality requirement is amplified in situations that require high-trust relations among people who do not know each other well. As a result, these environments tend to have a very standardized appearance and protocol (Kelly refers to this as "hypernormalization"). For example, the usual trappings of a doctor's office—nutritional posters, white overcoats, eye charts, pastel walls—are there to put the patient in a surrounding that will be immediately familiar, the "doctor's office." Everyone knows what a "doctor's office" looks like. Deviation from the pattern would suggest that things are somehow not "normal," and this would immediately cast suspicion on the doctor.

So when agents want to establish their trustworthiness, the best way for them to do so is to "do being normal." There are a variety of reasons why people want to be trusted. In part, it is because being trustworthy gives them access to cooperative arrangements that can be enormously beneficial to them. But it is also experienced by many as a straightforward moral obligation. Being normal puts other people at ease, it makes them comfortable, allows them to enjoy themselves, let down their guard, and so on. By following the rules, one makes others happy. Violating the rules, on the other hand, immediately raises questions about one's motives. People have no way of telling whether someone is breaking the rules because she has some kind of principled objection to them, or is rationalizing her self-interest, or is acting out some antisocial tendencies. As a result, it is one thing to criticize a particular social norm in the abstract, it is something else entirely to start violating it in practice. People may well agree that a given practice is unfair to them, that it is exploitative, and so on. But acting on this opinion may involve sacrificing social relationships that are highly valued, for either personal or instrumental reasons. As a result, even people who reject a particular social norm, and who recognize that it treats them, or some other social group, unfairly, may still choose to "play along" with it.

From an instrumental perspective, the advantage of being normal is that it provides access to cooperation. Others will treat you as a "team player," and not as someone who likes to "rock the boat." In extreme cases those who don't play along will be ostracized from the group or community (this is the case with women who are not "circumcised" in societies in which this is the norm—they are often unmarriageable). There are also somewhat more indirect advantages to securing people's trust. For example, participating in "shop talk" is extremely valuable to anyone seeking to advance his or her career. In a male-dominated corporation, women who challenge prevailing practices and the ambient corporate culture too directly will often exclude themselves from shop talk with male colleagues. This may not take the form of direct ostracism. Shop talk occurs when people are relaxed, when they're whiling away time in the corridors or unwinding in the hotel bar. If a man suspects that something he says may be "used against him" by a female coworker, for example, as part of a sexual harassment grievance, then he will not be relaxed in her company. Women who understand the disadvantage this places them in will often make deliberate use of profanity or sexist language, precisely to signal to the men around them that they will not fault them for doing the same. A woman can establish herself as "one of the boys" by conforming to the rules of a corporate culture that demeans her own gender. Doing so may help her to gain the trust of her coworkers.

The other major advantage of "being normal" is that it reduces the level of anxiety of those around you. Despite the fact that people often complain about rules, most people find normatively unregulated interactions highly vexatious. Unfortunately, when a particular set of rules is challenged, it is seldom the case that a new set of rules springs right up to take their place. It usually takes a lot of negotiation and a certain length of time before people begin to settle into a new pattern—before a new pattern becomes "normalized." In cases where there is less than universal agreement about what this new pattern should be—and this is most cases—it can be a long time before a new set of rules becomes entrenched. In the meantime, people are left to negotiate their interactions in an ad hoc manner, without the benefit of settled expectations. Most people find this to be, if not intensely anxiety provoking, at least highly demanding. It creates enormous room for misunderstanding, simply because no one knows exactly what the other believes it is appropriate to do, and so cannot tell if the other is trying to "send him a message" by either living up to, or failing to live up to some expectation. Normatively unregulated interaction also requires more interpretive effort, and so more time and attention, both of which are intrinsically scarce resources.

As a result, people often resent those who challenge the rules, even when they do not derive any particular benefit from the terms of the existing institutional arrangements. The benefit they receive stems from the mere *existence* of an established institutional arrangement. Having settled expectations allows them to "get on with it," without having to worry about the details. This creates an inherent resistance to the problematization of interaction patterns. It can also lead to the characteristic "backlash" phenomenon that accompanies attempts to effect social change. If an old set of rules becomes discredited, but a new set of rules does not spring up quickly enough to replace them, people may start to revert to the old ones, simply because bad rules are better than no rules.

Consider the example of the controversy over the book, appropriately named *The Rules*.[17] This was a handbook of rules, aimed at a female audience, specifying how to go about courtship, dating, and marriage. Many social commentators were distressed by the retrograde character of these rules, along with their enormous popularity. The rules basically encouraged women to adopt the traditional passive feminine role, to "let him chase you," make him pay for your meals, and so forth. The reason these rules became popular, however, was not that everyone found them appealing, but simply that some rules were better than none. While the sexual revolution of the 1960s and 1970s succeeded quite well in destroying all of the traditional relationship protocols, it failed to produce many new ones. The absence of such rules turned out to produce a lot more anxiety than freedom. Thus the sexual revolution imposed significant inconveniences upon the generation that came of age in the late 1970s and 1980s, who were largely left without cultural norms to guide them through the difficult transition to sexual maturity.[18]

These examples show how people can choose to follow rules that they do not endorse, and so reproduce practices that it is ultimately not in their "interest" to retain. The fact is that cooperation offers significant advantages, and so securing cooperation under unfavorable terms is often superior to securing no cooperation at all. Furthermore, attempts to change social institutions can generate anomic conditions, which lead to failures of cooperation or coordination. Individuals may retain social practices, or seek to restore discredited ones, simply because replacement institutions have failed to materialize. Again, having a bad set of rules is often better than having no rules. Finally, it is an important component of all socialization practices that individuals come to feel some responsibility for the comfort level of those with whom they interact. Opposing entrenched social practices may generate anxiety, tension, misunderstanding, and even hostility in one's interaction partners. Often the discomfort that norm-violations cause in others, including significant others, may lead agents to decide that their broader social objectives are simply "not worth it."

4 Adapted Preferences

The final, and perhaps trickiest, set of problems involves the phenomenon that social theorists refer to as *adapted preferences*. Most people's goals and desires are strongly influenced by their social environment. The most general reason is that desires are propositional attitudes, and so the range of desires that one can have is internally connected to the vocabulary through which these desires are expressed.[19] Similarly, the range of outcomes that we can imagine achieving are constructed using a set of ideals, roles, and scenarios provided by our culture. Our culture provides the horizon within which we plan our life-projects. As a result, the kinds of things that we want are strongly influenced by what those around us happen to want, or encourage us to want.

It is sometimes felt that this "social construction" of preference creates an opportunity for individuals to exercise undue influence over one another. For instance, critics often complain that the advertising industry cultivates inauthentic desires in consumers, allowing companies to sell people goods that they don't "really" need. But this kind of criticism must be advanced with care. Apart from its inherently paternalistic structure—the implicit claim that people are not the best judge of their own needs—this argument trades on a distinction between authentic and inauthentic desires that is far from clear. Every desire beyond the most primitive physical urge is socially constructed, and so no *particular* class of them can be discounted by virtue of that fact. The desire to drink single-malt Scotch and read nineteenth-century Russian literature is just as artificial as the desire to drink Budweiser and wear Nike shoes. Most of what passes for "culture criticism" under this guise is just the expression of class distinction.[20] If preferences are to be of interest to critical social theory, they must be handled at a more theoretically sophisticated level.

What the concern over adapted preferences points to is not the mere fact that preferences are culturally endogenous, but that they are also *ambition-sensitive*. In order to protect themselves against disappointment, people usually try to develop "moderate" or "realistic" expectations. In particular, parents often encourage their children to cultivate desires that they have some chance of satisfying—to set their sights high, but not too high. As a result, the goals and desires that people wind up with are usually constrained by what they or others consider it possible for someone in their situation to achieve, or what it is reasonable to expect. As a result, many people who come from disadvantaged backgrounds have downwardly adapted expectations.[21] They do not want a lot, because they could not reasonably have expected a lot.

The problem with preferences of this type is that they can serve to reproduce inequality, and the effects of discrimination, even after the institutional barriers to advancement have been lifted. So while the first generation of a particular social group might be forced to occupy a particular role, or engage in particular activities, subsequent generations may continue to occupy that role simply because they have learned to like it. In particular, since parents often serve as role models, their children may base their aspirations and expectations on the kind of life that their parents have led. This would be the case, for instance, with women who seek to reproduce patriarchal family structures out of respect for their own mothers, or simply because their own sense of what is valuable in life is tied up with fulfillment of traditional gender roles.

The second major consequence of downwardly adapted preferences is that they may lead members of disadvantaged groups to be too easily satisfied. In a bargaining situation, people generally start out by presenting high initial demands, with the expectation that these will be scaled back as part of the bargaining process. It is in one's interest to make an initial demand that is quite high, because this leaves more room for concessions. However, it is very important that the initial demand not be *unreasonably* high, since this usually signals a lack of seriousness or good faith. As a result, people with poor background expectations may start out with demands that are in fact much lower than others would be willing to entertain. (For example, people with little work experience generally make salary demands that are too low.) They will wind up with outcomes that are much worse than those that could be obtained by someone with higher initial expectations. They may also give up on their claims far too easily. One of the most commonly noted characteristics of the upper classes is their extraordinary sense of entitlement. For example, the rich often get a higher level of service simply because they alone have the presumption to demand it. As a result, social inequalities can be projected into the future simply because people have adapted their expectations in response to such inequalities in the past.

The other major problem with preference adaptation occurs when individuals are trying to break out of a particular social role, but are unwilling or unable to break with some of the preference patterns that this role has induced. This can be called the problem of *partially adapted preferences*. In the typical case, an individual has decided that he or she does not want to occupy a particular social role, but retains some collateral preferences associated with it. In the milder cases, this can simply impose welfare losses on that individual. In the extreme, it can actually have the effect of dragging the individual back into a social role that he or she does not want to occupy.

Examples of this phenomenon can be seen in the adjustments that women must make in order to enter the workforce. A lot of attention has been paid to the "second shift" that working women perform.[22] The explanation for this is usually thought to reside in the fact that traditional gender norms define certain jobs as "women's work" and thus assign much of the domestic labor to women. This assumes, however, that couples blindly "act out" the roles that their culture assigns to them. In most relationships, however, the division of household labor is a source of considerable conflict. Rather than "play along" with some standard set of rules, couples usually develop a long-run equilibrium through a combination of strategic action and bargaining. Some recent feminist theorists have argued that part of the explanation for the second shift is that women's own preferences sometimes disadvantage them in this bargaining process.[23]

Take, for example, the issue of household cleanliness. Whatever the reason, men often have a higher tolerance for filth than women. It is a general characteristic of bargaining scenarios that whoever can "hold out" the longest has a strategic advantage over the other.

Whenever there is a mess to be cleaned up, and no settled agreement on who is to do it, a conflict of interest arises. The person who cleans up does all the work, but then both parties enjoy the satisfaction of living in a clean home. Because of this free-rider incentive, no one will move immediately to clean up, because both will be hoping that the other will do it. But as the house gets messier and messier, the cost of this bargaining stance for each individual increases as well. Eventually, someone will "break down" and do it. The person who experiences the greatest welfare loss from the messiness will generally be the first to break down. Since this is usually the woman, men in heterosexual relationships are often in a strong bargaining position when it comes to cleaning, since both sides know that in a war of attrition, the man can probably hold out longer, and at a lower psychological cost.

Part of the reason for this difference between men and women has to do with women's own values. In the age when women were expected to engage in full-time housework, a woman's social status was intimately connected with how she managed the home—and in particular, how clean she kept it. A filthy home reflected poorly on the wife, not the husband. This has resulted in many women feeling responsible for housework, even as they explicitly renounce this social role. For example, many women who work full-time employ cleaning services. Despite this fact, it is not unheard of for women to "pre-clean" the house before the maid arrives (a compulsion that men generally find baffling). This is an example of how some individuals, despite having officially renounced a particular social role, may not be fully adapted to its renunciation.

Inadequately adapted preferences can also generate unanticipated consequences. For example, in the traditional patriarchal "marriage market," a woman's primary asset was her beauty, whereas for a man it was his wealth. Many people look to marriage as a way of enhancing their social status. Among men, this has meant intense competition for beautiful women, and among women, competition for men with significant wealth or earning potential. There is evidence that this preference pattern has persisted, despite the mass entry of women into the labor force. For example, a study of Stanford MBA graduates showed that men earned an average salary of $144,461, while women earned $101,204. Here one can see a typical "gender gap" in earnings. Even more startling, however, is the gap in what their spouses earned. The female MBA's husbands earned $120,124 on average, while the average male MBA's wife earned only $30,323.[24] The message is fairly clear—despite making extremely high salaries, most of the female MBAs in this study still managed to marry men who earned more than they did.

The full explanation for this type of marriage pattern must obviously involve a complex set of factors (which will include the gender gap, along with the fact that women tend to marry men who are older than they are). According to Rhona Mahoney, however, one important factor that must be taken into consideration is straightforward preference:

I suspect that many hard-driving women believe so strongly in the value of hard work in a challenging field that a man who takes a more relaxed approach may seem second-rate. A man who earns very little, because he is a community organizer or struggling writer, may even seem lazy or suspect. For example, in one study of how sixty-three women made decisions about their careers and their marriages, most women said they were not interested in marrying a househusband. The women who were very devoted to their paying work wanted a man who was, too.[25]

This preference structure, where it occurs, can have unanticipated consequences. It is hard for women with careers—who must take specific evasive action to avoid becoming housewives—to resist the tendency to *devalue* housework. As a result, they do not want to marry househusbands, precisely because they want to marry someone whose life-choices they respect. But marrying someone who makes more money than you is tantamount to marrying someone with more power than you. This kind of power asymmetry may not become salient until many years into the relationship. For example, when child-rearing responsibilities begin to exert time pressure on the household, the person most likely to cut back on work responsibilities is the person with the lower salary. As a result, women who show preference for men with "high-powered" careers have a preference structure that is often not fully adapted to their own ambitions.

The underlying phenomenon here simply reflects the fact that social change can often be very complicated. Social practices are supported by a vast network of behavior and preference, whose functional connection to the reproduction of any particular practice may be very difficult to discern *ex ante*. This means that changing a practice may involve far more extensive revisions in individuals' preferences than anyone ever anticipated. As a result, a social practice may persist despite enjoying very little expressed support. This may be because individuals remain attached to preferences and behavior patterns that indirectly support it, or that reproduce it through consequences that begin to be felt only in the very long term.

The general goal of this paper has been to examine why individuals sometimes act in ways that are contrary to their own interests. The problem of adapted preferences arises when people have *interests* that are, in some sense, contrary to their interests. But in developing a critical analysis of this problem, I have resisted the temptation to appeal to some external conception of what individuals' "real" interests are. This kind of high-handed—not to mention epistemologically suspect—maneuver is by now thoroughly discredited. I have focused on cases where the preferences that individuals have are in tension with one another (partial adaptation), or else cases where the way that these preferences interact with those of others generates lower overall levels of preference-satisfaction (downward adaptation). Neither of these critical strategies requires any second-guessing of the agent's own self-conception, or involves any suggestion that the agent is somehow irrational for failing to recognize where her "real" interests lie.

5   Conclusion

The explicitly stated goal of this paper has been to wean social critics from their attachment to the concept of ideology. The general concern is that, through an excessively uncharitable attitude toward their subjects, critical theorists have had a tendency to undermine the credibility of their own views. In the background, however, has been another concern. Many social critics succumb to a sort of tacit cultural determinism. This is reflected in the widespread assumption that social practices directly reflect people's values, or that they express some set of beliefs about how people should act. If this were the

Joseph Heath

case, then the key to changing social institutions would indeed be to change people's values or beliefs. Unfortunately, while some social practices are directly "patterned" by the cultural system, many more are reproduced through very loosely constrained strategic action. These interactions are integrated only indirectly, and so the associated outcomes may not reflect any specific set of values or beliefs. In this case, social criticism alone will not change anything.

The more serious problem for critical theory arises as follows: after having presented the criticism, and having it widely accepted, the critic expects to see some kind of social change. When none is forthcoming, the critic begins to suspect, not that there is a practical problem preventing implementation of the desired improvements, but that the criticism itself was too superficial, that it didn't get to the root of the problem. The ideology must be more pervasive than originally suspected. Perhaps the original criticism was insufficiently radical, because it used concepts that were in general circulation, and hence complicit in the ideological system. The solution may be to deconstruct these concepts, and form an entirely new set.

Once this line of thinking has been engaged, the critical theory becomes increasingly baroque, increasingly obscure, and of course, increasingly unlikely to change anything. This can generate a vicious cycle of theoretical self-radicalization, in which critics respond to the increasing irrelevance of their theories by further radicalizing them, making the entire apparatus more and more remote from the concerns and the vocabulary of everyday life. The goal of this paper has been to suggest one way in which critical theorists can engage in social criticism without pricing themselves out of the market. More attention to the structure of social interaction, the practical mechanisms through which undesirable interaction patterns are reproduced, has the potential to generate more useful theoretical interventions.

Notes

1. Ludwig Feuerbach: "Every limitation of the reason, or in general the nature of man rests on a delusion, an error." *The Essence of Christianity*, trans. George Eliot (New York: Harper, 1957), 7. Karl Marx: "In all ideology men and their circumstances appear upside-down as in a camera obscura." *The German Ideology* (Moscow: Progress Publishers, 1976), 42.

Problems in the Theory of Ideology

2. Donald Davidson, "On the Very Idea of a Conceptual Scheme," *Inquiries into Truth and Interpretation* (Oxford: Clarendon Press, 1984), 183–198.

3. Lucien Lévy-Bruhl, *How Natives Think*, trans. L. A. Clare (London: Allen, 1926).

4. E.g. Sigmund Freud: "Religion would thus be the universal obsessional neurosis of humanity," *The Future of an Illusion*, trans. W.D. Robson-Scott (New York: Anchor 1961), 70–71.

5. Karl Mannheim, *Ideology and Utopia*, trans L. Wirth and E. Shils (New York: Harvest, 1936), 75–83.

6. Freud's inner circle often conducted theoretical disputes by analyzing each other's motives for disagreement. See Peter Gay, *Freud: A Life for Our Time* (New York: W.W. Norton, 1988).

7. Figures reported by Edward E. Zajac, *The Political Economy of Fairness* (Cambridge: MIT Press, 1995), 29.

8. See Allen Buchanan, "Revolutionary Motivation and Rationality," in *Marx, Justice and History*, ed. M. Cohen , T. Nagel, and T. Scanlon (Princeton: Princeton University Press, 1979), 264–287.

9. Mancur Olson, *The Logic of Collective Action* (Cambridge: Harvard University Press, 1965).

10. These figures and calculations are from Naomi Wolf, *The Beauty Myth* (London: Vintage, 1991), 88–89.

11. Ibid, p. 83.

12. Ibid, 6.

13. Ibid, 87. Here Wolf is conforming to one of the stranger unwritten rules of twentieth-century social criticism, namely, that it is okay to call people stupid as long as you blame someone else for their stupidity.

14. See Yael Tamir, "Hands off Clitoridectomy," *Boston Review* 21/3 (1996).

15. For defense of this claim see Joseph Heath, "Foundationalism and Practical Reason," *Mind* 106 (1997): 451–473.

16. Terrence M. Kelly, "Rationality, Reflexivity and Agency in the Critique of Everyday Life" (unpublished Ph.D. diss., St. Louis University, 1998). Much of this discussion is indebted to Kelly's analysis.

17. Ellen Fein and Sherrie Schneider, *The Rules: Time Tested Secrets to Capture the Heart of Mr. Right* (New York: Warner, 1996), and their follow-up, *The Rules II: Living the Rules* (New York: Warner, 1998).

18. A situation memorably dramatized in the film "The Ice Storm." This is in part what motivates the often noted "ironic" disposition that characterizes members of this generation. Irony allows people to follow "old" rules without being taken to endorse them.

19. Charles Taylor, "Interpretation and the Sciences of Man," *Philosophy and the Human Sciences: Philosophical Papers 2* (Cambridge: Cambridge University Press, 1985), 15–57.

20. See Pierre Bourdieu, *Distinction*, trans. R. Nice (Cambridge: Harvard University Press, 1984).

21. See Jon Elster, *Ulysses and the Sirens* (Cambridge: Cambridge University Press, 1979). See also G. A. Cohen, "Equality of What? On Welfare, Goods, and Capabilities," in *The Quality of Life*, ed. M. Nussbaum and A. Sen (Oxford: Clarendon Press, 1993), 9–29.

22. Arlie Hochschild, *The Second Shift: Working Parents and the Revolution at Home* (New York: Viking, 1989).

23. See Rhona Mahoney, *Kidding Ourselves* (New York: Basic Books, 1995).

24. For further discussion, see Mahoney, 143–145.

25. Ibid., 146. The study referred to is from Kathleen Gerson, *Hard Choices: How Women Decide about Work, Career, and Motherhood* (Berkeley: University of California Press, 1985).

II

Conceptions of Autonomy and the Self

8

Competent Need-Interpretation and Discourse Ethics

Joel Anderson

Jürgen Habermas has argued that the justification of moral norms requires a maximally inclusive process of argumentation among real individuals under ideal conditions. As he is well aware, there is a tension here. If the critical and epistemic force of the process of moral justification is to be retained, it must not be reduced to the de facto conditions, given how distorted they often are. But if the justificatory process he terms "practical discourse" is to avoid the presumptuousness of imagining what others would find acceptable, it must retain the requirement of actual dialogue.[1]

In his attempts to address this tension, Habermas typically focuses on idealizations involving unlimited time, unrestricted participation, and sameness of meaning, but he has said little about requirements regarding the competence of participants. In this essay, I focus on one set of capacities that participants in practical discourse clearly expect of one another, namely, the capacity to perceive and express their own needs, desires, interests, feelings, and concerns. Habermas is very clear that "need-interpretation" is an essential aspect of practical discourse, but less clear about what I propose to call "need-interpretive competence." Once it is recognized that participants in practical discourse demand this set of capacities of one another, the tension between the real and the ideal reemerges. This puts pressure on Habermas to revise his discourse ethics in a way that better appreciates the pragmatic nature of the presuppositions of practical discourse.

Joel Anderson

I begin by reconstructing an account of need-interpretive competence, on the basis of what Habermas says about need-interpretation and about the idealizing presuppositions of practical discourse. I then note several unwelcome implications of this requirement, focusing on what I call the "trilemma of inclusive and stringent consensus." I go on, in section 3, to consider several attempts that Habermas could make to avoid this trilemma, none of which succeeds. I then reexamine the three horns of the trilemma and argue that although two of them should be avoided, the third horn is not a threat to discourse ethics, although it does involve reconceptualizing the idealizing presuppositions of discourse in a way that is *normative all the way down.*

1   Need-Interpretive Competence as a Presupposition of Practical Discourse

The basic outlines of Habermas's discourse ethics can be stated as follows. Discourse ethics is a proceduralist account of moral rightness, as Habermas's "discourse principle" makes clear: "Only those norms can claim to be valid that meet (or could meet) with the approval of all affected in their capacity *as participants in a practical discourse.*"[2] If this approval is to be part of a process that participants can consider rational, the process must meet certain conditions that, upon examination, turn out to be rather demanding, including freedom from coercion, unlimited time, and the availability of all relevant information.[3] These conditions are not, however, externally imposed criteria developed by the moral theorist. Rather, they are found within the attitudes of the participants themselves. For in order for participants to be able to think of the justificatory process as good enough for what they agree on to count as fully valid, they must consider each other to have met these conditions. They may discover, of course, that these conditions do not hold, but this does not diminish their critical potential. As Habermas puts it:

The idealization of justificatory conditions that we undertake in rational discourses constitutes the standard in terms of which reservations can be raised at any point regarding the degree of decentration [that is, inclusion] attained by that justificatory community. . . . When those affected are excluded from participation, or topics are suppressed and relevant contributions pushed aside, when compelling interests are not forthrightly articulated or convincingly formulated, when others are not respected in their otherness, we have to reckon with the fact that a rationally motivated position will not be forthcoming or even broached.[4]

Thus a norm can count as valid only if agreement on it can be reached under conditions that no participant finds at all objectionable. On Habermas's current formulation of the key discourse-ethical principle (U), "A norm is valid when the foreseeable consequences and side effects of its general observance for the interests and value–orientations of *each individual* could be *jointly* [*gemeinsam*] accepted by *all* concerned without coercion."[5]

For my purposes here, the crucial points in the two passages just quoted are, first, that participants' "interests and value-orientations" are decisive for acceptability of a norm and, second, that these concerns must be "forthrightly articulated" and "convincingly for mulated." It is here that we see the roots of the requirement of need-interpretive competence.

The first point is straightforward. It is hard to see how a defensible form of moral justification could neglect the needs, interests, desires, values, feelings, and self-understanding of individuals. As I read him, Habermas uses the terms "needs" and "interests" in a broad way, to include this variety of instantiations of the "partiality that determines our subjective attitudes in relation to the external world."[6] Although he has, at various points, preferred talk of "needs" or "generalizable interests," his current writings suggest a broader view:

The phrase "interests and value-orientations" points to the role played by the pragmatic and ethical reasons of the individual participants in practical discourse. These inputs are designed to prevent the marginalization of the self-understanding and worldviews of particular individuals or groups and, in general, to foster a hermeneutic sensitivity to a sufficiently broad spectrum of contributions.[7]

Indeed, it fits best with his antifoundationalist approach to justification that Habermas avoids privileging any particular class of considerations as especially morally relevant and instead conceives of moral discourse in a way that is open for a variety of inputs.[8] To highlight this variety, I will typically use the phrase "needs, desires, interests, feelings, and concerns."

Talk of "need-interpretation" should be understood to be similarly broad. Moreover, as Habermas has emphasized from his first writings on discourse ethics, a person's needs, desires, interests, feelings, and concerns are not given but are subject to reinterpretation. Because they "are accessible only under interpretations dependent upon traditions, the individual actor cannot himself be the *final* instance in developing and revising his interpretations of needs."[9] This public contestability of need-interpretations does not, however, displace the need for individual competence and effort, for there is, as Habermas might say, "no functional equivalent" for the subject's own expression, articulation, and interpretation of her needs, desires, interests, feelings, and concerns.

This leads to a second and less frequently noted point. If participants are *unable* to articulate their concerns, practical discourse will not be fully rational, any more than if they were being excluded or interrupted. This point is crucial. It would be easy to misunderstand discourse ethics' "freedom from coercion" requirement as a moral prohibition against coercion. But this is actually an epistemic point about what conditions stand in the way of a fully rational justificatory procedure. And these conditions include not only the presence of interfering factors but also the absence of sustaining conditions, such as full information, adequate time, and the ability to perceive and express one's needs. And to the extent to which participants in practical discourse lack this last-mentioned ability—what I am calling "need-interpretive competence"—the process will be epistemically deficient. That is, participants will have reason to view their deliberations as inconclusive.

What does the requirement of need-interpretive competence entail? Because this question can only be answered as a reconstruction of the presuppositions of discourse participants, there are no substantive criteria to be specified theoretically.[10] As a hypothesis, however, I would propose characterizing full need-interpretive competence as the ability to provide interpretations of one's needs, desires, interests, feelings, and concerns that are complete, non-illusory,

articulate, and intelligible. (And this is to leave to one side the crucially important *interpersonal* capacities that are also necessary for give-
and-take about one's need-interpretations.[11])

To satisfy the first requirement, that of *completeness*, need-interpretively competent individuals must be able to introduce into practical
discourse all their needs, desires, interests, feelings, and concerns, insofar as they are relevant to the discussion of the norm in question.
This will typically involve the acquisition of self-awareness, the re-
moval of pathologically repressive mechanisms, and the development of sensitivities to the subtleties of one's inner life.

Second, those with full need-interpretive competence not only
leave nothing out, they also don't include anything extra. They must
filter out the needs, desires, interests, feelings, and concerns that are
based in *illusions*, whether cases of outright (self-)deception or the
more subtle cases in which one mistakes low-priority whims and urges
for the needs and values that really matter to one.[12]

A third feature, *articulation*, is crucial for interpreting components
of one's "inner nature" in such a way that their status as morally relevant considerations can become clear. In part, this is a matter of ac-
curacy, since one's needs, desires, interests, feelings, and concerns
are often complex. One must have the language to disambiguate
them and to capture their nuance and tone. In addition, articulate
self-interpretation is a condition for the possibility of gaining access
to the normative character of certain needs, desires, interests, feelings, and concerns. This is because, as Charles Taylor has shown,
"certain modes of experience are not possible without certain self-
descriptions," and this is especially true of "import-bearing" modes
of responding to situations.[13]

Fourth and finally is the requirement of intelligibility, the inclusion
of which has the most far-reaching implications. Intelligibility is necessary in both a *cultural* and a *personal* sense. Culturally, the evaluative
language one uses to articulate one's needs must resonate with others: "Evaluative expressions or standards of value have justificatory
force when they characterize a need in such a way that addressees can,
in the framework of a common cultural heritage, recognize in these
interpretations their own needs."[14] For example, if I appeal to my
neighbor not to chop down her tree on the grounds that the loss of

shade would leave me feeling "exposed to the sun in a demoralizing way," this appeal has justificatory force only if my reaction is recognizable and not some bizarre phobia. This need-interpretation must also be intelligible in the *personal* sense. The avowed importance of my neighbor's tree must find support in the rest of my life. If I hacked down my *own* shade trees without remorse or spend most of my vacations in desert landscapes, the authenticity of my appeal would be undermined. In general, one must be able to situate one's needs, desires, interests, feelings, and concerns both vertically, as part of one's life-story, and horizontally, as cohering with what else one cares about.[15]

Despite the breadth of this account of full need-interpretation, it should be distinguished from what Habermas discusses under the rubric of either "personality" or "ethical-existential discourse." Unlike need-interpretive competence, personality is a personal resource that enables a person to negotiate conflicting demands of morality and inclination, as well as different role obligations. And even where personality and character are involved in dialogically transforming an agent's needs, desires, interests, feelings, and concerns in a way that reconciles them with the demands of morality, it is still the quite different *epistemic* capacities for articulation and interpretation that are at the heart of need-interpretive competence.[16]

It is a bit more complicated to distinguish need-interpretation from what Habermas calls "ethical-existential questions," since they involve the questions we ask ourselves about what we *really* want. Habermas makes clear that the capacity and willingness to engage in reflection on ethical-existential questions is not a generally required presupposition but rather an optional lifestyle choice, one that "already presupposes, on the part of the addressee, a striving to live an authentic life. . . . In this respect, ethical-existential discourse remains contingent on the *prior* telos of a *consciously* pursued way of life."[17] However, although individuals who are interested in such self-clarification are more likely to have need-interpretive competence, the status of the imperative is quite different. For unlike a commitment to ethical-existential self-clarification, need-interpretive competence is an unavoidable presupposition of practical discourse.

As usual, the unavoidability of this presupposition is revealed in cases where it is disappointed. Our attempts to resolve practical conflicts discursively run aground as soon as it becomes clear that our interlocutors are unable to make crucial distinctions between passing whims and serious needs, who respond rigidly in the face of ambiguous or ambivalent emotions, or who have been brutalized in ways that leave them unable to trust their own intuitions about what their own preferences are.[18] Cases of small children, victims of brain injury, or sociopaths provide examples, but the decisive factor is not the fact that someone fits some category of psychopathology but rather that, in these cases, the presuppositions underwriting an attitude of discursive engagement with that person can no longer be sustained.[19] Once the evidence of need-interpretive incompetence accumulates and cannot be explained away, we can no longer think of our deliberations as meeting the standards of rational justification. We may still have the option of treating others *as if* they had the relevant competence—and, under certain circumstances, this may even be ethically required of us—but that is already a different attitude, and not one that can sustain genuine discourse.[20]

In sum, I have argued that Habermas's conception of practical discourse entails the view that participants in discourse presuppose of one another that they are able to interpret fully and accurately their needs, desires, interests, feelings, and concerns. Insofar as they cannot sustain this presupposition, conditions of practical discourse are not met and the process of justification must be viewed as incomplete and inconclusive. There are back-ups and alternatives—institutionalized political discourse, compromises, and so on—but the standards of *discourse* have not been met.

2   Some Potential Difficulties with the Requirement of Need-Interpretive Competence

It is perhaps not surprising that Habermas has not elaborated a requirement of need-interpretive competence as a presupposition for practical discourse, for such an elaboration brings to the surface several thorny issues for discourse ethics, some familiar and some new.

In this section, I will mention several difficulties and the initial responses to them that Habermas might offer. My analysis leads up to what I see as the central trilemma generated by the inclusion of need-interpretive competence as a presupposition of practical discourse.

(a) The first difficulty has to do with the familiar objection that the conditions for justification are unrealizable. Thus including the requirement of need-interpretive competence might appear as the final straw in undermining the plausibility of ever realizing genuinely discursive conditions. Avoiding manipulation, exclusion, and faulty information is improbable enough. Including the requirement of need-interpretive competence adds a component that is particularly difficult to realize, given that it is a set of skills and attitudinal dispositions developed over time. After all, we all have pockets of rigidity, unexplored regions of the subconscious, and feelings we can't quite get a handle on.

Habermas would likely reply that this objection, at least as it is stated, misses both the point and the pragmatics of discursive presuppositions as *counterfactual idealizations*. Their point is to keep alive the anticipation, built into the claims to rightness we actually make, of full and unrestricted validity. These presuppositions do *not* function as certificates of authentification that license us to think we have the final answer. Rather they are constitutive of the gamble that is made with any assertion about what is morally defensible, namely, that it could meet with acceptance even (or perhaps only) under conditions that are indefinitely improved beyond what we now have. "As the gerund 'idealizing' already reveals, idealizations are operations that we must undertake here and now, but *while performing them* we must not vitiate their context-transcending meaning."[21] Thus, rather than providing grounds for dropping the requirement of need-interpretive competence, the awareness that we fall short of the ideal reveals its relevance. While this reply is, I think, successful as it stands, it does not address some deeper problems in such idealizations, which I take up in section 3 below.

(b) A second, more political challenge is that this model of moral discourse seems to privilege those who have greatest access to what Nancy Fraser has called the "socio-cultural means of interpretation and communication."[22] If participation in practical discourse requires all the need-interpretive skills outlined above, then those less well educated into the hegemonic discourse and those who have grown up under difficult circumstances stand less chance of qualifying, as it were, for practical discourse.

This objection misses its mark. To begin with, it is a mistake to think of presuppositions as entry requirements, in the sense that some get to participate and others don't. Unless *everyone* affected is competent to participate, conditions for discourse are not met, and no parties to any actual agreement reached under those circumstances can legitimately think of themselves as knowing what is right. Instead, under such circumstances, we must settle for the epistemically inferior status of "advocatory" deliberations.[23] Discourse ethics has much work still to do on the topic of advocacy, and the de facto unequal distribution of competence adds urgency to the question of who is supposed to advocate for whom—and of how such asymmetries could be defended. But these points do not apply to practical discourse proper. Against the objection that some idiolects of need-interpretation might be hegemonic and exclusionary, Habermas very clearly insists that the language of need-interpretation is open to being challenged. As with other presuppositions of discourse, no charges of linguistic exclusion may remain standing if the discourse is to count as genuine.

Perhaps the most important issue raised by this objection—one I cannot address here—is the more general question of how much would need to be done to move current conditions closer to the idea of genuine discourse. The serious inequalities of access to acquiring need-interpretive competence pose an enormous challenge for such a task. Habermas has held such discussions at arm's length, in order to avoid having conditions of discourse be misunderstood as a *goal*, but Karl-Otto Apel, Axel Honneth, and others are right to call for more work on bridging the gap between the ideal of full competence and the current reality of widespread inequality.[24]

(c) A third difficulty for discourse ethics lies in the possibility that requiring need-interpretive competence for practical discourse would radicalize a point made by Thomas McCarthy regarding intractable disagreements. As I mentioned earlier, for participants to consider each other need-interpretively competent, they must find one another's need-interpretation to be intelligible. However, since needs, desires, interests, feelings, and concerns are interpreted "in the light of cultural values,"[25] and because these cultural values are so divergent within and between contemporary cultures, the prospects for the agreement on need-interpretations appear dim:

> So consensus could be achieved only if all participants could come to agree on the authentic interpretation of each's needs, and they would have to do so from the very different hermeneutic starting points afforded by a pluralistic and individualistic culture.[26]

In other words, if it is true, as Habermas himself suggests, that needs interpretation requires "thickly" evaluative language, then it is hard to see how one can jointly assess the consequences of a norm's general observance as long as there is disagreement about how to interpret the needs, desires, feelings, and interests affected by acting in accordance with that norm. As a result, the validity of moral norms seems to presuppose a prior ethical agreement on substantive values.

It might be thought that this conclusion could be avoided by separating "agreeing with someone's need-interpretation" from the seemingly weaker "finding someone's need-interpretation intelligible." Couldn't one know what a person meant without agreeing with him? In the case of factual assertions, this may be unproblematic. But in the case of evaluative claims, understanding them means appreciating what is being presented *as* worthy (or not). There is something incoherent about saying, "I don't see what could be ennobling about driving a sport utility vehicle, but it makes sense to me when others say they find it to be so." As with the appreciation of material inferences, the evaluative claims central to need-interpretation have intelligibility only once one is already within what one might call the "space of values," to adapt a phrase of Wilfred Sellars.[27] Hence mutual assessment of intelligibility requires that interlocutors situate themselves in the same broad space of values, which involves achieving some degree of agreement.

Nor will it work to counter that differences are typically local or relatively minor issues, such as whether to cut down a shade tree, and thus that it would be no problem to concede that these issues are resolvable only within restricted contexts. But substantive differences of this sort are at the heart of disputes of an undeniably moral nature. This is clearly the case, for example, with regard to norms about sexual harassment. To identify and express the relevant considerations that bear on such norms, we must be able to sort out desires and emotions that are often complex or ambivalent. Moreover, such norms involve a highly contested evaluative language for discussing sexuality, physical attraction, and the sense of personal space. Although these disagreements are also about how to *apply* agreed-upon norms, the disagreements cannot be relegated to "application discourse," since what is central to the discourse-ethical justification of norms, as we have seen, are "the foreseeable consequences and side effects of its general observance for the interests and value-orientations of *each individual*"[28]—and these "consequences and side effects" can be assessed only in terms of need-*interpretations.*

Once it is clear how intimately substantive values are involved in the justification of norms, the implications of McCarthy's analysis become serious. For unless participants in discourse come to agree on their substantive "ethical" value-commitments—something antithetical to the formalism of Habermas's moral theory—they will not be able to reach agreement on moral norms in practical discourse. McCarthy's analysis focuses on reaching agreement on the need-interpretations themselves. These are disagreements about the subject matter in dispute or about the relative weights of various considerations as reasons for or against adopting a norm. But these disagreements bring with them a deeper dissensus at the level of the very *presuppositions* of discourse. This is because being competent cannot be separated from being appropriately viewed as competent, and thus competence itself is something that requires intersubjective agreement.

Seeing this requires understanding how, as a normative or "deontic" status, need-interpretive competence differs from other capacities, such as basic color vision or the ability to run a four-minute mile. Whereas these latter capacities can be separated from the ability to tell whether one has succeeded in exercising it, intrinsically normative capacities, such as those for need-interpretation, practical reasoning, or language use, can be had only *within* a web of status-attributing attitudes. Just as one cannot be "the go-ahead run on second base" outside the nexus of rules, events, judgments, attitudes, and so on that make a baseball game a legitimate baseball game, such normative capacities as need-interpretive competence do not come into view except within the "game" in question.[29] Michael Dummett illustrates this point with the following joke: A man turns to a woman and asks, "Do you speak Spanish?" "I don't know," she replies, "I've never tried." As Dummett points out, what has gone humorously wrong here is that if the woman doesn't *already* speak Spanish, she won't be able to know whether the sounds she makes are Spanish sounds or not.[30] In this sense, being a competent language-speaker is inseparable from already being in the game, that is, being able to discriminate between when one is speaking the language and when one is uttering gibberish. It is not enough, of course, simply to *think* that you are making the right moves. Your judgments must accord with those of other competent judges. Thus, you are a Spanish speaker only if, in your interaction with other Spanish speakers, you make what are considered to be the right moves. Similarly, I am suggesting, you are need-interpretively competent only if you can make what count as the right moves in the language-game of need-interpretation. And one must earn—as an ongoing accomplishment—the ascription of competence from consociates, whose competence is similarly dependent on your finding them to be competent.

As McCarthy's analysis makes clear, however, in pluralistic societies it is likely that in at least some important domains, reasonable interlocutors will find one another's need-interpretations unintelligible enough to suspend the attribution of full need-interpretive competence. And to the extent to which this would continue to be the case under otherwise ideal conditions, large areas of social conflict will not be discursively resolvable.

This suggests a trilemma at the heart of discourse ethics: Habermas must (a) loosen the requirements of agreement and mutual intelligibility, particularly of having to agree for the same reasons, or (b) accept that agreement on norms will be attainable only if we limit the scope to those who share our evaluative language, or (c) lower the expectations of need-interpretive competence as a presupposition of discourse. At least at first sight, none of these is an attractive option for Habermas. Thus, before examining whether Habermas would actually be advised to take one of the horns of this trilemma—which I will refer to as the "trilemma of inclusive and stringent consensus"—it is worth asking what resources Habermas has for avoiding it altogether.

3   Can Discourse Ethics Avoid the Trilemma?

In this section, I consider two ways in which Habermas could try to argue that discourse ethics does not actually face this trilemma. The first involves understanding discourse about need-interpretations and discourse about the validity of a norm as distinct but complementary undertakings, such that substantive value conflicts can be relegated to a nonmoral context of justification. The second strategy involves reasserting the *counterfactual* nature of idealizing presuppositions of discourse mentioned earlier. I argue that both attempts are unsuccessful.

This first argumentative strategy can be seen as a response to McCarthy's charge that Habermas is committed, despite himself, to making moral discourse dependent on ethical discourse: "The separation of formal procedure from substantive content is never absolute: we cannot agree on what is just without achieving some measure of agreement on what is good."[31] This is a problem for Habermas, who insists on the priority of the right over the good. One reply open to him is to grant that need-interpretation involves discussions of substantive values, but that they should be thought of as a supplement to moral discourse, without displacing the priority of moral discourse. Indeed, Habermas himself mentions the possibility of such complementary relationships between types of discourse: "The different forms of argumentation form a system precisely to the extent that they *refer internally to one another* owing to their need for supplementation."[32] Although he rejects, in this passage, Martin Seel's proposal for a form of discourse that would mediate between moral, ethical, and other forms of discourse,[33] he still allows for the idea that the need might arise *within* the context of moral argumentation for the resolution of issues that are best addressed in a different context of argumentation, say, of deliberations about need-interpretation. In this way, Habermas could "outsource" the reliance on substantive values to a separate domain and drop the idea that need-interpretive competence has to be a presupposition of participants in practical discourse. In cases of breakdown of communication or the need for further clarification, participants could shift to an "ethical" mode, but they would not have to agree on evaluative standards of intelligibility as a *precondition* for moral discourse.

Upon reflection, however, it is unclear whether this proposal can meet McCarthy's objection in a way Habermas could accept. The separation of the two contexts cannot be too sharp. The results of deliberations in the domain of need-interpretation must still be construed as relevant input into and correctives on moral discourse, at least to the degree that application discourse is. To this extent, moral discourse remains dependent on need-interpretive discourse. Moreover, this would not eliminate the problem-generating need for convergence on the substantive values, since participants in moral discourse have grounds for accepting the results of the need-interpretive discourse only if they can accept the intelligibility of the perspectives raised. Habermas could, alternatively, adopt an approach parallel to McCarthy's suggestion that "*in practice* political deliberation is not so much an interweaving of separate discourses as a multifaceted communication process that allows for fluid transitions among questions and arguments of different sorts."[34] But at that point the complementarity would have been absorbed into a single, inclusive discourse. However sensible such a view is, it would amount to giving up the hoped-for possibility of exporting value disagreements out of practical discourse proper.

The second way in which Habermas could try to avoid the trilemma of inclusive and stringent consensus is by arguing that the trilemma is based on a misunderstanding of the *counterfactual* nature of the presuppositions of practical discourse. I have been speaking as if contexts of moral and political deliberation would break down if we did not attribute full need-interpretive competence to one another. But this is obviously not true. Despite deep and sometimes violent conflicts over moral issues, there is remarkable stability in those discussions and increasingly widespread acknowledgment of the legitimacy, in principle, of human rights claims. The explanation, it could be argued, is that when conditions are less than ideal, the presuppositions of discourse are not thereby falsified. They retain, as I noted earlier, their essential corrective status.

But in light of the account I have offered of need-interpretive competence, the talk of counterfactuals is a bit more complicated, for what participants anticipate is not easily represented as the progressive reduction of limitations. In the case of time limits, we know what it would mean to "counterfactually presuppose unlimited time for discussion," for it is simply an extension of familiar experiences, such as extending the length of a meeting in order to handle new business. Similarly, we can imagine a situation free from coercion by abstracting away the forms of manipulation with which we are all too familiar. Requirements of competence are, however, quite different. Not only does idealization presuppose the teleological anticipation of where a developmental process is heading, the state of affairs being "counterfactually presupposed" is one that involves participants *actually* viewing each other as competent. This follows from the earlier point that being need-interpretively competent is a normative status that emerges within a nexus of attributive attitudes. But this makes the very notion of "idealizing" competence problematic. For the state of the world in which full need-interpretive competence would be attained would also be a world in which there was agreement, among competent attributors, on the evidence. But, since the relevant evidence is that others' need-interpretations are intelligible in light of shared value-commitments, the idealization presupposed in practical discourse is of conditions incompatible with reasonable pluralism about values.

One response open to Habermas, which he has taken in his debate with McCarthy, is to insist that we *can* anticipate, as an idealizing presupposition of discourse, a context of pure communication unimpeded by any difficulties of translation, including those between evaluative vocabularies. In his discussion of Bernard Peters's model of a society characterized by "purely communicative social relations," Habermas suggests that, as a "methodological fiction," we can still conceptualize a situation unburdened by differences in competence, attention, or even language.[35]

The fact that this is a *counterfactual* presupposition doesn't solve the problem, however. Many critics will, of course, view such a leveling of difference as precisely the nightmare scenario that they have always suspected Habermas's view to entail. But one doesn't have to be a post-modernist to be concerned. For if ideal conditions for discourse include full need-interpretive competence, and if that requires mutual attribution of the competence—which in turn requires convergence on essentially evaluative standards of intelligibility—then the realization of ideal conditions would seem to involve a situation in which we share the same evaluative standards and vocabulary. Unfortunately, at the conceptual level, realizing that condition would entail the elimination of competing and incommensurable value-orientations. But such evaluative diversity just *is* what reasonable pluralism about values involves. In this way, discourse ethics seems to be at odds with a commitment to the legitimacy of value pluralism.

Habermas can respond in two ways to this line of critique, by showing that sharing an evaluative language does not amount to cultural homogenization and by emphasizing that discourse not be thought of as "concrete."

For Habermas, the idea that our evaluative vocabularies form unbridgeable divides is a decidedly *unpragmatic* position, rooted in "culturalist" assumptions about language as "world-disclosing" rather than problem-solving.[36] Rather, in contexts of communication, interlocutors face the joint and symmetrical task of finding a language in which to address the issue at hand. Indeed, progress on this task must already be made before the issue can come up as one that is shared. In a recent response to McCarthy, Habermas emphasizes this point.

The everyday hermeneutics of mass communications actually constitutes a melting pot, in which subcultural value-orientations *interpenetrate* and in which the evaluative vocabularies of public language are subjected to constant revision. To this extent, the common language in which citizens reach understanding regarding the interpretation of their needs is always already a fact.[37]

In part, this is a matter of the usual task of finding the language in which to proceed communicatively. But, as William Rehg emphasizes, there is also an epistemic component to this task of finding a mutually acceptable way of formulating the issues and the considerations raised. A focus on the world-disclosing or "constitutive semantic power of language," as in Charles Taylor's approach,

. . . does not do justice to the fact that such [evaluative] languages, in constituting answers to moral questions, thereby raise validity claims the illocutionary force of which goes beyond the boundaries of the language in which the answer was first formulated. . . . [In cases of conflict,] neither side can rest content, in a cognitive sense, with the constitutive power of *its* language, but must enter into a dialogical reflection with the others so as to reach a consensus settling both the cognitive uncertainty and the practical conflict."[38]

Once we recognize that, like other value differences, conflicts over the attribution of need-interpretive competence are not *necessarily irresolvable owing to essential differences between persons or cultures*, then we can treat such conflicts as practical problems that must be faced by individuals seeking a fair basis for coordinating their action—and thus as conflicts that can be resolved *legitimately* only by finding a *mutually* shared language. Nor is there any suggestion here of assimilating what the other says into one's own language, since finding common ground typically means moving to new ground.

Despite its pragmatic character, this "melting pot" approach still represents ideal conditions as involving convergence of evaluative languages, and this might be considered incompatible with an endorsement of pluralism. But a further rejoinder can be found in Habermas's insistence on avoiding an overly "concretistic" understanding of ideal conditions of discourse. Rather than anticipating a single moment of global fusion, the idealizing presuppositions are best understood in terms of a decentered process that includes a variety of contexts of argumentation, to a variety of audiences, to resolve a variety of concrete conflicts, in a variety of evaluative languages. The idealization of discursive inclusivity—in many ways the key idea of discourse ethics—is decidedly *not* to be thought of as a large meeting but rather as a decentered and ongoing process.[39] Only if one forgets this, Habermas could argue, is there anything to the charge that realizing ideal conditions of discourse would require negating pluralism about values.

Compelling as this approach is, it is not clear that Habermas is willing to accept the implications of such a thoroughgoing decentration. In particular, this pragmatist decentration of the process of finding agreement seriously undermines the grounds for expecting that these dispersed agreements will involve reaching agreement *for the same reasons.* For example, as part of developing such a decentered approach, Rehg suggests that "it is possible to conceive of universally valid claims that nonetheless must be defended in terms tailored to particular audiences."[40] This means that agreement on one norm could be reached within different communities of discourse on grounds that might not be acceptable to all. Thus the advantages of understanding practical discourse in terms of a decentered process are to be purchased at the price of a looser connection between the acceptability of the norm and acceptability of the reasons for the norm. This is not a conclusion that Habermas has been willing to accept. At the very least, this is not a strategy for avoiding the trilemma, since giving up the requirement of agreeing for the same reasons was one of the horns of the trilemma. It remains to be seen, however, whether taking this horn is the best available option for Habermas.

4 Shared Reasons, Abstract Principles, and Modest Expectations

Once it is granted that Habermas cannot escape the "trilemma of inclusive and stringent consensus," the question becomes which of the three horns is least problematic. That trilemma, again, is that (a) unless Habermas weakens his conception of agreement by giving up the view that normative rightness is established only by participants in practical discourse agreeing *for the same reasons*, then either (b) participants will find agreement on norms only with those who share their substantive value-commitments, or (c) participants must lower their expectations and adopt less stringent requirements for ideal discourse.

(a) As I have mentioned, Habermas insists that the validity of a norm depends on participants in practical discourse agreeing on the norm for the same reasons. His motivation for this is complex, but the key argument is that the "binding/bonding force" of mutual understanding requires that interlocutors find each other's speech act offers acceptable not merely for their own, sometimes strategic, reasons, but for reasons that make the speech act offer acceptable in general.[41] In any event, it is clear that Habermas would resist taking the first horn of the trilemma.

McCarthy has, however, provided reasons for reconsidering Habermas's sharp divide between agreeing for the same reasons and making a strategic compromise. There is, he suggests, room for "*rationally motivated* agreement" that "may well involve elements of conciliation, compromise, consent, accommodation, and the like."[42] Understanding this alternative requires appreciating the status of participants in practical discourse as "reflective participants." McCarthy argues that although, as participants in discourse, we cannot avoid presupposing that agreement could be reached, we also have access to an *observer* perspective. And if, from that observer perspective, we have reason to believe that conditions for agreement are unfavorable, that insight will affect our expectations: "As 'participants,' to use Habermas's terminology, we want to justify our actions to others on grounds that all could rationally accept. As 'observers,' however, we note the fact of reasonable pluralism and anticipate that some of the reasons acceptable to us will be unacceptable to others."[43] In the case of attributing need-interpretive competence, we may know that, even if conditions of discourse are otherwise ideal, our interlocutors are so far from sharing our standards of intelligible need-interpretation that the only way to reach any agreement at all is to "bracket" critical consideration of their reasons for the avowed urgency of their needs, desires, interests, feelings, and concerns. In general, McCarthy is urging Habermas to move in the direction of John Rawls's view that, in light of the "fact of reasonable pluralism," individuals must assume the "burdens of reason" and become tolerant and self-restrained in their judgments about others' "comprehensive doctrines."[4]

Habermas's response to this proposal has been sharply critical, claiming that if we follow McCarthy's proposal, "we end up with something resembling Carl Schmitt's understanding of politics."[45] While this accusation goes too far, I think Habermas is right to argue that settling for rationally motivated agreement (without agreement for the same reasons) is acceptable only if doing so is licensed by a more fundamental principle on which there *is* agreement for the same reason. Whenever we agree to disagree, the agreement providing the parameters for legitimate disagreement demands agreement for the same reasons.[46]

Joel Anderson

Moreover, as McCarthy himself says about Rawls's approach, it is important not to let the observer's perspective push out the participant's perspective. Although McCarthy is enough of a Kantian to know that neither the observer nor the participant standpoint is "more true" than the other, there is still a tendency in his account of reflective participation to assume an asymmetry between the two. The observer perspective is presented as putting a check on participants' performative presupposition that agreement could be reached. It offers a dose of realism that serves to correct the participant perspective that is caught up in its own engaged perspective, the way one might get caught up in a conversation and lose track of time. This makes it seem as if the participant's perspective is something to which one succumbs, rather than a source of insight. Indeed, it is only against the background of the assumed privilege of the observer perspective that the expectations of disagreement could be treated as grounds for scaling back our discursive presuppositions. The danger is that normative judgment about the presuppositions of discourse is held hostage to concerns about stability.[47]

One final reason for avoiding this first horn of the trilemma, despite McCarthy's arguments, has to do with the difficulties in extending this view to the toleration of less-than-full competence. Although I have tried to extend McCarthy's proposal to contexts in which we withhold the attribution of need-interpretive competence owing to value difference, it is much easier to accept the idea of agreeing to disagree about our value-orientations than to agree to ignore relative incompetence. Being more tolerant of value differences may, however, be of a piece with rethinking what is required for "competence," and so I shall return to this point below, in applying the idea of reflective participation to the third horn of the trilemma.

(b) Perhaps, then, we should consider accepting the possibility that agreement will be found only among those who share value-orientations. Such a concession seems antithetical to the universalism of discourse ethics until one considers the way Habermas distinguishes "morality" from "ethics."[48] Morally valid norms—as well as the fundamental principles underlying democratic political procedures—are those that could meet with universal acceptance. Thus, on one reading, taking this second horn of the trilemma simply involves acknowledging that there will be relatively few norms and principles on which everyone can agree. Indeed, this is exactly the position Habermas takes in response to McCarthy: "The sphere of questions that can be answered rationally from the moral point of view shrinks in the course of the development toward multiculturalism within particular societies and toward a world society at the international level."[49] Habermas thus appears to grant McCarthy's point that some common ground may be needed but believes we can still hold fast to moral universalism. This is because we have no reason to believe that we could never find agreement on enough core norms and procedures to establish the backbone for a system of norms and values that would prohibit most of the violence, coercion, and inhumanity that drive our moral intuitions. And that, he argues, is all that is needed, since abstract principles can be sufficiently powerful to preserve universalism as a bulwark against the parochial abuses that contextualism permits.

While I think Habermas is right to emphasize the power of abstraction to provide differentiated integration of the moral world, there are several problems with the way he develops this approach, including the view that it is an "empirical question" whether an issue such as abortion is a *moral* issue, depending on whether universal agreement can actually be found regarding this issue.[50] Most relevant for my purposes, however, is the difficulty that the narrow but adequate common ground on which these core moral norms come to be accepted must still meet the ideal conditions of practical discourse, including, I have argued, the mutual attribution of need-interpretive competence. Thus what would have to be assumed is that by moving toward more abstract norms, it becomes more likely that participants in practical discourse will mutually attribute need-interpretive competence.

I see no reason to think, however, that either the give-and-take of disputed reasons or the ongoing reciprocal assessment of need-interpretive competence will be any easier in discussions of abstract principles. Assuming that establishing the validity of these more abstract norms and principles is not to be conceptualized as overlapping consensus but rather as the result of agreement in practical discourse, Habermas cannot ignore the dynamics of practical discourse even about abstract norms. Given how much weight such principles are designed to carry, one would expect the dynamics to be at least as contentious. This is not a psychological point, but a point about the level at which the abstraction is occurring. That is, the thinness and the abstractness of the norms under discussion may allow one to move away from contentious substantive values *at the level of what is being discussed*, but this is quite a different matter from the business of attributing need-interpretive competence, since that requires the broader sort of person-oriented evidence described in section one above. To resolve this issue, discourse ethics seems to need something analogous to thinner and more abstract norms. And this is just what is involved in taking the third horn of the trilemma.

(c) The third horn involves weakening the notion of the ideal standards for practical discourse. It might be argued that the real source of the problematic dissensus I have identified lies with the stringency of the standard of full need-interpretive competence. Perhaps discourse ethics would do better with a less demanding standard here. Indeed, Habermas does talk about conditions needing to be "sufficiently ideal."[51] But simply scaling back on the standards would be problematic. It would require discourse ethics to provide criterial specifications that define "sufficiency" and the perspective from which one assesses it. This requirement would ultimately force us to give up on the key discourse-ethical understanding of "ideal conditions" as calling for the constant improvement of real discourse. To be acceptable, then, any moderation of the stringency of presuppositions for discourse will have to be conceptualized in a way that does not undermine the pragmatics of idealizing presuppositions as always reaching beyond the given context.

The way to do this is to focus again on the attributive and deontic status of need-interpretive competence. The requirement of need-interpretive competence is the requirement that one count as someone to whom it is appropriate to attribute that competence. In the dynamics of social contexts, including practical discourse, that attribution is presupposed and retained as long as interlocutors provide the evidence that, for all practical purposes, they have the relevant capabilities. As McCarthy has emphasized more generally, the key move lies in the idea that discourse requires no more than the mutual attribution of need-interpretive competence as an *ongoing achievement* of *engaged participants* for *all practical purposes.*[52] Once this is understood, it becomes clear that more evidence is relevant in some contexts than in others. And this opens up an interesting possibility for addressing the difficulties that intractable value dissensus poses for the requirement of need-interpretive competence.

The key to this solution lies in noticing that the degree of evidence that we expect of one another as backing for our attributing need-interpretive competence varies across contexts. In some situations, straightforward evidence of the ability to register acute pain might be adequate (although even *that* could become disputed under some circumstances). In other circumstances, the potential for disagreement on the attribution of need-interpretive competence diminishes because less evidence is necessary for practical purposes. A natural way of thinking about the variation in the requisite evidence is in terms of two continua running in tandem. One continuum represents the degree of stringency of expectations regarding the evidence of need-interpretive competence.[53] The other continuum represents the degree of inclusiveness of the discourse that can be expected to secure agreement, that is, the degree to which disagreements over substantive values stand in the way of individuals recognizing each other as competently participating in discourse. In terms of the issue at the heart of the trilemma we have been discussing, this second continuum has to do with the reduced potential for agreement that comes with including an increasing number of participants of diverse value-orientations.

The interesting question is whether these two continua map onto each other. If we could think of contexts in which the least evidence is expected as also being contexts in which the greatest inclusivity of participation—that is, the most universal norms—is to be expected, and if we could think of contexts in which expectations are highest as the contexts in which one need only convince the narrower ethical community of "significant others,"[54] then this approach might give us universality and particularity in just the right places. This approach achieves much of what Habermas intended with his morality-ethics distinction: the thinly evaluative demands of moral discourse allow for maximal inclusiveness in practical discourse, whereas the demands for a richer, more substantive account would hold in contexts where it is less important that everyone be consulted. If we think of these two continua mapping onto each other in this way, we seem to have a palatable way of taking the third horn of the trilemma and thereby accommodating the substantive nature of need-interpretation within a universalistic moral theory.

As I argued above regarding the trilemma's second horn, however, it is still not clear why the two continua should map onto each other in this way. Why should it be the case that discussions of universal moral norms require less evidence of need-interpretive competence? Some account is still needed here.

One answer builds on McCarthy's account of reflective participation. We could think of the level of evidence expected as informed by the observer's knowledge that, under some circumstances, intractable differences of substantive values mean that we are not likely to get evidence to meet demanding standards of need-interpretive competence. Like context-sensitive travelers who soften their usual reactions to the seemingly bizarre behavior of others, reflective participants could scale back their standards of evidence for need-interpretive competence when they know that the cultural context is marked by disagreement about evaluative language. If we know, for example, that our interlocutors are ethically opposed to viewing sexuality in the language of "basic needs," then we have grounds to view their relative silence regarding the impact of a norm on their potential for sexual satisfaction as something other than a repressed relation-to-self. Given that it is appropriate, adopting this less demanding standard of evidence provides an increased basis for reflective participants viewing each other, *for practical purposes*, as competent. At the same time, by insisting that the attribution of need-interpretive competence still has to be *earned*, this approach differs from the blanket liberal suspension of judgment. Thus, if a person's silence about issues of sexuality is complete and rigid, that might still count as evidence of a lack of need-interpretive competence.

Although this approach views the relationship between the potential for agreement and the demandingness of our expectations as an ongoingly negotiated feature of the pragmatics of argumentation, it ultimately means that we scale back our presuppositions for discourse out of a concern for stability. Consequently, it appears that we have given priority to the observer perspective and empirical predictions of where agreement is likely—just the problem I noted in McCarthy's proposal above.

The way to avoid this, I suggest, is to realize that the pragmatics of idealizing presuppositions is *normative all the way down*. The level of competence to be expected, on this view, is determined neither by an independent criterion nor by the social need to find agreements. Rather, it is determined by judgments that admit of degrees of appropriateness. Instead of assuming that there is a fact of the matter about how much evidence for need-interpretive competence to expect under what conditions, judgments about the appropriateness of how much evidence to expect are subject to challenge and admit of argumentation. Sometimes the social norms license attributing need-interpretive competence on the basis of relatively little evidence; at other times, they demand more.

Consider the parallel normativist account that could be offered for the *point* behind the liberal presumption against making personal tastes, say in sweaters or cars, objects of intersubjective criticism. It's not that there is something about tastes themselves that induces our liberal reservation to criticize them. Rather, certain judgments are constituted *as matters of taste* by the way in which they fit into certain normative patterns of judgment. We find it important to allow for this sort of leeway, and there is a whole array of norms, practices, institutions, customs, and inculcated dispositions that define and reinforce this normative pattern. It is crucial to get the order of explanation the right way around. The norms constitute "matters of taste" as such; they are not a response to any fact about tastes.[55]

Similarly, my proposal involves treating expectations regarding the degree of evidence to be expected regarding need-interpretive competence as answered in terms of the norms governing such expectations. Thus the question of how much agreement on substantive values to expect as part of the conditional presupposition of need-interpretive competence is a context-sensitive matter governed by higher-order expectations, that is, expectations about what it is appropriate to expect.[56] For example, we may not expect that, when dealing with issues of sexuality, we will be able to find everyone to be equally open about their feelings, whereas when it comes to issues of painful or denigrating mistreatment, we have high expectations of convergence regarding the evidence for need-interpretive competence. In this context, expectation is not a matter of thinking that agreement is empirically likely but is rather a directly normative judgment that strong evidence of need-interpretive competence is appropriate.

This approach does, of course, represent a departure from the quasi-transcendental character of Habermas's reconstruction of the presuppositions of practical discourse.[57] Rather than building an account of the idealizing presuppositions on the basis of purported universals about "what we cannot help but expect," the present proposal grounds the presuppositions only in the normative judgments of the participants, that is, in what we view as *appropriate* to expect of others. Does this move involve a slide into conventionalism—are we basing the key critical standard of idealizing presuppositions on whatever norms happen to have currency? It does entail a more *constructivist* account of the presuppositions of practical discourse, at least regarding the requirement of need-interpretive competence. But such an account need not be problematic, as long as we understand its standard of appropriateness as caught up in a complex and inescapable web in which competence as well as the authority to attribute competence is intersubjectively attributed, contested, revised, and so on. That is, my proposal need have no relativistic implications.[58] In many domains, the results will probably not depart from the claims of Habermas's reconstructive universalism. But the analysis will be different, for the question of whether disagreement is problematic will depend not on whether the question is a moral or ethical question or an empirical prediction about the chances for agreement but rather on whether, for relevant purposes, the disagreement is viewed as problematic in a cognitive sense.

Taken together, these considerations suggest that taking the third horn of the trilemma might be the best option, whatever complexities it might bring with it. If it is true, as I have argued throughout this essay, that need-interpretive competence is an unavoidable presupposition of practical discourse, and if it is true, as McCarthy has argued, that the disputes over substantive values are implicated in moral discourse because of the evaluative nature of need-interpretation, then some account is needed of how agreement on moral norms is still possible within pluralistic societies. The normative account just sketched offers one promising and pragmatic avenue for filling this gap within discourse ethics.[59]

Notes

1. Jürgen Habermas, *The Theory of Communicative Action*, 2 vols., trans. Thomas McCarthy (Boston: Beacon Press, 1987), vol. 1, 95.

2. Habermas, "Discourse Ethics: Notes on a Program of Philosophical Justification," in *Moral Consciousness and Communicative Action*, trans. C. Lenhardt and S. W. Nicholsen (Cambridge: MIT Press, 1990), 66.

3. For one proposed list of such conditions, see Robert Alexy, "A Theory of Practical Discourse," trans. D. Frisby, in *The Communicative Ethics Controversy*, ed. S. Benhabib and F. Dallmayr (Cambridge: MIT Press, 1990), 163–176.

4. Habermas, "Richtigkeit versus Wahrheit: Zum Sinn der Sollgeltung moralischer Urteile und Normen," in *Wahrheit und Rechtfertigung: Philosophische Aufsätze* (Frankfurt: Suhrkamp, 1999), 298.

5. Habermas, "A Genealogical Analysis of the Cognitive Content of Morality," in *The Inclusion of the Other*, ed. C. Cronin and P. DeGreiff (Cambridge: MIT Press, 1998), 42 (emphasis in the original). For the earlier, better-known version, which does not include a reference to "value-orientations"; see "Discourse Ethics," 65.

6. Habermas, *Theory of Communicative Action*, vol. 1, 92. Indeed, the breadth of the German original [*Bedürfnisstruktur* or *–natur*] is highlighted in McCarthy's translation as "desires and feelings" (ibid., 20) and William Rehg's rendering as "appetitive structures" [in *Insight and Solidarity: The Discourse Ethics of Jürgen Habermas* (Berkeley: University of California Press, 1994), 49–54].

7. Jürgen Habermas, "A Genealogical Analysis of the Cognitive Content of Morality," 42; cf. "Richtigkeit versus Wahrheit," 309–311.

8. William Rehg suggests a slightly different view, according to which needs and interests operate at different levels: "Whether one finds the constraints and impacts of a norm's general observance acceptable or not depends on how one understands certain interests, which in turn depends on one's need interpretations." (*Insight and Solidarity*, 55). Although I doubt that much depends on this difference, it seems important for avoiding foundationalism that discourse ethics avoid introducing distinctions of levels among morally relevant considerations.

9. Habermas, *Theory of Communicative Action*, vol. 2, 96. This is already clear in "Moral Development and Ego Identity," in *Communication and the Evolution of Society*, trans. T. McCarthy (Boston: Beacon Press, 1979), 69–94. See also Habermas, "Genealogical Analysis of the Cognitive Content of Morality," 42, and "Discourse Ethics," 67–68. On the intersubjective contestation of need-interpretation, see also Seyla Benhabib, "The Generalized and the Concrete Other: The Kohlberg-Gilligan Controversy and Femi-

nist Theory," *Praxis International* 5 (1986): 402–424; Nancy Fraser, "Toward a Discourse Ethic of Solidarity," ibid., 425–429; and Thomas McCarthy, "Practical Discourse: On the Relation of Morality to Politics," in McCarthy, *Ideals and Illusions: On Reconstruction and Deconstruction in Contemporary Critical Theory* (Cambridge: MIT Press, 1991), 181–199.

10. On the difficulties with criterialist approaches, see Michael Williams, *Unnatural Doubts* (Princeton: Princeton University Press, 1996), chap. 3; and Joseph Heath, *Communicative Action and Rational Choice* (Cambridge: MIT Press, 2001), chap. 5.

11. Habermas has increasingly acknowledged the importance of empathy for discourse ethics [see "Morality, Society, Ethics: An Interview with Torben Hviid Nielsen," in *Justification and Application: Remarks on Discourse Ethics*, trans. C. Cronin (Cambridge: MIT Press, 1993), 174–175], and now speaks of "unrepressed openness to others' self-interpretations and situation-interpretations" ("Richtigkeit versus Wahrheit," 311). The need for this account is stressed by Matthias Iser in "Habermas on Virtue," in *Proceedings of the Twentieth World Congress of Philosophy*, vol. 7 (Bowling Green, Ohio: Philosophy Documentation Center, in press). Habermas's recent emphasis on empathy goes some way toward vaccinating discourse ethics against criticisms from Levinasians or Asian ethicists, to the effect that the responsibility of being competent lies with the listener, not the speaker [see June Ock Yum, "The Impact of Confucianism on Interpersonal Relationships and Communication Patterns in East Asia," *Communication Monograph* 55 (1988): 374–388].

12. Eliminating illusions from one's need-interpretations—and thus increasing one's need-interpretive competence—is typically the subject of what Habermas calls "therapeutic critique"; see *Theory of Communicative Action*, vol. 1, 20–21. Elijah Millgram usefully distinguishes the sort of conative state that deserves uptake in practical reasoning (what he calls "genuine desires") from mere whims, wishes, etc. in *Practical Induction* (Cambridge: Harvard University Press, 1997).

13. Taylor, "What Is Human Agency?" in *Human Agency and Language*, vol. 1 of *Philosophical Papers* (New York: Cambridge University Press, 1985), 37. For a further discussion of Taylor's views in this regard, see my "The Personal Lives of Strong Evaluators: Identity, Pluralism, and Ontology in Charles Taylor's Value Theory," *Constellations* 3 (1996): 17–38.

14. Habermas, *Theory of Communicative Action*, vol. 1, 92; see also ibid., 16–17, regarding the distinction between problematically "idiosyncratic" expressions of sensibilities and those that are "innovative."

15. See my "Starke Wertungen, Wünsche zweiter Ordnung und Intersubjektive Kritik: Überlegungen zum Begriff ethischer Autonomie," *Deutsche Zeitschrift für Philosophie* 42 (1994): 97–119.

16. On the separation of justificatory and motivational capacities, see Habermas, "Questions and Counterquestions," trans. J. Bohman, in *Habermas and Modernity*, ed. R. Bernstein (Cambridge: Polity Press, 1985), 214; "Moral Consciousness and Communicative Action," in *Moral Consciousness and Communicative Action*, 182; and "Morality and Ethical Life: Does Hegel's Critique of Kant Apply to Discourse Ethics?," ibid., 207–209. For formulations that suggest a more transformative model of practical discourse as personally liberating, see "Moral Development and Ego Identity," 78 and, very recently, "Richtigkeit versus Wahrheit," 312.

17. Habermas, "On the Pragmatic, the Ethical, and the Moral Employments of Practical Reason," in *Justification and Application*, 12.

18. On rigid personality structures, see David Shapiro, *Autonomy and Rigid Character* (New York: Basic Books, 1981). On how rape and torture can cut victims off from viewing their felt needs as supporting legitimate claims, see Axel Honneth, *The Struggle for Recognition: The Moral Grammar of Social Conflicts*, trans. J. Anderson (Cambridge: Polity Press, 1995), chap. 6; and Trudy Govier, "Self-Trust, Autonomy, and Self-Esteem," *Hypatia* 8 (1993): 99–120.

19. On the notion of having to switch to a different mode of interaction when certain presuppositions cannot be sustained, see especially Peter Strawson, "Freedom and Resentment," in *Freedom and Resentment and Other Essays* (London: Methuen, 1974), 1–25.

20. This distinction is not made clearly by Seyla Benhabib when she writes that "every communication with an infant counterfactually presupposes that that infant is a being who must be treated as if she had fully developed wants and intentions" ["In the Shadow of Aristotle and Hegel: Communicative Ethics and Current Controversies in Practical Philosophy," in *Situating the Self: Gender, Community and Postmodernism in Contemporary Ethics* (New York: Routledge, 1992), 58]. As an ethical stance toward those lacking need-interpretive competence, this seems to be largely right. But we must not confuse the ethical imperatives governing concrete contexts of interaction with the very different matter of the idealizing presuppositions necessary for engaging in discourse about the validity of a norm.

21. Habermas, "Reply to Symposium Participants, Benjamin N. Cardozo School of Law," in *Habermas on Law and Democracy: Critical Exchanges*, ed. M. Rosenfeld and A. Arato (Berkeley: University of California Press, 1998), 452 (hereafter cited as "Cardozo Reply"). The idea of referring to an assertion as a gamble is Michael Dummett's ["What Is a Theory of Meaning?" in *Truth and Meaning*, ed. G. Evans and J. McDowell (Oxford: Clarendon, 1976), 126.]

22. See Fraser's "Toward a Discourse Ethic of Solidarity" and "Struggle over Needs: Outline of a Socialist-Feminist Critical Theory of Late Capitalist Political Culture," in Fraser, *Unruly Practices: Power, Discourse, and Gender in Contemporary Social Theory* (Minneapolis: University of Minnesota Press, 1989), 161–190. For an excellent discussion of inequalities in deliberative political contexts, see James Bohman, *Public Deliberation: Pluralism, Complexity, and Democracy* (Cambridge: MIT Press, 1996), esp. chap. 3.

23. On advocatory discourse, which also applies to those who will be affected in the future but are not now, see Micha Brumlik, "Über die Ansprüche Ungeborener und Unmündiger: Wie advokatorisch ist die diskursive Ethik?" in *Moralität und Sittlichkeit: Das Problem Hegels und die Diskursethik*, ed. W. Kuhlmann (Frankfurt: Suhrkamp, 1986), 183–193. Decision making in representative democracies has similarities with advocatory discourse; see Habermas's *Between Facts and Norms: Contributions to a Discourse Theory of Law and Democracy*, trans. W. Rehg (Cambridge: MIT Press, 1996).

24. See, e.g., Honneth, *The Struggle for Recognition*; Karl-Otto Apel, *Diskurs und Verantwortung: Das Problem des Übergangs zur postkonventionellen Moral* (Frankfurt: Suhrkamp, 1988); and Bohman, *Public Deliberation*, esp. chap. 3.

25. Habermas, "Discourse Ethics," 67–68.

Joel Anderson

26.McCarthy, "Practical Discourse," 191. Cf. Habermas's concurring restatement of this in his "Replik," *Revue Internationale de Philosophie* 49 (1995): 557 (hereafter cited as "*Revue* Replik").

27. On the notion of the "space of reasons," see Sellars, "Empiricism and the Philosophy of Mind," in *Science, Perception, and Reality* (London: Routledge, 1963), pp. 140ff. John McDowell has done much to make articulate the force of this metaphor, e.g., in *Mind and World* (Cambridge: Harvard University Press, 1994), as has Charles Taylor in his talk of "horizons of value" in *Sources of the Self: The Making of Modern Identity* (Cambridge: Harvard University Press, 1989), part 1.

28. Habermas, "A Genealogical Analysis of the Cognitive Content of Morality," 42.

29. Robert B. Brandom, *Making It Explicit: Reasoning, Representing, and Discursive Commitment* (Cambridge: Harvard University Press, 1994), 230–231.

30. Michael Dummett, "Soll der Begriff der Wahrheit der fundamentale Begriff der Semantik sein?" interview by Sven Rosenkranz and Thomas Sturm, *Information Philosophie* (June 1996): 22–30, here 22. Dummett attributes the joke to P. G. Wodehouse.

31. McCarthy, "Practical Discourse," 192. See also Rehg, *Insight and Solidarity*, 54–55.

32. Habermas, "Reply," in A. Honneth and H. Joas, eds., *Communicative Action: Essays on Jürgen Habermas's "The Theory of Communicative Action,"* trans. J. Gains and D. L. Jones (Cambridge: Polity, 1991), 226, emphasis in the original (hereafter cited as "*Communicative Action* Reply").

33. Seel, "The Two Meanings of 'Communicative' Rationality: Remarks on Habermas's Critique of a Plural Concept of Reason," in *Communicative Action*, ed. Honneth and Joas 36–48. See also "Das Gute und das Richtige," in C. Menke and M. Seel, eds., *Zur Verteidigung der Vernunft gegen ihre Liebhaber und Verächter* (Frankfurt: Suhrkamp, 1993), 219–240.

34. McCarthy, "Legitimacy and Diversity: Dialectical Reflections on Analytical Distinctions," in Rosenfeld and Arato, eds., *Habermas on Law and Democracy*, 135.

35. Habermas, *Between Facts and Norms*, 322–326.

36. Habermas, "*Communicative Action* Reply," 215–222.

37. Habermas, "*Revue* Replik," 558. See also Davidson, "On the Very Idea of a Conceptual Scheme," in *Inquiries into Truth and Interpretation* (Oxford: Clarendon Press, 1984), 183–198.

38. Rehg, *Insight and Solidarity*, 156. On the contestability of the vocabulary for interpreting needs, see Habermas, "Remarks on Discourse Ethics," 58, 90, and 96–105 and *Between Facts and Norms*, 312–314; Fraser, "Struggle over Needs"; Richard Rorty, "Feminism and Pragmatism," *Michigan Quarterly Review* 30 (1991): 231–258; and Honneth, *The Struggle for Recognition*, 126–128.

39. Habermas, "Remarks on Discourse Ethics," in *Justification and Application*, 103–105.

40. Rehg, *Insight and Solidarity*, 243. Other writers on discourse ethics who have defended such a decentering appear to accept a loosening of the requirement that rational agreement must be "for the same reasons." See McCarthy, "Legitimacy and Diversity"; and Heath, *Communicative Action and Rational Choice*, chap. 6, sec. 4.

41. Habermas, "Some Further Clarifications of the Concept of Communicative Rationality," in *On the Pragmatics of Communication*, ed. M. Cooke (Cambridge: MIT Press, 1998), 328.

42. McCarthy, "Practical Discourse," 197.

43. McCarthy, "Kantian Constructivism and Reconstructivism: Rawls and Habermas in Dialogue," *Ethics* 105 (1994): 58. See also "Practical Discourse," 196; and "Legitimacy and Diversity," 146f.

44. McCarthy, ""Kantian Constructivism and Reconstructivism." Rawls's view can be found in *Political Liberalism* paperback edition (New York: Columbia University Press, 1996). See also his debate with Habermas (ibid., 372–434) and Habermas's contributions (*The Inclusion of the Other*, chap. 2–3).

45. Habermas, "Cardozo Reply," 395.

46. Habermas, "Cardozo Reply," 402; see also "*Revue* Replik," 558–559.

47. This is not to say that stability cannot be a relevant concern, but only that it should not be made foundational with regard to issues of legitimacy.

48. On the morality-ethics distinction, see esp. Habermas, "On the Pragmatic, Ethical, and Moral Employments of Practical Reason," in *Justification and Application*, 1–17.

49. Habermas, "Remarks on Discourse Ethics," 91.

50. Habermas, "Remarks on Discourse Ethics," 59, 91.

51. See, for example, Habermas, "Remarks on Discourse Ethics," 55–57.

52. See McCarthy, "On the Pragmatics of Communicative Reason," chap. 3 of David Couzens Hoy and Thomas McCarthy, *Critical Theory* (Cambridge, Mass.: Blackwell, 1994).

53. See Rehg, *Insight and Solidarity*, 102: "Moral norms have an internal relation to individual need interpretations, such that the values by which those norms are expressed—in terms of which they are internalized as 'needs'—lie along a continuum of values stretching from the more particular to the more universal."

54. See my "Überlegungen zum Begriff ethischer Autonomie," 117–119; and Rainer Forst, *Kontexte der Gerechtigkeit: Politische Philosophie jenseits von Liberalismus und Kommunitarismus* (Frankfurt: Suhrkamp, 1994), 393–395.

55. The example of taste in sweaters and cars is actually Habermas's, in a passage in which he seems to make the mistake of thinking that there is something about such questions involving "trivial preferences" that must be accommodated by refraining from criticism; see Habermas, "Employments of Practical Reason," 4. Closer to the

view I am defending is his discussion of "private autonomy" in *Between Facts and Norms*, 120. Cf. Elizabeth Anderson, *Value in Ethics and Economics* (Cambridge: Harvard University Press, 1993), 91–103.

56. For a parallel, see Allan Gibbard's discussion of "higher-order norms" in *Wise Choice, Apt Feelings: A Theory of Normative Judgment* (Oxford: Clarendon, 1990), 168–170. Note that there need be no regress here, since the supposition is not that all authority for expectations at level n comes from an expectation at level $n+1$.

57. See, e.g., Habermas, "Philosophy as Stand-In and Interpreter," in *Moral Consciousness and Communicative Action*, 1–20.

58. One very good model for this "web" is Brandom's discussion of the I-thou sociality underwriting the proprieties that govern deontic scorekeeping practices; see *Making It Explicit*, esp. chap. 9.

59. For discussion of earlier versions of this essay, I wish to thank Pablo De Greiff, Joseph Heath, Pauline Kleingeld, Kevin Olson, Christopher Zurn, William Rehg, and audience members at the 6th Critical Theory Roundtable in Toronto.

9

Into the Sunlight: A Pragmatic Account of the Self

M. Johanna Meehan

Liberalism once did the work of emancipation. But it was so influenced by a heritage of absolutistic claims that it invented the myth of 'The Individual' set over in dualistic separation against that which is called 'The Social.' It obscured the fact that these words are names for traits and capacities of human beings in the concrete. It transformed that which they actually name into entities by themselves. It thereby obscured, indeed prevented, recognition of the fact that actual realization of these traits and capacities depends upon the specific conditions under which human beings are born and in which they grow up.
—*John Dewey,* Philosophy of Education

Social cooperation requires the ongoing accomplishment, in ever changing circumstances, of stable meanings, an objective world known in common, a shared social world whose constitutive norms are recognized as legitimate, and individual identities capable of finding authentic expression.
—*Thomas McCarthy,* Ideals and Illusions

The Sleep of Reason Produces Monsters—The Dream of Reason Produces Monsters
—*Title of an Etching by Francisco Goya*

As I have listened to and read the work of Thomas McCarthy over the years, the phrase "into the sunlight" has echoed again and again in my mind like the words to a favorite song. I don't know where my mental trope originated, but the three words seem to capture for me the brightness of McCarthy's intellect, the quicksilver of his temperament, and the directness of his emotions. They also capture his ability to illuminate what other philosophers often seem to prefer to obscure. He has continued to eschew the rhetorical devices so common in Continental philosophy, constructing cogent arguments, and carefully identifying the presuppositions, the assumptions, and the often unacknowledged and unjustifiable ideals of those with whom he disagrees. The phrase also captures for me McCarthy's unabashed commitment to the emancipatory role of social political theory. In the last three decades, when postmodernism made rationality, subjectivity, and ideals of democratic consensus unfashionable, McCarthy has reminded his students and readers, that, in the last analysis, social theory minimally ought to be able to help us make sense of real people in the real world and maximally ought to be able to contribute to realizing a public sphere less marked by relations of domination and more directed by rational consensus. McCarthy's commitment to emancipatory social theory motivates his remarkable efforts to introduce American audiences to Jürgen Habermas's postwar critical theory, which warns that it is only the development of the modern capacity for communicative rationality and the institutions that embody it that stand between us and moral, social, technical, and political disaster. It was in that context that, with McCarthy's help, I first came to grips with Habermas's critical theory. In this opening part of my essay I recall the theoretical and personal context in which the questions driving this essay arose for me. It is these questions, which concern the constitution of the gendered self, that led me to the pragmatic conception of the self that I then sketch in the subsequent parts, before I conclude by drawing some broader implications for critical theory.

Like Habermas, McCarthy believes that reason is "embodied, culturally mediated, and interwoven with social practice, and that the embeddedness and variability of basic categories, principles, procedures and the like mean that the critique of reason has to be carried out in conjunction with social, cultural, and historical analysis."[1] Relinquishing Kantian pure reason as an artifact of an Enlightenment dream does not for McCarthy—again like Habermas—mean relinquishing rationality per se. In fact, central to McCarthy's philosophical commitments is the belief that "the social-practical analogues of Kant's ideas of reason are so embedded in our form of life as to make doing without them unimaginable, and undesirable."[2] McCarthy understands rationality as the human capacity to organize thought and experience in terms of ideas. Ideas and experience cannot be disconnected because ideas organize experience, though experience is not reducible to ideas. As Kant put it, they are regulative, but not constitutive, of experience.

To forget this and to attribute an ontological status to Reason or to its "Other" is to be guilty of the same metaphysical fallacy that Western philosophy has revisited time and again since Plato. To deny an ontological status to ideas, however, is not therefore to declare them unreal, but rather, to understand them as the "idealizing suppositions we cannot avoid making when attempting to arrive at mutual understanding—suppositions, for instance, of the intersubjective availability of an objectively real world, of the rational accountability of interaction partners, and of the context transcendence of claims to truth and moral rightness."[3] If we make the pragmatic turn that McCarthy recommends, the post-Enlightenment critique of reason shifts from a focus on abstract ideas to a focus on the social practices in which they are embedded. These practices can then be evaluated in light of the gap between, on the one hand, the regulative ideals that make those practices possible in the first place and, on the other hand, the social realities these practices make actual. Regulative ideals of reason generate what McCarthy terms the "'normative surplus' of meaning, which points beyond what we agree to here and now" and, to paraphrase Habermas, acts as "a thorn in the flesh of social reality."[4] Thus, our understanding that actual social and political conditions do not realize the aspirations shaped by our ideas fuels social critique and political movements.

Much of the feminist theorizing being published in the 1970s and in the 1980s when I was a doctoral student working with McCarthy sprang from the gap feminists identified between the ideals and aspirations of the social movements of the 1960s and the multiple and varied social practices that constituted women as irrational, essentially embodied, inferior, and Other. Feminists by the score were engaged in precisely the kind of theorizing McCarthy was defending. They criticized women's exclusions from jobs and professions, from schools and playing fields, from the Senate and the battlefield in the name of some abstract norm of justice, autonomy, or emancipation. Feminists made their arguments by pointing to the actual social practices that devalued women; they pointed to the way gendered language and its pretended universalism constituted men as the unmarked subject, women as the marked; to the gender-distinct requirements for bodily dress, adornment, and comportment; to the different behavioral expectations for nice girls and good boys, the sexual double standard; to the way the male gaze in advertising, film, and pornography constituted men as subjects and agents, and women as objects and passive reactants. As a young woman not always enchanted with the very male philosophical world I found myself part of or, as I felt more often, at the edges of, I was often convinced of the aptness of the feminists' descriptions of the practices and shared their convictions of the wrongness of the results. At the same time, I found myself rejecting their varied understanding of the roots or remedies of the gender injustices they described so well. It came to seem obvious to me (if not then to the sometimes philosophically skeptical, but always personally supportive, McCarthy) that my ever-deepening feminist commitments could be theoretically wed to my ever more deeply held critical theory commitments. I'd like to say that it was an immediately blissful relationship but in fact, like many fundamentally sound relationships, it has taken a lot of effort to make it work.

That critical theory did not rush to embrace feminism was not in itself something I viewed as a notable obstacle. Aside from some important exceptions, Marxist theorists were not enthusiastic either, yet feminists had successfully used Marxism as a theoretical framework. Simone de Beauvoir had managed to bend even the recalcitrant framework of Sartrean existentialism to useful feminist effect. Feminist defenders of liberalism have had to cope with a Western tradition that, as Susan Okin made clear in *Women and Western Political Thought*, was not very woman friendly.[5] Feminist psychoanalytic theorists haven't had it easy either. In addition to Freud's misogyny, they have had to respond to criticisms of the white, middle-class, heterosexual, privatistic slant of his theorizing, but still have managed to produce feminist masterpieces like Chodorow's *The Reproduction of Mothering*,[6] Gilligan's *In a Different Voice*,[7] and Benjamin's *The Bonds of Love*.[8] By the late 1980s, Foucault and even Lacan had been made to serve the feminist cause as well.

I knew all these texts because, while my male graduate student counterparts were beginning to work on dissertation proposals, I was reading and teaching all the books not taught in our graduate school program, searching for a theoretical paradigm that would make better sense of what I had come to know and think about justice, rationality, subjectivity, gender, and emancipation. To McCarthy's relief, I finally did write a proposal for a dissertation, clunkily entitled, "An Analysis and Critique of a Communicative Theory of Ethics." An inordinate number of years later, to McCarthy's even greater relief, I defended a dissertation with the equally clunky but different title, "An Analysis and Defense of a Communicative Theory of Ethics."[9] In the years between my proposal and defense, my confidence that McCarthy's pragmatic reading of Habermasian critical theory could serve my feminist theoretical and political interests grew.

Three things explain my continued theoretical commitments to Habermasian theory. The first is the absolute break it makes with the Western tradition's account of the subject as a monadological consciousness. Habermas embraces Marx's understanding that the self is intersubjectively constituted through linguistically mediated, historically rooted social relations. This seems to me to be a fundamental starting point for any effort to understand the sex/gender system,[10] the role power plays in organizing it, and the way it constitutes men as men and women as women. Second, Habermas's experience of national socialism had given rise to passionate normative commitments that satisfy my own sense of the importance of ethical theory in the face of both the positivism and the mania for consumption that marked the post-sixties social world. I also understand feminism to involve demands for more humane forms of life, demands that are political in form but often ethical in substance. Finally, I find Habermas's distinction between technical reason and communicative reason compelling. While I understand the link between reason and domination sketched by Weber, and then Adorno, Horkheimer, and Marcuse, on the one hand, and feminist theorists like Gilligan and Benjamin on the other, unlike many feminists I have been unwilling to view rationality as either inherently masculine or dominative. Habermas's distinction between strategic or instrumental reason and reason directed toward mutual understanding seems a way to retain critiques of modernity and masculinity that I find insightful, while still acknowledging reason to be integral to an emancipatory theory.

There were other features of Habermas's theory that were not attractive to me. Habermas's insistence that there is no subject prior to socialization opens a way to understand that gender identity is not just a behavioral overlay but implicated in the very constitution of subjectivity. But his gender-blind account of social role-taking fails to recognize that getting gender right—both in one's own identity constitution and performance and in interpreting the identity of others—is almost as fundamental a precondition for the intelligibility of speech and action as is mastering the other pragmatic rules coordinating intersubjectivity. Because social roles are gendered, the gender-blind standard of reciprocity that Habermas extrapolates from his analysis of reciprocal role-taking cannot be used to capture or reveal the complex power relations of men and women. Reciprocity, therefore, expresses an incomplete ideal of emancipation because the sex/gender system (like the race subsystem) enforces a distinction between males and females, such that the role of the differently gendered (or raced) is one that human beings are unable to fully grasp let alone take up.

A second problematic aspect of Habermas's account of the subject is that although he acknowledges the significance of the emotional/psychic relations of attachment as prerequisites for the ability to take up social roles, his emphasis on linguistic socialization makes it difficult to theorize the physical, affective, and psychic aspects of identity. The non- and prelinguistic aspects of socialization are crucial to accounts of gender formation.

A third feature of Habermas's account that seemed uncongenial to my feminist project was his increasing tendency to identify morality with rationality, rationality with postconventional moral reasoning, postconventional moral reasoning with legal norms, and legal norms with democracy. Such an account didn't seem to be able to address feminist critiques that were directed not only at issues of social justice but at men's ego failings as well, including the way in which inadequate development of emotional intelligence can blind men to their prejudices, dispose them to violence, and limit their relational capacities. How could an account that identified morality with rationality and legality address Gilligan's insistence that morality involves not just rationality and the universal principles it can arrive at, but affective and empathetic responses to particular and distinct human beings?

My dissertation was an attempt to answer these questions. In it I argued that Habermas's then recent work on the relation of morality and rationality, work that leaned heavily on the work of Kohlberg and Piaget, suggested that for morality the only aspect of the intersubjective constitution of the self that was important was the development of a specific form of principled reasoning. Such an account ignored the development of the empathetic and imaginative abilities integral to identity formation and to the exercise of full communicative rationality and morality. It also failed to thematize the intersubjective constitution of our psychic selves and the way that families, communities, and gender are fundamentally linked to the selves we become. Such accounts were not only consistent with the Habermasian project, but they were crucial to it. While McCarthy was tolerant of these views, and even Habermas acknowledged that they were in some ways legitimate, more doctrinaire Habermasians were often less receptive and much less gracious.

The central issues for my dissertation were the relationships of empathy, compassion, and moral imagination to rationality, autonomy, and discourse ethics. Yet while I was writing about the self and its identity and capacities for morality, the very notion of the self was under increasingly intense attack, particularly from the feminist quarter. These discussions tended to pit a notion of the self understood as a subject differently located in various discursive practices and regimes against a modernist conception of the self, figured as autonomous, reflective, and self-constituting. To many participants in the fray, it seemed not to matter that the battle lines had been drawn between, on the one side, a position committed to the emancipation of subjects its adherents didn't have the theoretical or normative resources to articulate or defend and, on the other side, an antiquated conception of the self that hasn't really been defended by anyone since the nineteenth century. At one job talk in which I explicated the idea that the self is intersubjectively constituted, I was taken to task for suggesting that the development of rationality was a historically contingent achievement. A week later, at a different school, I was chided for failing to recognize that the idea of the self is a fiction, one of power's many ruses. Though defending a pragmatic account of the intersubjective constitution of subjectivity has often put me between the proverbial rock and a hard place, I am still convinced that it is the right account and that it is one that can embrace the best insights of postmodernist accounts of the role of power in identity formation without relinquishing the recognition that human beings are selves and that rationality, empathy, domination, and recognition are capacities of such selves.

A Pragmatic Account of the Gendered Self

The pragmatic account of the self that I defend holds that the self is neither a mere discursive effect of power, nor is it freely autonomous. The self is constituted in and through complex psychic and social processes, but it is constituted as an agent that negotiates its identity intersubjectively within socially specified, shifting parameters. Gender is currently one aspect of self-identity. The process of self-constitution including the construction of gender is not best captured under the rubric of subjectification with its connotations of docile subjects who are the mere effects of power and lack internal coherence or continuity—an account favored in one form or another by many postmodernists. The self is better understood as continuously constituting and constituted, and thus always changing, though it is also in some ways the same as it always bring its past with it—albeit a past that is always being reinterpreted and thus always understood differently. The shape that the self takes—its characteristic and hence recognizable patterns, performances, and desires—results from its negotiations with physical, social, and psychic experience. The nature of the self I am describing can be illuminated by a dream I have had. In the dream I enter a room that I know I have been in before, though at the same time everything seems different. While I am there the shimmering translucent things in the room seem to shift and change so I can't really be sure it is the same room but I seem to know my way around. In the dream most of the room is vibrant and the colors are beautiful but the familiar and unfamiliar feel of the place makes me nervous and I am vaguely aware that there are dark corners full of shadows that also shift in an uncanny way. Like the room in my dream, the self as I conceptualize it is both the same over time and different: the same inasmuch as its past psychic constitution is taken up in the present, different because this past is shifted with every encounter. In other words, recognizable and characteristic aspects of the self are part of what negotiates the uptake and effect of the self's new experiences of itself and others. Because these negotiations are continuous and because they cause the self to shift and change in response to them, the self is always in the process of becoming and is to that extent discontinuous, but because already present and characteristic psychic aspects of the self negotiate these experiences, the self is also continuous and can experience itself to be so in its relations to itself and to specific others, to its body, and to the physical and social world. In the contemporary social world, one of the negotiated aspects of the self's identity is gender. The negotiations that produce the genderedness of our psychic and social identities are sometimes conscious and sometimes unconscious, sometimes deliberate and sometimes fortuitous; our genders are variously constructed and differently enacted in different social locations marked by shifting relations of power and expectations.

The process of the intersubjective forming of gendered selves minimally involves three analytically distinguishable but experientially mingled and ongoing self-constitutions. The first is the acquisition of a conscious and unconscious sense of bodily subjectivity, the second is the psychic sense of self that is established in socially saturated intersubjective relations, and the third is what I think of as cultural subjectivity. This last term refers to the subject positions that the individual can take up in actual social settings, in discourses, factual or fantasied. Each of these aspects of identity formation involve the individual's uptake of gender, but each also lays patterns that have an impact on the many other aspects of what makes us such different individuals, each of us uniquely different from anyone else. Identity is never finally established and thus self-constitution is never completed, except with death.

In some sense, identity does not begin with an individual's own birth either. Instead we are born into an ongoing human community with a history and with preestablished structures and meanings that we negotiate but do not invent, and often cannot change. It is for this reason that Hannah Arendt argues that we are the actors in, but not the authors of, our life story. In another sense, however, our identities begin with our conscious and unconscious processing of the sensual, cognitive, and emotional experiences of our bodies, our minds, and our emotions. These experiences are mediated by our relationship with others, their responses to us and ours to them. They are also mediated by particular human bodies and minds, whose physical condition they both made possible and affect. Any adequate account of the self must acknowledge the significant role of the body and mind, and of intimate emotional relationships, as well as the economic, social, and political conditions in which the self is constituted and maintained. In what follows I elucidate various aspects of what minimally must be included in a pragmatic account of the constitution of the gendered self.

Infancy and Childhood

Because the nature and experiences of the infant and child are so obviously important to the constitution of selfhood, it has always struck me as strange that philosophers have paid no real attention to these ontogenetic origins of subjectivity. None of them have really thought about babies. Some—Plato and Rousseau come quickly to mind— have reflected on the significance of children's education on identity formation, but their interest was in an already constituted social subject, albeit a still immature one. Hegel purported to be interested in the development of consciousness, but his pivotal accounts of the stages of development begin with adults, not infants. Until Freud, the origins of the self were not really theorized, and though Freud attributes much to infants and infancy, few of his claims seem to have been based on real study. Perhaps it is not surprising that the earliest theoretical work on infants and small children is that of Melanie Klein, Anna Freud, and Margaret Mahler, all women. Their monumental contributions to our understanding of the way infants come to be selves triggered a great deal of observation and theorizing about the development of human subjectivity from infancy through adulthood. Thus the best working description of the self I have found comes from this tradition. Infant researcher and psychoanalyst Daniel Stern argues that even if we can't agree what the self is:

As adults we have a very real sense of self that permeates daily social experience. It arises in many forms. There is the sense of self that is a single integrated body; there is the agent of actions, the experiencer of feelings, the maker of intentions, the architect of plans, the transposer of experience into language, the communicator and sharer of personal knowledge. Most often these senses of self reside out of awareness, like breathing, but they can be brought to and held in consciousness. We instinctively process our experiences in such a way that they can appear to belong to some kind of unique subjective organization that we commonly call a sense of self.[11]

This description suggests some of what must be explored when considering the constitution of the self: the ways in which selves come to be in complicated relations to their own bodies; the ways in which the infant self first experiences others semiprelinguistically, in virtue of its capacity for hearing; and the self-constitution that occurs through the conceptual and social apparatus of language, through cultural and individual fantasy represented in image and narrative.

The tradition of research that theorizes human subjectivity from infancy on has a great deal to teach us about the earliest stages of the intersubjective constitution of the self. I will first consider how one can integrate the empirical research on the earliest aspects of the organization of self (as rooted in mental and bodily capacities and realized only in social relations) into an account of a self constituted in and through socially and linguistically mediated relationships.

The Proto-Self

The first sense of self we develop is rooted in the experience of *our bodies* and in the cognitive processing of bodily sensation. Much of the integrative work important for establishing a coherent sense of self distinct from all others is, at this stage, biologically driven, though these organically rooted capacities are socially mediated in important ways.

M. Johanna Meehan

Claims about a prelinguistic organization of identity have been based on observations of infant responses and behaviors. This empirical evidence supports the claim that, in the absence of physical abnormalities, a rudimentary non-reflective sense of self begins developing in the early months of life. This preliminary experience of self provides a kind of organizational skeleton that will be filled out and layered over as the infant develops. From the earliest weeks of life, the biologically intact infant experiences a nonreflective unity of self and experience that is biologically driven, but socially mediated by the infant's caregiver. Research indicates that from birth on, infants are "predesigned to be able to perform a cross-modal transfer of information that permits them to recognize a correspondence across touch and vision."[12] In other words, infants are born with the capacity to unify the experiences of different and distinct sensations. After sucking on a previously unseen particularly textured nipple, infants could visually identify the nipple: they were able to translate oral sensation into visual representation. At three weeks, infants can match light intensity with sound intensity, can match auditory temporal patterns and visual temporal patterns, and can imitate an adult sticking out his or her tongue. At two days, infants can imitate smiling, frowning, or surprised looking adult models. Without "knowing" they have a face, or what their expressions look like, and without having a cognitive grasp of "imitation," two-day-old infants can act as agents of their own bodies, and distinguish self from other enough to make self resemble other.

Perceptions and sensations provoke feeling states in infants, much in the way hearing music or watching dance provokes feelings in adults. These feeling states can be associated cross-modally so that the child that experiences the patting of a soothing mother at the same time as the voice saying "there, there" perceives not two caregivers, a patting one and a vocalizing one, but one "soothing vitality affective mother." Thus cross-modal unification of sensation lays the ground for not only a unified self that experiences itself as one entity experiencing in two different modalities, but for grasping other selves as unified as well, though they too are experienced across different modes.[13] Thus the self's ability to unify across sensation makes possible a preliminary unification of the other, as well as the preliminary experience of a unified self.

This account of the self's origins is very unlike ones offered by many developmental and psychoanalytic theorists. Though these too view the construction of the self, or the ego, as a project initiated at birth, they see it as realized in the context of a never completely resolved conflict between the needs of attachment to and separation from the original and compelling power of the infant-mother bond. These accounts posit an infant whose self-identity is initially merged with that of its primary caregiver; thus the infant advances from a state of original oneness to a state of separateness. This model makes the achievement of identity an intrapsychic accomplishment of the infant, a position that is not supported by empirical studies, which indicate that infants experience the distinctness of self and other early on. The only model of development consonant with the empirical data is an intersubjective one that recognizes both the biological and social/psychic processes of self-formation. Furthermore, the intrapsychic view makes it impossible to distinguish being merged with another from being in a relationship with another. Relationship can never be viewed as something accomplished over time between two distinct selves in an intersubjective process. Thus, in this account, relationship is always a threat to the achievement of identity through separation. A very different understanding of self/other relationships and their inherent difficulties follows from the intersubjective account of the formation of the self.

The Psychic Self

Though the human infant is biologically equipped to become a self, this biologically rooted possibility can only be realized intersubjectively in psychically sustaining relationships with others. That selfhood and indeed life itself cannot be sustained in the absence of these relationships was first made clear by René Spitz's essay "Hospitalism." It described in wrenching detail the psychic and physical damage sustained by institutionalized newborn infants who were physically cared for but deprived of ongoing emotional connection with a caretaker. He found that, if emotional starvation continues for more than three months, eye and motor coordination deteriorates, a frozenness of expression develops, and rocking and headbanging ensue followed by withdrawal and increasing listlessness, and eventual refusal or inability to eat. Of the children Spitz observed, one third of them had died by the end of the second year. Of the children who did survive, few could sit, stand, walk, or talk at age four. Spitz argued that what caused this profound developmental retardation was not just a lack of perceptual or tactile stimulation. "We believe," he wrote, "that they suffer because their perceptual world is emptied of human partners, that their isolation cuts them off from any stimulation by any persons who could signify mother-representatives for the child at this age. The result . . . is a complete restriction of psychic capacity by the end of the first year."[14] Spitz's findings make dramatically clear that self-formation is dramatically dependent on attachment relationships.

William Fairbairn's clinical work with abused children prompted him to conclude, against Freud and Klein, that it is not the drives toward pleasure and away from pain that are most fundamental to human infants, but rather those directed to the establishing of attachment relationships.[15] The reason is that no coherent sense of self or other could be sustained in the absence of such relationships, leaving the child alone and in unendurable solitude. He found that a maintenance of attachment was so critical for abused children to be able to construct a sense of themselves, that they had to split off the good in the parent to have a parent to whom they could remain attached, leaving the bad parent to be internalized as part of themselves. Anna Freud theorized that children's acceptance of their own badness results from the child's internalization of an abusing parent, through which the child identifies not with himself as the child victim, but with the powerful aggressor parent. In part this is done because to identify with the child victim would be just too psychically painful, but also because constructing a self-identity and not being left alone requires a sense of a coherent parental other. A parent who is both good and bad is experienced as incoherent, and thus as not fully present. The behavioral discontinuities that undercut experiencing the necessary other as present are erased by ascribing the badness not to the parent, who can then be retained as the needed loving other, but to the child whose badness can then be understood as causing the abuse. The child thus sustains a relationship with the parent who is necessary for selfhood to be sustained by constructing a self whose consistent badness accounts for the parent's abuse.[16]

In the complete absence of an attachment that good parenting makes possible, experience of others is entirely incoherent and no unified sense of self can emerge. Thus extreme abuse or lack of attachment caused by extended institutionalization, for example, can result in children who seem to lack the coherent subjectivity that make conscience possible. Some of these children can only briefly gather their psychic fragments around a multiplicity of shifting identities, borrowed from acquaintances, television and movie characters, or even strangers.

Thus the self is a psychic derivation made possible by biology but made real only in attachment relationships with other human beings. This is because a self becomes a self through a process of assimilating and "using" selves outside itself, splitting them into good, bad, desired, or repudiated, taking such parts, whether real or imagined, and either identifying with them or projecting them back onto their source or onto other selves. This does not occur in any simple way. First, the external other must be distinguished from the fantasized other, though the self may confuse or deny this distinction. Second, external others are not typically imported as complete entities. Indeed, in such cases, one might argue that a real self is not formed, but a false self is incorporated instead; normally bits and pieces of the real or fantasized other are incorporated into the already existing but ever changing self. Mere interaction between selves is not relationship. It is for this reason that babies require more than casual interaction with human beings taking care of their bodily needs. Relationship requires an awareness of the other that arises neither from projection nor repudiation. It is possible only when the I and the other recognize each other to be fully external and therefore not to be assimilated to themselves. Benjamin describes this as recognizing that the other is "an equivalent center of destruction."[17] That is, both selves must recognize that just as I am distinct from your mental fantasy of me, so too you are distinct from my mental fantasy of you, that is, the actual other must be distinguished from the intrapsychic other.

M. Johanna Meehan

Benjamin's description reveals the extent to which recognition, despite its psychic rewards, can involve a struggle between two separate wills. While Spitz, Fairbairn, and Anna Freud had made clear that the self needs to experience the reality of an independently existing other, Benjamin, following Winnicott, reminds us that the self's awareness that it is not alone brings at the same moment the awareness of the possibility of mutual recognition and relationship and the awareness that it may be opposed, limited, or denied. This tension between the need for the independent existence of others and the threat that their independence signifies is a tension that inheres in all relationships, a tension expressed in the self's need both to recognize and to deny the extrapsychic existence of the other. When the balance tips in favor of recognition, the other is recognized as a "like subject," as a being apart from my projections and repudiations of it. When the balance tips the other way, the self views the other, whether positively or negatively, in the delusive fantasies of a romantic crush or in the lethal politics of sexism, racism, or homophobia, as a split-off part of the self to be consumed or destroyed.

It is crucial to understand that in Benjamin's account negation, breakdown, and repair are viewed neither as obstacles to mutual recognition nor as opposed to it, but as essential aspects of its achievement. They are necessary because our way of being in relation to others is to use them intrapsychically and to relate to them as outside others. When we take up the other in fantasy, we are always negating them as real others, even when we idealize them. As Benjamin puts it, "from the intersubjective standpoint, all fantasy is the negation of the real other, whether its content is negative or idealized—just as from the intrapsychic view, external reality is simply that which is internalized in fantasy."[18] Thus intersubjectivity always involves a struggle between recognition of an unassimilated other and the omnipotent assimilation of the other to the self's fantasy of it. Our urge to omnipotence drives assimilating fantasy, our need for an external other drives recognition. The need for separation is expressed in bids to omnipotence, driving the self to domination and inviting the other to submit, resist, struggle, or retaliate. The need for relation, the dissolution of separation, can motivate relationship but can also motivate assimilation, domination, or submission. This dynamic of intersubjectivity, the struggle between self/other, separation/connection, recognition/assimilative domination is part of the fabric of the human psyche and hence a feature of all relationship. Thus it is impossible even in the most harmonious relationships to "take the sting from the encounter with otherness."[19]

If the self's origins are rooted in the biological nature of the human organism and then realized in the crucible of (an always socially, and thus, linguistically) mediated intersubjectivity, how is gender to be understood, and how do human beings become gendered?

Culture and the Gendering of the Self

Accounts of gender tend to fall into some version of the following three: either gender is viewed as identical to sex and the differences ascribed to human females and males are attributed to biology; gender is held to be a psychic identification with masculinity or femininity resulting from the conditioning of individuals to take up social roles organized around a distinction drawn on the basis of biology; or gender is seen to be a discursive effect of power. To my mind, none of these accounts does justice to the complexity of the meaning of human gender or to the processes by which human beings come to be or to enact a gender.

Just as biology plays a role in the ability of human beings to become selves, I believe biology—that is, hormones, breasts, penises, wombs, vaginas, and so on—is not wholly unrelated to gender. But just as the constitution of the self is only made possible by human biology but requires intersubjectivity for its realization, so too gender is made real and acquires its meaning and significance only in and through relationships with others. Because human meaning is symbolically expressed and transformed, gender is rooted in psyche, informed by fantasy, mediated by symbolic systems, and regulated by power in a variety of forms.

Like all aspects of self-formation, gender involves a coming to terms with real differences mediated by fantasy, and with fantasied differences articulated individually and socially. While the earliest distinction an infant must make in the process of becoming a self is that between self and other, culture and the relationships in which culture is specifically refracted demand that children master another distinction as well, that captured by the binaries of male/female and masculine/feminine. Children are born into a social world that views selves as gendered, ascribes one gender or another to them, conceives of gender in a host of often contradictory ways, and in different settings rewards or sanctions different gender performances differently. How gendering contours different selves, how the meaning of gender is elaborated in and through selves that are continuously being formed and reformed depends on a host of psychic, individual, and cultural confluences and practices. The fully pragmatic account to which I am committed does not view gender to be a mere discursive effect of power. It views gender as a cultural collection of meanings loosely attached to anatomical differences that are made more or less real in the psychic contouring of shifting selves and embodied in social practices or, to use the language of Foucault, in power/knowledge regimes.

How does the gendering of the self happen? Just as most human beings achieve selfhood in the context of intimate relationships, gender identity too is first negotiated in relationships with others with whom children have intense affective relationships. This should not be taken to mean that psychic relations with intimate others are outside culture or preserved from the social meanings ascribed to gender. The understanding and enacting of genders, and the conscious and unconscious beliefs about the child's gender on the part of the adults and the older children with whom the child emotionally interacts, are personally negotiated but culturally saturated. Because the self is formed in the context of intimate relationships with others whose own identities are the shifting results of intersubjective relationships, inter- and intrapsychic fantasy, individual temperament, and the like, there is no family outside culture, or culture unmediated by individuals, families, and individual and/or social fantasy (what Castoriadis called the social imaginary).

The content of children's understanding of gender shifts and changes with age. Psychoanalysts have found that gender first becomes truly salient to the child just as the child's speaking abilities explode. The child begins to be aware of itself as an intentional willing agent—just as it is becoming more aware that the other, on whom it physically and emotionally depends, is separate from it and can thwart its will. The simultaneity of these developments and the fact that it is usually with women that infants experience their first intense emotional bonds turn out to be very significant to the emotions associated with femaleness and maleness. This is because "the struggle to differentiate becomes fatefully intertwined with the consolidation of gender identity."[20]

The tantrums so typical of the two- or three-year-old child are struggles to assert its will, but such assertion is important because it is in desiring to have or do something that a child discovers its subjectivity. It is in willfulness that children discover themselves to be distinct from others and in so doing, discover difference, plurality, and opposition. When the parent says no to some trifling thing, the child's sense of self is clarified precisely by the experience of opposition. Because the child experiences this "no" as an attempt to obliterate its will, its identity is suddenly brought clearly into focus. It is for this reason that the parent's "no" provokes such rage. From the child's perspective, what is at stake is not a bath, or a toy, or drinking milk. The parental "no" is a refusal of recognition, a denial of the child's independent selfhood. The parent is experienced as a powerful, dominating other who in failing to accept the child's bid for domination, fails to recognize the child as an autonomous being. Both male and female children engage in these nursery struggles, and if identity were not gendered, the outcomes of these struggles would not be imbricated in the structure of gender. Identity in our world is gendered, however, and wars in the nursery are most often between women and children. Women are what must be separated from, but precisely because of children's dependence on them, it is from women that it is most difficult to be separated. Existing as a self distinct from the mother is as threatening as is the possibility of maternal engulfment: if she is not me, then I am alone, if she is all, then I do not exist.

Boys may use maleness as a way of asserting an identity distinct from women on whom they are emotionally dependent. If this maleness is viewed as a difference disallowing identification with any aspects of a female caregiver, femaleness comes to be viewed not just as different from maleness, but in opposition to it and thus threatening to it. The more heightened the difference between the culturally mandated performances of maleness and femaleness, the more heightened this opposition and the greater the threat that femaleness poses to maleness. With the experience of threat comes anxiety that can provoke hostility, contempt, and aggression.

Girls too engage in a struggle to separate from female caregivers and assert their independence. While they can assert difference on many fronts including unruliness in relation to gender norms, they cannot appeal to a conventionally recognizable sex difference. This does not mean that the struggle for independence will be less intense than that of boys, or the resolution more harmonious—just the opposite is possible—but it does mean that the anxiety and hostility provoked by the struggle for autonomy does not play itself out along the axis of gender in quite the same way. Femaleness per se is not as often opposed to masculinity per se and thus misogyny is not as frequently the outcome of a girl's struggle, though it can be. Any number of girls grow to be women who feel contempt and loathing for other women and overly esteem and value maleness.

For both girls and boys the female caregiver is a figure in relation to which ambivalence about connection and independence is enacted. A mother that is too close threatens to smother and destroy the independence that the child struggles to establish. But a mother that is experienced as too distant provokes frightening feelings of abandonment. Complicating the child's task and contributing to its volatility are both the emotional intensity of the mother-child bond and the effects of the patriarchal positioning of women as less than fully autonomous agents. Irigaray argues that since heterosexual gender identity constructs femaleness as an identity achieved through the desire of a male, the child finds it difficult to grasp the mother's independent subjectivity. Children understand that in the context of current heterosexual gender arrangements, women's identity, like their desire, is refracted through the prism of male desire, male names, male identity. But the child has a further reason for refusing to recognize the mother's independent subjectivity, namely the defensive desire to protect its own subjectivity from threat. In addition to limiting the threat posed by a truly external and potentially hostile or abandoning other, this defensive attitude also allows the child to retain the mother as a place to which to return when the desire to be independent and autonomous gives way to the desire for security and nurturance. Max, the boy hero of Maurice Sendak's much beloved children's book, *Where the Wild Things Are,* can go and be king of the wild things safe in the intuitive grasp that he isn't likely to meet his mother there enacting the wild desires of her independently existing subjectivity. She will be safely in the place to which he returns, her identity fully expressed in being his mother and fulfilling his desires, that is, keeping his dinner warm and waiting for him.[21]

But what about men? What role do they play for children in their struggles with the psychic twins, autonomy and connection? How do children psychically take the meaning of maleness embedded in the psychic and social imaginary? In the traditional families that are the subject of the heterosexual middle-class narratives of stories, films, and television plots, men have typically played the role of the exciting figures—figures that are interesting and sometimes frightening— figures more clear of the intense emotional shoals of the nursery than are women. Both girls and boys turn to these exciting male figures as outside others who might be useful in supporting their efforts to become subjects. By identifying with male figures and recreating their characteristics and exploits both actually and in fantasy, children open up a space of difference between themselves and the emotionally entangled figures of the nursery. For boys this process of identification can embrace a shared gender, for girls identification can be thoroughgoing but gender difference creates an often-uneasy divide between the girl child and the male with whom she identifies. Even when a girl is warmly supported in her bid to identify with a male figure, someone who allows her to imagine herself as him despite her different gender, it remains a precarious business for her to establish in reality the subjectivity she achieved in fantasy by identification—especially as the heterosexual positionings implicit to current gender constructions become more salient during and after puberty. Even before puberty, conventional gender arrangements can abruptly undercut her fantasies of sameness. I remember watching just this happen to a small girl in Chicago's O'Hare Airport. She was giggling happily as she walked behind her father, imitating the way he swung the small suitcase he was carrying. All was well until they reached the restroom doors and socially mandated difference interrupted her fantasy of sameness. She was dragged off to the women's room with her mother and had to relinquish her dad to her older brother who of course could use the men's restroom with him. While a girl can use a positive relationship with a male to support her in imagining herself playing like he does, thinking like he does, and winning like he does, heterosexual gender positioning requires that when it comes to viewing herself as a heterosexual sexual being, she identify not with his desire and thus not with his sexual subjectivity, but rather with those whom he desires, with women, those who are not themselves viewed as desiring agents but as the objects of male desire.

Fantasy plays a crucial role in the development of the self and it is crucially important to the gendering of the self. We can see its importance if we examine children's play, something Bronwyn Davies has studied extensively. She found that in play the nuances and ambiguities of actual gender performance are eclipsed by highly stylized narratives that exaggerate the oppositional content of masculinity and femininity. Analyses of children's play, the fantasy narratives that structure it, and children's responses to stories read to them make it clear that for children "male power equals domination in public spaces, particularly of females but also of smaller boys. Their power relies heavily on the use of violent symbols such as guns and fire."[22] In order to position themselves as recognizably masculine, boys must at least occasionally engage in the play that is culturally sanctioned as signifying maleness. While girls are occasionally drafted to play victims, a significant percentage of the violent shooting, hitting, burning, destroy-or-save games boys play are enacted with and against other boys. In the narratives of the boys' fantasy as it unfolds on many playgrounds around the world, one can discover that

> . . . the forms of discourse, the emotions and the bodily state that is required to participate in the narrative from the position of power have become something known. These boys know well the feelings and the narratives that go with power. They are good at it and they clearly enjoy it. It was the form of dominant masculinity that many of the children called on to interpret the stories that I read to them and . . . even if the form of masculinity is not achievable in one's own behavior, it constitutes an ideal through which the category male and its relation to the category female will be understood.[23]

In the boys' narratives, boys and men can act from positions of power and can act powerfully. Play mediates reality in the minds of children; thus little boys use these narratives in the service of establishing subjectivity through fantasized identifications. Through enacting these narratives in play, boys learn the feelings, attitudes, and strategies necessary for positioning themselves as powerful subjects. In the boys' fantasies, females play the supporting cast, the romantic interests, the victims of violence, or the vulnerable maidens to be rescued through the benevolent heroism of males.

While girls were allocated positions of weakness in boys' play, the girls Davies observed did enact narratives in which they dominated. These were primarily domestic narratives of motherhood, housewifery, and to a lesser extent that of sexual or romantic love. Boys who wanted to play house or dolls with girls had to be willing to play the supporting cast. The power that devolves upon girls via their domestic power is not experienced as power in the same ways as boys experience power in the violent shooting, burning, and hitting fantasies they enact. The power of the wife and mother, particularly in the middle and upper classes, "is only legitimately expressed in forms of persuasion. Naked power battles are taken as an expression that she has failed as a mother."[24] Mothers are expected to be nice and loving to their children and husbands even as they exercise control over how things are done. Thus even if girls physically discipline other children or dolls as they play house, it is legitimated by appeals to love and order. The unwillingness of grown women to use physical force except to protect another person, particularly a child, points to the extent to which femininity is understood as agency expressed in the care of others and not in self-assertion.

Girls' exercise of power in their representations of domesticity is also limited because the narratives of motherhood and household administration in which girls dominate are cast within the broader narrative of heterosexual romance and marriage in which men are the controlling agents. Thus in children's play, domestic narratives involving home and children are inextricably bound to narratives of beauty and romantic and sexual love. The subversive feminist children's story *The Paper Bag Princess* plays on this in its opening lines, "Elizabeth was a beautiful princess. She lived in a castle and had expensive clothes. She was going to marry a prince named Ronald." As Davies points out, the usual resolution of a story that begins this way is for the princess to achieve a domestic space of her own (usually with staff) through the agency of a male rescuer. Cinderella, because she is found beautiful and feminine, gets her prince and a castle. Snow White, through the agency of the woodsman, moves from her father's castle to the dwarfs' cottage, then to the absolute passivity of "sleep," and finally to the arms of her prince who also provides a castle. Davies discovered that very few of the children she talked to seemed to think that the prince's worthiness of a girl's love was an important part of the romance-domesticity fantasy. Elizabeth, the paper bag princess, decides that a prince who only estimates her worth on the basis of her appearance, and who cannot love and appreciate her merely because she is wearing a paper bag, is not worth having. Thus she rejects him and "does not get married after all." The children Davies interviewed thought that the book ended wrongly and offered new endings in which Elizabeth tidied up, bought new clothes, and married the unworthy Ronald after all. (One child did think Ronald should be made to apologize before the wedding.)[25]

It is interesting to note that in four recent Disney retellings of classic children's stories, *Beauty and the Beast, The Little Mermaid, The Hunchback of Notre Dame,* and *Pocahontas,* the "prince" is required to demonstrate not only traditional heroic characteristics, but also tenderness and affection toward the heroine. The heroines in these remakes are also sporadically positioned as bold and daring agents, albeit within the parameters of still easily recognizable girl positionings. In *The Little Mermaid,* for example, though the little mermaid Ariel initially positions herself as a desiring agent in active pursuit of her prince, she is forced (by a more powerful, but less desirable and thus spiteful older woman) to sacrifice her agency, figured in this movie by her compellingly beautiful voice. As a result, she must wait to be appreciatively noticed by him, that is, she must become the object of his desires, thus recouping the expected gender positionings.

The highly stylized fantasies of the narratives that constitute children's play obviously echo the literary culture of children, the stories read to them at home and school. In these stories, the princess is always beautiful, princes never need to be rescued, the bad guys are always bad, the good guys always good, and most of the guys are definitely still guys. Boys come to see themselves, at least ideally, in the cultural fantasy of masculinity, positioned as physically or agentially powerful beings, whereas girls learn that what power they can exercise has to be obtained via a male agent, a father, a prince, a dwarf, a kindly woodsman. These discourses have an extraordinary impact on children's ideas about the content of gender identity. Children have been known to declare that girls can only be nurses and men doctors, despite themselves having a mother who is a physician; to insist that boys are stronger than girls, despite obvious and present counter examples; or to maintain that only women can take care of babies, no matter that their actual experiences belie the truth of such claims.

Children who feel constrained by and unhappy with the discursive descriptions of masculine and feminine, or with the way traditional discourses position them, can attempt to negotiate new discourses and new positions that better suit their version of gender. But this is a difficult task. Children, like all members of the social world, are constrained by the demand that they demonstrate social competence, that is, the ability to navigate through the social world by getting things, at least the essential things, right. One of the earliest and most important things that must be gotten right is gender. One cannot by fiat completely rewrite the gender script, for social interaction is made possible by the implicit know-how of social actors. Identities that are not based on an asymmetric gender dualism require not only new performances and new discourses in which personhood can be constituted, but something much trickier—the recognition and thus the legitimation of those performances by others. The need for social recognition and legitimation means that new performances and new discourses require concerted social and political shifts in the social imaginary. One may perhaps imagine such possibilities privately, but one cannot institute them singlehandedly.

While absolutely novel gender performances are often met with lack of recognition or acceptance, and often with violence—one need only think of Teena Brandon—every individual interpretively constructs his or her gender by psychically identifying with specific men and women, introjecting some aspects of them, and repudiating other aspects. Every human being responds differently to the social fantasy, which gives gender its content, taking it up, interpreting it, repudiating it, or taking it as an ideal. Although gender has thus far been constitutive of a fundamental aspect of the selfhood of all historically recorded people, each individual has a unique version. An individual's gender-identity arises from the shifting contents of a social imaginary whose available contents change with one's social locatedness; from the individual psyche with its unique desires configured in intimate relations and by the broader social world; and finally, from the structuring of disciplinary powers which legitimate the narratives that not only sustain socially dominant fantasied contents of gender by legitimating some subject positions in cultural and political narrative and delegitimating others, but that also punish social incompetence and prevent gender rebellion.

The Personal, the Political, and the Future

The pragmatic account of the gendered self that I offer understands human identity to be constituted by biological beings whose intimate relationships, particularly those of childhood, are crucial to the individual's psychic structure, the meanings of his or her emotions and responses. Equally crucial, however, are our relations to culture and the intersubjective relations that are constitutive of our relationship with culture. These interactions reconstruct, deconstruct, and shift other psychic contents. The discursive narratives that are expressions of the social imaginary both enable and limit the meanings we ascribe to selves, to identities, to gender. The disciplinary apparatus of the social world, from the taunts of small children on the school yard, to the murderous rage of those who kill gender transgressors, to the schools, hospitals, churches, and courts of law, patrol the borders for those whose desires violate accepted social norms, making it difficult to shift the content of what is accepted. It is for this reason that change vis-à-vis the content of the meaning of identities is most effectively undertaken by political movements initiated by those who have imagined the possibility of different narratives, different subject positions, and different fantasies.

It is not just contradictions in the normative claims of a society that make cultural and political change possible. Social change is also brought about by shifts in the social imaginary that make it possible for political movements to grow to include more than the handful of people who first articulate another vision of what could be the real. Just as a little girl can identify with her father or a male hero (a skill girls must learn early on, given that almost 80 percent of children's books have a male protagonist), so too can we imaginatively identify across race, gender, and age, with a fictional social reality, with what is not but might be. Despite the contradictions that such identifications produce between the self one understands oneself to be within the parameters of what is socially tolerated, and the self one imagines oneself capable of becoming, that imagined identity is thenceforth part of who one is and may play a more or less important part in the person one becomes. Martin Luther King appealed to just such imaginative identification when he invoked a dream world of racial integration in the face of an actual world where the racial other is too often the fantastical creature of fear and hatred. He appealed not just to the contradictions in our norms of equality and our racist practices but also to an alternative narrative of a yet-to-be-made-real subjectivity.

While psychic identifications with fantasy can produce the impetus for emancipatory social movements, they can also produce dreams of omnipotence, of obliterating those imagined as "other," of the thousand-year Reich, white supremacy and the Aryan Nation, of masculinity as domination and femininity as submission. Technical rationality orchestrated the nightmare of the death camps, but it was fueled by a fantasy of omnipotence, the dream of establishing a fantastical "pure" German volk, as masters of the master race.[26] Fantasy (like rationality), whether that of the individual or the collective, is not necessarily directed toward either the benign or the destructive.

How then can we even know why dreams of reason can produce monsters and how reason can make peace with our dreams?[27] Habermas has given us an answer to the first question. Because instrumental reason can be effectively employed to any end, the fact that its development has led to ever more efficient means of destruction is unsurprising. Only when we understand that reason is Janus-faced and distinguish communicative rationality from instrumental rationality will we be able to locate the link between reason and emancipation. Having identified this link, leftist political theory undertakes to lay out the institutional means of achieving communicative rationality, and to reveal the social/economic/political obstacles to its achievement, among which is the domination of communicative rationality by instrumental rationality. What Habermas has not done is to answer the question of the relation of communicative rationality to the other parts of our psychic selves—our emotions, desires, fantasies, and fears.

When Habermas made the linguistic turn in an effort to escape all the shortcomings of the philosophy of consciousness, he did it so thoroughly that the self he described originated in and through relationships that were not just linguistically saturated but were themselves linguistic. The self he describes is not just a self whose identity is accessible only through the mediation of language, it is a self that is wholly linguistic. Although Habermas may be able to argue that communicative action is directed toward mutual understanding, and although he can offer an account of the institutional procedures that would make it a social possibility, he is unable to explain either the origins of the murderous ends that instrumental reason has been made to serve or the psychic motivations for choosing to engage in practices of communicative rationality. We must not stop with the question of why human beings should choose to be Habermasian subjects rather than the lords of death that they can just as easily desire to be. More fundamentally, we must ask how one conceptualizes the kind of selves that can so easily have both of these desires.

I have not yet decided what kind of difference it would make to Habermas's political project as a whole if he were to recognize the inadequacies of the linguistic self and embrace the kind of model of the self I propose. It is possible, and I suspect even likely, that much of it would remain as it is. His main focus as a social theorist has been to clarify the legal and political institutions that preserve democracy. Following Hannah Arendt, in whose understanding of political power he locates the inspiration for his distinction between instrumental and communicative rationality, Habermas understands the goal of democracy to be the preservation of human plurality through the establishment of conditions in which differences can flourish because normative agreements are reached that preserve the interests of all. The end of these institutions is the creation of what Arendt would have described as a world, a shared space that both gathers and separates us, bringing us into a relationship regulated by communicative norms that limit the fantasized assimilation of the other.

While Habermas believes that the development of social institutions grounded in communicative rationality are the best hope for the realization of the political conditions that allow for intersubjective relationships, like Arendt he is not always sanguine about the possibility of our creating such a world. Thomas McCarthy has spent a good part of his intellectual life defending the emancipatory ideals that he is well aware may never be realized. It is for this reason that McCarthy's insistence that we must continue to focus on their possibility has never seemed naïve or shallow, but is instead a refusal to succumb to a mood of despair, a refusal to live in a world where "the best have lost all hope." While my intellectual interests and commitments have diverged from McCarthy's to some extent, I am deeply indebted to him as a mentor and a friend. As a mentor, he offered lessons not just in critical theory, but in intellectual and personal integrity; as a friend he lent them a special humor and grace. As I have been writing this paper, I have come to understand that the light of the sun that I associate with McCarthy is neither the light of reason nor that of normativity, but the light radiated by human decency. I am grateful to have had the experience of it.

Notes

1. Thomas McCarthy, *Ideals and Illusions* (Cambridge: MIT Press, 1991), 1.

2. McCarthy, *Ideals and Illusions*, 2.

3. McCarthy, *Ideals and Illusions*, 3.

4. McCarthy, *Ideals and Illusions*, 5; cf. Jürgen Habermas, *Postmetaphysical Thinking*, trans. W. M. Hohengarten (Cambridge: MIT Press, 1992), 47.

5. Susan Moller Okin, *Women in Western Political Thought* (Princeton: Princeton University Press, 1979).

6. Nancy Chodorow, *The Reproduction of Mothering* (Berkeley: University of California Press, 1978).

7. Carol Gilligan, *In a Different Voice* (Cambridge: Harvard University Press, 1982).

8. Jessica Benjamin, *The Bonds of Love: Psychoanalysis, Feminism, and the Problem of Domination* (New York: Pantheon, 1988).

9. Johanna Meehan, "Justice and the Good Life: An Analysis and Defense of a Communicative Theory of Ethics" (Ph.D. diss., Boston University, 1989).

10. This is the appellation coined by Gayle Rubin in her groundbreaking 1975 article "The Traffic in Women: Notes on the 'Political Economy' of Sex," in *Feminist Theory: A Reader*, ed. W. Kolmar and F. Bartokowski (London: Mayfield, 1999), 228–244.

11. Daniel Stern, *The Interpersonal World of the Infant* (New York: Basic, 1985), 6.

12. Ibid., 48.

13. Ibid., 59.

14. René Spitz, "Hospitalism: An Inquiry into the Genesis of Psychiatric Conditions in Early Childhood," *The Psychoanalytic Study of the Child*, 1 (1945), 68.

15. W. Ronald Fairbairn, "The Repression and the Return of Bad Objects (with Special Reference to the 'War Neuroses')," *Psychoanalytic Studies of the Personality* (London: Tavistock, 1952), 59–81.

16. Anna Freud, *Ego and Mechanisms of Defence*, trans. C. Barnes (New York: International Universities Press, 1946).

17. Jessica Benjamin, "Recognition and Destruction: An Outline of Intersubjectivity," *Like Subjects, Love Objects* (New Haven: Yale University Press, 1995), 28.

18. Ibid., 45.

19. Ibid., 47.

20. Benjamin, *Like Subjects, Love Objects*, 120.

21. See Maurice Sendak, *Where the Wild Things Are* (New York: Scholastic, 1963); Luce Irigaray, "This Sex which Is Not One," trans. C. Reeder, in *New French Feminisms*, ed. E. Marks and I. de Courtivron (New York: Schocken, 1981), 99–106.

22. Bronwyn Davies, *Frogs and Snails and Feminist Tales: Preschool Children and Gender* (Sydney, Australia: Allen and Unwin, 1989), 91.

23. Ibid., 109.

24. Ibid., 78.

25. See Robert N. Munsch, *The Paper Bag Princess* (Toronto: Annick, 1980).

26. Charles Mills, *The Racial Contract* (Ithaca: Cornell University Press, 1997), 66.

27. David Couzens Hoy and Thomas McCarthy preface their book *Critical Theory* (Cambridge, Mass.: Blackwell, 1994) with a discussion of Francisco Goya's painting. In it they lay out the argument that the Enlightenment conflated instrumental rationality with communicative rationality and thus failed to understand that the dream of reason could produce the myriad disasters of the twentieth century.

10

Mutual Recognition and the Work of the Negative[1]

Joel Whitebook

1   Introduction: The Truth Content of Hobbesianism

Hobbesianism was not entirely wrong—despite what the new inter-subjectivist orthodoxy would have us believe. While there is no doubt that the intersubjective turn was a decisive event in the development of social and political philosophy, something important is missed when the mode of theorizing that preceded it is rejected *in toto*. Indeed, now that intersubjectivism threatens to become the dominant theoretical bias of our day—which is as uncritically adhered to and confidently brandished as the Hobbesianism that it replaced—there is reason for concern. My aim in this essay is therefore to loosen the grip that the intersubjective paradigm has on the current theoretical imagination. This in turn will allow us to retrieve some of the truth content of Hobbesianism that has been lost along the way. Here I construe Hobbesianism broadly, as the approach that takes isolated, naturally driven, asocial, and strategically oriented individuals as its basic constituents.

Although my broader critique is directed against central proponents of the intersubjectivist program in the critical theory camp, Karl-Otto Apel and Jürgen Habermas, I will focus on the work of Axel Honneth. His thinking is more internally conflicted and therefore more open with respect to the questions I'm concerned with. Moreover, Honneth is one of the only critical theorists who is still actively engaged with psychoanalysis. And his attempt to link it with an intersubjective position—this is one of the sources of the tensions—makes Honneth's work relevant to my project of redirecting critical theory toward a psychoanalytically oriented anthropology that would combine the empirical findings of the human sciences with philosophical reflection. After setting out the broader theoretical context in this section, I will turn to Honneth's discussions of Hegel and Mead. And then in the conclusion I will return to the broader issues.[2]

Within critical theory, the self-confidence of the intersubjectivist approach has largely resulted from the interpretive scheme, adopted by Apel and Habermas, that models itself on the history of science in the Kuhnian mode and conceptualizes the history of Western philosophy as a series of paradigm shifts. According to their view, the three major paradigms of philosophy are ontology, the philosophy of consciousness [*Bewusstseinsphilosophie*] or of the subject [*Subjektphilosophie*], and the philosophy of language.[3] However, as Dieter Henrich has argued, the application of the Kuhnian approach to the history of philosophy tends to be overly schematic and misleading.[4] Unlike natural science, philosophy does not progress in such a way that a later position represents an unequivocal advance over an earlier one. Earlier philosophical positions may not therefore simply be relegated to "the mere prehistory of truth."[5] Rather than being "solved" with the move to a new paradigm, perennial philosophical problems typically emerge transfigured in a different theoretical context. For example, the question of the unity of substance in the ontology paradigm is first reconfigured as the unity of the subject in the consciousness paradigm and then as the unity of the speaker (or language community) in the linguistic. The preemptory rhetoric of paradigm shifts—with its temptation to use dismissive epithets rather than arguments to reject legitimate objections—often obscures these displacements, thus giving rise to the impression that the earlier problem has in fact been dealt with. This, in turn, has the effect of suppressing and evading serious challenges.[6]

Hegel—who might be viewed as the first philosopher of paradigm shifts—was aware of this problem and tried to exploit the polysemy of the German term *Aufhebung* to address it. As is well known, the term not only has the connotation of negating, superseding and surpassing, but also of lifting up and preserving. Hegel used these different meanings to introduce a distinction between abstract and concrete negation: whereas the former simply nullifies or abrogates an earlier paradigm, the latter takes up and preserves its truth content and tries to do justice to it in a more adequate way. Put in Hegelian language, my thesis is the following. Despite his warning against an "undialectical rejection of subjectivity,"[7] Habermas's move from a monological to a dialogical position—which has been at the heart of his program since its inception—often amounts to an abstract negation. Because of this false overcoming, the truth content of what I am calling Hobbesianism is often lost, and certain fundamental difficulties are avoided. However, before describing that truth content in greater detail, let me say something about the rationalism behind Habermas's intersubjectivist view.

There are three interconnected and problematic politico-philosophical reasons for the Habermasians' tenacious defense of the "strong intersubjectivist" program.[8] (1) In spite of everything we have learnt about the depths of human irrationality and destructiveness—theoretically from thinkers like Nietzsche and Freud and historically from the events of the past century—they want to defend the traditional philosophical notion that a human being is essentially a rational animal, a *zoon logikon*. I suspect they believe that the establishment of this rationalist conceit can serve as an effective prophylactic against further barbarity. (2) The rationality claim in turn requires the defense of another thesis: namely, "the per se social character of the self."[9] Unless the self is socially, that is to say, intersubjectively constituted all the way down, the status of the rational animal is seen to be in jeopardy. There is a tendency therefore to systematically deny the existence of any pre- and extrasocial dimension of the self. Again, as in the traditional conception, the Habermasians think that the *zoon logikon* and the *zoon politikon* go together. (3) Finally, the Habermasians see these first two points—which radically mitigate the positive role of the irrational in human affairs—as necessary philosophical and anthropological presuppositions for a political program of radical democracy. It is not self-evident, however, that this assumption is correct even logically, much less politically. But, beyond this, there is a more significant problem. These presuppositions lead to a restricted vision of democracy. As Jonathan Lear has articulated, there is a far more interesting question to be examined: how can one "both take human irrationality seriously and participate in a democratic ideal"?[10] An answer to this question can help us to avoid two equally one-sided positions that play a significant role in the current scene, namely, postmodernism, with its skepticism toward democracy, and left Rawlsianism, with its rather pallid defense of it.

The Habermasian emphasis on communicative rationality and sociability contrasts sharply with the Hobbesianism defined above. The latter conception is typically criticized for mistaking the conditions prevailing in modern capitalist society for the human condition per se. The war of all against all doesn't represent the situation in a state of nature, but in the capitalist market. And I in no way want to deny the validity and force of these criticisms.

There is, nevertheless, a truth in Hobbesianism that often drops out of sight in the move to the intersubjectivist position. For capitalism didn't create human egoism, aggression, and acquisitiveness; the potential for these forces was always there as part of our anthropological and psychological makeup. Capitalism only set them free from traditional constraints so that they could expand in a relatively unhindered way. Almost without exception, premodern societies understood the human capacity for aggression and acquisitiveness and the threat it posed to their traditional forms of ethical life based on communal (intersubjective) solidarity. They therefore sought to keep it in tight check. Thus they strove to keep the economy firmly "embedded," as Karl Polanyi put it, within a larger institutional framework, so that economic concerns would always remain strictly subordinated to—and contained by—larger religious, communal, and political values.[11] An essential feature of the emergence of modern society was precisely the "disembedding" of the economy from the larger institutional framework, which is to say, the emancipation of the capitalist market. This, in turn, had the effect of unleashing human acquisitiveness and aggression in the way premodern societies had feared. Indeed, it has taken place on a scale they could hardly have imagined.

There are two points I want to make about this phenomenon, both of which run counter to received left-liberal opinion. The first is that human aggression—which I will later subsume under the larger category of negativity—is not simply the by-product of an irrational social order (or unenlightened childrearing), which could be eliminated in a more enlightened society (or family formation). It is indeed "a piece of unconquerable nature"[12]—though perhaps not in the way Freud meant—that every society, past and future, must "take into account"[13] and attempt to come to terms with in its own way. To be sure, there are forms of society that encourage its expression and those that inhibit it—but it can never be eliminated.

My second point is that the unleashing of aggression accompanying the emancipation of the market is a disturbingly ambiguous phenomenon. I do not need to convince anyone of the destruction modern societies have visited on the globe. What needs to be stressed, however, is the amount of creativity—in science, art, technology, philosophy, law, and even in the economy—engendered when "all that is solid melts into air." Indeed, it is not implausible to suggest that in modernity the magnitude of creativity and destructiveness has been equal. The daunting problem is how to retain the former without the latter. From radical ecologists to neofundamentalists there are those who would sacrifice the dynamism and creativity and return to a more contained form of existence. But, even if that were desirable—which I don't think it is—it's probably impossible. The genie is out of the bottle.

2 Hegel and the Struggle for Recognition

Both Habermas and, following him, Honneth returned to the writings of the young Hegel in an attempt to recapture some of the lost intuitions of the Jena period. Despite the obvious inadequacies of these early writings, they see something less rigidified, and therefore potentially more fertile—and also something more materialistic—in Hegel's work before the *Phenomenology of Spirit*. Habermas offered an account of the relative advantages of the *Jungendschriften* in his own early and important programmatic essay "Labor and Interaction: Remarks on Hegel's Jena Philosophy of Mind."[14] His thesis was that, by the time Hegel wrote *The Phenomenology*, his thinking had consolidated into a monistic idealism that saw Spirit as the sole subject of development. The different heterogeneous realms of history had come to be understood as emanations of this monistic subject. In contrast, an internally differentiated naturalism or materialism, bearing striking similarities to the Marx of the 1844 Manuscripts, characterized Hegel's thinking during the Jena period. According to this scheme, history unfolds through the interaction of three "equally original," which is to say, heterogeneous and irreducible "media,"[15] namely, language, labor, and interaction. Spirit is seen, not as the subject of development but as itself the product of the workings of actual history.

Habermas returned to the Jena writings to try and recapture the intuitions of the young Hegel and correct some errors of the latter's mature work. And with the help of postmetaphysical philosophy and the social sciences, he attempted to recast those ideas from the Jena period into an intersubjective form of critical theory. In a somewhat complicated genealogical scheme, Honneth returns to the same Jena writings in an attempt to revive the spirit of the early Habermas's conception of critical theory—which Honneth believes was lost along the way. As he tells us, he had become dissatisfied with "the direction in which Habermas himself pursued his original idea, employing universal pragmatics as the theoretical means for analyzing the normative presuppositions of social interaction."[16] In Honneth's opinion, as Habermas's theory matured, the dimension of everyday experience, psychic life, the body, and, most importantly, (individual and collective) struggle—all of which were dismissively subsumed under the epithet "praxis philosophy"—increasingly dropped out of Habermas's theory.[17]

Moreover, the struggle for recognition represents for Honneth an attempt to preserve the truth-content of Hobbesianism, just as it did for Hegel. (I will argue that Honneth doesn't go far enough.) He argues that "the exceptional, even unique place" of Hegel's Jena writings derives from the fact that he "appropriated Hobbes's model of interpersonal struggle"[18] and used it against him in his immanent critique of Hobbes's position. More precisely, Hegel's original move in modern political philosophy consisted in retaining the notion of struggle from Hobbes, while simultaneously detaching it from its atomistic, anti-Aristotelian presuppositions in order to give it a new meaning. Against Hobbes, Hegel argued that there is no way to de-

rive an adequate conception of association from a multitude of atomistic a- or antisocial individuals focused on self-preservation (construed in the wide sense); the best that could be gotten from that
starting point was a "mere heap." Furthermore—and this is Hegel's
decisive claim—a situation such as the one described by Hobbes
could never exist on its own but presupposes a form of supra-indi-
vidual intersubjective life [*Sittlichkeit*]. It does not represent an independent state of nature but a particular sphere of modern society
that was constituted by and presupposes its intersubjective institutions, that is to say, the modern system of property and law. The point
is that even atomistic individualism has its intersubjective presuppositions. Or to put it differently, even the Hobbesian state of nature—
like all forms of human life—is already a form of second nature and
has its Aristotelian presuppositions.

At the same time as Hegel uses the Aristotelian idea that the "existence of intersubjective obligations" is "a quasinatural precondition
for every process of human socialization" to break the atomistic
Hobbesian assumptions of modern political theory, he uses another
Aristotelian doctrine to help him appropriate Hobbes's theory of
struggle for his own purposes: namely, the "teleological process in
which an original substance gradually reaches its full development."[19] For Hegel accepted Aristotle's premise that a preexisting
form of ethical relations underlies every society, but he only accepted
it as a general assumption and provided it with his own distinctive
content. As they existed in premodern societies or in the modern
family, those *sittliche* relations are, he argued, simply natural or in-
themselves; their full ethical potentiality has not yet been developed
out of them. This requires the moment of difference—that is, the destruction of the given level of ethical equilibrium and the experience
of alterity—and the reestablishment of a more mature, differentiated
and self-conscious form of *Sittlichkeit* at a higher level of integration.
Unlike the natural law and social contract theorists, Hegel doesn't
have to explain "the genesis of mechanisms of community formation
in general"—communities are always already there. What he has to
account for, instead, is "the reorganization and expansion of embry-
onic forms of community into more encompassing relations of social
interaction."[20] To do this, Hegel must conceptualize the nature of

the original social substance in such a way that it not only already possesses an ethical nature, but that it also contains the potentiality and dynamic for further ethical development. This means it must contain both the potentiality for sociation and the potentiality for individuation. It is at this point that Hegel introduces the notion of recognition, as a constituent mechanism for both self- and community-formation.

On the recognition model, the subject does not comprise a need-bearing self with a preformed identity, which must be inserted into a social matrix, essentially external and/or antagonistic to it. Rather—and this is the key assertion—the self is intersubjectively constituted to begin with. A subject acquires articulated needs and an identity only by having its incipient needs—we will consider the crucial question of the incipient self later—and its capacities and qualities recognized by another. According to Honneth, this process of recognition has both an integrating and an individuating moment. That is, rather than being opposed to each other, socialization and individuation work in tandem. Insofar as an individual's recognition by the other represents a form of reconciliation between two subjects, it provides the basis for social cohesion—that is, sociation. But to the extent that a subject also "comes to know its own distinctive identity" by being recognized, "it comes to be opposed . . . to the other as something particular." Considered in this respect, recognition is a vehicle for individuation. Furthermore, the element of negativity that destabilizes any given state of ethical equilibrium, which is to say, the dynamic element, arises, Honneth argues, from inadequate recognition. "The reason why subjects have to move out of" the immediate "ethical relationships in which they find themselves is that they believe their particular identity to be insufficiently recognized." In other words, the injury and suffering that results from insufficient recognition propels individuals to abandon a given level of ethical life and struggle to create new relations in which their identities are more adequately acknowledged—a process Honneth calls a form of "moral-practical learning."[21]

It is true that the young Hegel appropriates Hobbes's claim that struggle is a basic fact of social life. However, as he did with Aristotle, he also radically reinterprets Hobbes's position. For Hobbes, the basic agon of social life involves "self-preservation," that is, the acquisitive and aggressive drives. For Hegel, in contrast, struggle pertains to "the intersubjective recognition of dimensions of human individuality," which is to say, to identity.[22]

Hegel first analyzed how the immediate solidarity and natural form of ethical relationship, found in the family and based on need and affect—that is to say, on love—passes over into the "unethical" realm of civil society, characterized by differentiation, cognition, and formal autonomy. He then set out to identify a higher, reflected, and uniquely modern form of *Sittlichkeit* that would overcome the one-sidedness of each of the previous phases. Because its "mode of recognition" would be "affect that has become rational," it would integrate intuition and insight.[23] And because it would combine individuality and solidarity, this reflected form of ethical life would represent a condition of differentiated unity that would preserve the elaborations of civil society. Honneth believes that the desideratum, which emerged from Hegel's unprecedented synthesis of Aristotelian and Hobbesian motifs during the Jena period, was basically sound. But he sees Hegel's claim to have found its fulfillment in the modern state as ideological and spurious. Honneth's project, therefore, is to drop the Hegelian mystifications and—using the resources of the social sciences—reinterpret the notions of the struggle for recognition and modern ethical life in terms of the contemporary historical and political problematic. He attempts, moreover, to go beyond both left-Rawlsianism and economistic Marxism and to integrate identity politics and communitarianism—into a political vision that is more robust than the liberal alternative.

As I said above, Honneth, like Habermas, believes that in important respects the *Phenomenology of Spirit* constitutes a regression behind "the extraordinary program that [Hegel] had pursued in ever new and always fragmentary versions in the Jena writings."[24] Not only does Hegel replace his proto-Marxian materialism with a *Geistmetaphysik* and severely restrict the scope of the struggle for recognition so that it only pertains to the lordship-bondage dialectic, but—perhaps most unfortunate of all—he backslides from his intersubjective approach to the philosophy of consciousness. I would argue, however, that the apparent return to the philosophy of consciousness—if, indeed,

Honneth's reading doesn't constitute an oversimplification of Hegel's aims in the *Phenomenology*—only counts as a regression if the intersubjective standpoint is taken as the standard against which all philosophical positions must be measured.[25] Viewed in a different light, Hegel's move has merit: it can be seen as an attempt to preserve the materialist and psychological truth content of the Hobbesian approach. Just as dropping the concept of love and the idealization of the Greeks after the Jena period marks the end of a certain youthful naiveté on Hegel's part, so the apparent return to the philosophy of consciousness might suggest a new sense of psychological and political realism.[26]

Indeed, if you didn't know better, you'd think that, in addition to studying Plato, Aristotle, Ferguson, and Smith, Hegel had also been reading Melanie Klein during his sojourn in Jena. For in the *Phenomenology*, self-consciousness appears to go through the whole repertoire of manic defense mechanisms—adumbrated by Mrs. Klein—in its attempt to maintain its omnipotent self-sufficiency and deny its dependency on, and the independence of, the object. Unlike the Jena writings, the necessity for mutual recognition in the *Phenomenology* is forced on self-consciousness when its omnipotent program breaks down. Because of the strength of the reality-denying force in self-consciousness—the "work of the negative"[27]—the struggle for recognition, as it is conceived in 1807, is much more conflictual—that is to say, much more of an agon, a struggle—than it is in the earlier writings. Honneth's use of the early Hegel as opposed to the Hegel of the *Phenomenology* (and his use of Mead as a source of reference as opposed to Freud) serves to radically reduce the conflictual nature, and therewith the intensity, of the struggle in the quest for recognition.

The first fact to be noted is that, in the *Phenomenology*, the struggle for recognition arises from the dynamics of Life and Desire. I take this as a clear indication on Hegel's part that the self and Spirit—subjectivity and intersubjectivity—have their unsurpassable fundaments in the biological substrata of human existence, a point that must not be forgotten. Moreover, as an emergent phenomenon of life, self-consciousness tenaciously manifests "being for-itself"—"closure"[28]—with respect to its surround, and a significant element of that for-itselfness will adhere to it through all of the later, more humanized or socialized *Aufhebungen* it will undergo. The rhetoric of interaction suggests, however, that because the subject is, to a large degree, inter-subjectively constituted, the self is already an interlocutor—a "being 'for-others,'" as André Green has suggested[29]—thus disregarding its significant dimension of closure and for-itselfness. Indeed, this may be the central fallacy of the intersubjectivist position. In contrast to the external or passive unity of the inanimate object, the living thing preserves its "self-identical independence," that is, its identity, by actively maintaining its boundary—its "shape" or "form" [*Gestalt*]—vis-à-vis the flux of the surrounding environment.[30] For Hegel, Desire emerges as a result of self-consciousness's "intention" [*Meinung*] to achieve and maintain its autarchic unity, its omnipotent self-sufficiency, with respect to "the independent object"—which, as something independent, can only appear as negative. Put in Kleinean terms, we can say that the object is "bad" simply in virtue of its independence. Self-consciousness can only affirm itself, then, by consuming the object: "Self-consciousness is thus certain of itself only by superseding this other that presents itself to self-consciousness as an independent life; self-consciousness is Desire. Certain of the nothingness of this other, it explicitly affirms that this nothingness is for it the truth of the other; it destroys the independent object and thereby gives itself the certainty of itself as true certainty, a certainty which has become explicit for self-consciousness itself in an objective manner."[31] In psychoanalytic terms, this can be likened to the oral-cannibalistic stage of development.

A glance at the French reception of Hegel is illuminating in this context. As Gadamer has recognized, there is a tendency in the French tradition of Hegel interpretation—that is, Kojève, Hyppolite, and Lacan—to play down the biological dimension as Hegel originally introduces it and to humanize or socialize Desire at an inappropriately early stage of its development. (Like the French, Habermas also tends to debiologize Hegel but for contrary reasons.) As Gadamer points out, the German term *Begierde* has strong "carnal" or appetitive connotations that are absent in the French term *désire*. Had Hegel wanted the connotations of the French term, Gadamer suggests, he would have used the German word *Verlangen*, which has more of the connotation of "yearning."[32] The choice of *désire* constituted a deliberate interpretative decision, which rested on substantive anthropological assumptions. As Hyppolite, who translated the *Phenomenology* into French, explicitly states, "We have translated *Begierde*, the word Hegel uses, as 'desire' [*désire*] rather than as 'appetite' [*appétite*]" because although "it merges initially with sensuous appetite, it carries a much wider meaning,"[33] namely, "the desire for the desire of the other." This claim is, however, inaccurate. Instead of saying, "it carries . . . " Hyppolite should have said "it comes to acquire a much wider meaning," for the specifically human desire for the other's desire only emerges out of the impasse of appetitive desire. (Whereas Desire as such is introduced in ¶168, the desire to be recognized by another doesn't emerge until ¶178.)[34]

There is something confusing about the French school's interpretation that needs to be sorted out. The radical aura surrounding French Hegelianism, which was in fact launched by a Russian émigré living in Paris—as well as "French Freud" that, via Lacan, is significantly derivative from it[35]—results from the following fact. In contrast to the Habermasian reading of Hegel, which stresses mutual recognition, the French tend to celebrate the centrality of desire and negativity rather than reconciliation and consensus—a tendency reinforced by the influence of Surrealism. Yet, at the same time as they emphasize negativity, they "dematerialize" or "intersubjectivize" desire; with Lacan, it becomes the desire of the recognition of the other.[36] Given French philosophy's penchant for the erotic, one might expect the negativity of Desire to derive, at least in the first instance, from bodily strivings. Instead, it arises from a purely psychosocial fact, namely, the impossibility of achieving mutual recognition owing to the inevitability of mis-cognition (*mésconnaissance*).[37] Thus, in their eagerness to avoid biologism, both the Habermasians and the French Hegelians (and Lacanians) move in the same direction, namely, sociologism.[38] But—and here's the twist—where Habermas turns to the social (and the linguistic) to soften the work of the negative, the French take the same approach to strengthen it.

Returning to the text of the *Phenomenology*, Hegel argues that the gratification of appetitive Desire is, by its very nature, transient and unsatisfying, unable to secure the plentitude and self-sufficiency that self-consciousness is after. For not long after the object has been consumed, Desire—hunger, privation, dissatisfaction—inevitably returns. Self-consciousness, in the form of appetitive desire, is embedded in the infinite circularity of the life cycle and therefore fated to repetitiously reproduce itself along with its object. The constant repetition of this experience—compare it with Freud's notion of the repeated "non-appearance of the breast"—constitutes an "education to reality."[39] Through it, self-consciousness comes to learn that the "essence of Desire" is outside of, "something other than," self-consciousness. In other words, it grasps "the independence of the object." This impasse, however, does not stop self-consciousness from pursuing its pure for-itselfness. Instead, a new condition emerges that must be fulfilled if self-consciousness is to advance in its program. Self-consciousness requires an object that can both be negated and abide—"that can cancel itself in such a fashion that it does not cease to exist"[40]—and only another self-consciousness can meet this condition. As self-consciousness, B, like A, has the ability to negate itself. But because it "effects the negation within itself,"[41] that is, volitionally, B is not annulled as a result of affirming, which is to say, recognizing A. It remains self-subsisting and can continue affirming A even while negating itself. "Self-consciousness," therefore, can achieve "its satisfaction only in another self-consciousness."[42] More specifically, "self-consciousness exists in and for itself when, and by the fact that, it so exists for another; that is, only as something that is recognized."[43]

I would like to call attention to three points at this juncture in the development. First, self-consciousness doesn't turn to another self-consciousness because of innate intersubjectivity or sociability, but because it is compelled to by the inner logic of its narcissistic program. Second, Hegel views the recognition of A by B as a self-negation on B's part. Recognition—at this point at least—appears to be a zero sum game: to recognize another is to deplete yourself. Third, in ¶ 177 Hegel provides us with a sketch of self-consciousness' further itinerary: "What still lies ahead for consciousness is the experience of what Spirit is," namely, "'I' that is 'We' and 'We' that is 'I.'" He tells us, moreover, that when it arrives at the level of Spirit, self-consciousness will "leave behind the colorful show of the sensuous here-and-now and the nightlike void of the supersensible beyond." That is, in achieving the standpoint of Spirit, self-consciousness will move beyond what, for Hegel, are the two aporetic alternatives within the philosophy of consciousness, namely, the false concreteness of empiricism and the airy ephemerality of Kantianism. But this is privileged information "for-us," that is, for Hegel and the reader of the *Phenomenology*. It is something that self-consciousness will have to discover through its own experience. Because of this situation, Honneth's claim that the *Phenomenology* represents a return to the philosophy of consciousness is simply inaccurate. The structure of the book indicates that "in the order of being"—or, "for-us"—Spirit (or intersubjectivity) has priority over consciousness (or subjectivity), but "in the order of knowing," consciousness and subjectivity still retains an important priority. Just as the child must go through a *Bildungsprozess* that will decenter its infantile omnipotence and locate itself in a social world, so through its Odyssey, self-consciousness must learn that it has its presuppositions in, and can only be satisfied through, Spirit. In other words, although Spirit may be a presupposition of consciousness, it has to learn this fact. And this requires a struggle.

The bind is, of course, that B desires to be recognized by A every bit as much as A does by B. Each would like to use the other as an object for its desires—as a narcissistic object—but cannot because the other "has an independent existence of its own." Monological or strategical "action by one side only would be useless because what is to happen can only be brought about by both." Hence, the necessity of mutual recognition: "They recognize themselves as mutually recognizing one another," Hegel explains.[44] We can once again see, however, that mutual recognition doesn't arise out of a prior experience of mutuality but is forced on the subjects by the inner dynamics of their monological experience. As with Hobbes's social contract and Freud's primal horde, insight into a structural impasse compels the subjects to mutually renounce their omnipotence and enter into a relationship with one another.

It would be a mistake to think, however, that this realization is achieved through civilized dialogue or by merely cognitive means. On the contrary, insight into the necessity of mutual recognition is the culmination of a learning process that begins in the most affectively charged way imaginable, namely, with a life-and-death struggle—not a Hobbesian struggle for self-preservation, but, as in the Jena writings, a struggle for identity. For Hegel, the fact that the subject is willing to risk its life shows that self-consciousness has transcended its attachment to mere *zoe*, in the Aristotelian sense, and is primarily concerned with identity. Indeed, self-consciousness's transcendent freedom consists in the fact that it can abstract itself from or negate "its objective mode."[45]

By emphasizing the work of the negative and the psyche's striving for omnipotence, however, I do not mean to be totalizing—or nihilistically celebrating—the role of power and conflict in human affairs, as Michel Foucault tended to do at one phase in his career. I do, however, want to stress another point. Not only are the omnipotent strivings of the psyche a major source of human destructiveness, but—in their tendency to reject the given world and their wish to fashion a counter-cosmos of their own—they are also a source of creativity. Although it isn't easy, we must resist the form of theoretical splitting that sees omnipotence as either all good or all bad. It is necessary, instead, to hold on to the idea that human destructiveness and human creativity have the same source in these omnipotent strivings. Psychoanalytically, there is no getting around the fact that the "lowest" and the "highest" in human life have their roots in the same soil. Left unsocialized and unmediated, omnipotence can lead to horrifying destructiveness and barbarity; sublated and sublimated, it can result in the most exalted creations of the human Spirit.

3 The Inadequacy of the "I" in Mead's Social Psychology

For systematic reasons, the topic of individuation, creativity, and spontaneity presents a formidable problem for the philosophy of intersubjectivity. These same reasons, moreover, continually threaten the linguistic approach with the danger of relativism, conservatism, and conventionalism. As we will see, this is not the case for the philosophy of the subject. Although the connection between the two may be contingent, the philosophy of the subject has generally been associated with the Enlightenment project of critique. For as Mark Sacks has observed, the philosophy of the subject envisions a "sharp dichotomy between the self and everything other than it"[46]; it thus pictures a self that can stand outside the world—outside any given traditional world—and evaluate it. And this capacity, in turn, has generally been viewed as a necessary anchorage point for critique.

This critical potential appears in at least two areas. First, with respect to social psychology, *Subjecktphilosophie* does not see the socialization process—in post-traditional societies, at least—reaching down into all the strata of the self; society is not, as Sacks puts it, "fully empowered to structure the individual."[47] Therefore it can count on a pre- or extrasocial dimension of the psyche that can react against the inevitable pressures to conform to the mores of the "tribe." Indeed, the counter-pressure exerted on the group by those who deviate from the statistical norm often acts as a source of dynamism, innovation, and creativity, without which societies would be stagnant. Second, with regard to normative deliberation, because the subject is deemed capable of divesting itself of all accidental empirical determinations, it can adjudicate "what counts as rational thought, what counts as a good reason, or as an end worth pursuing."[48] (The Husserlian epoché or a Rawlsian veil of ignorance are examples of this theoretical divestiture.) In other words, a transcendental self, in one form or another, has been seen as the necessary precondition for establishing the universally binding norms that are necessary for evaluating any actually existing normative state of affairs.

Whatever other advantages it might provide, however, the dialogical model offers "no such naked, core individual such that they could step back from all socio-cultural structuring as a free thinker."[49] This fact doesn't present a problem for the conservative representatives of the intersubjectivist tradition. On the contrary, they tend to see the idea of a thoroughly decontextualized self as not just mistaken—as a central error of the Enlightenment—but as invidious and potentially terrorist as well. Likewise, they have no trouble with the charge of relativism. For that is exactly their claim: no tradition-transcending standpoints exist, and, furthermore, rationality and the Enlightenment are themselves traditions. Their claim "can be captured by saying, simply, that there are only traditional societies."[50] However, for thinkers who want to pursue a strong intersubjectivist program and simultaneously remain faithful to the critical intentions of the Enlightenment, as the contemporary critical theorists do, these considerations present an enormous problem—that is, unless you are Richard Rorty. As Sacks puts it: "If the self, or at least the substantial self, is an intersubjective construct all the way down, the individual cannot transcend his or her socio-historical setting. There remains no trace of the Enlightenment self that can step out of the community in which it is embedded, taking its critical capacities with it, to make an independent judgment about that community. The norms of critical judgment would themselves have been left behind."[51]

With respect to the problem of normative validity, Habermas and Apel have attempted to provide a solution that is both audacious and unique. As opposed to varieties of hermeneuticists, communitarians, late Wittgensteinians, neopragmatists and so on, they try to maintain a position that is both intersubjective and universalist by relocating the source of normativity from the structure of consciousness to the pragmatic preconditions of intersubjective communication itself. However, by embracing the strong intersubjectivist program, they have inherited the problems concerning spontaneity and creativity that come along with it.

The difficulties become particularly perspicuous with Honneth, in large part, because—to his credit—he refuses to leave the claims of psychoanalysis behind as he pursues his communicative program. As we have seen, Honneth believes that the intuitions that animated Hegel's "extraordinary program"[52] of the Jena years were basically sound and his plan is to reinterpret them in a way that can be defended in today's postmetaphysical philosophical context. For him, this would mean reconstructing the development of the self and the ethical community as an intersubjective "inner-worldly process occurring under contingent conditions of human socialization," which is to say, "in the light of empirical social psychology."[53] And Mead's theory of socialization appears to fit the bill to a tee. Indeed, Honneth sees Mead—who had in fact studied philosophy and psychology in Berlin[54]—as attempting "to develop a nonspeculative solution to the problems of German Idealism."[55] Mead raises what for Honneth is "the essential psychological problem" concerning the formation of the self: namely, how can self-consciousness develop? "How," in other words, "can an individual get outside himself (experientially) in such a way as to become an object to himself?"[56] And Mead's answer, as is

well known, is that an individual accomplishes this by taking the attitude of the other—a process that occurs primarily in language. The
self is constituted, according to this model, through the internalization of the attitude of the generalized other, which takes on the character of an intrapsychic agency [*Instanz*], in Freud's sense. Mead calls
this the "me."[57] And when Mead tells us that the internalization of
the expectations of the generalized other—that is, of the demands of
the community—"builds up" the child's self and creates the "unity"
of the subject by giving him control of "his particular response[s],"[58]
it does in fact appear that society is dominant and the self ancillary.
Indeed, Tugendhat believes that the conformist implications of the
"me" are so strong that it "comes close to" Heidegger's concept of the
They (*das Man*).[59]

Mead's theoretical wish to assert the priority of the social factor in
the formation of the self, however, threatens to get him into trouble
politically. For, although he wants to stress the centrality of cooperation in social practice, Mead is no conservative communitarian who
can accept the possible traditionalist and conventionalist consequences of the intersubjectivist position. On the contrary, he was an
active progressive and sought to promote social and political experimentation and innovation.[60] To counteract the conventionalist tendencies of his theory of socialization and emphasis on the "me,"
Mead offers the theory of the "I." If the "me" comprises the intrapsychic institutionalization of society's demands and is hence a
major source of social homogeneity, then the "I" is the aspect of the
self that continually responds to the demands of the "me" in its own
idiosyncratic way. As such, it is a source of individuation. The main
question, as we shall see, concerns the source of those idiosyncratic
reactions.

The relationship between the "I" and the "me" can, moreover, be
more or less harmonious or conflictual within a given individual
and/or a given society. At one extreme is the conventional individual, whose "ideas are exactly the same as those of his neighbors," and
who is "hardly more than a 'me.'" At the other extreme we find "a
definite personality," who "replies to the organized attitude in a way
which makes a significant difference." In this case, the "I" is "the
more important phase of experience."[61] Similarly, traditional soci-

eties place greater emphasis on the integrative forces of the "we" and "individuality is constituted by the more or less perfect achievement of a given social type." By contrast, modern postconventional societies tend to regard individuality as "something more distinctive and singular"[62]; moreover, they often place a high premium on nonconformity.[63]

When the conflict between the "I" and "me" crosses a certain threshold and the demands of the "me" are experienced as painfully constricting or seen as unjust, the individual has three options: (1) accept the status quo, which can lead to ordinary everyday unhappiness or psychopathology; (2) attempt to transform oneself autoplastically through various forms of askesis or therapy; and (3) fight back by attempting to make the external world more hospitable to the demands of the individual's "I." It is the third alternative that interests us. When it is successful not only is the allosplastic solution generally the most gratifying for the individual, but it is also the one that can make the greatest contribution to the transformation of society.[64] For Mead, "leaders"—a concept that can include artists, politicians, thinkers, and religious prophets—are those individuals "who make the wider society a noticeably different society"[65] by dint of the impact of their "I" on the public sphere.

A sizeable gap between the "I" and the "me"—between the private world of the *kosmos idios* and the shared world of *kosmos koinos*—does not by itself, however, guarantee the emergence of a leader; it can just as easily result in severe psychopathology, that is, idiocy in the strict sense. Potential leaders must also possess considerable talent that allows them to articulate the private demands of their counter-*kosmoi* in the public arena in such a way that it resonates with the inchoate and frustrated yearnings of a significant segment of the community. On top of that, moreover, they generally need a healthy dose of phronesis. For they must have the social and political skills to promote their visions once they have been articulated into public works. This consideration gives some credence to the postmodern claim that "power" (i.e., "marketing") and not transcendent value determines which works become inscribed in the canon.

Though Mead obviously draws on the tradition of aesthetic expressivism,[66] he is no devotee of the romantic cult of genius. As a pragmatist and democrat, he is primarily concerned with the everyday creativity of the ordinary citizen. The model of the genius, or leader, is illuminating for him because, as an example of creativity writ large, it reveals the structure of the innovative potential of every citizen's "I" vis-à-vis the community. Leaders "are simply carrying" that potential "to the nth power."[67] In this regard, Mead's ideas invite comparison with Winnicott's important reflections on the capacity to live creatively, which the British analyst sees as an essential feature of psychic well being. For Winnicott, creative living—which is the opposite of "compliance," that is, submission to the "we"—results from the ability to invest quotidian experience with fantasy and thereby infuse it with vitality and meaning.[68] There is, however, a major difference between the two thinkers, and this difference points to the fundamental difficulty with Mead's concept of the "I." Whereas Winnicott offers a developed theory—which includes such concepts as transitional phenomena, primary creativity, the true self, play and so on—to provide an explanation of creativity, Mead does not. Charles Taylor is only exaggerating slightly when he says that "Mead's 'I' has no content of its own." After Mead has stressed the intersubjective constitution of the self, he "recognizes that this cannot be the whole story" and, as Taylor puts it, "that something in me must be capable of resisting or conforming" to the demands of the generalized other.[69] Mead's introduction of the "I" is supposed to account for this capability. But because this is not where the theoretical or polemical weight of his thinking lies—and because it would have unsettled his primary commitment to the intersubjective constitution of the self— the concept remains little more than an empty marker.

The indeterminate nature of "I" provides different interpreters of Mead with a wide margin to construe it to suit their own theoretical and political purposes.[70] It allows Honneth, for example—who originally acknowledged its ill-defined character—to steer Mead's theory in the direction of psychoanalysis. Thus, in *The Struggle for Recognition*, Honneth writes that the "I," which stands for "the sudden experience of a surge of inner impulses," has "something unclear and ambiguous about it." And, he goes on, "it is never immediately clear whether [those impulses] stem from presocial drives, the creative imagination, or the moral sensibility of one's own self."[71] In a more recent paper, however, he overlooks the ambiguity and claims that Mead's "I" is "hardly different from the 'unconscious' in psychoanalysis." It "is the agency of the human personality which is responsible for all impulsive and creative reaction and which as such is never able to reach the horizons of consciousness."[72]

If this claim were true, it would solve several central problems confronting Honneth's own theory. First, the assimilation of the "I" to the unconscious would allow the Meadian position, which Honneth wants to appropriate, to piggyback on the psychoanalytic account of motivation and creativity. And, second, the equation of the "I" and the "unconscious" makes it possible for Honneth to subtly insinuate the following entailment: if Mead has constructed a successful theory of the intersubjective constitution of the self, and if his concept of the "I" is equivalent to the unconscious, then there is no fundamental incompatibility between the psychoanalytic unconscious and an "intersubjectivity-theoretic approach."[73] A claim of this magnitude, however, must be demonstrated rather than simply implied.

Honneth explicitly situates his movement in a more psychoanalytic direction in the context of the long train of theorists who, in one way or another, have forecast "the end of the individual"—that is, Adorno, Marcuse, Foucault, and Luhmann. According to them, the dynamic of modernity leads to the inexorable absorption of the "I" into the impersonal collective, without remainder. Their predictions would indeed bring the "me" close to Heidegger's *das Man*, as Tugendhat suggested. Against this tradition, Honneth tells us he was trying to formulate a theory that would show why the "struggle for recognition cannot be silenced."[74] And in his attempt to construct such a theory, he turned "to a particular tradition of psychoanalytic theory," namely, the one represented by Castoriadis. Honneth believes that the central idea of Castoriadis's psychoanalytic social theory—namely, "the hypothesis of an enduring unconscious, which again and again confronts us with the fantasies of an unattainable reconciliation"—explains how "the individual's claim to recognition is anchored in every subject as an enduring motive which is continually capable of being activated."[75]

Whether or not the equation of the Meadian "I" with the Freudian id or unconscious can be textually validated—I don't think it can—

is of secondary importance. The important substantive question concerns the difficulties that a psychoanalytic reading of the "I" creates for the strong intersubjectivist program. But we do not have to go as far as Castoriadis, who probably takes the most uncompromising position on the question of omnipotence within psychoanalytic theory—or even to Freud, for that matter—to encounter the difficulties. Even with Winnicott's position, which Honneth uses extensively and sees as dovetailing with Mead's "intersubjectivity-theoretic approach," the problem of omnipotence—that is, the tendency to totalize one's position and deny recognition of the other—is still central. It is instructive to note that the intersubjective or relational psychoanalysts often use two of Winnicott's most important contributions to claim him for their position. The first is his famous aperçu that there is no infant without a mother. This means that the infant can only be understood in the context of its interaction with its caretaker and that Freud's use of the model of the autarchic ego to elucidate the earliest phases of development is severely deficient.[76] The second is his stunningly original theory of transitional phenomena, which pertains to the space between—that is "intra"—subjects. The claim, however, that Winnicott is a strong intersubjectivist, who has abandoned Freudian theory—with its Hobbesian tendencies—ignores a decisive point. The "good enough" mother and the transitional object allow the child to overcome its original state of omnipotence. Indeed, though the mother's ultimate task is to "disillusion the infant" in tolerable doses, she can succeed only if she has sufficiently "illusioned" it, that is, confirmed its experience of omnipotence in the first place.[77] Furthermore, the whole notion of the transitional object would not make sense without the presumption of an original state of omnipotence, for omnipotence is precisely the problem it is designed to address.

To his credit, Honneth doesn't make it easy on himself. In contrast to many intersubjective theorists and relational analysts, he makes it clear that he has no intention of eschewing the concept of omnipotence. On the contrary, he views the idea of an original undifferentiated state of development "as the specifically psychoanalytic contribution to the modern understanding of the subject." He believes, therefore, that "a lot of effort ought to go into refuting" the claim of contemporary infant researchers—notably, Daniel Stern—to have invalidated "the assumption of a primordial state of symbiosis."[78] (Again, intersubjectivist and relational psychoanalysts generally see Stern's research as a cornerstone of their position.) How, then, does Honneth try to reconcile the existence of a symbiotic phase, and its attendant sense of omnipotence, with his adherence to an intersubjectivist program? He does so by equating "symbiosis" with "a phase of undifferentiated intersubjectivity."[79]

In all fairness, this equation cannot simply be dismissed as a terminological subterfuge. The very nature of "the primal psychical situation"[80]—which must have its differentiated and undifferentiated dimensions—has forced its most important theorists to introduce paradoxical formulations. For example, Margaret Mahler refers to a "dual unity" and Hans Loewald to an ""undifferentiated psychic field"[81] in characterizing the earliest phase of development. Nevertheless, a number of distinctions must be insisted on, for Honneth's use of the term "intersubjectivity" smuggles in too much content. To begin with, "interaction" must be distinguished from "intersubjectivity."[82] The conflation of the two implies that subjects already exist when the baby and mother interact in this early phase, when the genesis of the subject is exactly what has to be explained.[83] Honneth in fact acknowledges as much when he notes that the purpose of the transitional object is to lessen the pain of separation that is part and parcel of "the emergence of intersubjectivity."[84]

Even more importantly, the use of the term "intersubjectivity" also implies that the initial phase is already a state of "sociability." To run these two concepts together would deprive the ideas of symbiosis and omnipotence of their reality-rejecting force, that is, their negativity. It would indeed constitute the situation, described by Green, where the intersubjective constitution of the self is thought to entail the consequence that it is essentially "for-us," that is, social per se. Again, as with the concept intersubjectivity, the emergence of sociability—"the accession of the individual ego to culture"[85]—has to be accounted for. Furthermore, Honneth's use of Mead's theory of internalization also mitigates the work of the negative in a way that Green cautions against. For Honneth, "the individual psyche" is understood "as an inwardly transposed communication structure."[86] The self is formed through the internalization of "communication relation[s]"[87] with the significant figures in the child's environment. They, in turn, become institutionalized, as it were, as the different agencies [*Instanzen*] of the psyche, and intrapsychic life is composed of the communication between them. On this view, the goal of development is not "efficient ego strength," but the "enrichment of the ego through a communicative loosening of inner life."[88]

Up to this point, I have no objections to Honneth's conceptualization of the self. Things become problematic, however, when he refers to this communicatively conceived ideal of psychic well being as the "intrapsychic capacity for dialogue [*Dialogfähigkeit*]."[89] Freud's use of the term notwithstanding, "communication" was already perhaps too imprecise to describe the interaction (or intercourse) between the agencies. But the assimilation of "communication" to "dialogue"—with its overtones of moderation, nonviolence, and symmetry—is downright misleading. Instead of the idea of a dialogue, Green uses the notion of a "polemic" to describe the interaction between the parts of the psyche. (He explicates it with the terminology of the topographical model, but this does not affect the basic point.) Psychoanalysis, Green argues, postulates a "psychic activity other than consciousness" that acts "in tandem with it." And "unlike the neutral ideality of symmetry," which informs a dialogical conception, psychoanalysis presupposes a "polemic between the two states, one being conscious, the other not, and sees them as struggling for power."[90] The ubiquity of intrapsychic polemics and power struggles—which makes up the stuff of everyday clinical experience and is a touchstone of the analytic conception—is simply not a systematic feature of Mead's social psychology. And when Honneth tries to integrate Meadian psychology and psychoanalysis, the pragmatist's dialogical commitments trump those polemical realities.

4 Conclusion

In conclusion, I want to return to the discussion of paradigm shifts in philosophy with which we began. As I have been arguing, the strong anti-Hobbesian current creates a constant theoretical pressure for the Habermasians to socialize the self all the way down, so that in one way or another the full existence of a prereflective or presocial intuition of the self is denied. The logical problem is parallel, whether we consider the theoretical or the psychological self. (This is why the conceptual conundrums of German Idealism reappear in infant research.) Thus, Habermas claims that the ability of the inter-subjectivist paradigm to eliminate the aporiai of self-consciousness, which plagued the philosophy of the subject, is one of the central advantages that favors its adoption. But this is one of the cases where the shift to the new paradigm simply results in a displacement of the problem. Indeed, the displacement seems so obvious that it is difficult to understand how Habermas denies it.

One way to formulate the aporiai of self-consciousness—which can be traced to Fichte's attempt to provide content to Kant's transcendental unity of apperception[91]—is as follows. The self is generally understood as that unique entity which is constituted by forming a representation of itself. This would mean that no self can exist before it takes itself as an object and forms such a representation. The very locution, "before it takes itself as an object," however, points to the problem: it presupposes a previously existing X—a preself of some sort—that could do the taking. But this is ruled out ex hypothesi—that is, unless you challenge the definition of the self as necessarily representational and argue for the existence of a prereflective or prerepresentational intuition of the self. By suggesting a form of non-representational acquaintance, however, this move appears to reintroduce a notion of intellectual intuition that would regress behind Kant's critical philosophy. Habermas, who is deeply suspicious of any hint of intellectual intuition, claims that because the communicative model explains the genesis of the self through interaction rather than self-reflection, the "problem is rendered pointless by a change of paradigm."[92] But the interactive paradigm presupposes an initial intuition of the self no less than the consciousness paradigm. For example, with Mead's conception, if assuming the attitude of the other generates the self, then there must already be an X, in some form, to do that assuming. That X must not only be able to take the perspective of the other, but also to pick out those features that count as part of itself when it has adopted that position. As Dews puts it, "interaction cannot generate" a self-relation; like self-reflection, it

Joel Whitebook

"presupposes the primary self-acquaintance at the core of self-consciousness."[93]

Habermas's response to this line of criticism is a strange act of simultaneous affirmation and denial, reminiscent of a famous story recounted by Freud. When a man is accused of having returned a kettle that he had borrowed in a broken condition, he offers the following surefire defense. First, he had returned it undamaged, second, the kettle already had a hole in it when he received it, and finally he had never borrowed it to begin with.[94] Similarly, Habermas seems to be saying both that there is no prelinguistic intuition of the self and that it is trivial. Consider, for example, this particularly tortured passage: "Prelinguistic subjectivity does not need to precede the relations-to-self that are posited through the structure of linguistic intersubjectivity . . . because everything that earns the name of subjectivity, even if it is a being-familiar-with-oneself, no matter how preliminary, is indebted to the unrelentingly individuating force possessed by the linguistic medium of formative processes."[95] It is not clear whether Habermas is making a factual statement claiming that all "being-familiar-with-oneself" is of a linguistic nature or a normative-transcendental statement concerning what should be dignified with the name of—that is to say, count as—subjectivity. The latter exercise would be close to the one Donald Davidson undertakes in his paper "Rational Animals," where he says he is not interested in addressing which beings are and are not rational—or the borderline case of the prelinguistic child—but only what the criterion is for rationality. (For Davidson it is the possession of propositional attitudes.)[96] But the transcendental question regarding the strict criterion for subjectivity is, on its own, of limited interest—especially to the postmetaphysical, naturalized, and psychoanalytically oriented social theorist. For, whatever the transcendental philosophers tell us, we know that empirically there is much that goes on before and alongside subjectivity in strictu sensu that is of enormous importance in human life.

That Habermas is primarily interested in the transcendental question is clear in the following passage: "By no means does this exclude prelinguistic roots of cognitive development for early childhood: even with primitive rule consciousness, a rudimentary relation-to-self must already develop itself. Such ontogenetic assumptions do not, however, prejudice the description of the function of metacognitive abilities at the developmental stage of the mastered mother tongue, where achievements of intelligence are already linguistically organized."[97] Here Habermas clearly acknowledges the existence of a "rudimentary relation-to-self." He then goes on to claim, however, that this assumption doesn't "prejudice"—a very fuzzy term indeed— our "metacognitive abilities," once we have acquired language and are within its circumference. (What about our first-level cognitive abilities?) But this claim ignores two crucial facts. First, researchers from a number of theoretical orientations have shown that the prelinguistic self must undergo an enormous amount of development simply to establish "the child as an interlocutor,"[98] who can enter into language in the first place. Furthermore, much of this development is distinctively non-cognitive and affective in nature—it is semiotic rather than symbolic, in Kristeva's sense of the terms.[99] Second, Habermas's claim assumes that this prelinguistic experience doesn't remain encoded in the mind and exert enormous force on linguistic structures after language has been acquired. But this goes against psychoanalytic experience as well as more recent research in cognitive science, which envisions multiple codes operating in the mind simultaneously and interacting with one another.[100]

Habermas's compulsion to linguistify—which is to say, socialize— the mind leads him to a form of linguistic monism. He appears to be claiming that language constitutes a self-sufficient cosmos, so that, once in its circle, we have no access to the pre- and extralinguistic forces that act on and distort it. But, unless I'm mistaken, this was Gadamer's thesis that Habermas worked so hard to refute over thirty years ago.

Notes

1. I am grateful to the students in my class "Psychoanalysis and the Philosophy of Recognition" at the New School for Social Research for their contribution to this paper. Their challenging questions and thoughtful suggestions helped me to formulate my position.

2. I am in sympathy with the general thrust of Dieter Freundlieb's diagnosis of the current state of critical theory, although my psychoanalytic approach differs from his

return to metaphysics. See Dieter Freundlieb, "Rethinking Critical Theory: Weaknesses and New Directions," *Constellations* 7 (2000): 80–99.

3. See especially Karl-Otto Apel, "The Transcendental Conception of Language-Communication and the Idea of a First Philosophy: Towards a Critical Reconstruction of the History of Philosophy in the Light of Language Philosophy," *Karl Otto-Apel: Selected Essays*, vol. 1, ed. E. Mendieta (New Jersey: Humanities Press, 1994), 83–111. The move from the philosophy of consciousness to the philosophy of language is often seen as similar to the move from the intrapsychic to the interpersonal, or from "one-person" to "two-person" psychology in psychoanalysis. See André Green, "The Intrapsychic and the Intersubjective in Psychoanalysis," *The Psychoanalytic Quarterly* 69 (2000): 1–40.

4. See Dieter Henrich, "The Origins of the Theory of the Subject," in *Philosophical Interventions in the Unfinished Project of Enlightenment,* trans. W. Rehg, ed. A. Honneth et al. (Cambridge: MIT Press, 1992), 29–38. See also Peter Dews, "Communicative Paradigms and the Question of Subjectivity," in *Habermas: A Critical Reader,* ed. Peter Dews (New York: Blackwell, 1999), 112–13, and "Modernity, Self-Consciousness and the Scope of Philosophy: Jürgen Habermas and Dieter Henrich in Debate," *The Limits of Disenchantment* (New York: Verso, 1995), 169–193.

5. Henrich, "Origins," 33.

6. For an impassioned criticism of this style of philosophizing, which nevertheless remains deeply appreciative of the magnitude and significance of Habermas's achievement, see Dieter Henrich, "What Is Metaphysics—What Is Modernity? Twelve Theses against Jürgen Habermas," *Habermas: A Critical Reader,* 291–319.

7. Jürgen Habermas, *The Philosophical Discourse of Modernity,* trans. F. Lawrence (Cambridge: MIT Press, 1987), 337.

8. Axel Honneth, *The Struggle for Recognition,* trans. J. Anderson (Cambridge: MIT Press, 1995), 30.

9. Hans Joas, *George Herbert Mead,* trans. R. Meyer (Cambridge: MIT Press, 1985), 110.

10. Jonathan Lear, "On Killing Freud (Again),"*Open Minded* (Cambridge: Harvard University Press, 1988), 31. Within the critical theory camp, Hans Joas has been moving in a similar direction with his notion of "creative democracy," though he would no doubt object to the term "irrational" as a residue of rationalist theory of action with its Cartesian presuppositions. See Hans Joas, *The Creativity of Action* (Chicago: University of Chicago Press, 1996).

11. Karl Polanyi, "Aristotle Discovers the Economy," in *Trade and Market in the Early Empires,* ed. K. Polanyi et al. (Chicago: Regnery, 1957), 64–94; also my "Pre-Market Economics: The Aristotelian Perspective," *Dialectical Anthropology* (1976): 1ff.

12. Sigmund Freud, *Civilization and Its Discontents,* in *The Standard Edition of the Complete Psychological Works of Sigmund Freud,* ed. and trans. J. Strachey (London: Hogarth, 1953–1974), vol. 21, 86. Hereafter the works of Freud will be cited by title and volume number in the standard edition (S.E.) series.

13. See Cornelius Castoriadis, *The Imaginary Institution of Society,* trans. K. Blamey (Cambridge: MIT Press, 1987), 290.

14. Jürgen Habermas, "Labor and Interaction: Remarks on Hegel's Jena Philosophy of Mind," *Theory and Practice*, trans. J. Viertel (Boston: Beacon Press, 1971), 142–169. Already in this early article, Habermas mentions G. H. Mead as representing a "naturalized" reformulation of Hegel's interactive program. On the importance of Mead as providing Habermas with a third "basic alternative model" beyond Marx and Kierkegaard, see Dews, "Communicative Paradigms," 100.

15. Habermas, "Labor and Interaction," 152.

16. Axel Honneth, "Author's Introduction," *The Fragmented World of the Social*, ed. C. W. Wright (Albany: SUNY Press, 1995), xiii.

17. See Axel Honneth, *The Critique of Power*, trans. K. Baynes (Cambridge: MIT Press, 1991), 284.

18. Honneth, *The Struggle for Recognition*, 10. See also Judith Butler, *Subjects of Desire* (New York: Columbia University Press, 1987), 242 note 18.

19. Honneth, *The Struggle for Recognition*, 15.

20. Ibid., 15.

21. Ibid., 16–17.

22. Ibid., 17.

23. Ibid., 25.

24. Ibid., 62.

25. See Freundlieb, "Rethinking Critical Theory," 81.

26. Cf. Max Horkheimer, "Egoism and Freedom Movements: On the Anthropology of the Bourgeois Era," *Between Philosophy and Social Science*, trans. G F. Hunter, M. S. Kramer, and J. Torpey (Cambridge: MIT Press, 1993), 49–110.

27. See André Green, *The Work of the Negative*, trans. A. Weller (London: Free Associations Press, 1999).

28. Castoriadis notes that while intersubjectivity is a possibility for human beings, it is, from the larger perspective, a rare anomaly that goes against life's tendency toward closure: "The for-itself may be thought of as an enclosed sphere—that is what closure means—whose diameter is approximately constant. . . . Human subjectivity is a pseudoclosed sphere that can dilate on its own, that can interact with other pseudospheres of the same type, and that put back into question the conditions or the laws, of its closure. . . . Genuine interaction with other subjectivities signifies something unprecedented in the world: the overcoming [*dépasement*] of mutual exteriority." Cornelius Castoriadis, "The State of the Subject Today," *World in Fragments*, trans. D. A. Curtis (Stanford: Stanford University Press, 1997), 169–179.

29. Green, *Work of the Negative*, 15.

30. See G.W.F. Hegel, *The Phenomenology of Spirit*, trans. A.V. Miller (Oxford: Oxford University Press, 1977), ¶168–¶170 (hereafter referred to as PhS). See also Hans

Jonas, "Is God a Mathematician? The Meaning of Metabolism," *The Phenomenon of Life* (New York: Delta Books, 1966), 79ff.

31. PhS, ¶174. Julia Kristeva refers to the "paranoid" character of self-consciousness's desire; see *Revolution in Poetic Language*, trans. M. Waller (New York: Columbia University Press, 1984).

32. Hans-Georg Gadamer, "Hegel's Dialectic of Self-consciousness," *Hegel's Dialectic*, trans. P. C. Smith (New Haven: Yale University Press, 1976), 62 note 7.

33. Jean Hyppolite, *Genesis and Structure of Hegel's "Phenomenology of Spirit,"* trans. S. Cherniak and J. Heckman (Evanston, Ill.: Northwestern University Press, 1974), 160.

34. Despite her strong orientation toward the French, Judith Butler recognizes that appetitive, or what she calls "consumptive," desire is prior to the desire of the Other's desire; see Butler, *Subjects of Desire*, 33.

35. See Jean Hyppolite, "Hegel's Phenomenology and Psychoanalysis," *New Studies in Hegel's Philosophy*, ed. W. E. Steinkraus (New York: Holt, Rinehart and Winston, 1971), 57–70, and Green, "Hegel and Freud: Elements for an Improbable Comparison," *The Work of the Negative*, 26–49.

36. Lacan carries the tradition of interpretation through translation one step further when he equates *désire* with Freud's concept of the wish [*Wunsch*], thus assimilating psychoanalysis to an already dematerialized Hegelianism. See Jacques Lacan, *Écrits*, trans. A. Sheridan (New York: W.W. Norton & Co, 1977).

37. On the relationship between the emphasis on paranoia, mis-cognition, and the gaze in twentieth-century French thought see Martin Jay, *Downcast Eyes* (Berkeley: University of California Press, 1993), passim.

38. Jean Laplanche points out the necessity of avoiding both these extremes. See Laplanche, *New Foundations of Psychoanalysis*, trans. D. Macey (Oxford: Blackwell, 1989), 17ff. Both Green and Kristeva have tried to correct this tendency in Lacanian thought by reintroducing the affects and the body after Lacan's linguistic turn.

39. Sigmund Freud, *The Future of An Illusion*, S.E., vol. 21, 21, 49.

40. Gadamer, "Hegel's Dialectic of self-consciousness," 61.

41. PhS, ¶175.

42. Ibid. (emphasis in the original).

43. PhS, ¶178 (translation modified).

44. PhS, ¶182.

45. PhS, ¶187.

46. Mark Sacks, "The Conception of the Subject in Analytic Philosophy," 3 (unpublished manuscript).

47. Ibid., 6.

48. Ibid., 3.

49. Ibid., 5.

50. Ibid., 18.

51. Ibid., 17–18.

52. Honneth, *The Struggle for Recognition*, 62.

53. Ibid., 67 and 68.

54. See Joas, *G. H. Mead*, 18ff.

55. Honneth, *The Struggle for Recognition*, 71.

56. Ibid., 138.

57. Mead's notion of the "me," which does not essentially go beyond Piaget's concept of decentration, presents an extremely limited, cartographic conception of the self that lacks depth. What is essentially missing in both Mead and Piaget is an adequate examination of the self's intercourse with its interior dimension. The cartographic conception of the self informed Habermas's thinking almost from the beginning of his dialogical investigations. Consequently, it is not surprising that his account of individuation through socialization is similarly impoverished. See Jürgen Habermas, "Individuation through Socialization: On George Herbert Mead's Theory of Subjectivity," *Postmetaphysical Thinking*, trans. W. M. Hohengarten (Cambridge: MIT Press, 1992), 149–204; Axel Honneth, "Decentered Autonomy: The Subject After the Fall," *The Fragmented World of the Social*, 261–271; for a critique see Charles Taylor, "The Dialogical Self," *Rethinking Knowledge*, ed. R. F. Goodman and W. R. Fisher (Albany: SUNY Press, 1995), 57–66.

58. G. H. Mead, *Mind, Self, and Society from the Standpoint of a Social Behaviorist*, ed. C. W. Morris (Chicago: University of Chicago Press, 1934), 160. Consider also: "If we use a Freudian expression, the 'me' is in a certain sense a censor." Ibid., 210.

59. Ernst Tugendhat, *Self-Consciousness and Self-Determination*, trans. P. Stern (Cambridge: MIT Press, 1986), 251.

60. See Joas, *G. H. Mead*, chap. 2.

61. Mead, *Mind, Self, and Society*, 200.

62. Ibid., 221.

63. Ibid., 209.

64. It is in fact a conceptual abstraction to separate autoplastic and alloplastic solutions from one another completely. For it is more common that they work in tandem, with a mutual feedback mechanism operating between them. For example, transfor-

mation of the self can lead to a new capacity for constructively intervening in the world, which in turn can contribute to the further reshaping of the self.

65. Mead, *Mind Self, and Society*, 216.

66. See Joas, *The Creativity of Action*, 21.

67. Mead, *Mind, Self and Society*, 216; see also ibid., note 23. The relentless quality of Habermas's intersubjectivism forces him to miss an important distinction concerning the oppositional capacities of the exceptional individual. Habermas rightfully agrees with Mead's observation that independent prophets, political rebels, and iconoclasts of all sorts do not maintain their opposition to the existing order in an attitude of radical isolation. On the contrary, they must appeal to a larger ideal community to obtain the consensual validation necessary for maintaining their position. Consider a heroic dissident like Nelson Mandela, who must have sustained the almost unimaginable courage required for his opposition to the actually existing society by identifying with such a counter-factual community. Habermas, however, then goes on to adduce this fact to support the claim that "the self from which these independent achievements are expected is socially constituted through and through." But Mead's observation about the necessity of appealing to an ideal community only concerns the *maintenance* of one's opposition to the given social order. It doesn't concern the *source*—for example, the "I," the id, or the unconscious—from which that individual opposition originates. And this argument in no way excludes the existence of presocial sources of the self. See Habermas, "Individuation Through Socialization," 183.

68. See D.W. Winnicott, "Creativity and Its Origins," *Playing and Reality* (New York: Tavistock, 1971), 65–85.

69. Taylor, "The Dialogical Self," 64.

70. Furthermore, a number of different accounts of the "I" can be found in Mead's writings. For example, in "The Definition of the Psychical," he understands the "I" as a breakdown product that emerges when our habitual unreflective approach to a task is frustrated. At that point, our integrated experience dissolves into conflicting impulses, and it is the task of the "I" to reconstitute those elements into a new self, which, at the same time, involves a reconstitution of our perspective on the object, and, to this extent, creates a new object [in George Herbert Mead, *Selected Writings*, ed. A. J. Reck (New York: Liberal Arts Library, 1964), 53 ff.]. In *Mind, Self, and Society*, on the other hand, Mead understands the "I" as the part of the self that constantly trails the experience of the "me" and reacts to it. As such it is always after the fact—*nachträglich, après coup*—and can never itself be captured in experience (see 173 ff.). We should note that on neither account is the "I" understood as something existing prior to experience, which could therefore bring its own distinct input to it. Nor is it conceived as having any conative pressure—*Drang* in Freud's sense—that could propel experience.

71. Honneth, *The Struggle for Recognition*, 81.

72. Honneth, "Decentered Autonomy," *Fragmented World of the Social*, 267. And even more recently, he equates the "I" with the Freudian id: see Axel Honneth, "Object Relations Theory and Postmodern Identity: On the Supposed Obsolescence of Psychoanalysis," 8–9 (unpublished manuscript).

73. Axel Honneth, "Object Relations Theory and Postmodern Identity," 7.

74. Honneth, "Author's Introduction," *Fragmented World of the Social*, xxiv.

75. Ibid., xxiv–xxv. See also Axel Honneth, "Rescuing the Revolution with an Ontology: On Cornelius Castoriadis' Theory of Society," *The Fragmented World of the Social*, 168–183. Habermas, in contrast, counters the thesis of the end of the individual by arguing that socialization is simultaneously a process of individuation, which is intensified by the modern division of labor. Honneth also asserts the socialization-as-individuation thesis. But by using a Castoriadian argument, he simultaneously adopts the strategy of the Freudian Left, which sees an uneliminable opposition between "Desire" and the "Law." This is, of course, the very strategy Habermas saw as a remnant of praxis philosophy and the production paradigm and sought to make unnecessary with the socialization-as-individuation thesis; see Habermas, "Excursus on Cornelius Castoriadis: The Imaginary Institution," *The Philosophical Discourse of Modernity*, 327–335. See also Whitebook, *Perversion and Utopia* (Cambridge: MIT Press, 1995), chap. 4.

76. See D.W. Winnicott, "The Theory of the Parent-Infant Relationship," *The Maturational Process and the Facilitating Environment* (New York: International Universities Press, 1965), 39 note 1.

77. D.W. Winnicott, "Transitional Objects and Transitional Experience," *Playing and Reality*, 11. In a statement that invites comparison with Castoriadis's notion of the "monadic core of the psyche," Winnicott writes: "I am putting forward and stressing the importance of the idea of the permanent isolation of the individual and claiming that at the core of the individual there is no communication with the not-me world. . . . This preservation of isolation is part of the search for identity, and for the establishment of a personal technique for communicating which does not lead to violation of the central self." D.W. Winnicott, "Communicating and Not Communicating Leading to a Study of Certain Opposites," *The Maturational Process*, 189–190.

78. Honneth, "Object Relations Theory and Postmodern Identity," 10.

79. Honneth, *The Struggle for Recognition*, 98.

80. Sigmund Freud, "Instincts and Their Vicissitudes," S.E., vol. 14, 134.

81. Margaret Mahler et al., *The Psychological Birth of the Human Infant* (New York: Basic Books, 1975), 55; also Hans W. Loewald, *Papers on Psychoanalysis* (New Haven: Yale University Press, 1980).

82. Judith Guss Teicholz insists on the crucial distinction between the terms "interactive," "interpersonal," and "intersubjective" and between "mutual regulation" and "mutual recognition." Much of the confusion in current psychoanalytic controversies—and polemical shenanigans—results from the failure to distinguish systematically between these terms. One would be hard put to find an analyst of any persuasion who maintains that early development—or the clinical situation—isn't interactive. But it doesn't follow from this that it is already interpersonal or intersubjective. Likewise, few analysts would deny that mother-infant and analyst-analysand interaction involves mutual regulation. But again, mutual regulation is not the same as mutual

recognition, and, in narcissistic transference, can actually be used to impede the latter. See Judith Guss Teicholz, *Kohut, Loewald and the Postmoderns* (Hillsdale, N.J.: Analytic Press, 1999), 181, 172–172, 182–189.

83. Honneth could have used Thomas Ogden's concept of the "autistic-contiguous position," which is designed to designate an early stage of development that is interactive but not yet intersubjective. See Thomas Ogden, "The Dialectically Constituted/Decentered Subject of Psychoanalysis II: The Contributions of Klein and Winnicott," *The International Journal of Psycho-Analysis* 73 (1992): 616.

84. Honneth, "Object Relations Theory and Postmodern Identity," 12.

85. Green, *The Work of the Negative*, 27.

86. Ibid., 6.

87. Ibid., 8.

88. Ibid., 6. Cf. Castoriadis, *Imaginary Institution of Society*, 104.

89. Honneth, "Object Relations and Postmodern Identity," 12.

90. Green, *The Work of the Negative*, 17.

91. See Dieter Henrich, "Fichte's Original Insight," trans. D. R. Lachterman, in *Contemporary German Philosophy*, vol. 1, ed. D. Christensen et al. (University Park, Pa.: Pennsylvania State University Press, 1982), 15–55; Robert Pippin, "Fichte's Contribution," *The Philosophical Forum* 19 (Winter-Spring, 1987–1989): 75–96 and Frederick Neuhouser, *Fichte's Theory of Subjectivity* (Cambridge: Cambridge University Press, 1990), chaps. 3 and 4.

92. Jürgen Habermas, "Metaphysics after Kant," *Postmetaphysical Thinking*, 25.

93. Peter Dews, "Modernity, Self-Consciousness and the Scope of Philosophy," 178; also Sacks, "The Conception of the Subject," 8, and Henrich, "What Is Metaphysics— What Is Modernity?" Theses 9 and 10.

94. Sigmund Freud, *The Interpretation of Dreams*, S.E. vol. 4, 119–120.

95. Habermas, "Metaphysics after Kant," 25.

96. Donald Davidson, "Rational Animals," *Dialectica* 36 (1982): 319–327.

97. Habermas, "Metaphysics after Kant," 27 note 18.

98. Bénédicte de Boysson-Bardies, *How a Child Comes to Language*, trans. M. DeBevoise (Cambridge: MIT Press, 1999), 73. See also Jerome Brunner, *Child's Talk* (New York: W.W. Norton, 1985), chap. 2, and Hans Loewald, "Primary Process, Secondary Process, and Language," *Papers on Psychoanalysis*, 178–206. Or as Henrich puts it: "This would require us to speak of an implicit self-relation, which already appears or functions at the most elementary level of language acquisition. For it is clear that the capacity to use the grammatical first-person singular (the pronoun 'I') is acquired

only at a late stage in the process of language acquisition." Dieter Henrich, "What Is Metaphysics—What Is Modernity?," 311.

99. Kristeva, *Revolution in Poetic Language*, Part I. See also de Boysson-Bardies, *How a Child Comes to Language*, passim.

100. See especially Wilma Bucci, *Psychoanalysis and Cognitive Science* (New York: Gilford Press, 1997).

III

Engagements with Political Theory and Problems of Pluralism

11

Taking Ethical Debate Seriously

Georgia Warnke

In an essay on Jürgen Habermas's discourse ethics entitled "Legitimacy and Diversity: Dialectical Reflections on Analytical Distinctions,"[1] Thomas McCarthy further examines an issue he raised earlier in "Practical Discourse: On the Relation of Morality to Politics" as to whether Habermas's discourse ethics can serve as a "realistic normative ideal for democratic theory."[2] While Habermas emphasizes the scope of moral consensus even within pluralistic and multicultural societies, McCarthy looks to the potential for ethical dissensus and examines its implications for moral agreement. In this essay, I want to explore aspects of this difference between McCarthy and Habermas and I want to consider McCarthy's suggestion of a democratic decision-making process that takes disagreement seriously. I shall begin with McCarthy's comments on Habermas's account of law and democracy.

Habermas ties the legitimacy of law to deliberative and decision-making procedures that involve three analytically distinguishable modes of discourse: pragmatic, ethical, and moral. Pragmatic discourses consider legal norms and political proposals with regard to their utility and efficiency in reaching certain preestablished goals or ends. Thus if a society wants to provide a social safety net for its members or defend them against external or internal threats, pragmatic discourses consider only the efficiency of various strategies in achieving these goals. Ethical discourses, in contrast, consider norms and programs in terms of a group's understanding of who it is and what

Georgia Warnke

it wants to be. In this case, questions about proposed legal-political norms and resolutions are concerned with whether they are suitable for the group or, in other words, whether they accord with who it thinks it is and what is important to it. For Habermas, this sort of collective self-understanding mirrors an individual self-understanding. Conscientiously deciding what kind of life I want to lead requires that I reflect on who I am, what sort of life will appropriate my values and heritage, what these values are, and what parts of my heritage are important to me. Similarly, a collective determination of the appropriate life for us as a community requires that we reflect on our collective values and intersubjectively shared cultures and traditions. Accordingly, what Habermas calls ethical-existential discussions involve our understanding of our individual identities and goods while what he calls ethical-political discussions have as their goal "the clarification of a collective identity."[3]

Moral discourses examine possible laws and policies from the perspective of a third set of questions, those concerned with justice. These questions are not directed at whether a proposed legal or political norm is likely to be effective or whether it reflects our common conception of who we are; instead, they are directed at whether it is just. Moreover, Habermas insists that these questions have priority. As he writes, "The making of norms is primarily a justice issue, subject to principles that state what is equally good for all. Unlike ethical questions, questions of justice are not inherently related to a specific collectivity and its form of life." Moral discourses rather attach questions of justice to a universal consensus on the rightness of norms. Only those norms are valid ideally to which everyone could assent under conditions that exclude coercion, secure the freedom and equality of participants in challenging, raising, and redeeming validity claims, and allow only for the force of the better argument. Democratic decision making takes this ideal as a regulative one for securing the validity of legal-political norms. "The law of a concrete legal community must, if it is to be legitimate, at least be compatible with moral standards that claim universal validity beyond the legal community."[4]

McCarthy has three criticisms of this conception. In the first place, he argues that while Habermas characterizes his account of moral, ethical, and pragmatic modes of discourse as one that picks out different aspects of decision making with regard to legal-political issues, he also thinks of the modes of discourse as independent forms of discourse. Furthermore, he tends to identify legal-political discussions primarily with moral discourse. As a result, McCarthy argues, Habermas fails to attend adequately to the degree to which discourses are situated in particular communities with particular histories, self-conceptions, and traditions. Thus whereas Habermas claims that questions about matters of justice are not "inherently related" to specific collectivities and their forms of life, McCarthy points out that they arise only within them. Further, whereas Habermas emphasizes the dimension of justice, McCarthy emphasizes the dimension of value. "For legal norms are not meant to be context-transcendently valid in the same way as moral norms; though they must be in accord with the latter, they must also give expression to 'the particular wills of members of a determinate legal community' and to their 'intersubjectively shared form of life.'"5

Yet in the pluralistic and multicultural societies most individuals in the West now inhabit, how are legal norms to give expression to intersubjectively shared forms of life? The populations of these societies do not share forms of life; common self-understandings are rather limited to smaller groups and communities and Habermas attempts to move beyond the scope of ethical points of view for just this reason. If ethical-political discussions look to "the clarification of a collective identity," then in pluralistic and multicultural societies this sort of discussion will not be able to assist deliberation and decision making for the society as a whole. Instead, different groups will begin from different cultural, racial, religious, ethnic, or gender-defined starting points and they will possess different values and different conceptions of what parts of their heritage and tradition are important.

Accordingly, Habermas moves from the ethical aspects of discourse to the moral. On the one hand, the norms on which pluralistic and multicultural societies will be able to agree will be increasingly general and abstract.6 On the other hand, the very generalness and abstractness of such norms will allow for consensus on the level of principles, rights, and procedures while permitting variety and disagreement with regard to ethical conceptions of the good. As McCarthy puts the point, "general agreement on legal-political procedures may coexist with irresolvable disagreements on matters of ethical substance."[7] Habermas's example is the controversy over abortion:

Insofar as what is at issue is in fact a moral matter in the strict sense, we must proceed on the assumption that in the long run it could be decided one way or the other on the basis of good reasons. However, *a fortiori* the possibility cannot be excluded that abortion is a problem that cannot be resolved from the moral point of view at all. . . . it might transpire that descriptions of the problem of abortion are always inextricably interwoven with individual self-descriptions of persons and groups, and thus with their identities and life projects. Where an internal connection of this sort exists, the question must be formulated differently, specifically, in ethical terms. Then it would be answered differently, depending on context, tradition, and ideals of life. It follows, therefore, that the moral question, properly speaking, would first arise at the more general level of the legitimate ordering of coexisting forms of life. Then the question would be how the integrity and coexistence of ways of life and worldviews that generate different ethical conceptions of abortion can be secured under conditions of equal rights.[8]

In this analysis, the moral aspect of discourse effects agreement on matters of equal rights such as the right to the free exercise of religion and to freedom of conscience. Differences can be sustained at the ethical level in the different identities, projects, and understandings of abortion that different cultural and religious groups possess. Yet McCarthy raises two questions. First, if different communities within a multicultural society can disagree in their understandings, identities, and life projects, why assume that these disagreements will not "carry over to more general questions concerning 'the legitimate ordering of coexisting forms of life'?"[9] Why not assume that if we disagree over abortion we will also disagree over a number of issues that are meant to reside along the moral dimension of our deliberations: for example, in descriptions of what counts as the securing of equal rights, in differing views of who the subject of equal rights is, fetuses or women, in what the free exercise of religion involves, and what counts as a religion? Second, McCarthy asks whether the sorts of disputes like that over abortion might not be more widespread than Habermas recognizes. McCarthy then argues that "democratic deliberation would normally be shot through with ethical disputes that could not be resolved consensually at the level at which they arose."[10]

Habermas allows that moral consensus will extend along the level of general and abstract norms rather than along that of concrete ethical conceptions of the good life. Yet even this consensus is threatened by what seems to be the mutual entanglement of moral and ethical dimensions of discourse in which disagreement on the level of identities, self-understandings, and conceptions of the good can undermine agreement on norms. Moreover, if multicultural societies are riddled with disputes similar to the one over abortion and if these invade agreement over principles, rights, and procedures, then it remains unclear whether Habermas's starting point in the anticipation of rationally motivated consensus is adequate for democratic theory.

Habermas's response to this possibility is to emphasize the function of majority rule. Where citizens of a legal community cannot reach consensus on legal-political norms because of persistent disagreements in values and self-understandings and where these differences threaten a common adherence to procedures and principles, the function of decision rules such as the will of the majority is to defuse the threat by allowing for decisions to which most members of the society assent. If majority rule is really to defuse the threat, however, Habermas contends that it must be securely grounded in an anticipation of consensus. Hence, it is crucial that majority rule functions only as a provisional agreement within a continuing discussion where the trajectory of the discussion remains a rationally motivated agreement. The will of the majority is required for purposes of deciding how to proceed when the society must proceed one way or the other. Still, majority rule only temporarily suspends the discussion and the suspension serves only as a temporary stopping point on the way to a universal consensus on rational acceptability.

Yet McCarthy suggests that if we take the persistence of ethical disagreement seriously, then we must also understand majority rule differently. It functions, not as a provisional *agreement*, but rather as "the provisional *outcome* of a procedure intended to produce decisions even when there is no such agreement to be had." Moreover, the provisional character of the outcome does not refer to a trajectory of consensus on rational acceptability but rather "to the ongoing efforts by minorities to rationally persuade enough of the majority of the greater plausibility of their views to effect a change in the decision."

As McCarthy continues, under this analysis of majority rule, "deliberative procedures . . . would aim to enhance, as far as possible, the practically-rational character of the decisions that have to be made, while keeping open the possibility of ongoing contestation and eventual change."[11]

McCarthy thus understands majority rule in more practical terms than Habermas. If legal-political discussion is no longer exclusively connected to moral discourse, then we can also discard the idea that it can or should transcend cultural values or self-understandings. Instead, it remains situated in particular legal-political communities. Moreover, if we take seriously the possible scope of differences in values, identities, and self-understandings that can occur within such communities, we can understand the possible impact of the ethical aspects of discourse in undermining the possibilities for agreement along the moral dimension. Still, we need not limit the goal of legal-political deliberation to the telos of its moral dimension as rationally motivated consensus. We can, instead, stress mutual understanding and look to a continuing discussion that also anticipates the need for a decision. Hence, we can support majority rule but also remain open to challenges and possible changes to a particular majority decision, changes that may change the majority without anticipating or moving toward consensus. As McCarthy writes, "Reasonable participants will try to speak to (some of) [their] differences when rationally persuading others to support laws and policies they believe to be in the general interest. They will seek to accommodate (some of) them in the arrangement they propose. And they will learn to live with (all of) them in a nonviolent manner."[12]

McCarthy's account of democratic deliberation and decision making accomplishes five important tasks. First, it restores to those processes their full complement of pragmatic, ethical, and moral dimensions and, second, it questions whether their ethical and moral dimensions can be as clearly distinguished from one another as Habermas suggests. Third, McCarthy's account stresses the difference between ethical-political discussions and ethical-existential ones by indicating the way in which the former involve a potential for differences and conflict that the latter do not. Fourth, McCarthy's analysis indicates that the scope of intermixed ethical-moral conflicts might be greater than Habermas assumes and, fifth, it give us a way to think about persistent conflicts of this sort in democratic societies. If we give up on the two-tiered conception of a consensus on matters of right or justice together with dissensus on notions of the good life, we can bring our differences in values, projects, and self-understanding back into democratic debate. We no longer need to flush out the residue of values and aspirations in deliberating publicly on matters of justice. Rather than idealizing majority rule as a provisional type of closure on the way to rationally motivated, universal consensus we can think of it in more realistic terms as an open-ended process in which no ultimate consensus may be forthcoming. In that case, we shall need to speak both rationally and compellingly about both who we take ourselves to be as a community and what we take to be just in the effort to persuade and convince as many of our compatriots as necessary to create a new majority. Moreover, we shall have to be open to the possibility of opposition and redirection in evaluative approaches to our norms.

While Habermas claims that his discourse principle has both "the cognitive sense of grounding a presumption of rational acceptability" and "the practical sense of establishing relations of mutual understanding that are free of violence,"[13] crucial to McCarthy's conception is the latter: the commitment to mutual understanding and nonviolence. In the next part of this essay, I want to try to work out what this conception might involve by looking briefly at three current issues in American public life. I shall look first at the example of abortion that Habermas uses and then turn to two other issues, those of surrogate mothering and pornography, both of which revolve around similar issues of sex, women, materialism, and commercialization.[14]

Pro-life advocates in the debate over abortion claim that legal access to abortion should be denied because abortion is the murder of an unborn child. One cannot establish a definitive point in pregnancy before which a fetus is not a person and after which it is. Nor can a simple change in space mark a difference between the born and unborn. Hence, if it is wrong to kill a child, it is equally wrong to kill a fetus. For their part, pro-choice advocates argue that legal access to abortion is a right rooted in principles of freedom and equality. Women cannot be compelled by the state to give birth or not to give birth. Rather, they have the freedom to decide if and when to bear a child for whom they will be responsible. Moreover, to deny them this liberty would be to deny them equality, to impose "Good Samaritan" burdens of maintaining life that the state does not impose on men.[15] These opposing positions are usually expressed in terms of principles: in terms of the right to life versus rights to liberty and equality. At the same time, the debate contains deep ethical and attitudinal conflicts. Pro-life advocates are typically more religious than pro-choice advocates. Moreover, whereas pro-choice advocates tend to emphasize freedom, self-determination, and the equality of men and women, pro-life advocates typically stress family, responsibility, and the different roles of men and women.

Pro-life advocates reject a view of motherhood that attempts to prepare for it or to try to fit it into some preexisting life plan. Rather, what pro-choice women call "unwanted pregnancies" are simply "surprise pregnancies" for pro-life women. In the first place, pro-life women tend to rely on Natural Family Planning, a method of unassisted birth control in which couples abstain during fertile parts of the woman's cycle. However, NFP is valuable to them, not so much because it is meant to provide an effective form of contraception, but more precisely because it is not very effective and leaves open the possibility of creating life. In so doing, it instills what many pro-life advocates stress is the proper reverence for the act of sexual intercourse.[16] In the second place, a woman's life is specially related to the raising of children and to the provision of emotional support for the family. Since this is her life, pregnancies are never unwanted, even though they may come as a surprise. Pro-life women often work outside the home. Still, to the extent that a materialist culture links access to careers to access to birth control and abortion, pro-life advocates think that such a culture cannot properly recognize the importance of nurturing families and that it even sustains impulses toward greed, consumerism, and the neglect of family values. Making money and pursuing careers become the measure of a person's worth and, as a consequence, defending the right to abortion signifies what some pro-life advocates see as "a social denial of nurturance."[17]

For many pro-choice advocates, this set of attitudes is "medieval."[18] Respect for the act of sexual intercourse need not require the kinds of risks and reverence pro-life advocates attribute to it. It can be more than an athletic exercise even with the use of birth control and the availability of abortion. Moreover, if we ought, as a culture, to empha-size responsibilities as well as rights, then these responsibilities extend to bearing and raising children under circumstances in which they will be loved, cared for, and financially supported. Pro-choice advo-cates reject the idea that motherhood belongs to some quasi-natural framework and see it instead as optional and special.[19] Seeking to have children only when one is financially and emotionally ready to do so is not evidence of selfishness or materialism but of independent selfhood. The same holds for a woman's attention to her salary and career. By sacrificing her independence and self-sufficiency in tend-ing only to her family, a woman is, in the pro-life view, "only one man away from disaster."[20]

If this outline of the different sides in the debate over abortion is an adequate indication, then principles and values seem to be more intertwined within the debate than Habermas's account of demo-cratic deliberation admits. First, discussions of the principles at stake are deeply embedded in a "specific collectivity and its form of life." We cannot resolve the controversy over abortion by abstracting from this collectivity because we cannot appeal to norms proscribing mur-der or establishing liberty or equality without already prejudging questions about the appropriate descriptions or understanding of the activity in question: Is abortion murder or the nonacceptance of burdens that affect women disproportionally? Is the United States an overly materialist culture? What are the relative virtues of mother-hood and financial independence? Habermas suggests that we can resolve the abortion issue by seeing "how the integrity and coexis-tence of ways of life and world-views that generate different ethical conceptions of abortion can be secured under conditions of equal rights."[21] Suppose, then, that we secure different ethical conceptions under conditions that establish equal rights to freedom of con-science and religion. If this resolution permits different ethical conceptions of abortion as part of the equal right as stake, does it not already decide against the pro-life view and a description of abortion as murder? Does it not already decide against the relevance of prin-ciples of life? If access to abortion is secured under the right to the free exercise of religion, then different ethical conceptions of abortion are parts of different religious definitions of the sanctity of individual life. But, in this case, we have excluded the conception of abortion with which pro-life advocates begin. Conversely, if we begin with a description of abortion as murder, which conditions of equal rights secure coexistence of the way of life and world view of pro-choice advocates? Under this scenario, are women not forced to give birth to children whose illnesses or deformities might be so extreme as to violate their conception of respect for the sanctity of individual life? Are they not forced to carry pregnancies to term, which indicates a profound disrespect for the pregnant woman herself?

These questions thus indicate, second, that our ethical differences "carry over to more general questions concerning 'the legitimate ordering of coexisting forms of life,'" as McCarthy suggests. Evaluative questions seem not only to entwine themselves with moral questions but also to disrupt our moral consensus: we are supposed to possess a moral consensus that proscribes the taking of innocent life but if we disagree as to whether abortions take innocent life or instead, simply fail to save it, then what is our consensus a consensus on? We agree on principles that establish the freedom of conscience and the equality of men and women. Still, if we do not agree on how these principles apply to the case of abortion, what is the status of that agreement? What do freedom and equality mean? Finally, if we think of majority rule in Habermas's terms, we must assume that there is a right answer to these questions, that a legal or political decision in favor of some access to abortion is simply a temporary stopping point on the way to a decision that everyone can accept through the force of the better argument. Here McCarthy's view is more compelling. Why not assume that we will continue to differ on the question of abortion because we will continue to differ in how we define abortion, in what freedom, equality, and respect for the sanctity of life mean, and in how we conceive of good lives? If we think of our current laws on access to abortion as resolutions that track a open-ended, malleable will, as McCarthy suggests, then we must remain open to continuing debate and to efforts at understanding one another better than we do now.

Controversies over surrogate mothering raise similar concerns about the relation between moral and ethical dimensions of democratic decision making and they make similar reference to debates over the values of motherhood and materialism. In this case, our "general agreement on legal-political procedures" extends to rights of autonomy and the capacity to enter into binding contracts while our "irresolvable disagreements on matters of ethical substance" involve concerns about the meaning of procreation and parenting, as well as about commercialization, greed, and the degradation of women and children. The question is whether this distinction between an agreement on procedures and disagreement in ethical values helps us, as a society, decide what we ought to do about surrogacy contracts.

According to critics of surrogate mothering, the practice transforms women's bodies as well as children into commodities to be sold on the market. Women's labor in gestating and bearing children becomes just another form of productive labor, equivalent to producing goods and subject to the same exchange for a wage.[22] Children become objects for designer options. The "sponsoring parents" pick a surrogate with the features and genetic qualities they want in their child and then pay the surrogate to produce it. The relationship between surrogate mother and the child she bears is no longer one of love but, instead, one of profit. The relationship between child and sponsoring parents is no longer one that involves only cherishing, but instead one that lends itself to judging: did they get what they paid for? As Thomas H. Murray puts the point:

If children flourish best in stable, loving families, then we harm them by promoting a view of human relationship that equates the decision to initiate such a relationship with the decision to buy a wide-screen television or a medium-priced car . . . I like crusty bread so I chose a bread machine with that feature; you like hazel eyes and curly black hair, so should you choose your children by those characteristics?[23]

For supporters of surrogate mothering the practice appears very different, however. It is part of a general move in human relationships from status to contract, and this move is one that favors autonomy since individuals are free to have relationships and lives on the basis of choice rather than birth.[24] For surrogate mothers, this circumstance means that their sexuality is theirs to control as they want. Those who support surrogacy start with the understanding that women's sexuality has been controlled by men throughout most of human history and that this control has led to laws about adultery, custody, and marriage that subordinate and disenfranchise women; indeed, once they marry, their sexuality, their children, and their property have historically become their husband's. The same is not true for their husbands, however, who have typically engaged in adulterous relations with less punishment and retained custody of all the children of the marriage.[25] Options such as surrogacy restore women's bodies to them, on this view. Women's reproductive labor is not subjected to values of commercialization but is instead liberated from patriarchal restraints. For "sponsoring parents," as well, the practice of surrogate mothering means an increase in freedom. Not only are more options for parenthood available, in addition, the relationship they have with their children is one they freely intend and even seek out. The relation between parents and children is no longer based on biology or status, but is based on intent: those who intend to produce a child and who seek out the arrangements to do so are the true parents of the child.

The debate over surrogacy is sometimes framed as a debate over which law is to be the ruling authority: adoption law, where the deciding factor is meant to be the best interests of the child, or contract law, where the relevant questions are whether a particular contract is legal and, if legal, whether it has been performed. The New Jersey court that first decided one famous surrogacy dispute, the Baby M case, sided in favor of placing the child with the couple, Mr. and Mrs. Stern, who had sought out the surrogate mother, Mary Beth Whitehead, and did so primarily in accordance with prevailing contract law. The Supreme Court of New Jersey overturned this decision, however, claiming that the contract was not and could not be binding and that the decision on custody had to follow the best interests of the child.

Yet more is at stake here than whether contract or adoption law has controlling authority. Rather, the two different court decisions reflect different attitudes toward motherhood and different ideas about the value and meaning of family. Feminists who supported the original finding in favor of the validity of the surrogacy contract did so because it upheld the autonomy of surrogate mothers to enter into contractual relations. Moreover, it supported the capacities of most women, against stereotype, to make rational and autonomous decisions. Indeed, the lower court went to some length to show White-head's own irrationality and emotional instability: she was narcissistic in dyeing her hair and dressing herself and her older daughter alike; she was controlling in her marriage and, furthermore, deluded in her notions of proper infant play, offering the baby stuffed animals instead of pots and pans. For its part, the New Jersey Supreme Court admitted that the surrogate mother was "guilty of a breach of contract." Nonetheless, it concluded that the contract was invalid because it could not have reflected a voluntary, informed decision.[26] No surrogate mother could know in advance how she would feel about the child she was to bear for others and to require Whitehead to give up her child would be to require "something well beyond normal human capabilities."[27] Feminists who applauded this decision did so because it recognized the special bond between mothers and their children and even between pregnant women and their fetuses.

Habermas understands judicial decisions on the model of his account of majority rule. These decisions reflect "an interim report on the provisional state of an ongoing discussion seeking the one right answer to a . . . question but interrupted by institutional pressures for a decision."[28] But once judicial decisions are explicitly situated within "a specific collectivity and its form of life," it is not clear that this reliance on an eventual right answer makes sense. Instead, the Baby M case reflects the way in which courts can differ because their notions of a just solution are bound up with values and assumptions that affect their understanding of the legal issues involved. If one follows Habermas's attempt here to separate analytically the normative from the ethical aspects of these decisions and to concentrate on normative solutions that allow for individual choice in ethical solutions, the question arises as to whether one does not also risk overlooking the ethical assumptions that are surreptitiously part of the normative resolution. Thus if one looks only at the trial court's appeal to contract law, one misses the opportunity to consider the values (and, perhaps, vindictiveness) it brings to its understanding of the way mothers and women should behave. If one looks only at the New Jersey Supreme Court's appeal to adoption law, one misses the chance to consider the views (and, perhaps, stereotypes) it offers of motherhood and families.

Georgia Warnke

In contrast, McCarthy looks toward "a multifaceted communication process that allows for fluid transitions among questions and arguments of different sorts."[29] This form of democratic deliberation would seem to be much better suited for raising and revealing ethical assumptions and for allowing for reflection and forms of discussion that take them seriously rather than relegating them to a separate domain. In the debate over surrogate mothering, ethical views of the values of parenthood and good parenting seem to percolate up into moral claims about contractual or adoption rights. Rather than allowing them to do so unremarked, McCarthy's account of fluid and multifaceted processes of democratic deliberation and decision making gives us a way to include them as part of our discussions of rights. Those who favor surrogate mothering as a legal contract that instantiates principles of autonomy will have to speak to the worries others have about the commercialization of sacrosanct areas of life previously immune to contract law. Similarly, those who disagree will have to confront the way their notions fit with stereotypical views of women and mothers that may infiltrate our conceptions of equality. Neither side can simply recur to rights and principles without also discussing the values mixed into their understanding of what these rights are.

The last controversy I want to consider concerns the status of rights to free speech as they are affected by controversies over pornography. On the "general level of the legitimate ordering of coexisting forms of life," the resolution to the question of pornography appeals to universal rights. The government cannot restrict a person's or group's expression because other individuals or groups find it degrading to women, abhor its content, or disagree with what it says. The government can restrict expression that constitutes "a clear and present danger," but the application of this exception to free speech must succeed in showing that the speech in question will cause direct and imminent harm to a very important interest and that no other means short of suppressing speech will prevent this harm. In all other cases, "the fitting remedy for evil counsels is good ones."[30]

The terms that have historically applied to the principle of free speech speak to bravery and the courage to protect all speech, even hateful speech. Thus, Oliver Wendell Holmes declares that "if there is any principle of the Constitution that more imperatively calls for attachment than any other it is the principle of free thought—not free thought for those who agree with us but freedom for the thought we hate."[31] And Louis Brandeis insists that "those who won our independence by revolution were not cowards. To courageous, self-reliant men, with confidence in the power of free and fearless reasoning applied through the processes of popular government, no danger flowing from speech can be deemed clear and present, unless the incidence of the evil apprehended is so imminent that it may befall before there is opportunity for full discussion."[32]

Still, antipornography women bring a different set of values to their conception of free speech, not the courage of self-reliant "men," but a concern with the degradation of women for commercial purposes that can also lead to real harms. The argument for a free speech protection of pornography assumes that the right at risk in the dispute is that of those who consume and produce pornography. But suppose it is that of women? Suppose pornography helps to create a climate in which women cannot be taken seriously as equals in professional contexts and in which they are so pervasively considered sexual objects that their expressions of their needs and desires cannot be heard? The judge in a 1982 trial instructed the jury that "women who say no do not always mean no. It is not just a question of saying no."[33] Another judge in a 1990 trial did the same: "As the gentlemen on the jury will understand, when a woman says no she does not always mean it."[34] A man testified in court that he did not take his wife seriously when she said no and was acquitted on a consent defense even after the jury viewed a videotape that showed him having intercourse with his wife and penetrating her with objects while her hands and legs were tied with rope, her mouth was gagged, and her eyes were covered with duct tape.[35] For antipornography women, these instances indicate the extent to which pornography disempowers women. If speech-drowning hoots and jeers from hostile members of an audience can violate the free speech rights of the speaker and other members of the audience who wish to hear the speaker, then pornography violates the rights of women and those who want to hear them without disturbances in the field.

But if the two sides in the debate over pornography differ in their perspectives on the right to free speech, then how does appeal to this "general level of the legitimate ordering" resolve the issue? The two sides understand what is at issue in different ways and it is arguable that they do so because they approach the issue with different values and concerns. Those who argue in favor of free speech protections of pornography ask for courage, while those who argue against it ask for respect. Can we separate these different orientations and concerns from a normative consensus on the right at issue? These differences seem to "belong to different ways of life," lawyers and jurists, on the one hand, and activists in struggles for women's recognition, on the other. The differences also reflect different "world views," one which looks to a principled bravery and the other to respect for the individual and protection of the vulnerable. But do these different lives and world views not also disrupt the consensus on equal rights if they cannot tell us whose rights to protect and what that right means?

If so, then we are yet again directed to McCarthy's conception, to a multifaceted form of deliberation in which differences in value, self-understanding and identity are not excluded from discourses on justice but lead, instead, to a distinctive form of democratic deliberation, one that centers on fluid transitions in focus from values to general principles and back. While these foci might be analytically distinguished, it seems just as important to emphasize the extent to which they are always intertwined. If this is the case, then two consequences seem to follow. First, we should be as concerned with mutual understanding as we are with resolution and second, resolutions that reflect only the will of the majority will be justifiable along the lines McCarthy suggests rather than those that Habermas indicates. If our ethical differences cannot always be superseded by our moral agreement, then members of democracies might conceive of majority rule as an open-ended model of decision making that remains open to challenges and new perspectives. Its resolutions are not the right answers to our disputes or even points on the line toward right answers. They are rather decisions open to opposition and evolution.

In his conclusion McCarthy also refers to possibilities for accommodation arising from multifaceted deliberation:

It seems best . . . to acknowledge . . . a type of ethical-political dialogue aimed not at negotiated compromise, not at substantive agreement, and not at ethical-political consensus, but at forms of mutual accommodation that leave space for reasonable disagreements. We can imagine cultures that nourish the corresponding values and virtues, and practices that are predicated not on the assumption of one right answer but on respect for, and a desire to accommodate, ineliminable difference. We can imagine them because we already rely upon them in areas of our lives where it is important for us to maintain harmonious, cooperative, and mutually supportive relations with people with whom we do not always agree, whom we cannot always convince or be convinced by, and whom we do not want simply to outsmart. In multicultural democracies, they will inevitably play a larger role in political life as well.[36]

Yet, if we do have harmonious, cooperative, and mutually supportive relations with people with whom we do not always agree, why should we assume we can expand these to encompass the political community as a whole? What is it that might allow accommodations in debates such as those over abortion, surrogate mothering, and pornography—accommodations that allow different groups to maintain harmonious, cooperative, and mutually supportive relations, even as some draw on ethical values and moral principles in order to change the majority will while some draw on them to sustain it? McCarthy claims that "it would . . . be an important and interesting task to explore the logic of the ethical-political dialogue that could produce such mutual accommodation."[37] In concluding this paper, I want to argue that this logic is a hermeneutic one.

Both McCarthy and Habermas themselves connect the ethical-political aspects of discourse to hermeneutic processes of clarification and self-understanding. In Habermas's schema, these processes are separate from legal or moral debate. The question of who we are and what goods are important to us is separate from the question of whether our pursuit of our goods is compatible with what is equally good for all. Moreover, in the end it is the latter question that matters. In McCarthy's schema, hermeneutic processes of ethical clarification are reconnected to the determinations of moral and legal norms. Because ethical clarification leads to an awareness of differences in values, we are forced to give up on consensus as a normative ideal and reckon with persistent dissensus. In both conceptions, however, values, descriptions, and identities are the subject matter for hermeneutic reflection insofar as they are what we consider when we try to determine who we are and who we want to be.

Yet values and identities also serve as the framework for our reflections. We think in a certain ethical vocabulary, take certain commitments and allegiances seriously as touchstones, and appeal, consciously or not, to a certain heritage. This framework of values sets the context in which we understand the issues under dispute. Because we grow up in a Catholic tradition, we might understand abortion as murder. Because we grow up in a liberal one we might see it as the nonacceptance of burdens. Because of values we possess we can understand surrogate mothering either as a form of commercialization or as a valid contractual relation; we understand pornography as the degradation of women or as a form of obscenity that requires a courageous stand on principle. Differences in values ground differences in definition and understanding. Moreover, because we differ in what we take most seriously, we differ in the rights we take to be crucially at risk: life versus liberty and equality, adoption rights versus contract rights, and the free speech of pornographers versus the free speech of women.

But if our differences are differences in understanding that issue from differences in our evaluative orientations, then the logic of ethical-political dialogue is an interpretive one. What is at issue in ethical-political dialogue are our different interpretations of meaning. The logic of this kind of dialogue has at least two important features. First, a dialogue over interpretation need not converge on one right answer and, second, its point is mutual understanding and reciprocal development. I shall look at each feature in turn.

Interpretations of meaning are most familiar when they involve interpretations of texts; similarly, a dialogue about interpretations of meaning is most familiar as a discussion of the meaning of a text. Yet it would be bizarre to claim that the point of discussing the meaning of a text is to come to a rationally motivated consensus on the one right answer. We gather the arguments in favor of the interpretation we have of a given text, indicating the reasons we have for emphasizing certain aspects of it over others and showing how our perspective reveals the coherence, point, and insights that the text possesses. These arguments are not exclusive, however; they do not preclude a different perspective on the text or an emphasis on different elements of it. We assume, instead, that the text is open to a myriad of interpretations depending on the point of view we take toward it. Different interpreters can approach it from different theoretical perspectives and concentrate on the importance of different aspects of it.

Nor need these different perspectives be compatible with one another in the sense that they fit together like the pieces of a jigsaw puzzle. Rather, the text can be a very different text and reveal incommensurable meanings depending on the perspective from which one approaches it. Not any approach will be necessarily appropriate to it; nevertheless, a range of different approaches can reveal a range of meanings. Moreover, since historical developments, new texts, and new concerns will constantly give rise to new theoretical commitments and new perspectives, the range of possible interpretations will be a formidable one. If some established interpretations seem to become antiquated or remote, others become illuminating for a new age, a new set of circumstances, and a new set of interests.

What is the point of our discussions of texts if we are not converging on one right answer? In the first place, we come to understand perspectives other than our own; in the second place, we often learn from them. In anticipating the mutual understanding that ethical-political dialogue occasions, McCarthy seems to be primarily interested in the end to violence it permits. If we understand that those who support rights and access to abortion view it as the nonacceptance of "Good Samaritan" burdens, and if we try to understand their emphasis on self-reliance as well as on the psychological, emotional, and financial ability to bear the burdens of child-rearing in a responsible manner, we may still reject their perspective. Nevertheless, while we might continue to work to change their view, we cannot regard it as wrong or evil. We must rather regard it is as a potentially plausible interpretation, even if it is not the one we find most compelling. But if those who hold the interpretation are not wrong, then it is hard to see how bitterness or violence can be an intelligible response to their view.

The benefits of ethical-political dialogue conceived of in interpretive terms extend beyond the cessation of violence to include a reciprocal education. We can dispense with hostility because we recognize that the position we oppose is a plausible, though particular, interpretation, one rooted in particular concerns, values, and experiences. Moreover, we acknowledge the same status for our own understanding of the issue under debate. Yet because we recognize our understanding as only an interpretation we can also take an interest in interpretations other than our own. We are interested in alternative interpretations of texts because we are interested in what other perspectives can disclose about a text so as to confirm our own interpretation or help us to deepen or expand it. We also permit alternative interpretations of texts to show us the deficiencies of our own interpretation. In each case, however, the starting point is the same: we recognize that our understanding of textual meaning is an interpretive one that cannot exhaust the meanings the text can have.

The same would seem to hold for the issues of abortion, surrogacy, and pornography. Once we acknowledge that the different traditions, religious or otherwise, to which we belong and the different values we possess ground different orientations to and understandings of the issues under debate, we can also acknowledge the validity of different perspectives on them. Further, once we acknowledge the validity of different perspectives, we can try to learn from them. The point of doing so is not necessarily to converge on the one right interpretation of abortion or the right to free speech but, instead, to reflect further on our own understanding, to deepen it if we can, and to revise it if necessary. If we want to understand meaning, whether the meaning of texts or the meaning of our practices and principles, and if we acknowledge that understanding is never complete or exhausted, that new circumstances reveal new dimensions of meaning, then openness to alternative understandings of our principles and practices, to the dimensions of meaning they may be able to disclose seems to be not only defensible but appropriate.

Abortion is currently the most divisive of the issues considered in this paper. How might we conduct our debate over it if we were to allow for the kind of multifaceted forms of communication that McCarthy suggests, if we were no longer to anticipate consensus, and if we were to understand the logic of these forms of communication as an interpretive one? In the first place, we would abandon our present confrontation of inflexible, unyielding rights and include discussions of values and interpretations as permissible facets of the discussion. Rather than remaining cornerstones of the debate that resolution can only supersede, the values of care, on the one hand, and of self-reliance, on the other, would enter the debate as both starting points and legitimate subjects of discussion. Second, we might commit ourselves to trying to learn from one another. Critics of legal access to abortion might learn to understand abortion from a perspective that focuses on the active character of a decision to carry a pregnancy to term, where the default condition is one that ends the pregnancy rather than continuing it. Under this perspective, they might learn to understand a decision to continue the pregnancy in terms similar to decisions of family members to donate blood or bone marrow to other family members. Under current United States law, family members cannot be compelled to donate blood or organs even to their own children and even if the donation is necessary to save the life of their child. From a perspective that takes carrying a pregnancy to term to be the relevant decision rather than the decision to end it, deciding not to have an abortion appears as a decision not to use one's body to sustain life, on a par with a decision not to donate blood.

For their part, defenders of abortion might learn from its critics to take seriously the loss and tragedy that abortion can involve. They might learn not to defend it as a right but rather to conceive of it as a difficult decision under circumstances that do not allow the people involved to embrace the potential for life in a way that they think would respect it. Further, they might learn from the pro-life understanding to help with the effort to secure a place in American life for the virtues of care and nurturance, and to work with pro-life advocates in support of families. Lastly, they might learn to question presumptions that connect liberty with planning and control and to recognize the way unanticipated events or relationships can magnify and enrich one. In the end, both sides in the abortion debate might agree on a policy both can support. Such a policy would take the decision to bear a child seriously, as a decision rather than a default or natural position, and it would work to make American life and culture as supportive of children and families as it could be. We would underwrite the raising, nurturing, education, and medical care of children as a part of a social wage and we would encourage as far as we could the values of love and care in contrast to the commercialization of ever-increasing domains of life. In this way, our discussion of abortion might educate us with regard to surrogacy and pornography as well. In each case we could learn to question attempts to profit from a lack of sex, love, or child-bearing capacities and we could learn to value those parts of life we want to mean something more than our material good. We would permit abortion, however, when in a particular person's view the support of a generous social wage was not enough. And we would permit surrogacy and pornography as well, while working to make both superfluous by easing restrictions on adoption, continuing to equalize relations between men and women, and preserving not-yet-commercialized domains of life.

Still, common policies along these lines might not be forthcoming. In that case we would have to make do with the will of the majority as McCarthy conceives of it, as "the provisional outcome of a procedure intended to produce decisions even when there is no . . . agreement to be had." Supporters of the opposition might still engage in efforts to "persuade enough of the majority of the greater plausibility of their views to effect a change in the decision." They would employ arguments and attempt to convey the force of their interpretations. They would, as McCarthy continues "aim to enhance, as far as possible, the practically-rational character of the decisions that have to be made, while keeping open the possibility of ongoing contestation and eventual change."[38] They would do so, however, in a nonviolent way that avoids the dogmatic use of an appeal to rights, attempts to understand alternative interpretations, accommodates conflicting values as far as possible, and, in short, participates in what all self-consciously recognize as interpretive debate.

Notes

1. "Legitimacy and Diversity: Dialectical Reflections on Analytical Distinctions," *Cardozo Law Review,* 17, nos. 4–5 (March 1996): 1083–1125. Reprinted in *Habermas on Law and Democracy: Critical Exchanges,* ed. M. Rosenfeld and A. Arato (Berkeley: University of California Press, 1998), 115–153. Hereafter cited as "Legitimacy and Diversity."

2. "Practical Discourse: On the Relation of Morality to Politics," in Thomas McCarthy, *Ideals and Illusions: On Reconstruction and Deconstruction in Contemporary Critical Theory* (Cambridge: MIT Press, 1991), 182.

3. Jürgen Habermas, "On the Pragmatic, the Ethical, and the Moral Employments of Practical Reason," in Habermas, *Justification and Application*, trans. C. P. Cronin (Cambridge: MIT Press, 1993), 16.

4. Jürgen Habermas, *Between Facts and Norms: Contributions to a Discourse Theory of Law and Democracy*, trans. W. Rehg (Cambridge: MIT Press, 1996), 282.

5. "Legitimacy and Diversity," 1105, quoting Habermas, *Between Facts and Norms*, 152 (McCarthy's translation).

6. Ibid., 1106.

7. Ibid., 1095.

8. Jürgen Habermas, "Remarks on Discourse Ethics," in *Justification and Application*, 59–60; cited in "Legitimacy and Diversity," 1095.

9. "Legitimacy and Diversity," 1096.

10. Ibid., 1095.

11. Ibid., 1109.

12. Ibid., 1110.

13. Habermas, *Between Facts and Norms*, 151; McCarthy's translation, cited in "Legitimacy and Diversity," 1109.

14. I also look at these three debates in *Legitimate Differences: Interpretation in the Abortion Controversy and Other Public Debates* (Berkeley: University of California Press, 1999), chaps. 2, 4, 5.

15. See Cass Sunstein, "Neutrality in Constitutional Law (with Special Reference to Pornography, Abortion, and Surrogacy)," *Columbia Law Review* 92 (1992): 1–52; also Eileen L. McDonagh, *Breaking the Abortion Deadlock* (Oxford: Oxford University Press, 1996).

16. See Kristin Luker, *Abortion and the Politics of Motherhood* (Berkeley: University of California Press, 1984), 167–168.

17. Faye Ginsburg, *Contested Lives: The Abortion Debate in an American Community* (Berkeley: University of California Press, 1989), 185.

18. Luker, *Abortion and the Politics of Motherhood*, 178.

19. Ibid., 182.

20. Ibid., 176.

21. See note 8.

22. See Elizabeth S. Anderson, "Is Women's Labor a Commodity?" *Philosophy and Public Affairs* 19 (1990): 71–92.

23. Thomas H. Murray, *The Worth of a Child* (Berkeley: University of California Press, 1996), 36.

24. See Carmel Shalev, *Birth Power: The Case for Surrogacy* (New Haven: Yale University Press, 1989).

25. Ibid., 27–28.

26. Phyllis Chesler, *Sacred Bond: The Legacy of Baby M.* (New York: Times Books), Appendix G, 198–199.

27. Ibid., 208.

28. "Legitimacy and Diversity," 1107.

29. Ibid., 1105.

30. Cited as Louis Brandeis in Nadine Strossen, *Defending Pornography: Free Speech, Sex, and the Fight for Women's Rights* (New York: Scribner and Sons, 1995), 48.

31. Strossen, *Defending Pornography*, 39.

32. Ibid., 48.

33. Quoted from *The Sunday Times* in Rae Langton, "Speech Acts and Pornography," in *The Problem of Pornography*, ed. Susan Dwyer (Belmont, Cal.: Wadsworth Publishing Company, 1994), 226.

34. Quoted from *The Sunday Times* in Langton, "Speech Acts and Pornography," 232, note 6.

35. See Catherine MacKinnon, *Only Words* (Cambridge: Harvard University Press, 1993), 114, note 3.

36. "Legitimacy and Diversity," 1124–1125.

37. Ibid., 1123–1124.

38. Ibid., 1109.

12

The Logic of Fanaticism: Dewey's Archaeology of the German Mentality

Axel Honneth

The "Western cultural" publisher, Anton Hain, had it right when he decided, just a few years after the founding of the West German *Bundesrepublik*, that the time was ripe for a translation of John Dewey's "German Philosophy and Politics."[1] With a policy of "re-education" in mind, the American occupation authorities had already launched the translation of some other humanities texts during the first years after the war, with the aim of exposing a demoralized population to the democratic spirit of the American tradition. But the only text of Dewey available at this time was a reprinted edition of his major work on education that had already appeared in German in 1930.[2] However, only a few people during those first few years of rebuilding a destroyed Germany knew that this same author had already grappled directly with the intellectual origins of German political aggression in the two world wars. The initial impact of American pragmatism was extremely slight.[3] Moreover, Anglo-American writings about Germany's peculiar aggressive path were always dismissed as works of propaganda and therefore were never able to exert any productive influence. Under such conditions, it must have seemed of the utmost importance to use this translation of Dewey's short studies to confront German-speaking readers of the 1950s with ideas formulated in 1914 and 1933 by one of the leading representatives of American philosophy. Perhaps the hope was that an interpretation of these texts could help intensify the urgently needed discussion over the intellectual heritage of the future Federal Republic, which was then in its founding phase. Looking back after nearly half a century, we can see this hope would be greatly disappointed. Dewey's booklet of fewer than a hundred pages had no real effect on the debate at that time. If there were a second attempt to republish Dewey in the transformed circumstances of the "Berlin Republic," it might be useful to explain the intellectual context and impetus of Dewey's text. This is because the German context presents considerable barriers to understanding, which must be overcome if readers are properly to accept a genealogy of Germany's twentieth-century politics of aggression that returns, not to Nietzsche or the Counter-Enlightenment, but to the idealism founded by Kant.

I

Although Dewey already possessed the reputation of being one of the leading philosophers in the United States, before the First World War he was hardly known as a political intellectual in the American public sphere. Despite a host of democratic implications in his central writings (including his *Psychology* and the first edition of his *Ethics*), the fifty-five-year-old author was scarcely recognized in the actual politics of the day.[4] That changed decisively once he yielded to Randolphe Bourne's insistence, during the early phases of the First World War, that Dewey apply his democratic theory publicly to questions of contemporary politics. A series of articles appeared in rapid succession in which Dewey argued (much to Bourne's disappointment) in favor of the United States entering the war in Europe. In this first phase of his engagement as a political intellectual, Dewey formulated his first essay on German philosophy and politics. Appearing as a book of lectures, this essay makes the impressive attempt to reconstruct the philosophical ideas that could explain the rise of a collective mentality able to morally legitimate a war of conquest. Naturally Dewey attends to a host of generalizations, which could easily awaken the suspicion that he has sloppily constructed a unified national consciousness. Indeed, one cannot simply dismiss the thought that the image developed here of the German mentality serves as propaganda insofar as it primarily aims to demonstrate the moral superiority of the American intellectual tradition. Nonetheless, Dewey is all too aware of the dangers that accompany this project for him not to provide at least an outline of a theory that makes it plausible to speak of a national mentality—some "German temperament," or the "spiritual disposition" of the German people. According to his own conception, philosophical ideas should be understood as idealized answers to practical and social challenges. These responses must be organized into a framework composed of stylized forms of action that could then become crystallized in the life habits of a population. Considered as a specific temperament, or a specific mentality, a national culture should be understood as an ensemble of habitualized patterns of reaction, the analysis of which attempts to show the mutual interaction between social problems and theoretically generalized ideas over a long period of time.

Such a concept of national culture permits Dewey to employ the history of ideas in his essay as an instrument in an archaeology of the German mentality. His audience is thus not specifically those intellectuals who could potentially take sides with the Germans; rather, he addresses his own comrades-in-arms who would make the wrong connections in their explanation of German aggression. As he also does in other, shorter, texts from the time of the First World War, Dewey here primarily opposes the tendency in Anglo-American analyses of the enemy to portray Nietzsche's metaphysics of power as the intellectual cause of the enthusiasm for war among the Germans. Instead Dewey argues that such an explanation fails to understand the history of ideas, particularly the epigonal position of Nietzsche in relation to an illusionary idealism that reaches back to Kant. The provocative yet central feature of Dewey's analysis derives from his viewing the aggressive German mentality as a consequence of the direction opened up for German philosophy by Kant's two-worlds doctrine. Despite the great cultural distance, his text touches upon the same concerns expressed in that famous passage on Kantian moral theory found in the chapter on Sade in the *Dialectic of Enlightenment*.[5]

The comparison with Horkheimer and Adorno's treatment of Kant can also establish the transition to the second essay printed in Germany as the introductory chapter to the volume on German politics. In this 1942 essay, Dewey extends his original interpretation of the German mentality in World War I to the rise of National

Socialism. After he had found his role as a public intellectual during the stormy debate over U.S. policy in the First World War, in the following years Dewey enthusiastically carried out the tasks that come with such a role. There was hardly an event of worldwide political significance, and hardly an occurrence touching on the moral self-understanding of the United States that Dewey didn't make an occasion for political analysis, in which his insights into the theory of democracy were worked into elements of a diagnosis of the times. Among the events Dewey treated were the prerevolutionary course of events in China, the efforts to build a League of Nations, the Stalinist terror in Russia, and U.S. imperialism in Mexico. Not surprisingly, Dewey also energetically followed the rise of the National-Socialist system of domination in Germany and must have feared that its wide support among the population was the first sign of a return of the typical German mentality. Only shortly after the beginning of the German war of aggression did Dewey use the debate about American involvement as an occasion for an analysis, turning to the history of ideas for constructing a genealogy of the National-Socialist worldview. Again he saw his essential task as contradicting those predominant Anglo-American interpretations that presumed that the Germans' readiness for war was simply due to the effects of an irrationalism traceable to Nietzsche. The global political constellation had now considerably shifted: besides the National-Socialist system of domination, Stalinist totalitarianism had been established as a political power structure. These events required a broadening of the perspectives on the contemporary German mentality to include cultural-historical developments that led to the increase in political barbarism and despotism. In the two articles to which Dewey had dedicated this theme, an outline of a diagnosis of the times takes shape. Despite the differences in form from the philosophy of history in *Dialectic of Enlightenment,* Dewey's diagnosis agrees entirely with its view that the crisis of human civilization is to be understood as a result of the combination of a zealous idealism and a morally oblivious positivism.[6] The genealogical analysis of the National-Socialist worldview, in the broader context of this theory of a "crisis in human history," assigns to Kantian idealism responsibility for the most catastrophic results in human history.

II

No one sufficiently familiar with the development of Dewey's philosophy should be surprised that in these two essays on the history of ideas he constantly leads us back to Kant's idealism to explain the beginnings of the German politics of aggression in the twentieth century. Developing intellectually under the strong influence of the British neo-idealism of F.H. Bradley and T.H. Green, Dewey first worked on a program of naturalized Hegelianism as a theoretical alternative not only to empiricism but also to Kant's transcendentalism. All the oppositions found in Kant's work and connected with the distinction between the noumenal and empirical worlds—whether the dualism of the "thing-in-itself" and appearance, of the transcendental and empirical ego, or of duty and inclination—are now to be overcome through the conception of an organism active in its own natural environment and conceived of simply as moments in conscious life. Already in the early writings, many clues make it clear how much Dewey saw in Kant the antipode of his own philosophical endeavors. In the "Outlines of a Critical Theory of Ethics," published in 1899, Dewey argues that the "absolute opposition of reason and inclination" in Kant's moral theory blocked any search for a starting point to determine morally right actions in the social world itself.[7] Kant's implicit psychology can be read in the same context and seen as much more primitive than many other approaches, because it ultimately reduces all human inclinations and drives to the goal of increasing pleasure or well-being.[8] Even as the influence of Hegel in Dewey's work begins to fade and the pragmatic motifs attain greater self-sufficiency, this constitutive demarcation from Kantianism loses none of its significance. Later, in addition to the original rejection of Kant, Dewey adds a cultural diagnosis that Kantian dualisms have left deep and long-lasting traces in the social lifeworld and have become real in the form of social disturbances or pathologies. Dewey still lacked a suitable conceptual model for clarifying what in social and political hindsight he considers the genuinely unfortunate implications of Kant's philosophy. Although the formulas of the independence of reason and the absolutization of obligation are already belabored, Dewey still lacked the illustrative material that could vividly confirm this negative chain of effects. In the end Dewey did not have to wait very long until historical developments themselves confronted him with the political need to prove, in a concrete case analysis, what had up until then remained merely vague conjectures. When the German population in 1914 began enthusiastically to support the war aims of the government, unlike the majority of his contemporaries Dewey saw it as an instance of the overwhelming effects that Kantian idealism established in the collective mentality of an entire people. His history of ideas should therefore be regarded as nothing less than a case study of the social and philosophical claim that the subordination of empirical reality under a priori reason inevitably engenders tendencies toward feelings of national superiority, especially when the emptiness of regulative rational principles is filled with the content of a suitably aggressive doctrine.

Dewey's image of Kant in his genealogical study is dominated throughout by his emphasis on the two-world metaphysics. To be sure, the cosmopolitan idea of a federation of states is mentioned positively,[9] as well as the intention of developing the concept of rational freedom for moral philosophy.[10] But little remains from Kant's three critiques beyond a foundationalist theory of the a priori status of reason. Dewey sees the "core" of this theory as the conviction that the physical world is made into the object of a legislative reason that is itself at home in the completely different world of transcendental subjectivity, through which the person (as an inhabitant of the noumenal sphere) masters the realm of the senses and of nature "as a sovereign is above his subjects."[11] On the one hand, the consequence of assigning such a predominant role to the inner activity of reason over empirical reality is a cult of interiority that the Protestantism of Luther, with its world-despising, inward stance, virtually revered as a kind of mythology. Kant merely conceptualized this inward orientation philosophically by selecting the realm of interiority in the concept of reason to be the determining ground of all justified relations to the world. On the other hand, however, along with increased value for inner ideals there arises an entirely profane sense for the technically adequate, the habitual equivalent for the utterly devalued world of what is merely given in nature. A form of disenchanted routine, even bureaucratic control, must dominate because

only then can one deal successfully with the determinism of the physical world. According to Dewey, the chain of influence that leads
from philosophical ideas to everyday habits of action in Germany
produced a collective mentality in which a pretentious idealism became harmonious with a devotion to the mechanical and organizational. In it the belief in the primacy of inner values and spiritual
ideals reigns supreme, along with a sober sense for what is technically
feasible.

With this separation of spheres as the starting point for the German mentality, Dewey sees its further development conditioned by
the fact that Kant develops his formalist concept of reason outside of
reality and thereby frees it from all content. Such an empty space can
be filled by those substantive definitions of rationality recommended
by the prevailing doctrines of the day. Dewey follows out the proces-
sion of insidious materializations of the formal principle of reason,
above all in Kant's concept of "duty" to which Dewey, as a successor
to Hegel, bears a great mistrust. However, in the context of his politically oriented archaeology, the critique of the very idea of a rational,
unconditional duty does not just serve to develop a moral philosophy
but, more importantly, gives us a more exact analysis of the German
mentality. The arguments that Dewey uses are in no way new, but
rather stem from his previously developed moral theory, here innov-
atively focused on the special case of Germany's intellectual development. Like Hegel before him, Dewey primarily emphasizes the
formalism of the Kantian theory of duty, in which the idea of the
moral fulfillment of duty seems to function as the only measure of
moral action; absent is any consideration of the different formulations of the categorical imperative, in which Kant himself sought to
avoid the crudest misunderstandings through the elucidation of the
principles of universalization. It is just a short step, Dewey argues, to
the possibility that the content of moral obligations could be set by
"social authorities." Thus, Dewey concludes that a Kantian ethic of
obligation can provide sufficiently fertile soil for a social cast of mind
in which the fulfillment of duties decreed by the state can be considered as if they were justified by the highest moral principle. Not
without a certain feeling of triumph, Dewey cites a passage of the
Prussian war-novelist Friedrich von Bernhardi in which universal

conscription is praised as the political legacy of Kantian moral philosophy. He summarizes his analysis in this way: "When the practical political situation called for universal military service in order to support and expand the existing state, the gospel of a Duty devoid of content naturally lent itself to the consecration and idealization of such specific duties as the existing national order might prescribe."[12]

This conclusion is to a large extent unclear, because it is not yet entirely certain whether it is supposed to emphasize the continuity in the history of ideas or a kind of perverted effective history. In the first case, Dewey could be reproached for ignoring the Kantian idea of reciprocal respect as a fundamental concept of moral duty. In the second case, however, we would be confronted with the interesting question of whether the structure of an ethic of duty could encourage the establishment of a frame of mind that is fixated on authority. Dewey's analysis certainly permits both alternative interpretations, even if the tone and brusque style of argumentation seem to favor the first interpretation. In this context, however, the essay that is published at the same time, "On Understanding the Mind of Germany," reveals Dewey's argument to be a middle position between both possible interpretations. Indeed, Kant himself was much too motivated by "noble aspirations" not to regard the fulfillment of moral duty as the realization of the ideals of the moral community of all human beings. Nonetheless, with his understanding of morality as an ethic of duty, he prepared the way in Germany for the eventual complete identification of moral obligations with obedience to government authorities.[13] A direct line leads, albeit unintentionally, from Kant over to the statist concept of obligation at the time of the First World War, during which the readiness of the Germans to submit to state command exceeded that of all other nationalities.

Dewey did not restrict himself in his archaeology of the German mentality merely to the emergence of a substantive ethic of obligation. On the contrary, he gives still greater weight to a second process of ideological development that also reaches back to Kant. The popularization of the idealism of reason is intertwined with the formation of a mental disposition that on the one hand consists of the belief in the power of ideas relieved of any connection to experience and, on the other, gives rise in moral theory to the ethic of obedience sketched above. Dewey also sees in this initial constellation the roots of a political philosophy oriented to the implementation of a priori reason as the goal of a state-run common existence. What Dewey means by this goal is best understood today with the help of the formulation of an "Ethicizing" of state functions. In his view, Kant had already delineated, in his writings on the philosophy of history, the distinction between "culture" and "civilization" that, once loaded with nationalistic content, immediately developed into the idea that the German state was uniquely destined to serve as a defense of ethical values against a merely technical, utilitarian civilization. In the course of the presentation of this process of development, Dewey necessarily departs from the narrow framework of an interpretation of Kant and turns toward the further development of German Idealism, in which he takes first Fichte's philosophy of the state and then Hegel's philosophy of history as the guiding themes for his subsequent analysis. However, the picture that he presents of Fichte's political philosophy as well as his rough sketch of Hegel's philosophy of history adds nothing new to conventional interpretations: with Fichte's political writings the German history of ideas takes a decisive turn, for now the moral task of the state is unambiguously furnished with nationalist features, in contrast to Kant's cosmopolitan ideals. Here Dewey finds the essential elements of the view that the German nation has been selected in times of cultural decline to represent universal ideas of reason. In Hegelian philosophy of history, Dewey finally sees this amalgamation of idealism and nationalism as adding a further legitimation of the equation of German mission with absolute spirit. Naturally Dewey does not ignore the fact that it was Hegel who conceived of war as a rational, purifying means for the realization of such a mission.

Even if the goal of educating the American reader about the most prominent basic thoughts of Idealist philosophy leads Dewey wide of the mark in his interpretations, he sticks closely and thoroughly to his central claim. Hardly a page goes by in which Dewey does not direct our attention again and again to the conceptual structure that led to the establishment of such a nationalistic philosophy of state and history. Had Kant not bifurcated reality and reason in his philosophical work, such that the physical came to stand here and the noumenal, spiritual world over there—then neither Fichte's idea of a German national culture nor the next step in Hegel's philosophy of history would have been possible. This is because both schemes are understood as attempts at the historical realization of an indeterminate principle of reason. Shortly before the end of a chapter that can be read as a summary of the history of philosophy, Dewey states that Fichte and Hegel had only helped "people the Kantian void of the supersensible with the substantial figures of the State and its Historical Evolution and Mission."[14] For Dewey, Kant remains "the philosopher of Germany,"[15] whose philosophical grounding of the belief in a priori reason was so subversive and so far-reaching that all subsequent intellectual developments in Germany were only variations on one and the same theme. The Romantics filled the ideal realm of formally determined reason with "poetic visions,"[16] the German Idealists detranscendentalized the void of the noumena and gave it the significance of a historically embodied reason, and the neo-Kantians finally restricted themselves to a "critique of the methodology of the sciences,"[17] whose principle was found in the idea of a constitution of reality through the activity of reason.

In light of such a history of ideas, it is not surprising that Dewey understands those authors who developed the spiritual heritage of a Kantian idealism of reason as representative of an intellectual mobilization in Germany at the time of the First World War. To be sure, Dewey does not name those important philosophers and sociologists whose undisguised advocacy of the aggressive war goals of Germany still irritate us today (Scheler, Simmel, Troeltsch),[18] but rather a series of second-rate, popular scholars who urged support for war. One finds not only Friedrich von Bernhardi but also the philosopher Rudolf Euken, who at the time enjoyed the international prestige that comes with the Nobel Prize for literature he received in 1908. In the cases named here, Dewey has no difficulty tracing the evidence for a direct appeal to Kant, nor in demonstrating the effects of rational-idealist motives: both Rudolf Euken and Friedrich von Bernhardi justified the goals of war with the argument that Germany as a state had the special task of an international advocate for the implementation of universalistic ideals of reason and morals. The scheme that intellectually oriented this legitimation of a war of aggression was, for Dewey, formally the same as the one that Kant originally imported into the world of philosophical ideas, only now mediated by a 100-year development that gives the original dualism its historical substance. Furthermore, such authors presuppose a sphere of merely physical, soulless reality that must be compelled by the will to achieve a principle of reason that lacks all reality. As Dewey says in reference to a contemporary writer, a "logic of fanaticism" is built into Kant's original idea of an a priori reason.[19] That is, as a sufficiently large collective emerges and becomes convinced of a growing resistance against inviolable principles of reason, it resorts to increasingly violent means if necessary, in order to impose rational ideals upon a soulless and uncultured reality.

In summary, this conclusion is best understood in terms of how Dewey employs a set of oppositions that are typically employed by historians of ideas to explain the development of German thought preceding the First World War. In Dewey's writings, the intellectual readiness to engage in war—the "German mentality"—is not explained by the consequences of the nineteenth-century countercurrents to the rationalist Enlightenment tradition. On the contrary, Dewey gives hardly any significance to the work of Nietzsche and *Lebensphilosophie* for the development of the German claim to leadership at the beginning of the twentieth century. The Kantian idea of an a priori validity of Reason, often considered the central bulwark against the irrational tendencies of the nineteenth century, is precisely what Dewey considers the spiritual cause of the fateful development of Germany. Whether one looks to Lukács or to Habermas, one finds among German speakers a constant tendency to view the tradition of rationalist idealism as a spiritual inheritance, without whose "destruction" by antirationalism the intellectual development of Germany might have taken a different—and politically preferable—direction.[20] Due to the stark difference in preliminary diagnoses, the therapy that Dewey indirectly recommends must, not surprisingly, be completely different from that of Habermas or Lukács. For Dewey, we need neither to reconnect with nor to renew the rationalist-idealist tradition, but finally to overcome it. Only a completely different form of rationalism can liberate the German mentality from the tendency to entrust their nation with a special cultural mission. The conceptual framework that he employs in his archaeology of intellectual history is not the opposition between rationalism and irrationalism, but rather between a problematic, a priori rationalism and a more limited, or "experimental" rationalism. On the few pages that Dewey dedicates to sketching out such an alternative rationalism, it becomes clear that the term "rational" should only apply to convictions that prove themselves worthy by providing solutions to concrete problems in the world of action.

III

This is not the appropriate place to discuss the many questions bound up with differences among the various diagnoses of the German mentality. In Dewey's treatment of the concept of duty, it is already clear that many of his theses depend on whether one is speaking of a perpetuation or a perversion of the fundamental Kantian idea. Dewey was doubtless certain that Kant's theory had precluded the possibility of political abuse to the extent that he linked the realization of practical reason with the idea of humanity as a "kingdom of ends." Although this grand idea is not suppressed in his writings on Germany, neither are the many theoretically mediating steps that were first necessary to turn the original program of transcendental idealism into a claim of national superiority. At the same time, Dewey remains unshaken in assigning objective responsibility for the German intellectual development that led to the ideas of 1914 to the scheme of thought that sets reason and reality in opposition to each other. Though completely independent from Kant's own moral intentions, his conception of an a priori validity of reason allows an individual, a group, or an entire people to believe themselves in possession of an inviolable truth independent of intersubjective scrutiny. To clarify this line of thought as the argumentative center of Dewey's archaeology remains a worthwhile endeavor, given the many examples of its use in political-philosophical reflections in the United States today. Michael Walzer warns of the danger of political elitism in the context-transcending intellectual, and Richard Rorty stresses how the idea of an objective reason can be used in the service of despotism.[21] These motifs echo Dewey's idea that a rationality placed beyond all experience can lead to the collective mentality evidenced by the German people in the First World War.

As Dewey himself thought, his analysis would carry even more weight after Hitler's seizure of power in Germany and implementation of an apparently different and incomparably brutal worldview. The confused writings of Hitler are also supposed to mirror a mentality that is in essence traceable back to the scheme of Kant's a priori reason.[22] In his extensive effort in gathering materials for his 1942 essay, Dewey focused on Hitler's confusions as evidence for his interpretation.[23] He indiscriminately cites *Mein Kampf* in order to show how from 1800 to 1914 and then to 1933 a unique constellation of ideas continuously developed on the basis of a characteristic opposition of spiritual world and simple reality. To be sure, Dewey can only countenance such continuity by undertaking a series of risky interpretive maneuvers that put the identity of this Kantian heritage in question. In three steps he defends the thesis that Hitler's worldview is to be understood merely as one more step in the unfolding of that fateful "logic of fanaticism" going back to Kant's idealism. First, he loosens up his discussion of the German mentality, no longer arguing that Kantianism is directly reflected in many of Hitler's writings. Dewey now speaks only of a certain relation of fit between those abstruse ideas and the spiritual situation of the German population. Here the premise is that Hitler's message and "creed" had found resonance with the majority of the Germans in virtue of a "pre-established harmony"[24] between the content of his statements and the intellectual aspect of their collective mentality. The second step argues that this elective affinity is found in Hitler's glorification of a spiritual sphere of the ideal beyond all ordinary, physically determined reality. Hitler's beliefs and intentions fit well with the "latent idealism"[25] of the German population, insofar as he wanted to cure the collective shame and humiliation after the First World War by unleashing ideals that were supposed to draw their revivifying and reunifying power through resistance against a contemptible reality. Dewey remains convinced that the formal ontology outlined in Kant's two-world theory is found once again in these thoughts of a national rebirth from ideals.

Up to this point of his argument, Dewey has said nothing about the specific components of the worldview that are reflected in the speeches and writings of Hitler. That occurs in the third step of his argument, in which he develops the thesis that carries the entire weight of his assertion of a historical continuity in mentality up to National Socialism. Hitler and his ideological party followers give content to the noumenal sphere (which Kant prudently had left merely formal) with aspects of the instinctual nature of humanity, aspects expressed by vitalistic concepts such as "blood," "life-force," and "race." The appeal to reason, which remained constitutive for National Socialism, could thereby acquire a content conjured up from natural forces, whose bearer moreover would be found in the long-standing model of the "German *Volk*." Although this is a most unusual explanation, Dewey argues that closer observation shows that the National-Socialist worldview contains two different elements that seem reasonable to keep apart. First, Dewey argues that National Socialism makes reason and nature equivalent and thus leaves the dualistic schema of Kantian idealism intact without having to renounce pride of place for the "most primitive" characteristics of life.[26] Natural human instinct is valorized by being endowed with the insignias of reason, all the constitutive characteristics of an ideal that is normatively in opposition to merely empirical reality.

Perhaps these thoughts of Dewey's can be rephrased most concisely in this way: in National Socialism, nature is not conceived as the "other" but as the embodiment of reason. Only with this reconciliation could nature become a conceptual ideal to which one may appeal with idealistic intonations because it belongs to a higher order of being than causally determined reality. However, Dewey must add a second component to this interpretive sketch in order to discover the specific characteristics of the National-Socialist worldview. That is, this nature that is unified with reason must at the same time function as a sphere to which the Germans—as a natural collective, as a *Volksgemeinschaft*— have a privileged access if they are to conceive themselves as a nation with a missionary task. Thus, in National-Socialist Germany, as Dewey sees it, a revival of idealism and nationalism together permit the replacement of formal rational values with primitive instincts of human nature. For Hitler, the Germans are a people charged with the mission of implementing, possibly with violence, a priori ideals. For unlike any other collectivity, they embody those powers of nature that epitomize the higher order of being. With this inference it should come as no surprise that Dewey often sees the actual meaning of the concept of race as having the epistemic function of securing for the Germans a monopoly on the articulation of the instinctive forces of nature.

In this context Dewey mentions for the first time those figures constantly given the most prominent place in alternative genealogies of the National-Socialist mentality. Beneath a citation of Heinrich Heine is a reference to the natural philosophy of Schelling.[27] Only a few lines later Richard Wagner is mentioned as the intellectual source from which Hitler drew his vision of a return to *Germanentum*. This frugal list again detours around the work of Friederich Nietzsche, even though Dewey himself several times used the concept "vitalism" to give a name to the intellectual core of Hitler's worldview. Every association with the founding father of *Lebensphilosophie* is avoided so as not to launch the genealogy in a false direction. One can only speculate about the motives that could have moved Dewey in 1942 to resolve not even to mention Nietzsche's name. Perhaps Dewey thought it only confused the historical line of intellectual responsibility. Reprimanding or even referring to Nietzsche would only produce a false move in the direction of antirationalism. Dewey's credo in 1942 is no different than in 1915—the fate of the German mind is not to unleash the critique of reason, but rather to pervert a rational idealism already ailing at its core. All objective responsibility for the authorship of the unfortunate development of the German mentality Dewey attributes to this single theme: the surpassing of the Enlightenment through the idea of an a priori reason. Without Kant's idea that reason is in principle strictly opposed to empirical reality, there would not have developed the fateful conviction that only the German nation is in possession of universally justified ideals to impose upon the rest of the world, with violence if necessary.[28] Thus Dewey must give precisely the interpretation of Hitler's worldview that he sought to outline in the few pages of his text—that with this last act in the completion of idealism, reason is made equivalent to its opposite, nature, so that the unleashing of natural instincts can now become a call to rational ideals.

The form of therapy that Dewey recommends for the Germans at the end of his analysis follows from the genealogical responsibility that he attributes to rationalist idealism. In bringing to fruition traces of reflections scattered in the 1914 text, the idea of an a priori reason is now opposed to a model of limited rationalism, whose core is presented as a procedure of "free and open communication." As soon as the rational is no longer presented as something located beyond reality in some noumenal realm, it requires forms of uncoerced, open discussion in order collectively to discover and validate what is "rational" in reality as given. Dewey's text ends with the advocacy of the normative ideals of American democracy; only those readers who believe the lack of a democratic sensibility was in no way responsible for Germany's catastrophic role in the twentieth century could consider such advocacy as propaganda: "I conclude, then, with expression of the belief that it is this method, the method of achieving community by processes of free and open communication, which is the heart and the strength of the American democratic way of living and that the weaknesses of our democracy all represent expressions of failure to live up to the demands imposed by this method. Prejudices of economic status, of race, or religion, imperil democracy because they set up barriers to communication or deflect and distort its operation."[29]

IV

The two essays by John Dewey discussed here naturally cannot keep pace with the vast wealth of literature on the twentieth-century German mentality, writings that were composed to a great extent by German exiles.[30] In contrast to George Herbert Mead, who had studied in Germany, this American pragmatist lacked an exact, first-hand knowledge of the German philosophical fraternity. As he himself occasionally mentioned,[31] he had to summon up a good measure of hermeneutical exertion in order to understand the normative horizon of a culture that seemed to him extremely far removed from the American way of life. This deep lack of understanding, coupled with his avowed propagandistic purposes, could have led him to some assertions about connections in the effective history of German thought that are more than merely problematic. Dewey never sufficiently distinguished between Kant's original theory and what the German nationalist tradition tried to make out of it. Nonetheless, it is precisely this outsider's viewpoint, this deep difference in cultural self-conception, that may possibly have placed him in a position to identify connections and inferences in the history of ideas that could not so easily be discerned from the inside. Dewey's unprecedented and perhaps unique analysis does not make Hegel's concept of the state nor Nietzsche's vitalism but Kant's two-world theory responsible for the German mentality in the two world wars. Whoever is not already inclined to believe that such genealogies display a high degree of arbitrariness, that they function somewhat like an adaptable reserve to be put to use in national controversies, must consider this diagnosis quite challenging. The core thesis holds that Kant's unbridgeable gulf between a merely empirical reality and a realm of transcendentally valid principles of reason is responsible for the German spiritual stance of the past 200 years and that philosophical innovations in more recent German philosophy were in the end mere variations of that two-world theory. The challenge for philosophy is then to prove one side or the other of the following dilemma with philosophical arguments: either that the accusation against Kantianism is in fact unjustified or that it is impossible systematically to do without such a distinction between reason and reality.

Translated by Jason Murphy

Notes

For advice and comments the author thanks Hans Joas.

1. Trans.—See John Dewey, *German Philosophy and Politics* (New York: G.P. Putnam's Sons, 1942). This appears in vol. 8 of John Dewey, *The Middle Works, 1899–1924*, ed. J. A. Boydston (Carbondale: Southern Illinois University Press, 1980); henceforth cited as *MW*. *EW* and *LW* refer, respectively, to John Dewey, *The Early Works, 1882–1898*, ed. J. A. Boydston (Carbondale: Southern Illinois University Press, 1967–1972) and *The Later Works, 1925–1953*, ed. J. A. Boydston (Carbondale: Southern Illinois University Press, 1981–1990).

2. John Dewey, *Demokratie und Erziehung* (Breslau, 1930; 1949). For the English, see *Democracy and Education* (New York: Macmillan, 1916); this is vol. 9 of *MW*. A helpful overview of the history of Dewey's publication in the German-speaking realm is Jean-Claude Wolf, "Dewey in deutscher Sprache" *Freiburger Zeitschrift für Philosophie und Theologie* 46, nos. 1–2 (1999): 287–294. However, Wolf's critical bibliography does not

Axel Honneth

mention the text at issue here nor the translation of "Freedom and Culture" that appeared in 1956: John Dewey, *Mensch oder Masse* (Vienna/Munich, 1956).

3. See Hans Joas, "Amerikanischer Pragmatismus und deutsches Denken: Zur Geschichte eines Mißverständnisses," in *Pragmatismus und Gesellschaftstheorie* (Frankfurt am Main: Suhrkamp, 1992), 114–115.

4. Robert B. Westbrook; *John Dewey and American Democracy* (Ithaca: Cornell University Press; 1991), chap. 7.

5. Max Horkheimer and Theodor Adorno, *Dialectic of Enlightenment*, trans. J. Cumming (Continuum Press: New York, 1972), Excursus 2, 81–120; *Dialectik der Aufklärung* (Frankfurt am Main, 1969), 88–127.

6. John Dewey, "The Crisis in Human History," *LW*, vol. 15, 210–223. For the intellectual context of these essays see Westbrook, *John Dewey*, 510–523.

7. See John Dewey, "Outlines of a Critical Theory of Ethics," *EW*, vol. 3, 239–388, especially 333–336.

8. Ibid., 250.

9. Dewey, *German Philosophy and Politics*, MW, vol. 8, 171.

10. Ibid., 156.

11. Ibid., 149.

12. Ibid., 164.

13. John Dewey, "On Understanding the Mind of Germany," *MW*, vol. 10, 216–233, here especially 227.

14. *German Philosophy and Politics*, 198.

15. Ibid.

16. Ibid.

17. Ibid., 199.

18. See Hans Joas, "Kriegsideologen: Der Erste Weltkrieg im Spiegel der zeitgenössischen Sozialwissenschaften," *Kriege und Werte: Studien zur Gewaltgeschichte des 20. Jahrhunderts* (Weilerswist: Velbrück Wissenschaft, 2000), 87–125; and Kurt Flasch; *Die geistige Mobilmachung: Die Deutschen Intellektuellen und der Erste Weltkrieg* (Berlin: Fest, 2000).

19. Dewey, *German Philosophy and Politics*, 159. (Trans.—The "contemporary writer" is not named by Dewey.)

20. See Georg Lukács, *The Destruction of Reason*, trans. P. Palmer (London: Merlin, 1980); also Jürgen Habermas, *The Philosophical Discourse of Modernity*, trans. F. Lawrence (Cambridge: MIT Press, 1990), chaps. 3 and 4.

21.Michael Walzer, *In the Company of Critics* (New York: Basic, 1988); Richard Rorty, *Philosophy and Social Hope* (New York: Penguin, 1999).

22. It should be stressed here again that Dewey is not arguing that Kant's writings themselves played a significant role in shaping the central ideology in World War I. As to the question of whether Kant's theory had an immunizing effect during the time of National Socialism or could be taken in by the dominant doctrine, different positions are possible. See Gereon Woltlers; "Der 'Führer' und seine Denker: Zur Philosophie des 'Dritten Reiches,'" *Deutsche Zeitschrift für Philosophie* 47 (1999): 223–251. In opposition to Woltlers is Volker Böhnigk, "Kant und der Nationalsozialism," *Bonner Philosophische Vorträge und Studien* 9 (2000).

23. (Trans.—From Dewey's "The One-World of Hitler's National-Socialism," *MW*, vol. 8, 421–446. This was the introduction to the second edition of *German Philosophy and Politics.*)

24. "The One-World of Hitler's National-Socialism," 421–422.

25. Ibid., 428.

26. Ibid., 440

27. Ibid., 428.

28. Only a single sentence from Thomas Mann's famous speech "Germany and the Germans" is cited here: "The Germans are a people of the romantic counter-revolution against philosophical intellectualism and the rationalism of the Enlightenment—an uprising of music against literature, of mysticism against clarity." In Thomas Mann, *An die gesittete Welt* (Frankfurt am Main, 1986), 717ff.

29. "The One-World of Hitler's National-Socialism," 444.

30. Helmuth Plessner, *Die verspätete Nation* (Stuttgart: Kohlhammer, 1959); and Karl Popper, *The Open Society and Its Enemies*, 2 vols. (Princeton: Princeton University Press, 1971).

31. See, for example, Dewey's "On Understanding the Mind of Germany," 218.

13

Political Pluralism in Hegel and Rawls

Andrew Buchwalter

One of the criticisms commonly made of any contemporary appeal to Hegel's political theory is that Hegel seems ill-suited to deal with current realities, especially the conditions of social and cultural pluralism that distinguish modern societies. Hegel is assumed to be committed to a view of political life that gives priority to organic unity, praises communal bonds, accentuates shared traditions, and exhorts patriotic engagement for communally valued ends. Moreover, this conception of political life is formulated as part of a general philosophy that champions monism, systematicity, absolutism, and conceptual closure. Such values are hardly consistent with the principles of tolerance, heterogeneity, diversity, novelty, open-endedness, and fallibilism that form the focus of so much discussion today in politics as in theory.

Yet while it is true that much in Hegel's philosophy is inimical to any pluralist rendering, his thought generally is less opposed to pluralism than is commonly assumed. A proper examination of his theoretical and, particularly, practical philosophy reveals that on many points he is as receptive to pluralist considerations as are those opposed to his alleged monism. Indeed, in some respects Hegel is more disposed to pluralism than many of those who present themselves as its proponents. Naturally Hegel should not be counted among the preeminent advocates of difference or agonism. Concepts like unity, identity, and reconciliation indisputably remain at the core of his thought. It is also the case, though, that Hegel's commitment to such concepts is inseparable from a simultaneous commitment to the principles of opposition, diversity, self-reflexivity, and open-endedness often associated with pluralist thought. For Hegel, a genuine account of holism is inconceivable without a concurrent affirmation of diversity, just as a genuine account of pluralism is inconceivable absent a thematization of unity and commonality. Little else is in fact conceivable for a writer whose thought is centrally committed to surmounting abstract dichotomies—above all, that between the one and the many.

In what follows I examine Hegel's conception of political pluralism by comparing it with that of John Rawls, whose theory of political liberalism is designed in large part to accommodate modern social and political pluralism. I defend four related theses: (1) not only does Hegel advance a developed conception of political pluralism, but he does so more robustly than does Rawls, whose political liberalism is conceived in part as an antidote to the purportedly antipluralist tendencies endemic to Hegelian thought; (2) while Hegel does accentuate the political centrality of a communal ethos and a common notion of the good, his aim is to fortify, rather than undermine, the pluralist principles that for Rawls are sustainable only by subordinating the good to the right; (3) although Hegel does accord special place in public life to the types of comprehensive doctrines Rawlsian pluralism banishes to the domain of the prepolitical, his aim is in part to provide for the functional conditions of a theory of political pluralism; and (4) while Hegel shares with Rawls a sensitivity to the "tragic" conflicts and oppositions characteristic of modern social life, he regards them less as "facts" than as sociocultural constructions, with the consequence that ethical conflict, however profound in modern life, is not deemed in principle irreconcilable. In broad terms this paper builds on the efforts of Thomas McCarthy, who has long sought to surmount the abstract dichotomies that beset contemporary social and political theory and who in recent years has done so admirably via a constructive engagement with the work of Rawls.

1. The concept of pluralism is central to Rawls's political philosophy as formulated in *Political Liberalism*.[1] Focusing on the sixteenth and seventeenth centuries' Wars of Religion, Rawls there advances a

notion of politics whose task is to accommodate the fundamentally pluralist conditions of modern life, in particular the profound conflicts regarding values and conceptions of the good that typify modernity. Political philosophy thus proceeds from the question: "How is a just and free society possible under conditions of deep doctrinal conflict with no prospect of resolution?"[2]

Already in this formulation, however, Rawls reveals a certain ambivalence toward pluralism, its social and political centrality notwithstanding. Rawls may embrace pluralism as part and parcel of the liberties of modern societies, presenting it "as the natural outcome of the activities of human reason under enduring free institutions."[3] At the same time, he regards it more as a condition to be managed than a value to be championed. Under modern conditions political philosophy is charged with devising principles of justice able to facilitate social cooperation among groups and individuals incapable of achieving agreement on fundamental values or "comprehensive doctrines." While political liberalism proceeds from social and political pluralism, it itself focuses on the principles of social order able to offset or "contain" the disorder and threat to stability imminent in modern pluralistic societies.[4] Rawls certainly claims, against conservatives, that pluralism is "not a disaster" and is "not an unfortunate condition of human life."[5] Yet this endorsement, if indeed it is one, attests to his ambivalence. Modern pluralism is not a disaster only because modern societies have fashioned "a new social possibility"—a constitutional order in which "social unity and concord" is now achievable despite the absence of any agreement on fundamental values and doctrines.[6] That modern societies might be distinctive because of their diversity is a view that finds limited expression in Rawls's thought.

Rawls does claim that principles of social cohesion are to be fashioned in a pluralist manner. At issue is not a "metaphysical" explication of the principles of justice but an intersectional composite generated from the diversity of existing values themselves. This is the basis for his rooting the principles of social cooperation in the idea of an overlapping consensus, yet this idea itself betrays ambivalence toward pluralism. For Rawls, an overlapping consensus and the principles of social order spawned by it are not conceived as a mere *modus vivendi,* a procedural compromise accepted by parties as a convenient means to safeguard private welfare and diverse interests. If principles of social cooperation are to claim the stability required of just institutions, if they are to "fit together into one unified system of social cooperation from one generation to the next,"[7] they must have "moral" status as well. Principles of justice must be affirmed not just for instrumental reasons but because they embody principles that are deemed intrinsically valuable. In Rawls's conception of a well-ordered society, citizens "desire for its own sake a social world in which they, as free and equal, can cooperate with others on terms all can accept."[8] Indeed, far from attending only to private goods, Rawls considers his notion of justice to express a principle of "common good," a set of "final ends" citizens of a well-ordered society share in common.[9] Yet if the principles of just social order are simply those that are commonly embraced and that proceed from what is held in common, the Rawls's endorsement of pluralism is only further qualified. Not only do such considerations raise questions about the degree to which political philosophy does in fact proceed from irreconcilable conflict; not only do they place a substantive premium on public reason construed as consensus rather than, say, dissensus; they also serve to withhold recognition from those doctrines unamenable to cooperative rearticulation. A political philosophy focused on an overlapping consensus bars from the outset those doctrines whose incommensurability precludes participation in a consensus predicated on a doctrine's ability to share "common ground."[10] Rawls himself acknowledges as much when noting that his is an account of "reasonable pluralism," one that, in opposition to "simple pluralism," bars all doctrines that are "unreasonable and irrational."[11] However incompatible otherwise, any such doctrine qualifies for public recognition only if it is reasonable, and thus committed to the values and obligations of social cooperation. Hence, while Rawls may start from the "fact" of irreconcilable pluralism, his own version of a rationally ordered society grants space only to views that at some level lend themselves to reconciliation; it is certainly not a vision in which diversity, difference, and heterogeneity play a defining role in the composition and identity of society. As one critic has noted, "Rawls's political liberalism can provide a consensus among reasonable persons who *by definition* are persons who accept the principles of political liberalism."[12]

When we look at Hegel on the same problems, we find that his position has much in common with Rawls, the latter's professed distance from Hegelian philosophizing notwithstanding.[13] Hegel's political philosophy also proceeds from the "fact" of modern pluralism, what Hegel terms bifurcation [*Entzweiung*]—something that, with Rawls (and Berlin), he also construes via the language of tragedy. Hegel also closely links modern pluralism with early modern religious conflict, a point noted by Rawls in fashioning his own position.[14] Further, Hegel sees the task of political philosophy as fashioning a theory of justice or right that can accommodate pluralism, acknowledging the impossibility of defining a modern political order in terms of any individual doctrine or creed. And like Rawls, Hegel asserts that the stability of a political order requires that its constitutive principles be collectively embraced as values that derive from the culture in which they are embedded.

At the same time, however, significant differences separate the two positions. Later we consider the sense in which the "common ground" to which Hegel appeals in anchoring pluralism is both richer and more variegated than that advanced by Rawls. First, however, let us note that Hegel's reception of pluralism is more robust and less ambivalent than Rawls's.[15] This is perhaps most pronounced in his version of a "rational" approach to politics, where, unlike both Rawls and his postmodern critics,[16] Hegel does not construe reason as a principle of harmony or cohesion juxtaposed to diversity. What characterizes such an approach—one based on reason [*Vernunft*] rather than the understanding [*Verstand*]—is precisely the effort to accommodate diversity. This is evident, *inter alia*, in Hegel's account of antinomies, which, for him, does not attest, as it did for Kant, to reason's illicit proclivity to exceed its proper boundaries. Instead, antimonies, together with the principles of dialectical opposition they express, assume the role of central and constitutive components of a genuine conception of reason, one dedicated to conceptualizing the basic features of experience and reality. Similarity, what distinguishes objective or absolute idealism from what Hegel sees as the subjective version proffered by Kant and Fichte is precisely an effort to fashion an account of unity that is genuinely whole, one that, far from simply supplying a formal framework of possibility, systematically seeks to incorporate and build on substantive difference and opposition. For Hegel, bifurcation is as much a factor in thought as it is in life.[17] Nor is his advance on his idealist predecessors merely a matter of extending the reach of a unifying framework. The sensitivity to "otherness" in Hegel's thought stems also from his effort to construe a totality not just from the perspective of theory but from that of the subject matter itself—or, as we might say today, from the perspective of the participants as well as the observer. The "product," he notes rather elliptically, "must be comprehended as a producing."[18] While Hegel may share with Rawls an inclination to prioritize cohesion and communality, the force of his position is that these are achieved because, and not in spite, of a commitment to pluralism. Accounting for holism is also "to look the negative in the face and tarry with it."[19]

The point can be made more concretely by turning to Hegel's theory of the modern state. It is now well recognized that Hegel's state is not a monolithic, homogeneous whole, but a complex and differentiated structure comprising a plurality of subpolitical occupational and preference-based associations, termed corporations and estates. The state is indeed an association of associations. Significantly, though, Hegel is not championing the idea of a central political "framework" that simply permits associated differentiation at the subpolitical level[20]; at issue is not something akin to Rawls's "social union of social unions."[21] Instead, associational differentiation is, at least in modern states, central to the very identity and "vitality" of a genuine polity. A "living relationship exists only in an articulated whole whose parts themselves form particular subordinate spheres."[22] This point is central to Hegel's very idea of a polity.

For Hegel, a polity consists and is constituted in the conjunction of structure and sentiment. A nation attains existence as such when legal-political structures are dispositionally embraced as a matter of social life, even as such dispositions are also shaped by institutional structures. In large, modern states, however, individuals cannot experience any direct identification with a central political order. The size, scale, and complexity of modern political institutions make such identification both impossible and undesirable. Any collective esprit de corps is now of a mediated nature, achieved through involvement in subpolitical associations where individuals can more tangibly perceive a correlation of their own interests and those of a whole. In modern states these formally sub- or extrapolitical entities become the "pillars of public freedom."[23] This is, to be sure, not to deny the role for Hegel of centralized legal-political institutions. The "oversight of public authority" is required to prevent intra- and intergroup domination.[24] Moreover, with de Tocqueville Hegel acknowledges that any public spiritedness generated at the local level can and should translate into broader forms of involvements. Still, the vitality and distinctive identity of a modern polity depends on and proceeds from what perforce is a multiplicity of extragovernmental bodies. The "proper strength of states resides in their communities [*Gemeinde*]."[25] For Hegel, the integrity of the modern state is sustained through associational pluralism.[26]

Hegel's commitment to political pluralism is also evident in his treatment of the concept of representation.[27] In opposition to much of the modern tradition, Hegel does not comprehend representation as the practice by which an individual seeks to articulate a view for and about the nation as a whole.[28] Hegel certainly does not follow Rousseau for whom political activity converts a multitude into a single person, for whom public life is akin to a relationship between me and myself. In line with a corporately differentiated account of the state, he maintains that a parliamentary delegate serves as a representative of a specific group, one whose voice is institutionally secured along proportional and nonterritorial lines. It is not a coincidence that he uses the language of *Mitwirkung* in describing representative activity, for the latter is just that practice of a delegate exerting an influence on individuals and groups with whom his views are not identical. Political representation presupposes and confirms a disjunction of part and whole.

Hegel, to be sure, does not claim that a representative acts on the basis of a mandate binding him or her to the views of a group. As a representative of "one of the essential spheres of *society*," the delegate must also deliberate on "matters of universal concern."[29] Hegel conceives parliament as "a forum for live exchanges and collective deliberations in which participants instruct and convince one another."[30]

This is one respect in which his position is distinguished from a feudal conception of estate representation, where a delegate is expected to fully articulate the will of a lord. On the other hand, the representative freed from a *mandat imperatif* is not thereby expected to attend to a putative common or national interest. Rather, collective deliberation is also a means by which to define and further solidify the various spheres of a differentiated polity. Not only does public deliberation serve to clarify and to obtain public recognition for group interests. In forging a *shared* consciousness, collective deliberation [*öffentliche Mitteilung*] differentiates even as it unifies. By taking part [*teilnehmen*] in public life, by having a share [*teilhaben*] in its outcome, individuals are able to develop an appreciation for the perspectival or partial nature of their own position, which in turn can accommodate openness to and appreciation of other perspectives. Kant defined pluralism as "the attitude of not being occupied with oneself as the whole world, but regarding and conducting oneself as a citizen of the world."[31] Whatever might be said of Hegel's views of cosmopolitanism, it is clear that, in linking representation to a process of shared deliberative activity, he too seeks to account for the establishment and maintenance of a pluralist public sphere. Like Hannah Arendt, whose republican theory of political pluralism proceeds from the notion that we are "localized in the world which we have in common without owning it,"[32] Hegel, through his notion of political representation, advocates a view of politics that ratifies differentiation even as it forges commonality.[33]

2. The notion that Hegel advocates pluralism may still seem curious in light of the priority he gives to the idea of *Sittlichkeit* and the principle of a communal ethos that he claims underlies societal existence. All societal life must have recourse to an "ethical substance" that serves as the "ground and starting point for the action of all."[34] It would be a mistake, though, to assume that such appeal precludes sensitivity to pluralism. Indeed, far from contravening pluralism, appeal to a communal ethos accommodates its possibility. When Hegel invokes the idea of ethical substance, he is not championing the values or traditions of a particular community. In line with his decidedly modern concept of *Sittlichkeit*, his idea of a communal ethos is characterized rather by a collective commitment to the general principles of a liberal-pluralistic-republican society—perhaps the very idea of a

genuine political order. Following Michael Walzer, we might say that Hegel's is a pluralist ethos,[35] one characterized by a sociocultural commitment to the values of individual rights, fairness, impartiality, tolerance, mutual respect, public debate, and a willingness to regulate action according to general principles.

A collective ethos of this sort is needed to counteract the threats to a modern polity emanating from its own midst. It is needed to prevent modern society's commitment to individual liberty from becoming so one-sided that it undermines the institutional structures these presuppose. It is also needed to prevent institutional development from assuming such power that it undermines the liberties it is designed to facilitate. Hegel thus invokes the idea of an ethos to safeguard modern societies, to prevent any one component "from becoming a self-constituting and independent power."[36]

So understood, Hegel's position may not appear much removed from Rawls's. Not only does Rawls also claim that the stability of modern society depends on a willingness of individuals to embrace the principles of a liberal polity; and not only does he claim that such embrace must be rooted in the values of the wider culture. With Hegel he also employs the language of republicanism in explicating the nature of this shared public culture. "The safety of democratic liberties requires the active participation of citizens who possess the political virtues needed to maintain a constitutional regime."[37] In this respect Rawls also speaks of a "duty of civility"—a public moral, albeit not legal, expectation that citizens exhibit "a willingness to listen to others and a fairmindedness in deciding when accommodation of their views should reasonably be made."[38]

Still, the differences between the two positions are also significant. What characterizes a genuine political ethos, for Hegel, is a wide-reaching coordination of norms, laws, and institutional principles on the one hand and everyday beliefs, values, and practices on the other. A notion of a political ethos conceived along these lines is not evident in Rawls's position, the concept of reflective equilibrium notwithstanding. In keeping with his "purely political" conception of justice, he demarcates everything associated with a political system of cooperation from the attitudes and practices found in the background culture. He also distinguishes valid norms from the conditions motivating their acceptance. The "principles of justice detach reasons of justice not only from the ebb and flow of fluctuating wants and desires but even from sentiments and commitments."[39] It is true that Rawls does link his account of justice to a "reasonable moral psychology," one where social virtues are part and parcel of the "ordinary human world" of a reasonable society.[40] These include "the willingness to propose fair terms of cooperation and to abide by them provided others do" and "the willingness to recognize the burdens of judgment and to accept their consequences for the use of public reason."[41] Yet while Rawls's characterization of these virtues is admirable, the fact remains that they are the virtues appropriate to the citizens of a reasonable political order, citizens who have already accepted its desirability.[42] Not adequately explained is the dynamic by which reasonableness and a reasonable political order are accepted in the first place. Nor is it clear how this can be properly explained, since assuming the "burdens of judgments" associated with citizenship consists precisely in suspending the private belief and attitudes one holds as an everyday member of society.

In response, Rawls relates the core principles of political justice to the values implicit in the political culture of a democratic society, a culture that includes appreciation of a "dualism" between private beliefs and public obligations.[43] Yet the function this intriguing claim performs in Rawls's thought remains unclear. Given that the public culture is also characterized by "deep conflicts of political values and conflicts between these and nonpolitical value," unqualified appeal cannot be made to the values of the existing culture. Instead, it is necessary to undertake a process of "abstraction," to construct an "idealized" version of a system of social cooperation, one which citizens might embrace "on due reflection" but which does not correspond to existing forms of cultural self-consciousness.[44] Yet in asserting this distinction between real and ideal, between genuine political culture and the social background culture, Rawls does not explain how norms of political justice may be embraced as a matter of everyday practice, how they can express the background "culture of daily life."[45]

For Hegel, however, the function of a political ethos is precisely to specify the connection between public principles and the attitudes and practices of everyday life, between the objective validity of norms and the conditions of their actual acceptance. It is to show the various ways in which principles of right can also and simultaneously be construed as features of a historically existent "second nature."[46] In particular, Hegel seeks to demonstrate both how public norms can be anchored in the wider political culture of a society and how in turn members of that society might be habitually disposed to accept and support them. Thus while he acknowledges that norms have a meaning that is not reducible to the values of a particular culture, he also maintains that they cannot claim their status as norms unless they express the values of a particular community. For Hegel, norms—universal norms included—are rules and principles that human beings must impose or be able to impose upon themselves. Norms have obligatory force only if individuals are free to act in accordance with them.[47] In this respect Hegel's position is not unlike Kant's, and indeed he asserts that "the merit and exalted viewpoint of Kant's moral philosophy" lies in its contention that "[i]n doing my duty I am with myself [*bei mir selbst*] and free."[48] Unlike Kant, however, Hegel maintains that the capacity of individuals to impose norms on their conduct is not defined via adherence to formal principles valid for all individuals irrespective of motivational considerations. A norm, for Hegel, is self-imposed only if individuals actually regard it as expressive of their own interests and values, only if they are indeed motivated to adopt it. "The universal does not attain validity of fulfillment without the interest, knowledge and volition of the particular."[49] Unless individuals are actually willing to adopt the norm for their conduct, it cannot claim binding force for that conduct.[50]

And if Hegel asserts that norms must find expression in the values of a culture, he also seeks to show that this specific culture—and here he speaks of modern culture—is so structured as to accommodate and nurture dispositions supportive of the legal-moral norms and principles. Consider impartiality. Although Hegel claims that impartiality is a central principle of modern liberal-pluralist societies, he does not present it as a norm that requires suspension or bracketing of individuals' values and commitments. Such a view disregards the uniquely "ethical nature of modern civil society" [*die Sittlichkeit in der bürgerlichen Gesellschaft*].[51] Modern civil society is notable not only in that it permits the societal emergence of the ideal of impartiality, but that it has forged the conditions whereby this ideal can be embraced as a matter of everyday practice and conduct. Guided by a commitment to the thorough interdependence of individual and community, universal and particular, modern civil society has created the conditions wherein one is acculturated and habitually disposed "to regulate one's will according to universal principles."[52] Hegel rejects Kant's abstract commitment to impartiality, but only because the modern world, with its systematic intertwining of universal and particular, is supportive of a type of cultural partiality to impartial judgment. Modern society has created the conditions whereby the principle of liberal neutrality itself can claim the status of a general societal value.[53]

Hegel, to be sure, is aware of the illicit nature of any unqualified ascription of ethical culture to modern societies. More so than most theoreticians of political modernity, he is aware that modern society unleashes pathologies destructive equally of communal bonds and individual liberties. Modern society gives rise to a nexus of instrumentalization and bureaucratization tantamount to a *Verlust der Sittlichkeit*, a loss of the very ethical life it occasions. In this regard Hegel would agree with Rawls, who, against what the latter terms "simple communitarianism,"[54] asserts that political philosophy must reconstruct rather than simply affirm values implicit in modern society. For Hegel, however, reconstruction does not consist in formulating a public political culture juxtaposed to the background culture of private individuals. If nothing else, this solution replicates the difficulties in question. His aim is rather to challenge the misconceptions and constricted forms of thinking contributing to modern pathologies. Proceeding from a systematic account of the modern concept of freedom, Hegel seeks to demonstrate the mutually implicative nature of such seeming oppositions as public and private, duty and inclination, law and culture. Only through this more extensive reconstruction of the values implicit in modern culture is it possible to fashion the type of "comprehensive" cultural ethos needed to ensure the "stability" of liberal-pluralist institutions.

Hegel's dispute with Rawls ultimately turns on the liberal affirmation of the "priority of the right over the good." Hegel is sufficiently tied to the tradition of modern political theory not to question the centrality of the concept of right. At the same time, however, appreciation of such centrality requires a corresponding assertion of the centrality of the good. Indeed, we might say that, for him, the two are co-primordial. If a focus on principles of political justice is central to societies characterized by a plurality of doctrinal beliefs and values, commitment to justice itself is tenuous unless that principle and those associated with it are collectively embraced and supported as valuable and desirable. While not fully disputing the view that the political stability of modern society requires subordinating the good to the right, Hegel also maintains that that same stability no less requires subordinating the right to the good. A well-ordered constitutional regime depends upon the presence of a comprehensive public culture expressive of the sentiments and commitments of a citizenry routinely disposed to embrace reasons of justice as their own.

The point can be restated by briefly comparing Hegel and Rawls on religion. At one level the two positions are remarkably similar. As Rawls himself notes, both see in Protestantism and modern religious conflict generally the basis for a notion of politics that is not only committed to the rights and liberty of the individual but also specifies principles of justice and cooperation that proceed from the absence of agreement on fundamental values. At the same time, however, Hegel would not accept Rawls's contention that the politics associated with Protestantism invalidates all public appeal to an emphatic conception of the common good. It may be true that politics revolving around a single doctrinal creed has been replaced by one focused on issues of right, liberty, tolerance, and the rule of law. What this means, though, is not that the good has been displaced by the right but that a new conception of the good has emerged, one needed for the stability of a modern political order. That order cannot be sustained over time unless it is rooted in an ethos supportive of its principles, an ethos in which modern principles of subjective freedom, mutual recognition, the rule of law, and the demands of rational and universal legitimation are collectively recognized as good and desirable. For Hegel, self-consciously writing in a "Protestant cultural context,"[55] that ethos finds preeminent expression in Protestantism. Not only is it the source of many of the principles of a modern polity; as a generally accepted set of beliefs that both anchors such principles in everyday attitudes and practices and relates those beliefs and practices to the normative principles of modern polity, it exemplifies the idea of an ethos able to conjoin public norms and their motivational acceptance. To be sure, Hegel's is a distinctive and even heterodox vision of Protestantism: it encompasses reform Catholicism, is ecumenical, is critical of much of what was accepted by practicing Protestants, and has little, if anything, in common with traditional theism. Indeed, Hegel asserts that this "religion of freedom"[56] can take wholly secular shape and "need not assume the form of religion."[57] On the other hand, what Hegel did find attractive about Protestantism on his understanding is that it introduced not only the principles of a modern liberal political order but the ethico-cultural conditions for its stability.

3. For his part, Rawls would likely say that any effort to accord public pride of place to principles of good is inimical to the very idea of political pluralism.[58] In a world characterized by diverse conceptions of the good, political philosophy must restrict itself to those principles of social cooperation that permit the private pursuit of individual conceptions of the good. Defining the conditions of a stable society in the modern world remains "a problem of political justice, not a problem of the highest good."[59]

For Hegel, though, the notion that societal commitment to a collective common good is antithetical to the reality of pluralism exemplifies precisely the dichotomous thinking he is determined to surmount. Two points are here in order. The first concerns the nature of the good. At issue is not a specific substantive value that invalidates appeals to other values. Hegel's idea of the good connotes a type of meta-value or second order value, one committed to the formal or procedural conditions for pluralist society itself.[60] Certainly, this is not to suggest that the highest good for Hegel reduces to a principle of liberal neutrality, a principle too "thin" to supply the desired motivation. It is the case that a modern political ethos is governed by commitment to certain substantive values. Yet this commitment has a decidedly reflexive character, focused on the conditions for pluralism itself. For Hegel, the basic communal value of modern, Western and, with increasing interconnections, global society is *freedom* or *autonomy*, understood both privately and publicly.[61] Only to the extent that this principle assumes the societal status of a principle of second nature is the long-term stability of a liberal-pluralist society comprehensible. Part and parcel of a society committed to value pluralism is the idea that goods are worthy of individual and social choice and this would not be possible without a prior cultural commitment to freedom as a common value.

Hegel's point, however, is not just that his notion of a substantive good accommodates pluralist values. He claims further that support of such a good itself serves to foster and effectuate a pluralist society. Collective affirmation of the underlying norms of a liberal-pluralist society cannot rest content with merely championing a prescribed set of norms. Even if one might want to claim, as Rawls does, that the meaning of basic constitutional norms or "essentials" are fixed "once and for all,"[62] their effectiveness and ongoing legitimacy is linked to processes by which they are applied to specific societal circumstances.[63] Yet processes of application are never univocal; they are instead always subject to differences in interpretation. This means, though, that the affirmation of such norms is perforce an affirmation of pluralism, for the meaning of norms in their concrete application cannot properly be detailed without acknowledging and accommodating the diverse views and beliefs surrounding that meaning. Moreover, such differences can begin to obtain proper resolution only in the context of a process of shared deliberation that itself gives voice to the diversity of views present in a society. Only such inclusive deliberation does justice to the idea of a *Volksgeist* characterized under modern conditions by its internal differentiation. Nor can such deliberation ever achieve closure. Given the "endlessly increasing diversity and complexity . . . of the material of civil society"[64] to which norms are applied, processes by which a culture interprets its basic values are necessarily ongoing and open-ended. It is not coincidental that, when speaking of legal adjudication, Hegel ultimately appeals not to the "limited" right of positive law, but to the "unrestricted" right of world history.[65] Even if he might affirm a common substantive value for modern societies, that affirmation itself triggers diversity-engendering processes of interpretation, mandates pluralist forms of public deliberation, and forges an openness to new and different perspectives.

Andrew Buchwalter

In this regard Hegel proposes a conception of politics clearly distinct from that of Rawls. Politics, for Hegel, focuses on more than the conditions for fair and just social cooperation among individuals in pluralist societies. It attends as well, and perhaps preeminently, to issues of collective identity, to processes by which a culture defines itself and its most basic values. At stake, however, is not an affirmation of some established ethos homogeneously infusing diverse practices, beliefs, and policies. Such a view might be required if one followed Rawls in juxtaposing a basic political structure to the forms of social life whose relationship that structure is assumed to facilitate. This is not Hegel's position. Given his focus on the need for ongoing application, politics is the process by which the identity of a culture—the spirit of a people—is routinely reshaped and "renewed" [*verjüngert*] [66]; it is the process by which the relationship between institutional norms and popular sentiment is recalibrated and reaffirmed. And inasmuch as processes of collective reassessment both depend on and trigger diversity in interpretation, attention to matters of collective identity is perforce affirmation of plural forces and tendencies—the very items that comprehensiveness in politics is presumed to undermine. Indeed, given that a politics committed to collective self-definition can subject to debate and deliberative scrutiny the central norms and values of society, it is arguably more hospitable to pluralism than is a notion of politics which, in its effort to safeguard pluralism, seeks to specify *ab ovo* underlying constitutional essentials.

4. Let me conclude by noting a final distinction between Hegel and Rawls. Proceeding from the "fact" of pluralism, Rawls claims that conflicts over fundamental values are in modern societies essentially irreconcilable. Political philosophy is indeed restricted to the question: "How is a just and free society possible under conditions of deep doctrinal conflict with no prospect of resolution?" [67] While the idea of reasonable pluralism attends to what is common among diverse values systems, the very need for a common framework flows from the notion that conflictual differences are insurmountable. In this regard Rawls seconds Isaiah Berlin's "tragic" vision of modern social relations: "That there is no social world without loss is rooted in the nature and values of the world, and much human tragedy reflects just that." [68]

This is not Hegel's position. While he is at least as aware as Rawls of the conflictual or "bifurcated" nature of modern societies, he does not regard such oppositions as an ontological fixture of social reality, a type of quasi-natural "fact" of modern life. In keeping with his criticism of appeals to immediacy, he regularly asserts that modern oppositions must be viewed against the backdrop of certain commonalities, commonalities that to some degree allow for their possibility. With Rousseau, for instance, he argues that modern social oppositions are as much the consequence as the cause of the tendencies toward uniformity in modern institutions. In establishing a common framework that encourages individuals to compare themselves with others, modern legal structures, with their focus of formality and uniformity, produce a drive for further refinement, distinction, and differentiation.[69] In addition, and more apposite here, Hegel maintains that oppositions are themselves the expression of a more fundamental social unity. While Hegel may understand modern life as essentially tragic, he does so with regard to a modern notion of tragedy, one where conflicts express not two radically incompatible principles but one principle at odds with itself. Giving pride of place to *Hamlet* or *King Lear* over, say, *Antigone*, he argues that modern tragedy focuses not on the opposition of two incommensurable ethical powers [*sittliche Mächte*], but on *die Tragödie im Sittlichen*, the tragedy internal to a single ethical principle. Tragedy now describes the process by which a totality sacrifices "a part of itself."[70] Accordingly, many of the conflicts that beset modern life—individual and community, public and private, self and other, reason and sensibility—are not to be understood as diametrically opposed polarities, but as consequences of a common framework that accounts for their very meaning and reality. Thus, for instance, a social world infused with a commitment to the principle of freedom contributes to the modern "dialectic" of individual and community. This principle gives expression to an individualism whose protection mandates structures of law and justice, whose developed size and scope in turn undermine the very freedom they are designed to protect.[71]

This recognition of the degree to which conflict may also express common identity is important in that it serves to call into question the notion that conflicts are irremediably irreconcilable. Understanding the modern, bifurcated world as a world "alienated from itself" gives rise to "the demand that such contradiction be resolved."[72] To be sure, Hegel is not proposing that conflict can or should be eliminated. As already noted, he claims that differentiation is central to the vitality and legitimacy of a modern social order. What Hegel does argue is that the opposition between political unity and social disagreement, identity and difference, should be construed in a manner less severe than is the case with Rawls. Among other things, an effort must be made to note the commonalities of seeming opposites, and to demonstrate the mutually implicative nature of such concepts as individual and community, self and other, public and private, duty and inclination, reason and sensibility, and the right and the good. Similarly, Hegel's "dialectical" view of the identity/difference relationship mandates a more capacious notion of political discourse. In noting a possible common ground for seemingly intractable oppositions, Hegel provides a mechanism and rationale for collective deliberation that accommodates and is sustained by markedly different values and doctrines. Such deliberation may not lead to consensus. Yet its possibility does demonstrate that the "fact" of modern pluralism in no way precludes a comprehensive politics that is attentive to the common ends of human and social life. Hegel once wrote: "According to Napoleon, . . . modern is distinct from classical tragedy in that what in the past was understood as fate is now a matter of politics."[73] In like manner he claims that the nature of modern social oppositions is such that conflicts are not *in principle* irreconcilable and that forging some measure of common identity while also accentuating social and cultural diversity is a central, if not *the* central, task of modern political action.

Notes

1. John Rawls, *Political Liberalism* (New York: Columbia University Press, 1996); hereafter *PL*.

2. Ibid., xxviii.

3. Ibid., xxvi.

4. Ibid., xvii.

5. Ibid., 144.

6. Ibid., xxvii.

7. Ibid., 11.

8. Ibid., 50.

9. Ibid., 202.

10. Ibid., 192.

11. Ibid., xvii.

12. Ibid., 250.

13. Ibid., 378f.

14. Ibid., xxvi.

15. Compare, however, Joshua Cohen, "Moral Pluralism and Political Consensus," in *The Idea of Democracy*, ed. D. Copp et al. (Cambridge: Cambridge University Press, 1993), especially 287f.

16. Chantal Mouffe, "Democracy, Power, and the 'Political,'" in *Democracy and Difference: Contesting the Boundaries of the Political*, ed. S. Benhabib (Princeton: Princeton University Press, 1996), 245–256.

17. G. W. F. Hegel, *The Difference between Fichte's and Schelling's System of Philosophy*, trans. H. S. Harris and W. Cerf (Albany: SUNY Press, 1977), 91, translation amended.

18. *The Difference*, 91.

19. G. W. F. Hegel, *Phenomenology of Spirit*, trans. A. V. Miller (Oxford: Oxford University Press, 1976), 19, translation slightly amended.

20. John Rawls, *Theory of Justice* (Cambridge: Harvard University Press, 1971), 528, herafter *TJ*.

21. *TJ*, 527.

22. *Hegel's Political Writings*, trans. T. M. Knox (Oxford: Clarendon Press, 1964), 263.

23. G. W. F. Hegel, *Elements of the Philosophy of Right*, ed. A. W. Wood, trans. H. B. Nisbet (Cambridge: Cambridge University Press, 1993) § 265, hereafter *PR*.

24. *PR*, §§ 252, 289Z.

25. *PR*, § 290.

26. This feature of Hegel's position, though still not fully recognized, was properly noted some time ago by Mary Follett: "True Hegelianism finds its actualized form in federalism." See *The New State* (New York: Longmans, Green and Co., 1920), 267.

27. For an instructive discussion of this matter, see Giuseppe Duso, *Der Begriff der Repräsentation bei Hegel und das moderne Problem der politischen Einheit* (Baden-Baden: Normos, 1990).

28. In this respect he is opposed to the modern idea of representation: "For where the self is merely represented [*repräsentiert*] or imagined [*vorgestellt*], there it is not actual; where it is delegated [*vertreten*], it is not" (*Phenomenology of Spirit*, 359, translation amended).

29. *PR*, §§ 311, 309, See also *PR*, § 255.

30. *PR*, § 309.

31. Immanuel Kant, *Anthropology from a Pragmatic Point of View*, trans. M. Gregor (The Hague: Nijhoff, 1974), 12. See also *Kritik der Urteilskraft* § 40, in *Immanuel Kant: Werke in Sechs Bänden*, vol. 5, ed. W. Weischedel (Frankfurt: Insel, 1957), 388ff.

32. Hannah Arendt, "Public Rights and Private Interests," in *Small Comforts for Hard Times*, ed M. Mooney and F. Stuber (New York: Columbia University Press, 1977), 104. See also Margaret Canovan, *Hannah Arendt: A Reinterpretation of Her Political Thought* (Cambridge: Cambridge University Press, 1992), 206ff.

33. See also Seyla Benhabib, *Critique, Norm, and Utopia* (New York: Columbia University Press, 1986), 348f.

34. *Phenomenology of Spirit*, 264.

35. Michael Walzer, *What It Means to Be an American* (New York: Marsilio, 1992), 10.

36. G. W. F. Hegel, *Natural Law*, trans. T. M. Knox (Philadelphia: University of Pennsylvania Press, 1975), 94, hereafter *NL*.

37. *PL*, 205.

38. Ibid., 217.

39. Ibid., 190.

40. Ibid., 54.

41. Ibid., 54.

42. It is a psychology "for expressing a certain political conception of the person and an ideal of citizenship" (*PL*, 87).

43. Ibid., xxiii.

44. Ibid., 43–46.

45. Ibid., 14.

46. *PR*, § 4.

47. Ibid., § 133.

48. Ibid., § 133.

49. Ibid., § 260.

50. For an insightful discussion on these issues, see Robert B. Pippin, "Hegel on the Rationality and Priority of Ethical Life." *Neue Hefte für Philosophie* 35 (1995): 95–126.

51. G. W. F. Hegel, *Encyclopaedia of the Philosophical Sciences* III (Oxford: Clarendon, 1971), § 552.

52. *PR*, § 209; see also Hegel's *Vorlesungen über Rechtsphilosophie 1818–1831*, ed. K.-H. Ilting (Stuttgart-Bad Cannstatt: Friedrich Frommann, 1973), vol. 4, 483a.

53. Terry Pinkard argues similarly that the charge of abstractness Hegel directs against Kant is based on the claims that universal ethics is already a part of the modern cultural tradition and only as such was it spawned: "Hegel's argument is that Kantian ethics can appear on the scene only when the claims of 'Abstract Right' and autonomy have made their *social* appearance." *Hegel's Phenomenology: The Sociality of Reason* (Cambridge: Cambridge University Press, 1994), 290.

54. *PL*, 44ff.

55. The phrase is that of Laurence Dickey, *Hegel: Religion, Economics, and the Politics of Spirit, 1770–1807* (Cambridge: Cambridge University Press, 1987), especially 1–32.

56. *PR*, § 270.

57. Cited in L. Oeing-Hanhoff's instructive essay, "Hegels Deutung der Reformation," *Hegel: L'Esprit Objektif, Aktien des 3. Internationalen Hegel-Kongresses* (Lille, 1968), 249.

58. *PL*, 175.

59. Ibid., xxv.

60. Compare Axel Honneth, who draws on Hegel to articulate the notion of a "formal conception of ethical life," though in a manner more Kantian than what is sketched here. See *The Struggle for Recognition: The Moral Grammar of Social Conflicts*, trans. J. Anderson (Cambridge: Polity, 1995), especially 171–179.

61. "Ethical life is the concept of freedom that has become the existing world and the nature of self-consciousness." *PR*, § 142. For a general discussion of these issues, see Albrecht Wellmer, "Bedingungen einer demokratischen Kultur," in *Gemeinschaft und Gerechtigkeit*, ed. M. Brumlik and H. Brunkhorst (Frankfurt: Fischer, 1993) 173–196.

62. *PL*, 233.

63. *PR*, § 211.

64. Ibid., § 213.

65. Ibid., § 30.

66. G. W. F. Hegel, *Vorlesungen über Naturrecht und Staatswissenschaft*, transcribed by P. Wannenmann, ed. C. Becker et al. (Hamburg: Meiner, 1983), § 134.

67. *PL*, xxviii.

68. Ibid., 197 note 32. For an extended discussion of the relationship of pluralism, political liberalism, and tragic conflict, see J. Donald Moon, *Constructing Community: Moral Pluralism and Tragic Conflicts* (Princeton: Princeton University Press, 1993).

69. *PR*, § 193.

70. *NL*, 104

71. See Christoph Menke, "Liberalismus im Konflikt: Zwischen Gerechtigkeit und Freiheit," in *Gemeinschaft und Gerechtigkeit*, 218–243. A somewhat different version of this argument is found in Menke's *Tragödie im Sittlichen: Gerechtigkeit und Freiheit nach Hegel* (Frankfurt: Suhrkamp, 1996).

72. G. W. F. Hegel, *Aesthetics*, 2 vols., trans. T. M. Knox (Oxford: Clarendon Press, 1998), 1: 54f.

73. G. W. F. Hegel, *The Philosophy of History*, trans. J. Sibree (New York: Dover, 1956), 278, translation amended.

14

Of Guests, Aliens, and Citizens: Rereading Kant's Cosmopolitan Right

Seyla Benhabib

Political Membership in Liberal Democracies

What are appropriate normative principles of democratic membership in a world of increasingly deterritorialized politics? Which practices and principles of political incorporation are most compatible
with the philosophical self-understanding and constitutional commitments of liberal democracies? Political membership, that is the
principles of incorporating aliens and strangers, immigrants and new-
comers, refugees and asylum seekers into existing polities, has rarely
been considered an important aspect of contemporary theories of domestic or international justice. The one exception here is Michael
Walzer who, in *Spheres of Justice* (1983), had pointed out that membership was the first social good that needed to be distributed, in that the
distribution of all other goods, such as income and positions, benefits
and opportunities, depended upon individuals being recognized as
members of a polity who would then be entitled to them. Yet ten years
later in his *Political Liberalism,* John Rawls would still assume "that a
democratic society, like any political society, is to be viewed as a complete and closed social system. It is complete in that it is self-sufficient ·
and has a place for all the main purposes of human life. It is also
closed . . . in that entry into it is only by birth and exit from it is only
by death. . . . For the moment we leave aside entirely relations with
other societies and postpone all questions of justice between peoples
until a conception of justice for a well-ordered society is on hand.

Thus, we are not seen as *joining society at the age of reason, as we might join an association, but as being born into a society where we will lead a complete life*" (Rawls 1993, 41; my emphasis).

Even if Rawls meant to use the model of a closed society as a counterfactual fiction, as a convenient thought-experiment in reasoning about justice, by not making conditions of entry and exit into the political community a central aspect of a liberal-democratic theory of justice, he assumed that the state-centric model of nations, with fairly closed and well-guarded borders, would continue to govern our thinking in international relations. This was made amply clear in the subsequent *The Law of Peoples:* "An important role of a people's government, however arbitrary a society's boundaries may appear from a historical point of view, is to be the representative and effective agent of a people as they take responsibility for their territory and its environmental integrity, as well as for the size of their population" (Rawls 1999, 38–39). Rawls adds in a note that "this remark implies that a people has at least a qualified right to limit immigration. I leave aside what these qualifications might be. . . . Another reason for limiting immigration is to protect a people's political culture and its constitutional principles" (Rawls 1999, 39). "The qualified right to limit immigration," marginal though it may appear in articulating a "law of peoples," is not so.

Transnational migrations, and the constitutional as well as policy issues suggested by the movement of peoples across borders, are central to interstate relations. Questionable here is not so much Rawls's claim that there "must be boundaries of some kind" (Rawls 1999, 39), but rather his disregard of the rights and claims of "others" as they relate to and affect the identity of the liberal-democratic polity. In not articulating explicit conditions of entry and exit Rawls is misconstruing the nature of membership in liberal-democracies. From a philosophical point of view, these issues bring to the fore the constitutive dilemma between sovereign self-determination claims on the one hand and universal human rights principles on the other.

In this essay I will argue that the rights and claims of others—strangers and foreigners, refugees and asylum seekers, immigrants and temporary workers—should be considered a central aspect of any understanding of membership in liberal democracies, and of theories of justice focusing on interstate relations generally. Recent contributions to international theories of justice from a neo-Kantian perspective have focused either on the obligations peoples owe to one another in the distribution of the world's resources and wealth (Thomas Pogge; Onora O'Neill), or they have challenged the relativism of Rawls's *Law of Peoples* and attempted to formulate a universalistic approach to human rights (Thomas McCarthy). My approach in this essay differs from both, though it agrees with these neo-Kantian theories in pushing international theories of justice, and in particular Rawls's own theory, in a more universalist and radical direction. I will claim that the normative issues raised by the practices of political membership can best be analyzed through an internal reconstruction of the dual commitments of liberal democracies to human rights on the one hand and collective self-determination on the other.

Democratic rule means that all members of a sovereign body are to be respected as bearers of human rights, and that the consociates of this sovereign freely associate with one another to establish a regime of self-governance under which each is to be considered both author of the laws and subject to them. Since Rousseau, however, we know that the will of the democratic people may be legitimate but unjust, unanimous but unwise. "The will of all" and "the general will" may not overlap either in theory or in practice. Democratic rule and the claims of justice may contradict one another.

Yet this paradox of democratic legitimacy has a corollary that has been little noted: every act of self-legislation is also an act of self-constitution. "We, the people" who agree to bind ourselves by these laws, are also defining ourselves as a "we" in the very act of self-legislation. It is not only the general laws of self-government that are articulated in this process; the community that binds itself by these laws, defines itself by drawing boundaries as well, and these boundaries are territorial as well as civic. The will of the democratic sovereign only extends over the territory that is under its power; democracies require borders. At the same time that the sovereign defines itself territorially, it defines itself in civic terms. Those who are full members of the sovereign body are distinguished from those who "fall under its protection," but who do not enjoy "full membership rights." Women and slaves, non-Christians and members of nonwhite races as well as servants and propertyless white males have historically been excluded from membership in the sovereign body. They are, in Kant's famous words, "mere auxiliaries to the commonwealth" (Kant [1797] 1996, 92).

Furthermore, as was the case with the American and French Revolutions, "we the people" who empower ourselves as the sovereign, do this in the name of truths held to be self-evident, namely that "all men are created equal and endowed by their creator with inalienable rights." The democratic sovereign draws its legitimacy not merely from its act of constitution, but equally significantly, from the conformity of this act to universal principles of human rights that are in some sense said to precede and antedate the will of the sovereign and in accordance with which the sovereign undertakes to bind itself. "We, the people" refers to a particular human community, circumscribed in space and time, sharing a particular culture, history and legacy; yet this people establishes itself as a democratic body by acting in the name of the "universal." The tension between universal human rights claims and particularistic cultural and national identities is constitutive of democratic legitimacy. Modern democracies act in the name of universal principles that are then circumscribed within a particular civic community. This is the "Janus face of the modern nation," in the words of Jürgen Habermas (Habermas 1998, 115). By focusing on this constitutive tension of democratic communities, I will articulate a vision of transnational political membership.

The neglect of this constitutive dilemma of liberal democracies, as between human rights claims and collective self-determination assertions, is characteristic of most neo-Kantian theories that do try to give a normative account of conditions of membership. Advocates of open borders and cosmopolitical citizenship, like Joseph Carens and Martha Nussbaum respectively, align themselves with the Kantian legacy of a world republic in order to articulate the transformative potentials of the present. From a moral point of view, national borders are arbitrary and the only morally consistent universalist position would be one of open borders. Joseph Carens, for example, uses the device of the Rawlsian "veil of ignorance," against the intentions of Rawls himself, to think through principles of justice from the standpoint of the refugee, the immigrant, and the asylum seeker (Carens 1995, 229–255). Are the borders within which we happen to be born, and the documents to which we are entitled, any less arbitrary from a moral point of view than other characteristics like skin color, gender, and genetic makeup with which we are endowed? Carens's answer is "no." From a moral point of view, the borders that circumscribe our birth and the papers to which we are entitled are arbitrary, since their distribution among individuals does not follow any clear criteria of moral achievement and moral compensation. Citizenship status and privileges, which are simply based upon territorially defined birthright, are no less arbitrary than one's skin color and other genetic endowments. Therefore, claims Carens, liberal democracies should practice policies that are as compatible as possible with the vision of a world without borders.

Cosmopolitical citizenship, as advocated by Martha Nussbaum, entails not so much a political practice but a moral attitude of not placing the affairs and concerns of one's immediate community ahead of those others who may be strangers to us, residing in faraway worlds. In Nussbaum's version, cosmopolitanism is a universalist ethic that denies the claims upon us of what is known in moral theory as "special obligations" (Nussbaum 1996 and 1997). These are obligations that emerge out of our situatedness in concrete human communities of descent or sympathy, genealogy or affiliation. Nussbaum denies that "patriotism," or a privileged commitment to a specific territorially bounded national community, constitutes such a special obligation. Patriotism does not trump "the love of humanity," and should not lead us to ignore the needs of others with whom we share neither culture nor descent, genealogy nor history (Nussbaum 1996, 12–17).

Even if we concede that such a cosmopolitical moral attitude has many arguments to recommend it in many circumstances, it is wholly unclear what political, as opposed to moral, practices cosmopolitical citizenship would assume, and which institutions, if any, would correspond to this mind-set. It is also interesting to note, as I will argue below, that this was not the meaning of cosmopolitanism for Kant himself. More significantly, these approaches avoid or skirt the paradox of democratic legitimacy; in doing so, they fail to illuminate the internal contradictions of liberal democracies and of an international order based upon state sovereignty.

I want to begin this argument via an examination of Immanuel Kant's articles for "Perpetual Peace." I then turn to a consideration of civic republican skepticism against political deterritorialization in order to show that, empirically speaking, fears that the new world order is threatening the core of democratic citizenship are exaggerated; philosophically, civic republicans like Walzer conflate the boundaries of the *ethical community* with those of the *democratic polity*. I conclude by maintaining that liberal-democratic practices of immigration and naturalization, far from undermining the civic community, can enhance the value of specific legal and institutional traditions by making erstwhile strangers and foreigners into *partners in a hermeneutic community of democratic interpretation and articulation.*

"Perpetual Peace" and Cosmopolitical Right—A Contemporary Reevaluation

Written in 1795, upon the signing of the Treaty of Basel by Prussia and revolutionary France, Kant's essay on "Perpetual Peace" has enjoyed considerable revival of attention in recent years. What makes this essay particularly interesting under the current conditions of political globalization is the visionary depth of Kant's project for perpetual peace among nations. Kant, as is well known, formulates three "definitive articles for perpetual peace among states." These read: "The Civil Constitution of Every State should be Republican"; "The Law of Nations shall be founded on a Federation of Free States"; and "The Law of World Citizenship Shall be Limited to Conditions of Universal Hospitality" (Kant [1795] 1914, 434–443; 1957, 92–103). Much scholarship on this essay has focused on the precise legal and political form that these articles could or would take, and on whether Kant meant to propose the establishment of a world-federation of republics or a league of sovereign nation-states [*Völkerbund*].

In his illuminating article, "On Reconciling Cosmopolitan Unity and National Diversity," Thomas McCarthy summarizes the gist of Kant's argument as follows: "Thus, the 'positive idea' of establishing a universal and lasting peace is the idea of a 'world republic,' the member states of which are themselves republics: a world republic of national republics. The 'public coercive' law of this world republic would regulate external relations among states, among individuals who are citizens of different states, and among individuals and states of which they are not citizens. This type of law is variously referred to by Kant as *Völker-Staatsrecht*, the right of a state of nations, and *Weltbürgerrecht*, the right of world citizens" (McCarthy 1999, 186).

Even in the light of McCarthy's lucid analysis, what remains frequently uncommented upon is the Third Article of perpetual peace, in fact the only one that Kant himself explicitly designates with the terminology of the "*Weltbürgerrecht*." The German reads: "*Das Weltbürgerrecht soll auf Bedingungen der allgemeinen Hospitalität eingeschränkt sein*" (Kant 1914, 443). Kant himself notes the oddity of the locution of "hospitality" in this context, and therefore remarks that "it is not a question of philanthropy but of right." In other words, hospitality is not to be understood as a virtue of sociability, as the kindness and generosity one may show to strangers who come to one's land or who become dependent upon one's act of kindness through circumstances of nature or history; hospitality is a "right" that belongs to all human beings insofar as we view them as potential participants in a world republic. But the "right" of hospitality is odd in that it does not regulate relationships among individuals who are members of a particular civil entity and under whose jurisdiction they stand; this "right" regulates the interactions of individuals who belong to different civic entities yet who encounter one another at the margins of bounded communities. The "right" of hospitality is situated at the boundaries of the polity; it delimits civic space by regulating relations among members and strangers. Hence the "right of hospitality" occupies that space between human rights and civil rights, between the right of humanity in our person and the rights that accrue to us insofar as we are members of specific republics. Kant writes: "Hospitality [*Wirtbarkeit*] means the right of a stranger not to be treated as an enemy when he arrives in the land of another. One may refuse to receive him when this can be done without causing his destruction; but, so long as he peacefully occupies his place, one may not treat him with hostility. It is not the right to be a permanent visitor [*Gastrecht*] that one may demand. A special beneficent agreement [*ein . . . wohltätiger Vertrag*] would be

Seyla Benhabib

needed in order to give an outsider a right to become a fellow inhabitant [*Hausgenossen*] for a certain length of time. It is only a right of temporary sojourn [*ein Besuchsrecht*], a right to associate, which all men have. They have it by virtue of their common possession [*das Recht des gemeinschaftlichen Besitzes*] of the surface of the earth, where, as a globe, they cannot infinitely disperse and hence must finally tolerate the presence of each other" (Kant 1914, 443; 1957, 103).

This remarkable passage expresses *in nuce* many of the dilemmas that still govern our reasoning about entry, residency, and membership conditions in polities. Kant distinguishes the "right to be a permanent visitor," which he calls *Gastrecht*, from the "temporary right of soujourn" [*Besuchsrecht*]. The right to be a permanent visitor is awarded through a freely chosen special agreement that goes beyond what is owed to the other morally and what he is entitled to legally; therefore, Kant names this a "*wohltätiger Vertrag*," a "contract of beneficence." It is a special privilege that the republican sovereign can award certain foreigners who abide in their territories, who perform certain functions, represent their respective political entities, and engage in long-term trade, and the like. The "*droit d'aubaine*" in prerevolutionary France, which granted foreigners certain rights of residency, the acquisition of property, and the practicing of a profession, would be a pertinent historical example. The special trade concessions that nations like the Ottoman Empire, China, Japan, and India granted westerners from the eighteenth century onward would be others.

The right of hospitality, by contrast, entails a claim to temporary residency that cannot be refused, if such refusal would involve the destruction of the other, for presumably this would involve a violation of the rights of humanity in the person of the other. To refuse sojourn to victims of religious wars, to victims of piracy or ship wreckage, when such refusal would harm them, is untenable according to Kant. What is unclear in Kant's discussion is whether such relations among peoples and nations involve acts of supererogation going beyond the call of moral duty, or whether they entail a certain sort of moral claim concerning "the rights of humanity in the person of the other." We may see here the juridical and moral ambivalence that affects discussions of "the right of asylum" and "the rights of refugees" to this day. Are the rights of asylum and refuge, "rights" in the sense of being *reciprocal moral obligations* which in some sense or another are grounded upon our mutual humanity? Or are these "rights claims" in the legal sense of *enforceable norms* of behavior that individuals and groups can hold each other to, and in particular, force sovereign nation-states to comply with? Kant's construction provides no clear answer. The right of hospitality entails a moral claim with potential legal consequences in that the obligation of the receiving states to grant temporary residency to foreigners is anchored in a republican cosmopolitical order. Such an order does not have a supreme "executive law" governing it. In this sense the obligation to show hospitality to foreigners and strangers cannot be enforced; it remains a voluntarily incurred obligation of the political sovereign. The right of hospitality expresses all the dilemmas of a republican cosmopolitical order, namely how to create quasi-legally binding obligations through voluntary commitments and in the absence of an overwhelming sovereign power with the ultimate right of enforcement.

When reflecting on the "temporary right of sojourn" [*Besuchsrecht*] Kant uses different strategies of justification from the ones he appeals to in discussing "the right to be a permanent visitor" [*Gastrecht*]. The one strategy of argumentation justifies the right of temporary sojourn on the basis of the capacity of all human beings [*allen Menchen*] to associate—the German reads: "*sich zur Gesellschaft anzubieten*" (Kant 1914, 443). The other strategy resorts to the juridical construct of a "common possession of the surface of the earth" [*gemeinschaftliches Besitzes der Oberfläche der Erde*], (ibid.). With respect to the second principle, Kant suggests that to deny the foreigner and the stranger the claim to enjoy the land and its resources, when this can be done peacefully and without endangering the life and welfare of original inhabitants, would be unjust.

The juridical contract of a purported common possession of the earth, which has a long and honorable antecedent in old European jurisprudence, functions as a double-edged sword in this context. It supports the fiction that the earth is a "res nullius," belonging to all and none until it is appropriated. To argue that the earth is a common possession of all human beings is, in effect, to disregard existing property relations of historically established communities on the land. The claim to property then shifts from the historical title that justifies particular property relations to the modes of appropriation whereby what commonly belongs to a particular historical community can then be appropriated as "mine" or "thine."

Recall here John Locke's argument in *The Second Treatise of Civil Government.* "In the beginning God gave the earth to men in common to enjoy." Private property emerges through the fact that the means of appropriation are themselves private: "The labor of his body, and the work of his hands, we may say, are properly his. . . . this nobody has any right to but himself" (Locke 1690 [1980], 19). In the context of European expansion to the Americas in the seventeenth century, Locke's argument served to justify colonial appropriation of land, precisely with the claim that the earth, being given to all "in common," could then be justifiably appropriated by the industrious and the thrifty, without harming existing inhabitants and, in fact, for the benefit of all.

Kant rejects the *res nullius* thesis in its Lockean form, seeing in it a thinly disguised formula for expropriating non-European peoples who do not have the capacity to resist imperialist onslaughts (Kant, 1957, 104; see also Muthu 1999 and 2000). Yet the right to seek human association, or in the literal translation of the German, "to offer oneself to civil association [*Gesellschaft*] with others" is for Kant a fundamental human right, and is to be distinguished from the *res nullius* thesis; in fact, the right to seek human association is at the core of what it means to be a "*Weltbürger.*" In true Enlightenment fashion, Kant celebrates the ship and the camel ("the desert ship," as he calls the latter) for reducing distances, breaking down barriers among local communities, and bringing the human race together. To deny "the possibility of seeking to communicate with prior inhabitants," or "*ein Verkehr zu suchen*" (Kant 1914, 444; 1957, 103) is contrary to cosmopolitan right. The terminology of "*Verkehr zu suchen,*" which can extend to commercial as well as religious, to cultural as well as financial contacts, reveals Kant's hope that, even if the motives of Western powers in seeking to encompass the face of the globe may be less than laudatory, through increased contacts with other peoples and culture, "the human race can gradually be brought closer and closer to a cosmopolitan constitution [*einer weltbürgerlichen Verfassung*]" (Kant 1914, 444).

Which of the two principles justifies then the right of temporary sojourn: the right to seek human association, which in fact could be viewed as an extension of the human claim to freedom? Or the juridical fiction of the common possession of the earth, which in its Biblical or theistic interpretation, and in the hands of natural law theorists such as Locke, has served to justify conquest and colonial expansion? Kant should have distinguished between the right of human association on the one hand and the claim to communal possession of the earth's surface on the other. That he did not do so can partially be attributed to his concern that denying common possession of the earth's surface would delegitimize commerce and contact across nations and peoples altogether. Kant's dilemma was how to justify the expansion of commercial and maritime capitalism in his time, insofar as these developments bring the human race into closer contact, without condoning European imperialism on the one hand or accepting the defensiveness of self-enclosed communities on the other. The cosmopolitan right of hospitality gives one the right of peaceful temporary sojourn, without entitling one to plunder and exploit, conquer and overwhelm by superior force those among whom one is seeking sojourn. But the cosmopolitan right is a right precisely because it is grounded upon the fundamental premise of the commonality of humanity in each and every person and the freedom of the will of each, which also includes the freedom to travel beyond the confines of one's cultural, religious, and ethnocentric walls.

Although Kant's focus fell, for understandable historical reasons, upon the right of temporary sojourn, my concern is with the unbridgeable gap he suggests exists between the right of temporary sojourn and permanent residency. The first is a right, the second is a privilege; granting the first to strangers is an obligation for a republican sovereign, whereas allowing the second is an "act of beneficence." The rights of strangers and foreigners do not extend beyond the peaceful pursuit of their means of livelihood upon the territory of another. What about the right to political membership then? Under what conditions, if any, can the guest become a member of the republican sovereign? How are the boundaries of the sovereign defined? Kant envisages a world condition in which all members of the human race become participants in a civil order and enter into a condition of "lawful association" with one another. Yet this civil condition of lawful coexistence is not equivalent to membership in a republican polity. Kant's cosmopolitan citizens still need their individual republics to be citizens at all. This is why Kant is so careful to distinguish a "world government" from a "world federation." A "world government," he argues, would be a "soulless despotism," whereas a world federation [*eine föderative Vereinigung*] would still permit the exercise of citizenship within bounded communities (Kant 1914, 453; 1957, 112).

Civic-Republican Skepticism and the Right to Political Membership

I have recalled at length Kant's argument concerning "the cosmopolitical right to temporary sojourn," because this discussion contains *in nuce* many of the dilemmas that still govern our thinking about foreigners and aliens, immigrants, refugees, and asylum seekers. We are still unsure whether the claims of refugees, and asylums seekers articulate international obligations, the violation of which should lead to sanctions against sovereign states, or whether such claims remain subject to the prerogative of the political sovereign. Although the right of asylum is guaranteed by the Geneva Convention relating to the Status of Refugees (1951), when the Italian government catches at sea Albanian refugees from neighboring Albania or Kosovo, and places them either in temporary detention camps and eventually repatriates them to their war-torn homelands; when the German government pays neighboring Hungary to accept refugees from the former Yugoslavia rather than letting them into the boundaries of the European Union; when the agreements of Schengen and Dublin seek to strengthen the walls of "the fortress Europe," or when the United States denies asylum to the Haitian refugees and instead imprisons them in Guantanemo Bay, international legal institutions as well as relief organizations are helpless to change the actions of national governments. The United Nations High Commissioner on Refugees takes note, seeks negotiations with the involved parties, monitors their activities, and publishes numbers and reports; it is more often than not impotent to bend the will of national governments.

In this essay I will accept the distinction between immigrants on the one hand and refugees and asylum seekers on the other, although in reality many immigrants become immigrants because they are made refugees by their home governments, whereas others, though not as many as their opponents would like to claim, demand political refugee and asylum status because they are, in truth, "economic refugees," that is, more properly immigrants. I uphold these distinctions, not because they are adequate to deal with the complexities of the flows of peoples in a globalized world, but because from the standpoint of international law as well as moral philosophy, the duties and obligations we owe to strangers who seek entry into our communities on the grounds that they are persecuted for their ancestry and ethnicity, beliefs or convictions, or because war, persecution as well as natural disasters, make their homes uninhabitable, are of a different kind than the obligations we owe others who *choose* to live in our midst. The claims of refugees and asylum seekers do generate stronger obligations of compliance on the part of receiving communities. Since to deny refuge and sojourn to refugees and asylees would involve a violation of a fundamental rule of human morality, namely to aid those in need, as well as violating the Geneva Convention, recipient communities must stand under a "stricter burden of proof" to show how or why such claims are not worthy of recognition or how or why recognizing them would jeopardize not just the economic standard of living but the very survival of the receiving communities.[1]

Current international practice, however, is much more lenient. Michael Walzer aptly summarizes common thinking about these matters: "Actually to take in large numbers of refugees is often morally necessary; but the right to restrain the flow remains a feature of communal self-determination. The principle of mutual aid can only modify and not transform *admissions policies rooted in a particular community's understanding of itself*" (Walzer 1983, 51; my emphasis). I think this formulation sets the bar of compliance for the involved governments quite low. What exactly counts "as admissions policies rooted in a particular community's understanding of itself"? Walzer is among the few contemporary theorists to have addressed the significance of questions of membership for theories of justice as well as democracy. Yet his position is built around one aspect of the paradox of democratic legitimacy that I articulated above, namely that of the collective self-determination of a democratic people, while leaving the dimension of universal human rights fully unrecognized. Walzer privileges the will of the political sovereign while seeking to leaven the possible injustices and inequities that may result from such acts and policies by considerations of fairness and compassion, sensitive contextual reasoning and moral openness. I want to argue that this strategy is inadequate and that dilemmas of political membership in liberal democracies go to the heart of the self-definition as well as self-constitution of these polities, precisely because, as liberal democracies, they are built on the constitutive tension between human rights and political sovereignty.

In an elegant passage that has been extensively quoted, Walzer writes: "To tear down the walls of the state is not, as Sidgwick worriedly suggested, to create a world without walls, but rather to create a thousand petty fortresses. The fortress, too, could be torn down: all that is necessary is a global state sufficiently powerful to overwhelm the local communities. . . . The distinctiveness of cultures and groups depends upon closure and, without it, cannot be conceived as a stable feature of human life. If this distinctiveness is a value, as most people (though some of them are global pluralists, and others only local loyalists) seem to believe, then closure must be permitted somewhere. At some level of political organization, something like the sovereign state must take shape and claim the authority to make its own admissions policy, to control and sometimes restrain the flow of immigrants" (Walzer 1983, 39).

There is a quick slide in Walzer's argumentation from "the value of the distinctiveness of cultures and groups" to the need for closure and to the justification for "something like the sovereign state" to control boundaries and set admissions policy. Walzer does not distinguish between the methodological fiction of a unitary "cultural community" and the polity. A democratic polity with pluralist traditions consists of many cultural groups and subgroups, many cultural traditions and countertraditions; furthermore the "national" culture itself is formed by the contested multiplicity of many traditions, narratives, and historical appropriations. Equally significantly, Walzer does not distinguish between principles of *cultural integration* and principles of *political integration*. Cultural communities are built around their members' adherence to values, norms, and traditions that bear a prescriptive value for their identity, in that failure to comply with them affects their own understanding of membership and belonging. Surely though there is always contestation and innovation around such cultural definitions and narratives—what does it mean to be an observant but a nonorthodox Jew? What does it mean to be a modern Moslem woman? What does it mean to be a pro-choice Catholic? Cultural traditions consist of such narratives of interpretation and reinterpretation, appropriation and subversion. In fact, the more alive a cultural tradition, the more contestation there will be about its core elements. Walzer invokes throughout much of his work, and not only in *Spheres of Justice,* a "we." This "we" suggests an identity without conflict; a unity without "fissure." It is a convenient methodological fiction, but its consequences for political argument can be invidious.

Political integration refers to those practices and rules, constitutional traditions and institutional habits, that bring individuals together to form a functioning political community. This functioning has a twofold dimension: not only must it be possible to run the economy, the state, and its administrative apparatus, but there must also be a dimension of belief in the legitimacy of the major institutions of societies in doing so. The *legal-rational* authority of the modern state rests on administrative and economic efficiency as well as a belief in its legitimacy. Precisely because modern states presuppose a plurality of competing as well as coexisting worldviews, precisely because in the modern state political life is one sphere of existence among many others with claims upon us, and precisely because the disjunction between personal identities and allegiances and public choices and involvements is constitutive of the freedom of citizens in liberal democracies, the principles of political integration are necessarily more abstract and more generalizable than principles of cultural identity. Of course there will be some variation across existing political communities as to what the constituents of such political integration will be: the typology of civic and ethnic nationalisms indicate such a range. Nonetheless, in liberal democracies *conceptions of human and citizens' rights, constitutional traditions as well as democratic practices of election and representation* are the core normative elements of political integration. It is to them that citizens as well as foreigners, nationals as well as resident aliens have to show

respect and loyalty, and not to the vagaries of this or that cultural tradition. Precisely because Walzer conflates cultural with political integration, many of his remarkably wise claims about immigration and
naturalization policy create the impression that they are the results of
what Kant would call "contracts of beneficence." Walzer cannot thematize the dual, fractured identity of the members of the modern
democratic sovereign, as bearers of human rights qua moral persons
and as bearers of citizen's rights as members of the sovereign. The dualism of universal human rights principles and the exigencies of sovereign self-determination are eliminated in his view in favor of the
right to collective self-determination. Repeatedly, citizens' identity is
given a thick cultural coating, while human rights are contextualized.
In a passage remarkably reminiscent of Edmund Burke's critique of
the French Revolution, Walzer writes: "Men and women do indeed
have rights beyond life and liberty, but these do not follow from our
common humanity; they follow from shared conceptions of social
goods; they are local and particular in character" (Walzer 1983, xv).
We may indeed wish to ask how a conception of "shared social goods"
is to provide a conception of rights, since pace Walzer, it is rights claims
that are invoked more often than not to arbitrate among conflicting
conceptions of social goods (see also Bader 1995 on Walzer).

The democratic people constitute themselves as sovereign because
they uphold certain principles of human rights and because the terms
of their association interpret as well as flesh out these rights. Of course,
the precise interpretation of basic human rights and the content of citizens' rights must always be spelled out and articulated in the light of
the concrete historical traditions and practices of a given society.[2] Nevertheless, these principles are not exhausted, either in their validity or
in their content, through their embodiment in specific cultural and
legal traditions. They have a context-transcending validity claim,[3] in
the name of which the excluded and the downtrodden, the marginalized and the despised mobilize and claim political agency and membership. The history of democratic reforms and revolutions, from the
workers' movements to the suffragists, from antidiscrimination to an-
ticolonial struggles widen the circle of addressees of these rights, as
well as transforming their content. It is precisely because these rights
claims have a context-transcending quality that they can be invoked by

those who have been excluded "from shared conceptions of social goods," and for whom the "local and the particular" have borne insignias of inequality, oppression, and marginalization.

I began this section by accepting the necessary as well as problematical character of the distinction between refugees and asylees on the one hand and immigrants on the other. Walzer, I maintained, represents the civic republican voice in debates around citizenship and immigration. He upholds the right of the democratic sovereign to define borders and boundaries, and to enclose the geographical as well as civic territory. Walzer confuses cultural with political norms of integration and for this reason, his perspectives on the political incorporation of foreigners and immigrants have the character of ad hoc considerations. In the final analysis, human rights claims become the thinnest of moral reeds in Walzer's seemingly sturdy thicket of cultural ties and bonds.

Principles of Political Incorporation in the Global Era

The urgency of articulating principles of political membership in the global era does not arise in the first place from an increase in migration figures. In absolute numbers, the middle of the nineteenth-century and the interwar period in Europe involved larger masses of population moving across continents than has been the case in Europe since World War II (Sassen 1999). Rather, this urgency arises from shifts in interstate relations through the emergence of an international regime of human rights and, especially in Europe, through the emergence of the European Union. The political and legal transformations brought about by the EU are creating economic, constitutional, and legal quagmires in this domain (Benhabib 1999b). Two other contributing factors are the patterns of changing migratory flows due to the geopolitics of the world's labor markets, and changes in sending and absorption patterns among countries. I treat each factor in turn.

Shifts in Interstate Relations

Within the European context, three developments are of particular note:

Seyla Benhabib

1. The acquisition by citizens of member states of the EU of a European pass and European citizenship.

2. The increasing discrepancy between the rights of EU citizens who reside in countries other than their countries of origin and Third Country nationals who are residents of EU member countries but who are not European citizens. While EU citizens can vote, run for, and hold office in local elections as well as in elections for the European Parliaments, Third Country nationals cannot do so.

3. The agreements of Dublin and Schengen, which liberalized border controls among the signatory countries (Belgium, the Netherlands, Luxembourg, France, and Germany signed the Schengen agreement in 1990; they were subsequently joined by Italy, Portugal, and Spain), also intended to "homogenize" asylum and refugee granting practices across the EU states.

Geopolitics of Labor Market Migrations

As Saskia Sassen notes "labor migrations are embedded in larger social, economic, and political structures, and . . . they are consequently bounded in geography, duration, and size. There is a geopolitics of migration and there is the fact that migrations are part of systems: both set parameters for migrations" (Sassen 1999, 155). Such migrations are now global phenomena. There are seasonal as well as long-term migrations from all over the Mediterranean basin countries, not only to northern Europe, but also to the oil-rich countries of the Gulf Region; likewise, the strong economic performance of Southeast Asian countries has created migratory flows to those countries from as far away as Australia and Germany.

Patterns of Sending and Absorption

With reference to recent patterns of immigration within and outside Europe, Rainer Bauböck has observed: "On the one hand, immigrants who settle in a destination country for good may still keep the citizenship of the sending society and travel there regularly so that the sending country rightly regards them as having retained strong ties to their origins. . . . Temporary migrants, on the other hand, often find it difficult to return and to reintegrate. Some migrants become permanent residents in destination countries without being accepted as immigrants and without regarding themselves as such; others develop patterns of frequent movement between different countries in none of which they establish themselves permanently. . . . International migration transnationalizes both sending and receiving societies by extending relevant forms of membership beyond the boundaries of territories and of citizenship" (Bauböck 1998, 26).

These three factors then—shifts in interstate relations, the patterned geopolitics of labor market migrations, and the transnationalization of immigration as a result of changes in sending and absorption patterns—all suggest that the question of political membership in the global era is a central aspect of the deterritorialization of politics.

The citizenship and naturalization claims of foreigners, denizens, and residents within the borders of a polity—as well as the laws, norms, and rules governing such procedures—are pivotal social practices through which the normative perplexities of human rights and sovereignty can be most acutely observed. Sovereignty entails the right of a people to control its borders and to define the procedures for admitting "aliens" into its territory and society. Yet in a liberal-democratic polity, such sovereignty claims must always be constrained by human rights, which individuals are entitled to, not in virtue of being citizens, but insofar as they are human beings *simpliciter*. What kinds of immigration, naturalization, and citizenship practices then would be compatible with the commitments of liberal democracies to human rights?

The irony of current practices in most liberal democracies in the world, including the United States, is that whereas social rights and benefits—such as unemployment compensation, retirement benefits, some form of health insurance, and in some cases educational and housing subsidies—are granted to citizens as well as legal aliens and residents, the transition to "political rights" and "the privileges of membership" proper remains unbridgeable (Benhabib 1999b, 720ff). Once again, though, political practice is changing slowly but surely. In Denmark as well as Sweden, foreigners, that is Third Country nationals, can participate in local and regional elections and be candidates for them. In Norway, Finland, and Holland these rights are granted at the local but not regional levels. Similar attempts in Berlin, Hamburg, and Schleswig-Hollstein to grant local election rights to those foreigners who have resided in Germany for more than five years have been declared "unconstitutional" by the German Constitutional Court (Weiler, 1995). What we are beginning to see is a "disaggregation effect," through which such constituents of citizenship as collective identity, political membership, and social rights and benefits are being pulled apart from one another (see Cohen 2000). One can have one set of rights and claims without the other—one can have political rights without being a national, as in the case of the EU. More commonly, though, one has social rights and benefits, in virtue of being a foreign worker, without either sharing in collective identity or having the privileges of political membership. The danger in this situation is that of "permanent alienage," namely the creation in society of a group that partakes of that society's property regime and civil society without having access to political membership. It is the privilege of political membership that now must be recognized as a right, and not just as a status granted to some by a "contract of beneficence," in Kantian terms. This means bridging the gap between "civil" and "political citizenship."

Contemporary societies are complex, fragmented, and contradictory social structures. In such societies human conduct and interactions assume many and diverse forms. We are equally authentically members of a family, of a neighborhood, of a religious community, of a social movement, and citizens of a national or multinational state or of a federation. While the modern democratic state remains a possible structural expression of democratic self-determination, the complexity of our social lives integrates us into associations that lie above and below the level of the nation state. These associations mediate the manner in which we relate to the state. If we stop viewing the state as the privileged apex of a form of collective identity, but instead view it "as a union of unions" (Wilhelm von Humboldt), then citizenship should also be understood as a form of collective identity that is mediated in and through the institutions of civil society. In the European context this means foreigners' claims to citizenship in a political entity are established not through some hierarchical decision from above, but because individuals show themselves to be worthy of membership in civil society through the exercise of certain abilities and the fulfillment of certain conditions.

What are these abilities and conditions? Length and nature of residency in a particular country are undoubtedly foremost among such criteria. Minimal knowledge of the language of the host country as well as proof of a certain "civil knowledge" about the laws and governmental forms of that country are others. Criteria such as these can be formulated and applied reasonably.

The increasing analytical as well as institutional separation of the three dimensions constitutive of citizenship—collective identity, political membership, social rights and entitlements—suggests the need to rethink the "identity and virtues of citizens" from a normative point of view. In virtue of what do we prove our claim to the exercise of political rights? What abilities and competencies must we show to participate in and run for local elections? Increasingly, it is what one does and less who one is, in terms of one's origin, which will and should determine these claims. Applied to the case of contemporary Europe, this means very concretely: if an Italian or a Portuguese national can take up residence in Paris, Hamburg, or London and run for office as well as vote in local elections in those countries after about six months, what is the justification for denying similar rights to a Turkish or Croatian national, to a Pakistani or to an Algerian who has resided in these countries, who has participated in the economy and civil society of these countries, who has been a member of a trade union, religious group, school board, and neighborhood association? The liberal-democratic state is a "union of unions"; while the virtues and abilities that make an individual a good neighbor, a reliable coworker, an honest businessperson may not be immediately transferable to the virtues and abilities required by political citizenship, it is just not the case that there is an ontological divide between them. Walzer and other thinkers in the civic-republican tradition are wrong in their exaggerated attempt to segregate political from civic identities. As I have argued elsewhere (Benhabib 1992), the question is this: what are the social practices through which the qualities of mind of an "enlarged mentality" can be cultivated? This enlarged mentality allows us to exercise civic imagination in taking the standpoint of the other(s) into account in order to woo their agreement on controversial and divisive norms that affect our lives and interactions. Such an enlarged mentality, which I see as a sine qua non for the *practice, not the acquisition,* of democratic citizenship, is based upon the virtues of membership and association, the ability to negotiate conflicting perspectives and loyalties, and the ability to distance oneself from one's most deeply held commitments in order to consider them from the hypothetical standpoint of a universalistic morality. The democratic public sphere in which these virtues are cultivated is not opposed to global civil society but is an aspect of it.

The formation of a global civil society would be greatly enhanced if—in addition to making it constitutionally acceptable and legally easier for immigrants, refugees, and asylees who have fulfilled certain conditions to acquire citizenship—democratic participation rights were granted at the local and regional state levels to those who may be unable or unwilling to complete naturalization. The practice of dual citizenship, which is currently a murky constitutional and political practice, could be made clearer and more accessible. Surely, in such cases too there will be minimum residency, language, employment, and family status requirements. But even in the absence of the full recognition of dual citizenship status, granting resident foreigners the rights to vote and participate in local and state level elections, in addition to recognizing the link between civil and political citizenship, would ask these individuals, who already pay taxes as well as other dues, to accept the burdens as well as privileges of membership.

My conclusion suggests that the Kantian distinction between the "right of temporary sojourn" and "the right to form more permanent associations" is to be rejected. I am not suggesting that they are identical. To argue that they are identical would imply that first admittance should automatically lead to full membership. This is the logical consequence of an "open borders" position. Rather, I am suggesting "porous borders," which permit transition from first admittance to civil and then political membership, along a continuum of transparent, publicly articulated, and constitutionally consistent conditions (see also Bader 1997). Because human rights principles and sovereignty claims are the two pillars of the liberal-democratic state, practices of political incorporation must respect the fluidity of the boundaries between citizen and aliens, nationals and foreigners. There is a fundamental human right to exit[4] only if there is also a fundamental human right to entry, but not necessarily to admittance. Kant was correct on that point. While admittance does not guarantee membership, it does entail the human right to know how and why one can or cannot be a member, whether or not one will be granted refugee status or permanent residency and on what grounds. The actions of the liberal-democratic state should be consistent, transparent, and publicly accountable in its treatment of foreigners as well as citizens. In articulating such conditions, the liberal-democratic state must treat the other(s), the foreigner and the stranger, in accordance with internationally recognized norms of human respect and dignity.

Notes

1. In everyday politics, it is very common to assume that "foreigners, immigrants and asylees" are "taking our jobs." In Europe since the mid-1980s, as well as in the United States, the argument that a liberal immigration and asylum policy negatively affects the standard of living of the receiving population has been a staple of xenophobic sentiment. While I do believe that every immigration and absorption policy must balance self-interest and moral obligation, I also believe that the political economy of the international labor market is much more complicated than political folklore suggests. Cheap, immigrant labor, and in many cases, illegal immigrant labor have been the fuel in the engine of capitalist development (cf. Hollifield 1992; Sassen 1999) in many sectors of many industrialized countries—most notably in the agricultural and service sectors. Instead of cracking down on this secondary labor market, and obliging employers to pay fair wages, governments and political parties scapegoat migrant labor. As economic globalization proceeds, it will be extremely important to combine the protection of the standard of living of the working classes of the receiving countries with an immigration and absorption policy that is consistent with human rights and cosmopolitan in spirit (Pollin 2000). The status of migrant labor, which when legal pays taxes as well as benefits, is often confused with the aid paid too asylees and refugees. Illegal migrant laborers do not pay taxes, but by the same token, they save their employers from having to pay obligatory benefits to the state by way of health insurance premiums, old age pensions, and so forth. The amount of social aid paid to asylees and refugees, even if frequently conflated with the supposed costs of migrant labor, are usually miniscule in amount, compared to the national budget at large. Very often, the hidden agenda of the debates about the "burden placed by asylees and refugees" on national resources, concern either the boundaries of "cultural identity"—who are we?—or the cost sharing among federal and local agencies. The latter played a major role in asylum debates in post-unification Germany, as well as in the passing of Proposition 187 in California. For further clarification on the legal and cultural ramifications of this ostensibly economic concern, see Neumann 1993 and Fiss 1998.

2. The derivation, enumeration, and justification of basic (human) rights as well as citizens' rights pose undoubtedly one of the most challenging and difficult tasks of legal, moral, and political philosophy. In developing an argument about political membership on the basis of the dualism of rights claims versus sovereignty assertions, I am taking the self-understanding of liberal democracies at their own word, while attempting to avoid a specific material definition of certain rights. For example, to say that the right to asylum is a basic human right, recognized by the Geneva Convention, and justifiable by moral and legal philosophy, does not mean that there is also a "basic human right" to economic and social aid of a certain sort. A state may have a liberal asylum policy and delegate the responsibility for caring for asylees and refugees to civil society organizations, such as trade unions, ethnic associations, and church groups. By the same token a state may have a somewhat "illiberal" asylum and refugee policy, as the German government arguably does after the Reform of the *Asylgesetz* in 1992 and in 1993, while retaining the primary responsibility for the sustenance and social welfare of these groups in the period between their admission into the country and the resolution of their petition for asylum or refugee status. See Benhabib 1999b for further details on Germany's policy. The "human right to hospitality" does not entail the social and economic right to certain benefits; it only entails that one should not be prevented from seeking one's livelihood in the home country. Without access to the means of livelihood, the right of course would lose its material as opposed to its formal content (Habermas 1996, 122–123). Human rights issues are also at the heart of McCarthy's 1997 critique of Rawls.

3. In this paper I pass over the philosophical arguments concerning this claim; see Benhabib, *Situating the Self* (1992); cf. Baynes (2000) for a recent statement of the meaning of the transcendence of rights claims.

4. Although the U.N. charters do not recognize a human right to emigrate, to deny this right to citizens is compatible neither with human rights to liberty of movement nor with the self-understanding of liberal democracies.

References

Agamben, Giorgio. 1998. *Homo Sacer: Sovereign Power and Bare Life*, trans. D. Heller-Roazen. Stanford: University of Stanford Press.

Amin, Samir. 1997. *Capitalism in the Age of Globalization*. London: Zed Books.

Bader, Veit. 1997. "Fairly Open Borders." Pp. 28–60 in *Citizenship and Exclusion*, ed. V. M. Bader. London: Macmillan.

———. 1995. "Citizenship and Exclusion: Radical Democracy, Community, and Justice, Or What is Wrong with Communitarianism?" *Political Theory* 23: 211–246.

Baynes, Kenneth. 2000. "Rights as Critique and the Critique of Rights: Karl Marx, Wendy Brown and the Social Function of Rights." *Political Theory* 28: 451–469.

Benhabib, Seyla. 1999a. "Citizens, Residents and Aliens in a Changing World: Political Membership in the Global Era." *Social Research* 66: 709–744.

————. 1999b. *Demokratische Gleichheit und Kulturelle Vielfalt: Die Horkheimer Vorlesungen.* Frankfurt am Main: Fischer.

————. 1996. *The Reluctant Modernism of Hannah Arendt.* London: Sage.

————. 1992. *Situating the Self: Gender, Community and Postmodernism in Contemporary Ethics.* New York: Routledge.

Bauböck, Rainer. 1998. "The Crossing and Blurring of Boundaries in International Migration: Challenges to Social and Political Theory." Pp. 15–53 in *Blurred Boundaries: Migration, Ethnicity, and Citizenship,* ed. R. Bauböck and J. Rundell. Brookfield, Vt.: Ashgate.

————. 1994. *Transnational Citizenship: Membership and Rights in International Migration.* Cornwall: Edward Elgar.

Beck, Ulrich. 1998. *Was ist Globalisierung?* Frankfurt am Main: Suhrkamp.

Beck, Ulrich, Anthony Giddens, and Scott Lasch. 1994. *Reflexive Modernization: Politics, Tradition and Aesthetics in the Modern Social Order.* Oxford: Polity.

Bohman, James, and Matthias Lutz-Bachmann, eds. 1997. *Perpetual Peace: Essays on Kant's Cosmopolitan Ideal.* Cambridge: MIT Press.

Brubacker, Rogers. 1992. *Citizenship and Nationhood in France and Germany.* Cambridge: Harvard University Press.

Buchanan, Patrick J. 1998. *The Great Betrayal.* Boston: Little, Brown and Company.

Carens, Joe. 1995. "Aliens and Citizens: The Case for Open Borders." Pp. 229–255 in *Theorizing Citizenship,* ed. R. Beiner. Albany: SUNY Press.

Cohen, Jean L. 2000. "Changing Paradigms of Citizenship and the Exclusiveness of the Demos." *International Journal of Sociology,* vol. 14:3, 245–268.

Guehenno, Jean-Marie. 1995. *The End of the Nation-State.* Minneapolis: University of Minnesota Press.

Fiss, Owen. 1998. "The Immigrant as Pariah." *Boston Review* 23, no. 5 (October-November): 4–6.

Featherstone, Mike, Scott Lash, and Roland Robertson, eds. 1995. *Global Modernities.* London: Sage.

Friedman, Thomas. 1998. *Lexus and the Olive Tree.* New York: Basic Books.

Habermas, Jürgen. 1998. *The Inclusion of the Other: Studies in Political Theory,* ed. C. Cronin and P. DeGreiff. Cambridge: MIT Press.

————. 1996. *Between Facts and Norms: Contributions to a Discourse Theory of Law and Democracy,* trans. W. Rehg. Cambridge: MIT Press.

Heiberg, Marianne, ed. 1994. *Subduing Sovereignty: Sovereignty and the Right to Intervene.* London: Pinter Publishers.

Held, David, Anthony McGrew, David Goldblatt, and Jonathan Perraton. 1999. *Global Transformations.* Stanford: Stanford University Press.

Hollifield, James F. 1992. *Immigrants, Markets and States: The Political Economy of Postwar Europe.* Cambridge: Harvard University Press.

Jameson, Frederic, and Masao Miyoshi, eds. 1998. *The Cultures of Globalization.* Durham, N.C.: Duke University Press.

Jacobson, David. 1997. *Rights Across Borders: Immigration and the Decline of Citizenship.* Baltimore: Johns Hopkins University Press.

Kant, Immanuel. [1797] 1996. *The Metaphysics of Morals,* trans. M. Gregor. Cambridge: Cambridge University Press.

————. 1957. "Perpetual Peace," trans. L. W. Beck. Pp. 85–135 in *On History,* ed. L. W. Beck. Indianapolis: Library of Liberal Arts.

————. [1795] 1914. "Zum Ewigen Frieden: Ein philosophischer Entwurf." Pp. 343–386 in *Immanuel Kants Werke,* ed. A. Buchenau, E. Cassirer, and B. Kellermann. Berlin: Bruno Cassirer.

Locke, John. [1689] 1980. *Second Treatise of Government,* ed. C. B. Macpherson. Indianapolis: Hackett.

McCarthy, Thomas. 1999. "On Reconciling Cosmopolitan Unity and National Diversity." *Public Culture* 11, no. 1: 175–210.

————. 1997. "On the Idea of a Reasonable Law of Peoples." Pp. 201–218 in Bohman and Lutz-Bachmann, eds.

Miller, David. 1995. *On Nationality.* New York: Oxford University Press.

Moravscik, Andy. 1998. "Explaining the Emergence of Human Rights Regimes: Liberal Democracy and Political Uncertainty in Postwar Europe." *Working Paper Series. Weatherhead Center for International Affairs.* No. 98–17.

Muthu, Sankar. 2000. "Justice and Foreigners: Kant's Cosmopolitan Right." *Constellations* 7: 23–45.

————. 1999. "Enlightenment and Anti-Imperialism." *Social Research* 66: 959–1007.

Neumann, Gerald L. 1993. "Buffer Zones Against Refugees: Dublin, Schengen and the German Asylum Amendment." *Virginia Journal of International Law* 33: 503–526.

Nussbaum, Martha. 1997. "Kant and Cosmopolitanism." Pp. 25–59 in Bohman and Lutz-Bachmann, eds.

————. 1996. "Patriotism and Cosmopolitanism." In *For Love of Country: Debating the Limits of Patriotism,* ed. J. Cohen. Boston: Beacon.

Pollin, Robert. 2000. "Globalization, Inequality and Financial Instability: Confronting the Marx, Keynes and Polanyi Problems in the Advanced Capitalist Economies." Paper delivered at the Conference on "Globalization and Ethics." Yale University, March 31-April 2.

Rawls, John. 1999. *The Law of Peoples.* Cambridge: Harvard University Press.

———. 1993. *Political Liberalism.* Cambridge: Harvard University Press.

Rorty, Richard. 1996. "Global, Utopias, History and Philosophy." In *Cultural Pluralism, Identity, and Globalization.* Rio de Janeiro: Unesco/Issc/Educam.

Rosenau, James. 1997. *Along the Domestic-Foreign Frontier: Exploring Governance in a Turbulent World.* Cambridge: Cambridge University Press.

Sandel, Michael. 1996. *Democracy's Discontent: America in Search of a Public Philosophy.* Cambridge: Harvard University Press.

Sassen, Saskia. 1999. *Guests and Aliens.* New York: The New Press.

Soysal, Yasemin. 1994. *Limits of Citizenship: Migrants and Postnational Membership in Europe.* Chicago: University of Chicago Press.

Walzer, Michael. 1983. *Spheres of Justice: A Defense of Pluralism and Equality.* New York: Basic Books.

Weiler, Joseph. 1995. "Does Europe Need a Constitution? Demos, Telos and the German Maastricht Decision." *European Law Journal* 1, no. 3: 219–258.

Wright, Robert. 2000. "Continental Drift." *The New Republic.* (January 17): 18–23.

15

Beyond Liberalism: Toleration and the Global Society in Rawls's *Law of Peoples*

David M. Rasmussen

In John Rawls's newly revised essay entitled *The Law of Peoples*,[1] one discovers a curiously contradictory subtheme, namely the rejection of cosmopolitanism on the basis of a notion of reason that must be, in some sense, cosmopolitan. In an analysis of the original 1993 essay of the same title, Thomas McCarthy[2] has argued that when taking the long view of Rawls's work from the publication of *A Theory of Justice* on, one witnesses a certain weakening of Rawls's Kantian conception of reason. The basic move has been from reason to a conception of the reasonable that ends up relinquishing the relationship between reason and validity implicit in the Kantian conception of reason originally used by Rawls. I am basically sympathetic to this view. However, as I will show in a moment, specifically with regard to the development of *The Law of Peoples*, the process is somewhat complex and difficult to interpret. In the recent essay Rawls seems to break the link between reason and validity, specifically critiquing cosmopolitanism and ethnocentrism while, at the same time, attempting to justify a political (moral) conception of politics. Rawls in the first instance would have us dissociate him from a notion of reason that is critical, while in the second instance he wants to associate the Law of Peoples with an understanding of politics that has a moral component. Hence, in the second instance he associates himself with an idea of politics that bears within it a claim that is "utopian."[3] My working hypothesis is that this ambiguity stems from his notion of toleration. Rawls has argued in *Political Liberalism* that philosophy must apply the principle of

David M. Rasmussen

toleration to itself.[4] As Rawls has recently stated, toleration can be given both a comprehensive and a political justification. In my view, the theoretical consequence, with regard to the Law of Peoples, is a certain ambiguity. From a comprehensive point of view, toleration has reference to a form of justification that occurs within a comprehensive religious doctrine. For Rawls, this form of justification is based on interpretation or reinterpretation. His claim that a religious doctrine can be interpreted so as to correlate with a constitutional conception of human rights requires a certain religious reinterpretation of traditional doctrines.[5] But from a political point of view, toleration stems from a notion of reciprocity within public reason. While the former requires reasoning from "conjecture," the latter is purely a matter of public reason. If a comprehensive doctrine is amenable to a reasonable interpretation, it may then be understood as potentially justifying human rights, whereas a political justification of toleration, based on the notion of reciprocity, requires a certain kind of obligation to grant to others the same rights that are assumed to be one's own.[6]

So, in a liberal society where one expects people to be capable of distinguishing between a political and a comprehensive point of view as well as having a notion of public reason (which Rawls now says has a notion of toleration built into it), the justification of toleration with its basis in the reciprocal granting of rights works rather well. The real test will come when the Law of Peoples confronts nonliberal societies, which do not have the same political justification as liberal societies do. It would appear that Rawls thinks that from the comprehensive point of view a certain toleration of peoples could be granted if they were reasonable. But it would be difficult to give a political justification of toleration because there is no political reciprocity established and hence no notion of equal rights. Of course, one could perhaps carry on this entire discussion independently of human rights. But this is certainly not Rawls's intention. I state this because Rawls informs us at the outset of his discussion that the Law of Peoples refers to a "conception of right and justice" as well as to "principles and norms" of "international law."[7]

On a first reading, it appears that the Law of Peoples leads to two kinds of discourses, the first of which affirms the legitimacy of nonliberal peoples on almost apologetic terms, that is, that they should be tolerated because they function in accord with principles of decency, which is something like, although clearly not akin to, reasonableness. Here one would include the rejection of cosmopolitanism and ethnocentrism. But there is another discourse that identifies with a kind of utopian thinking stemming from Rousseau and Kant, which affirms a fundamental connection between morality and politics.

Given the kind of ambiguity present in *The Law of Peoples*, I first consider the model as it originates in Rawls's thought in a section entitled, "From the Law of Nations to the Law of Peoples." I then turn to Rawls's attempt to frame an idea of a liberal people or society in the context of what he claims to be a "realistic utopia." In the third section, I consider his anticosmopolitan argument for understanding a nonliberal people, his ideal people called "Kazanistan." Finally, I return to the question of two types of toleration and the ambiguities involved in the construction of two kinds of discourse.

1 From the Law of Nations to the Law of Peoples

Near the conclusion of his recently published *Law of Peoples*, John Rawls contrasts the view expressed therein with the cosmopolitan view that he characterizes as concerned with "the well being of individuals and not the justice of societies."[8] According to the cosmopolitan view, "there is still a question concerning the need for further global distribution, even after each domestic society has achieved internally just institutions."[9] This contrast with cosmopolitanism is rather curious given his original definition of the Law of Peoples, referred to a moment ago, which focuses on the concepts of "right" and "justice" in the context of international law. Indeed, he even cites Kant's *Perpetual Peace* as a model for his reflection in which the argument for "cosmopolitan right" has been presented.[10]

If we look at other societies from the point of view of the political conceptions that are derived from our own political society (as Rawls acknowledges he does), is not this a form of ethnocentrism?[11] "Not necessarily," says Rawls. For him this claim is associated with the "content" of the Law of Peoples as well as its "objectivity." The latter is associated with whether or not it fulfills the "criterion of reciprocity and belongs to the public reason of the Society of liberal and decent peoples."[12] I presume he means by this that the test is whether or not the Law of Peoples is a fair representation, or even interpretation of liberal and decent peoples. The further assumption is that it is fair with regard to other societies. "It asks of other societies only what they can reasonably grant without submitting to a position of inferiority or domination."[13] It does not ask "decent societies to abandon or modify their religious institutions and adopt liberal ones."[14] It only asks them to stand in a relation of "fair equality with all other societies."[15] In Rawls's view, that is not necessarily a "Western idea." One can begin to see how Rawls's previous writings on neutrality and toleration have begun to shape this discourse on international law. It would be inappropriate to take over the territory of the other in this international debate. Instead, it will be necessary to accommodate the position of other societies. This is obviously a strategic move that will belie a commitment to a certain view of toleration, legitimacy, and justification that, while not controversial in his earlier writings, certainly makes this text difficult to interpret. He must presume that rights are somehow givens, even in nonliberal societies.[16] He must assume that the idea of justice as the common good is adequate in nonliberal societies as well as that there is a parallel between decency and reasonableness. Whether or not it is possible to take such a neutral stance to nonliberal societies, particularly when fundamental human rights are at issue, is an open question. Certainly any of the controversial issues of the day would make this neutral stance problematic. But there is even a more basic issue regarding whether nonliberal societies have rights in the sense in which we modern westerners would want them—or whether rights are not just constructions that emerge from the transition to secular societies.

In order to understand how the Law of Peoples emerges as a model for reflection in Rawls's work it is necessary to go back to the original formulation of it as the "Law of Nations" in §58 of *A Theory of Justice*.[17] Curiously, the idea of a "Law of Nations" occurs in a discussion of the justification of conscientious refusal where Rawls takes up the question of how a "theory of political duty applies to foreign policy."

In order to treat this question he finds it necessary to "extend the theory of justice to the law of nations." Rawls frames the problem in a way that really has not changed much since the publication of *A Theory of Justice*. There he states the project in the following way: "Our problem, then, is to relate the just political principles regulating the conduct of states to the contract doctrine and to explain the moral basis of the law of nations from this point of view."[18] In order to do this, he uses (then as he does later) the original position a second time, although in the earlier statement he does not designate it as such. Also he shifts the focus from individuals to nations, using the difference principle as the mode of representation. The representatives in the original position know nothing of their situation within their own particular society, but they know enough to make a "rational choice to protect their interests." Under these circumstances the principles that would be chosen would be, according to Rawls, "familiar ones." Equality, nonintervention, self-determination, self-defense against foreign attack, the honoring of treaties, and the maintenance of just institutions rank among the principles that would be derived. What would not be legitimate, then as later for Rawls, would be the right to wage war for purposes of economic gain or the acquisition of territory.

The major transition in this formulation, as one moves to the later formulations of the model, is from nations to peoples. On the most elemental basis the reference is to the transition from the individual to the social. Hence, as actors in a democratic society are conceived nationally as citizens, so international actors are designated as peoples. This transition is already forecast in the idea of the Law of Nations. However, by choosing peoples over nations Rawls is clearly departing from the rhetoric of international law that distinguishes between citizens and nations or states. This is clear when he lists the "traditional principles of justice among free and democratic peoples"[19]:

1. Peoples are free and independent and their freedom and independence are to be so respected by other peoples.

2. Peoples are to observe treaties and undertakings.

3. Peoples are equal and are parties to agreements that bind them.[20]

Clearly, peoples, at least traditionally, don't respect other peoples as peoples, don't observe treaties, and are not parties to agreements that bind them. However, states or nations do have those functions. Hence, Rawls is replacing traditional rhetoric about states and the limits of state sovereignty with the term "peoples."

It would follow that this distinction between nations and peoples gives us the clue to how we should interpret the Law of Peoples. Essentially, it is a treatise on how nations or states should understand and relate to each other. But states are now conceived as peoples in order to avoid the principles set down by the treaty of Westphalia, namely, "traditional rights to war and to unrestricted internal autonomy."[21] More importantly, according to Rawls, in this treatise on international relations, peoples have basic features that cannot be attributed to states; principal among these is their "political (moral) conception of right and justice."[22] It is this latter point that grounds the underlying distinction between peoples and nations or states. "Liberal peoples limit their basic interests as required by the reasonable."[23] Nations are not so restricted. This is to claim that states do not have to be "stable for the right reasons," meaning that they do not have either to accept or act "upon a just Law of Peoples."[24] Nations or states can go to war while liberal peoples do not. "What makes peace among liberal democratic peoples possible is the internal nature of peoples as constitutional democracies and the resulting change in the motives of citizens."[25]

Apart from the transition from the concept of nation to that of people, there are two other key developments in the construction of the model that take this conception beyond the 1993 Amnesty Lecture by the same title[26]: the conception of a "realistic utopia" and the idealization of a nonliberal people under the name "Kazanistan." I want to deal with these additions in detail in the next sections. Suffice it to conclude this section by pointing out that the transition from "nation" to "people" involves the concept of reason or reasonableness. A people can be conceived of as a people in accord with a notion of reasonableness. In turn, reasonableness is linked to the notion of toleration, for even when evaluating a comprehensive doctrine, it is on the basis of reasonableness that a nonliberal people can be tolerated.

2 Realistic Utopia

Having so circumscribed the Law of Peoples to distinguish it from cosmopolitanism on the one hand and ethnocentrism on the other, one might be surprised to see Rawls's *Political Liberalism* reconstructed as a "realistic utopia." Although I'm not certain why he chooses to use such a designation, clearly he wants to dissociate himself from political realism while at the same time sustaining the Law of Peoples as a "hope" in spite of the "demonic possibility" represented by the Holocaust. In the case of political realism—which is based on the argument that "international relations have not changed since Thucydides' day"[27]—Rawls asserts that "there are political and social institutions that can be changed by people." This idea, of course, caused the democratic movement that began in Europe in the eighteenth century. Equally, "liberal people are not inflamed by lack of due self-respect."[28] With regard to the latter, Rawls counters the pessimism that could be engendered by the experience of the Holocaust with "hope for the future." But this is a hope based on working out a "reasonably just constitutional democracy that we have already formulated."[29] If this is done, Rawls concludes in a formulation that must be considered extraordinary, "No longer simply longing, our hope becomes reasonable hope."[30]

No doubt the concept of "realistic utopia" is something of a rhetorical device, but it is given a specific content and a particular history. He suggests that the idea stems from Rousseau, who was both realistic about human nature and optimistic about "constitutional and civil law."[31] In Rousseau's words, this is "taking men as they are and laws as they might be."[32] Equally, it becomes the rubric framing most of the basic arguments of *Political Liberalism*. Justice must be both realistic and utopian. To be realistic, it must achieve stability for the right reasons and it must be "applicable to ongoing political and social arrangements" without recourse to a theory of utility. But justice must also be utopian, which means that it will use "political (moral) ideas, principles and concepts to specify a reasonable society."[33] Under the utopian designation he places basic rights and liberties, "their priority with respect to claims of the general good" and "the requisite primary goods to enable [citizens] to make intelligent and effective use of their freedoms."[34] Here one also finds the criterion of reciprocity as well as public reason.

Regarding realistic utopia, he distinguishes between the political and the comprehensive, in light of the idea that "constitutional democracy must have political and social institutions that effectively lead its citizens to acquire the appropriate sense of justice as they grow up and take part in society."[35] Equally, citizens must acquire political virtues including "a sense of fairness," "tolerance," and a "willingness to meet others half-way."[36] Further, one finds here the argument for an overlapping consensus and a reasonable idea of toleration "drawn from the category of the political."[37] This latter designation is somewhat unusual given Rawls's reluctance to give content to the political as opposed to the comprehensive. He states: "The political conception will be strengthened if it contains a reasonable idea of toleration within itself, for that will show the reasonableness of toleration by public reason."[38]

One would assume that the major thesis of the text is that the designation of "realistic utopia" that characterizes a "constitutional democracy" can find its parallel in a Society of Peoples. Apparently, Rawls wants us to use for a second time the devices he has created in his reflections on the social contract as evidenced both in *A Theory of Justice* and *Political Liberalism*. Hence, on the side of realism he states: "The content of a reasonable Law of Peoples is ascertained by using the idea of the original position a second time with the parties now understood to be representatives of peoples."[39] It is likewise realistic in the sense that it is applied to "ongoing cooperative political arrangements and relations between peoples."[40] The Law of Peoples is utopian "in that it uses political (moral) ideas, principles, and concepts to specify the right and just political and social arrangements for a Society of Peoples."[41] Beyond that, in moving to the Society of Peoples Rawls wants to maintain the distance between the political and the comprehensive: he wants a parallel context for public reason and the idea of toleration. The hope is that there could be within a society of peoples a form of justification that would extend beyond mere force. "Political liberalism, with its ideas of realistic utopia and public reason, denies what so much of political life suggests—that stability among peoples can never be more than a *modus vivendi*."[42]

3 Nonliberal Peoples

Ideal theory, to be distinguished from nonideal theory, has two parts.
The first part constructs the Law of Peoples as a realistic utopia based
on an understanding of liberal societies. This part looks very much
like political liberalism except that the subject is peoples and not citizens. When Rawls turns to the second part of ideal theory he considers nonliberal peoples. As one might expect, the key concept is
toleration. "A main task in extending the Law of Peoples to nonliberal peoples is to specify how far liberal peoples are to tolerate nonliberal peoples."[43] It appears to be easy for Rawls to grant this
principle since his concept of toleration is dependent on the distinction between the comprehensive and the political. In his view, liberal people know how to make the distinction between the
comprehensive and the political. Whether nonliberal people have
that capacity is another question. When liberal people encounter
nonliberal people, they can reconstruct their own understanding in
the context of the neutrality of the political. But can they grant similar neutrality to nonliberal peoples who cannot make that distinction? Rawls attempts to construct an argument that sustains
toleration in the context of potential criticism of nonliberal by liberal
societies. To the argument for sanctioning nonliberal societies for
not treating their members as truly equal, Rawls responds with a
query regarding our foreknowledge of the need for sanctions: "How
do we know before trying to work out a reasonable Law of Peoples,
that nonliberal societies are always, other things being equal, the
proper object of political sanctions?"[44] Rawls thinks a similar argument can be made regarding the granting of self-respect to nonliberal by liberal peoples.

   At the level of the second stage there are two key concepts, which although common to the Rawlsian vocabulary, are inherently problematic in his attempts to make the case for toleration of nonliberal
peoples by liberal peoples. The first concept is the "common good
theory of justice" and the second is the relationship of decency and
reasonableness. The two notions are related, because justice in accord
with the doctrines of political liberalism is fundamentally related to
the reasonable. Rawls claims that a somewhat reasonable society of

peoples could have a decent consultation hierarchy. In his terms this would mean that "a decent hierarchical society's system of law be guided by what I have called a common good idea of justice."[45] Such a theory of justice grounded in religious and philosophical values would enable a certain form of representation for its members even though that representation would not be the same as liberal representation. The link is between justice and representation. But is it reasonable? This seems to bother even Rawls. A common good theory of justice is something other than a liberal conception of justice derived from overlapping consensus. One might say that to be fully reasonable, such a theory would have to meet the criterion of reciprocity,[46] but inasmuch as it is hierarchical, it cannot meet such a criterion. Rawls makes the rather modest claim that such a theory cannot be "unreasonable." Apparently, this means that such a theory is a "little bit" reasonable: "Among other things . . . these doctrines must admit a sufficient measure of liberty of conscience and freedom of religion and thought, even if these freedoms are not as extensive nor as equal for all members of the decent society as they are in liberal societies."[47] This seems to mean that this society of peoples must have a kind of religious freedom. Rawls states that "it is essential to the society's being decent that no religion be persecuted, or denied civic and social conditions permitting its practice in peace without fear."[48]

No doubt this issue involving the notion of equality is perplexing. Rawls ponders whether "the question might arise here as to why religious or philosophical doctrines that deny full and equal liberty of conscience are not unreasonable."[49] This is an interesting question. Why not say doctrines denying full and equal liberty of conscience are unreasonable? Rawls attempts to depart from the notion of critique implied in such a position. Whether he can totally depart from it is another question. His solution at this point is the following: "I do not say that they (the doctrines) are unreasonable, but that they are not fully unreasonable. One should allow, I think, a space between the fully unreasonable and the fully reasonable."[50] There has to be a correspondence between decency and reasonableness but it is difficult to specify within the theory precisely what kind of correspondence this is. To be decent is to be in some sense reasonable, but not reasonable like liberals in a liberal society are reasonable.

I grant the hermeneutic significance of the model Rawls presents to us. He seems to be claiming that in order to present an ideal type of a decent society that we can appreciate (in the sense of tolerate), that society must practice a form of justice that, although it may not be adequate from a liberal point of view, at least has sufficient identifiable characteristics to provide us with a sympathetic understanding. Hence Rawls's model, Kazanistan: this is an "idealized Islamic people" who "do not institute the separation of church and state," and who favor Islam inasmuch as "only Muslims can hold upper positions of political authority," but in which "other religions are tolerated and may be practiced without fear or loss of most civil rights except the right to hold the higher political and judicial offices."[51]

This idealization is based on an interpretation of the Ottoman Empire popularized most recently by Michael Walzer in his book, *On Toleration*. It is here in Kazanistan that we encounter a "decent consultation hierarchy." Essentially, this consultation hierarchy would assure, despite Muslim rule, that all groups would be consulted with the result that all interests would be represented. Hence, a certain kind of toleration would exist, sustained by a distinctive religious view of the world. Rawls admits that this idealized society would not be "perfectly just." However, one could expect, not unreasonably, that such a society "might" exist "especially as it is not without precedence in the real world."[52] In a peculiar turn of phrase Rawls defends Kazanistan as "the best we can realistically—and coherently—hope for."[53] One wonders why! The answer he gives is again somewhat surprising: "It is an enlightened society in its treatment of religious minorities."[54] Given the plethora of examples of so-called "enlightened," religiously oriented societies and their failures from the point of view of granting human rights, one might think Rawls is treading on rather thin ice with this defense. However, the intention of the creator of this ideal of a decent consultation hierarchy seems to be sustained in the following statement: "I think enlightenment about the limits of liberalism recommends trying to conceive a reasonably just Law of Peoples that liberal and nonliberal peoples could together endorse."[55] Rawls asks a great deal of his readers at this point. Given the actual examples of such societies, would it not be either necessary or desirable to endorse such a model? Rawls seems to think

David M. Rasmussen

everything rides on the embrace of this idealization. "The alternative is fatalistic cynicism which conceives of the good solely in terms of power."[56]

The culprit here is not only cosmopolitanism but also the way his thought has been used to support such a view.[57] The normal procedure would be to use a more or less Rawlsian model, which would include the distinction between the reasonable and the rational, the two moral powers, a global original position with the associated veil of ignorance and the working out of the first principle giving all people basic rights and liberties. He concludes, "Proceeding this way would straightaway ground human rights in a political (moral) conception of liberal cosmopolitan justice."[58] But this is clearly not the way he wants his position to be used. The problem for him seems to be that if one follows this procedure, the case for nonliberal societies has been rejected out of hand. The framework for thinking about this is, from Rawls's perspective, "foreign policy." But such a foreign policy would try to make all peoples into liberal peoples on the assumption "that only a liberal democratic society can be acceptable."[59] For him this means the following: "Without trying to work out a reasonable liberal Law of Peoples, we cannot know that nonliberal societies cannot be acceptable."[60]

Certainly Rawls has a point, an antiethnocentric point. No doubt recent ethnographic and anthropological research would support him on this point. However, the model he offers is somewhat problematic. Certainly, one can reconstruct the Ottoman example as an idealization. However, I would submit that most of us would find it less than desirable to have minority status in Kazanistan. To be sure, Rawls gives to Kazanistan "urgent rights," among which he includes "freedom from slavery and serfdom, liberty (but not equal liberty) of conscience, and security of ethnic groups from mass murder and genocide."[61] However, these so-called "urgent rights" could hardly be defended as, to use Rawls's own term, reasonable. For example, what does freedom from slavery and serfdom mean in the context of a consultation hierarchy? It would seem that the very term "hierarchy" would qualify the terms "slavery" and "serfdom." What does it mean to claim liberty (but not equal liberty) of conscience? Can there be a form of liberty of conscience that is not in fact measured by the notion of equality? And security from mass murder is important, but minimal, in the Hobbesian view, as the precursor for establishing rights. In any case, these rights are not, by Rawls's own definition, anything like political rights. Certainly, none of these rights is derived from a concept of reason that is self-legislating in meeting the criterion of reciprocity. Even Rawls admits that in actuality "hierarchical regimes are always, or nearly always, oppressive and deny human rights."[62] So Rawls's claim simply involves toleration, that is, "that decent hierarchical peoples exist, or could exist, and—they should be tolerated and accepted by liberal peoples as peoples in good standing."[63]

4 Two Kinds of Toleration

The Law of Peoples, as a work, illustrates how far Rawls has moved in developing the thesis that the task of political philosophy is to apply the principle of toleration to itself. This originally seemed, to this writer at least, to be a quite extraordinary position. However, upon examination it leads to a real ambiguity in Rawls's thought. His distinction between the comprehensive and the political—which seemed so persuasive in *Political Liberalism* with its correlate distinction between political and full justification—leaves behind traces of a particular understanding of toleration, the difficulties of which were not fully manifest until the publication of *The Law of Peoples.* With pluralism and overlapping consensus, Rawls was able to develop a notion of the political that became that neutral zone where citizens could justify themselves in political terms while they made their full justification to themselves, presumably through comprehensive doctrines. This way of distinguishing the political from the comprehensive suggests that the two realms are fundamentally, even organically, related. Rawls would have to claim that there is a certain reasonableness in the comprehensive doctrine, even though it was quite probably religious. Hence, the political is in some way the expression of a certain doctrine contained in the comprehensive.

Here Rawls echoes Locke in his attribution of the notion of reasonableness to Christianity. Toleration is more or less justified on this view in terms of the reasonableness of religion. But there is another view of toleration. Toleration can be conceived of as a hard-won value or norm whose justification exists independently of religion. Individual and social rights achieved as a consequence of the great religious conflicts of the West are to be achieved independently of religion and emerge as a consequence of the disenchantment of the world (to put it in Weberian terms). As a consequence, the right to self-legislation is essentially in conflict with prior comprehensive doctrines and it makes little sense to claim that, with regard to human rights, we can approach the claims of comprehensive doctrines uncritically. That is the hidden truth behind Kant's claim that we should act out of respect for the law.[64]

Rawls has attempted to account for this differentiation of law and morality in recent times by his more nuanced view distinguishing between two types of toleration. One accounts for the basic notions of justice within the context of a specific interpretation of a comprehensive doctrine. His concrete example relies on a specific reinterpretation of the Muslim Shari'a (divine law), which recasts that notion by changing the contexts of interpretation, focusing on the earlier Meccan, in contrast to the later Medinan, period of Islamic experience. By going back to the earlier period, one can interpret the Shari'a to teach the equality of men and women, freedom of religion—or at least choice in matters of faith—and equality before the law. Furthermore, constitutionalism, though not mentioned in the Qur'an, is essential for the implementation of the above principles and thus can be shown to be necessary for the realization of the principles of the Qur'an. Rawls goes so far as to suggest that inasmuch as constitutionalism can be supported by other justifications in this view, it is an example of overlapping consensus.

But clearly this is not the same as a political justification of toleration. Rawls has become relatively clear about this. As I stated earlier, there are two types of justification of toleration: one associated with public reason and the one just referred to that is associated with what Rawls calls "reasoning from conjecture."[65] According to Rawls, this form of reasoning appears when we reason "from what we believe, or conjecture, may be other peoples' basic doctrines, religious or philosophical, and seek to show them that, despite what they may think, they can still endorse a reasonable political sense of justice."[66]

There is a form of reciprocity here. It is the kind of reciprocity whereby, through conjecture, one takes the point of view of the other while at the same time attempting to reconceive or reconstruct that point of view in terms of one's own political point of view. Reasoning from conjecture appears to be a kind of hermeneutic fusion of horizons whereby one can reconstruct the view of the other in terms that will accommodate a political point of view. In other words, this is a hermeneutics of translation. But it is hardly benign and only moderately neutral. Even on the level of conjecture, one is still seeking to accommodate a political point of view. It seems that the point Rawls wants to make at this level is not so much an anticosmopolitan one as it is a pragmatic one. One cannot simply superimpose one's own political point of view on others without being sensitive to the moral claims of the other. At the same time the claims of the other can both be understood and translated into claims that we can understand. However, Rawls suggests that this procedure of conjecture is not the "ground" of toleration. "We are not ourselves asserting that ground of toleration but offering it as one they could assert consistent with their comprehensive doctrines."[67] Of course, this very statement sends us looking for the "ground" of toleration that must be the "purely political" notion of toleration. The purely political notion of toleration would conceive the comprehensive doctrine as part of the "background culture" that would be expressed in terms of a "public political culture." This, as I understand it, is *the proviso*. It appears, for Rawls, that in political terms the political notion of toleration would have a certain priority over the notion of toleration associated with the idea of conjecture. After all, the proviso "specifies public political culture as distinct from background culture."[68] Here another kind of reciprocity is specified, namely, one based on a purely political justification.

One may pose the question at this point, do these two notions of toleration conflict or do they constitute a harmonious view? Rawls would want to support the latter view. Hence, confrontation with nonliberal societies would follow the conditions specified by the proviso. He states early on in *The Law of Peoples* that "the idea of public reason for the Society of Peoples is analogous to the idea of public reason in the domestic case when a shared basis of justification exists and can be uncovered by due reflection."[69] Such a shared basis of justification could exist only when the conditions established by the proviso are followed. To the extent that this is the case, the second notion of toleration, namely the notion associated with public reason, predominates over the first. This would seem to be the case particularly when connecting international law and justice from the point of view of legitimacy. Hence, if a certain form of weak cosmopolitanism did not exist, we would have to claim that "stability among peoples can never be more than a *modus vivendi.*"[70]

Finally, it would seem that the logic of Rawls's notion of toleration would move us away from a notion of strict neutrality regarding the society of peoples and toward a notion of weak cosmopolitanism. I make this claim with regard to both types of toleration. According to the notion of toleration informed by the principle of conjecture, the standard of reasonableness is such that a comprehensive doctrine can meet the standards of interpretation only if it can accommodate itself to the criterion of reasonableness. Hence, the conjecture requires that a comprehensive doctrine can receive a political or even a constitutional interpretation, in the sense that the condition for the possibility of a particular interpretation would be a constitutional political arrangement. I would submit that so conceived, the conjecture harbors within it a weak cosmopolitan claim inasmuch as it presupposes a notion of justice associated with universal equality that would be correlated with certain rights. Certainly, if such phenomena were not discoverable within the comprehensive doctrine, then according to Rawls we could not call such a doctrine reasonable.

When one turns to the second notion of toleration found within public reason, one might assume that the cosmopolitan claim is even stronger. The reason for this would be that the standard of reciprocity is much more fundamental, being the ground for a political relationship. However, a certain ambiguity remains because one cannot expect that the standards of reciprocity apply to a society of peoples in the same way as they apply to a liberal society. To the extent that one can grant legitimacy to a comprehensive view from the point of view of a liberal society, it is difficult to see how Rawls could avoid the cosmopolitan label in accord with this second, stronger, notion of reciprocity. To put it simply, if the proviso is to be taken seriously from the perspective of public reason, then any comprehensive claim would have to be justified politically. I conclude that even if Rawls has sought to weaken the implicit claims of reason by reducing it to a form of reasonableness, the kind of reasonableness associated with toleration is one that gives priority to universal political claims. I do not see this form of cosmopolitanism to be a necessary weakness in Rawls's position. Instead, if this form of weak cosmopolitanism were acknowledged, *The Law of Peoples* would be in a much better position to speak about the universal claims of justice to which any society of peoples ought, in my judgment, to be able to subscribe. Certainly, it is this position that is in accord with the "realistic utopia" for which Rawls has so eloquently argued.

Notes

1. John Rawls, *The Law of Peoples* (Cambridge: Harvard University Press, 1999).

2. Thomas McCarthy, "On the Idea of a Reasonable Law of Peoples," in *Perpetual Peace: Essays on Kant's Cosmopolitan Ideal*, ed. J. Bohman and M. Lutz-Bachmann (Cambridge: MIT Press, 1997), 201–218.

3. My point here is that this is his term and not mine. As the argument will show later, Rawls is very much concerned to associate himself with the tradition of utopian thinking when questions of the "moral" content of politics arise. He tries, of course, to dissociate himself from the cosmopolitan implications of this same tradition. As I will show later, this stance of neutrality with regard to the Society of Peoples is inconsistent with his endorsement of the utopian tradition in political thought.

4. Rawls states, "The aim of justice as fairness, then, is practical: it presents itself as a conception of justice that may be shared by citizens as a basis of reasoned, informed, and willing political agreement. It expresses their shared and public reason. But to attain such a shared reason, the conception of justice should be, as far as possible, independent of the opposing and conflicting philosophical and religious doctrines that citizens affirm. In formulating such a conception, political liberalism applies the principle of toleration to philosophy itself." *Political Liberalism* (New York: Columbia University Press, 1993), 9–10.

5. Rawls, *Law of Peoples*, 151. This is the view that is present in the appendix "The Idea of Public Reason Revisited." At the end of this essay, I return to a detailed consideration of this orientation to comprehensive doctrines.

6. Following from justice as fairness, one would assume that equality is a basic right. This would mean that the notion of toleration, which is embedded in public reason, would sustain an obligation to grant basic human rights.

7. Ibid., 3. Significantly, the reference is to the first sentence of *The Law of Peoples*. As I interpret the text, I assume that this placement is not accidental and that it should be taken into account when trying to assess the significance of the text.

David M. Rasmussen

8. Ibid., 119. There is an issue regarding whether or not the question of cosmopolitan justice can be ascribed to societies. Rawls seems to think that, because he has focused on the notion of peoples and not citizens, the question of cosmopolitan justice can be avoided. Of course, there is the issue of whether rights are to be legitimated beyond the rights of citizens. As I will show, given the model of interpretation Rawls chooses, it is difficult to see how a form of cosmopolitanism can be avoided even from the perspective of "peoples."

9. Ibid., 119–120.

10. Ibid., 10.

11. I view this as a particularly important point in the argument and one that Rawls cannot so easily dismiss. He states, "In developing the Law of Peoples I said that liberal societies ask how they are to conduct themselves toward other societies from the point of view of their *own* political conceptions. We must always start from where we now are, assuming that we have all reasonable precautions to review the grounds of our political conception and to guard against bias and error." Ibid., 121. This is an important interpretative or hermeneutic point. From the point of view of interpretation, it is impossible to understand without assuming the perspective that is uniquely one's own. Some would argue that interpretation begins with a certain acknowledged prejudice. However, it is both acknowledging this stance and at the same time trying to neutralize it that causes trouble for Rawls when he attempts to encounter the "Society of Peoples." Rawls must assume the legitimacy of the liberal point of view. He will even go so far as to make it the standard for the interpretation of the Society of Peoples. Hence, it is difficult to see how he avoids the very ethnocentrism he criticizes.

12. Ibid., 121.

13. Ibid., 121.

14. Ibid., 120.

15. Ibid., 122.

16. The issue here is controversial. Regarding the question of rights, Rawls is assuming that nations who adopted the 1948 *Declaration of Human Rights* can be said to have rights. But this is a much more complex issue than Rawls is willing to grant. From a political point of view, the mere acknowledgement of justice as fairness would require the granting of the right to equality. Yet it is difficult to see that such rights could be granted in a "decent consultation hierarchy." The problem with this view is that it does not give an account of how rights are constructed. However, I believe the notion of justice as fairness could give such an account.

17. John Rawls, *Theory of Justice* (Cambridge: Harvard University Press, 1971), 331–335.

18. Ibid., 331.

19. *Law of Peoples*, 37.

20. Ibid.

21. Ibid., 27. Rawls has a definite historical interpretation of the nation-state in mind. After the Thirty Years' War (1616–1648), the powers of sovereignty involved a state's right to go to war as a "rational prudential interest" and the right to its own internal autonomy. After World War II, international law became "stricter," Rawls believes. "It tends to limit a state's right to wage war to instances of self-defense (also in the interests of collective security), and it also tends to restrict a state's right to internal sovereignty."

22. Ibid., 24.

23. Ibid., 29.

24. Ibid.

25. Ibid.

26. John Rawls, "The Law of Peoples," *Collected Papers*, ed. S. Freeman (Cambridge: Harvard University Press, 1999), 529–564. In this version Rawls makes the basic transition from nations to peoples.

27. *Law of Peoples*, 46.

28. Ibid.

29. Ibid., 23.

30. Ibid. The point is that this is a rather strong statement in defense of liberal principles for a position that tries to assume neutrality for a Society of Peoples.

31. Ibid., 13.

32. Ibid.

33. Ibid., 14.

34. Ibid.

35. Ibid., 15.

36. Ibid.

37. Ibid.

38. Ibid., 16.

39. Ibid., 17.

40. Ibid.

41. Ibid., 17–18.

42. Ibid., 19.

David M. Rasmussen

43. Ibid., 59.

44. Ibid., 44

45. Ibid., 71.

46. As I will show later, there are two kinds of reciprocity correlative with the two notions of toleration. I refer here to the notion of reciprocity specified by the idea of public reason; according to the proviso, this notion is the one that is the ultimate ground of toleration and reasonability.

47. Ibid., 74.

48. Ibid.

49. Ibid.

50. Ibid., 75.

51. Ibid., 70.

52. Ibid., 78.

53. Ibid.

54. Ibid.

55. Ibid.

56. Ibid. This is something of an unusual statement, since a model derived from the actual experience of the Ottoman Empire seems hopelessly inadequate, if one looks into its actual historical record. I believe Rawls can be here interpreted as addressing the question of legitimacy. The point seems to be that if we address the existence of other societies from the narrow perspective of the liberal West, we risk not only the accusation of being ethnocentric but we are also restricting ourselves to a perspective that can only be conceived of along the lines of a *modus vivendi*. Hence, our best hope would be to acknowledge Kazanistan as a legitimate Society of Peoples. The problem is that if we address that society from the point of view of international law and justice, is the model adequate to meet a legitimate standard of justice? I would argue that it is probably not adequate. Hence, it would be necessary to make a distinction between understanding and legitimacy.

57. The subtext is interesting. Apparently, Rawls does not approve of the way in which his thought has been interpreted, namely, from a cosmopolitan point of view. Hence, the references to Brian Barry, Charles Beitz, Thomas Pogge, and David Richards, all of whom have interpreted Rawls from a cosmopolitan point of view.

58. Ibid., 82.

59. Ibid., 82–83.

60. Ibid., 83.

61. Ibid., 79.

62. Ibid.

63. Ibid.

64. When one reflects on the distinction Kant makes between ordinary laws, which have the principle of obligation outside of them, and the unique law for which we can have respect because we are the authors of it, the consequential gap implied between the comprehensive and the political becomes significant.

65. Ibid., 152.

66. Ibid.

67. Ibid.

68. Ibid.

69. Ibid., 19.

70. Ibid.

Appendixes

Critical Theory Today: An Interview with Thomas McCarthy

Conducted by Shane O'Neill and Nick Smith

Perhaps we could begin by asking you some questions about your intellectual development. You are now well known as a leading proponent of critical theory. Has critical theory always been your main intellectual concern?

No. That interest developed later, as a result of the events and movements of the 1960s. Prior to that I had studied mathematics and then logic and the philosophy of science.

Would you like to tell us something about your own years as a student?

My undergraduate years were uneventful in political terms. I studied mathematics in the late 1950s, then decided to pursue graduate studies in philosophy. At the University of Notre Dame I worked primarily in logic and the philosophy of science, on the one hand, and in what later came to be called "continental" philosophy, on the other. These two interests came together in my Ph.D. dissertation, which dealt with Husserl's phenomenology from the perspective of the philosophy of logic and mathematics—a perspective that was central for him from start to finish. Part of the research was done in the Husserl archives at the University of Louvain in Belgium, where I was much impressed by Jean Ladrière, especially by the way he linked technical issues in the foundations of logic and mathematics to basic issues in the history of philosophy. While writing the dissertation I spent a year, 1966–1967, at Dalhousie University in Nova Scotia. One of my friends there was a Vietnamese political science student, who explained to me what was going on in his country. Together with the events of the American civil rights movement of the 1960s, that sparked a growing interest in social and political issues, but that interest was largely disconnected from my work in philosophy.

My first appointment, which I got while I was still writing my dissertation, was at the University of California at San Diego. Herbert Marcuse was a colleague there, and, as you can imagine, politically it was a very interesting situation. Angela Davis, for example, was still there, and Marcuse's students were very motivated politically. While I was at San Diego, between 1967 and 1968, Martin Luther King and Robert Kennedy were both shot. On one of my first political marches I was beside Marcuse walking through the streets of La Jolla, California.

At that time I became active in the Peace and Freedom Party, just when it accomplished the almost impossible task of getting on the ballot in almost every state. It was soon wiped out, however, when Eugene McCarthy and Robert Kennedy started running on antiwar platforms. Like most American students, though unlike those working with Marcuse, my political involvement at that time was not a theoretical engagement on the same level. My two lives, of philosophy and political interest, were almost entirely separate. That was not a problem in the United States since political activism was, generally speaking, very untheoretical in the European sense. When I went to Germany this began to change. I was at the University of Munich at the end of the 1960s and the beginning of the 1970s and the enormous amount of political activity there was bound up with theory. There I was motivated to bring my philosophical and political interests together.

When did you first come into contact with Habermas?

Habermas had just moved from Frankfurt to the Max Planck Institute in Starnberg. I was brought to Germany basically to teach philosophy of the social sciences in the Institute of Political Science at the University of Munich. At that time they were still borrowing from the American tradition, trying to reconstitute their own tradition after the war. That allowed me to spend a few years reading and teaching in the area of the social sciences. Up until that time I had been reading mainly in the philosophy of the physical sciences. One of the first things I was confronted with by the students was Habermas's critical social theory. It was 1968 and he had just published *Knowledge and Human Interests*. The year before he had published the essays which were translated as *Toward a Rational Society* and a couple of years earlier *Theory and Practice* had come out. Perhaps his most influential book was *The Structural Transformation of the Public Sphere* from 1962. He was still in his thirties but he was certainly, along with Adorno, *the* critical theorist whom students appealed to for contemporary approaches to social and political issues.[1]

I had brought with me all my Anglo-American training in the philosophy of science, which was largely logical empiricist. There may have been some twists and turns that were not standard but the ideas were basically mainstream. The arguments that the students kept bringing against me were coming out of Habermas's engagement in the ongoing disputes about positivism. I first read this material just to be able to answer some of the students' challenges. As a result, the first article I wrote set up an "encounter" between Habermas and mainstream Anglo-American philosophy of social science. I tried to be fair to both sides and thought of the outcome as a draw, but I think it would now read like the work of someone committed to a logical empiricist point of view on many of the basic issues. I sent a copy of the article to Habermas. As a person he is very much in tune with what he theorizes about and he loves to discuss philosophy and theory. He invited me to discuss my essay and later to attend some of the conferences in Starnberg, which is near Munich. I got more and more interested, and read more and more of his work. By the time I left, in 1972, I had decided I wanted to write a book about his thought.

Problems of Translation

You have translated some of Habermas's main works into English. As translations, these are held in high regard. Perhaps you could comment on the demands, difficulties, and rewards of translation.

When I returned to Boston, Beacon Press asked me to do a translation of *Legitimation Crisis* (1975), which I agreed to do. After that came

Communication and the Evolution of Society (1979), and then the back-breaking two volumes of *The Theory of Communicative Action* (1984, 1987), after which I swore I would never translate another word. To translate someone like Habermas, beside the usual linguistic resources, one needs a thorough familiarity with his thought, as one is repeatedly required to interpret passages in order to translate them correctly. You also need a certain intuition as to how the argument is going as you will typically make mistakes with passages you do not understand very well. That is usual with the translation of any theorist but it is particularly acute with philosophers because they put such an emphasis on precision and you have to duplicate that somehow.

Translating Habermas also presented some unusual challenges because of the vast literatures he worked with—think of the long and detailed discussions of Weber, Durkheim, Marx, Parsons, and others in *The Theory of Communicative Action*. You can't just invent terminology for all the areas he works in; for all these areas there is a well-established existing English terminology. That means, if he is writing a chapter on Weber you have to master Weber's terminology, and you cannot do that with a dictionary. It means you have to read Weber and the commentators and debates and so on. So I continued my education by translating these works. That was the greatest challenge and the greatest reward. You might say I had to educate myself in the grand tradition of social theory in order to translate Habermas.

Due to your own work and that of a number of others, most of Habermas's work is now available in English. Do you, however, believe that it is important for students to read Habermas in the original German?

I think that depends on the level of concern. Reading him in translation is adequate for most purposes. But if one wants to write, say, a dissertation on his thought, then obviously it would be of benefit to know German. On the whole, with the exception of *Theory and Practice*, the translation of his work is generally quite reliable.

America's Encounter with Habermas

Your first main work, The Critical Theory of Jürgen Habermas,[2] *has also played an important role in the dissemination of Habermas's thought in the*

English-speaking world. How intense, at the time you wrote, was the interest in Habermas in the USA and, more specifically, at your own institution?

As I was writing that in the mid-1970s, there was still only limited interest in his thought. At Boston University, where I was teaching, it did not predate my arrival. So the book—a long and rather detailed study of a still relatively obscure German writer—was something of a gamble. I simply thought that he had more of value to say on more issues than just about anyone doing social theory at the time, and I wanted to make his thought accessible to an Anglo-American readership. Given the widely scattered and then largely untranslated body of his writings, I felt that some synthetic overview would be necessary for a fruitful reading of his thought.

Was Habermas taught in many American universities at that time? Did his thought stimulate much interest among your own students?

So far as I know, he was taught only at a few places and only by a few people who had come to know his work on their own. For example, Dick Bernstein and Jeremy Shapiro in philosophy, Martin Jay and Paul Breines in intellectual history, among others. As I recall it, *Legitimation Crisis* was the first work to find a wider readership among social and political theorists—after its translation in the mid-1970s—though *Knowledge and Human Interests,* ably translated by Jeremy Shapiro, had earlier attracted a certain readership.

At Boston University, I started offering graduate courses on different aspects of his work in the early 1970s and interest gradually picked up. Of course, there was a long-standing interest in Marx and Marxism already in place there—built up by Marx Wartofsky and Bob Cohen. Seyla Benhabib joined us in the late 1970s, and there were other people doing related work in the philosophy department, particularly John Findlay teaching Hegel courses and Alasdair MacIntyre doing his thing in social and political theory. For about five years we had a first-rate program in political and social philosophy, until we all left at roughly the same time in the mid-1980s. During that period Boston University produced a number of doctoral students who have since made important contributions as critical theorists: Kenneth Baynes, James Bohman, Georgia Warnke, Steve Vogel, and Johanna Meehan, among others.

Did you face any obstacles in importing Habermas's thought into an American context? In particular, did Habermas's Marxism present obstacles that may not have arisen in a European context?

One of the main obstacles was disciplinary. Mainstream American philosophy was predominantly "analytic"—and that meant, to put it negatively, that very little European thought after Kant was being taught or written about in philosophy departments. There was almost no Hegel or Marx, Nietzsche or Heidegger, Weber or Durkheim, let alone Horkheimer or Adorno. So one usually had to begin at the beginning. And then it was not easy to find positions for our graduates in conventional departments. As you know, these aspects of institutional support or lack thereof play a big role in determining what gets taken seriously in American academic life. The political angle, the Marxist connection, only made that more difficult. But especially in the 1970s, a number of very talented, very committed young men and women chose to work in that track and succeeded in doing so largely by their own efforts.

I can't say, however, that American philosophy has changed in these respects. It is still overwhelmingly analytic in orientation. And American political science and sociology were and have remained largely empirical in orientation. Theory of *any* sort still exists on the margins, let alone Marxist theory. So, all told, Habermas and contemporary theory generally have never achieved canonical status in any discipline as practiced in the USA. They have been received on the whole by smaller groups—minorities—within a large number of different disciplines, so that while the community of those interested in working on such matters has grown, it has remained scattered across the academic archipelago. To my mind, an equally great obstacle has been the well-known American impatience with general theory. Very few people are willing or able to put in the considerable effort it requires to master a body of systematic thought of that range and complexity. Habermas is one of those thinkers, where, if you don't have all your t's crossed right at the start, something is going to go wrong in the argument somewhere. Even today, just about every talk I hear where Habermas comes up, a number of questions are based on serious, stereotypical misunderstandings. So one is constantly obliged to explain things people could have gotten clear on years ago, with a bit of work.

Would you say that the intellectual climate in the USA is now more receptive to Habermas's work than it had been, say, in the 1970s or early 1980s?

In some respects, no, in others, yes. On the one hand, the intellectual climate as a whole has become less hospitable to any form of Marxism, or to grand theory in general. Critical theoretical energy now flows much more into the politics of identity and difference, literary and cultural studies, while employing various poststructuralist and postmodernist approaches stemming mainly from France. Habermas is generally regarded by people working in these areas as an arch-modernist and thus often as an arch-enemy. He's every critic's favorite example of enlightenment universalism; if he did not exist they would have had to invent him.

On the other hand, Habermas's efforts over the years to engage with Anglo-American thought have gradually led to growing interest from that quarter—witness his recent exchange with Rawls in the *Journal of Philosophy*.[3] I think that *Between Facts and Norms*, which has just appeared in English translation, may well be the first of his books that mainstream Anglo-American political theorists will feel they *have* to read if they want to remain current.[4]

Critical Perspectives on Habermas

Perhaps we could now move on to ask some questions about your own contributions to contemporary critical theory. What do you see as the most significant differences between your own philosophical position and that of Habermas?

Speaking very generally, I would say that most of our disagreements derive from two or three differences in background and temperament. I am perhaps more pragmatic in the way I think about issues, more inclined to accept irresolvable differences regarding theory and somewhat more skeptical about the status of basic analytical distinctions. If you look at our exchanges over the years, you will find that these differences play a decisive role—for example in my criticisms of his labor/interaction and system/lifeworld distinctions, in my softening of his notion of rational consensus to accommodate irreconcilable differences, or in the more pragmatic version of the theory of communicative rationality I sketched in the exchange with David Hoy in *Critical Theory*.[5] To put it in another way, Habermas is more sanguine than I am concerning the extent to which the power of the classical ideas of Reason, Truth, and Justice can be preserved through reconstructing them in a universal pragmatics. That faith is, of course, a chief source of his greatness and of his irreplaceability in the present intellectual context.

Are there any elements of Habermas's early work, which he himself seems to have abandoned, but which you would still like to retain in your own thinking? We have especially in mind the emancipatory potential of hermeneutic reflection as it is stressed in Knowledge and Human Interests.

I do think that element is extremely important and am happy to see that it is again playing a role in Habermas's thought. It was occluded for a while by his focus on discourse ethics, which was in reality a discourse *morality* in the current sense of that distinction. But in recent years, starting with the essays in *Justification and Application*,[6] he has resuscitated concern with the specifically ethical dimension, in both personal and political life. Thus his categories of "ethical-existential" and "ethical-political" reflection and discourse provide points of reference, I think, for reappropriating and developing some of those earlier concerns.

As to other things, I think it is very important today for critical theory to get back in touch with its Marxist roots. "Iron laws" of political economy are emerging again as a central issue, this time at a global level, as in the period of national industrialization. This presents enormous problems of social dislocation, cultural degradation, political disempowerment, and just plain misery. Once again, "all that is solid again melts into air, all that is sacred profaned" and so on. What critical theory needs most now is something like a new Marx and I do not think we can think of Habermas in that way. What is more likely in the present organization of intellectual life is a new tradition of critical political economy. But that is not likely to be accomplished by philosophers.

You have criticized Habermas for drawing too uncritically on systems theory. Do you still see a democratic deficit in this aspect of Habermas's work? Does this appropriation of systems theory set unnecessary limits on the possibilities of democratizing the economy?

I think Habermas has since reversed himself on certain aspects of the system/lifeworld scheme of *The Theory of Communicative Action* as it was applied to the state apparatus. In *Between Facts and Norms,* he allows for a certain democratization of administrative initiatives—for instance, measures guaranteeing the participation of those affected in the process of implementing government programs. In regard to the economy, however, he is still skeptical of direct democratization and calls instead for indirect steering measures. Incidentally, this was not always his position. He changed his mind on this in the mid-1970s, not as a whim, but after studying several different schemes of self-organization (Yugoslavia, council organizations, and so on). He just came to the conclusion that it could not work. That meant that we would have to think about how we could live with the market.

My own view, which is far from being that of an expert in such matters, is that, as in the national case, effective centralization and effective politicization of the global economy are likely to go hand in hand. As long as no one seems to be in charge—as long as there is a deficit of recognized international laws, bodies, and agencies controlling the global economy—it will be difficult to gain a focus for efforts to politicize it. But that will come, inevitably I think, and then, it seems to me, one could reasonably hope for the development of some form of mixed economy on a global scale. I don't think Habermas would disagree.

Habermas's accommodation of systems theory is seen by many as an abandonment of Marxism. You mentioned the need for a "new" Marx but what, in your opinion, should critical theory retain from the "old" Marx?

Well, it should retain the critique of political economy as a general project. I never read the systems theory aspect of the theory of communicative action as an abandonment of Marxism. Marx was, in many ways, the first systems theorist of the capitalist economy amid the capitalist state. Habermas was, I think, trying to reconstruct that systemic aspect of Marx and to modify it somewhat by giving the life-world—as investigated for instance, by sociology, social psychology, political theory, and cultural studies—a kind of independent status. Of course, a big difference is that Habermas doesn't think that the economic and administrative systemic aspects of society can be superseded by an association of free producers. There is, for him, no realm of freedom on the other side of these realms of necessity. But then Marx never came close to a convincing account of what that would be like. On the whole, I agree with Habermas's diagnosis that we have to learn to live with markets and bureaucracies and that the task is to domesticate them, to get as much democratic control of them as we can, even if sometimes only by indirect means. What we need to get from Marx, I think, is a refocusing of theoretical energies on the workings of the global economy. It is a huge error to adopt an almost exclusively cultural focus, as much critical theory does today. And it is not enough to just complement cultural studies with legal and political concerns such as the ones dominant in Habermas's recent work. But then, twentieth-century critical theory was always much better on culture and politics than it was on economics. Philosophically trained intellectuals are not likely to be the ones to deliver the type of economic analysis required. Only Marx could pull that off.

One of the characteristics of Habermas's thought that is often challenged today, and this he does share with Marx, is an anthropocentric ethics of nature. Do you see this as a challenge that must be faced? If so, how is it best to be done?

I must confess that I am not convinced by any of the radical ecological alternatives on offer. When cast in philosophical terms, they often amount to a re-ontologizing of matters that post-Kantian philosophy has, I think, definitely de-ontologized. The major exception to this development in recent philosophy, Heidegger's later philosophy and its offshoots, does not convince me either. So here I basically agree with Habermas about the unavoidable anthropocentrism of an ethics of nature. Where I disagree, perhaps, is that I want to allow for scientifically informed *philosophies* of nature as a whole and of our place in it. Here I find some of the recent work by biological systems theorists very interesting. It forces us to view things in terms of larger ecological systems of which we are a part. But it remains that *we* have to decide in what kind of an environment we want to try to live.

In Ideals and Illusions *you engage critically with the deconstructive turn in Heidegger, Derrida, Foucault, and Rorty.[7] What, in general, are lessons that critical theory can learn from such an engagement?*

I will respond to a very general question with a very general answer. Critical theory from Marx to Habermas has tended to be somewhat overconfident about the reach of reason and somewhat underconcerned with its limits. There are notable exceptions, of course, such as Adorno, but on the whole, the idea of emancipation has been represented as a realization of reason, that is, as self-consciousness, self-determination, and self-realization. In this figure of thought, what deconstructivists refer to as "the other of reason" typically comes up short. So one lesson that can be learned is to attend carefully to what is inevitably left out of any conceptualization. But there are more particular lessons to be learned as well, especially from Foucault, whose methodologically diverse forays—archaeological, genealogical, ethical—suggest a multiplicity of models for critical-theoretical research. There is no need to deploy them in as one-sidedly negative a way as he typically does. Often it is the ambiguity of rationalization processes that has to be articulated.

In recent essays you have discussed the problems that moral conflict raises for an account of democratic legitimacy. Could you tell us how your own proposals are designed to avoid the difficulties you have highlighted with Habermas's strong conception of a rational consensus?

Once reason is "detranscendentalized" and seen as deeply and inextricably implicated in history and tradition, language and culture, body and desire, practices and institutions, then the idea that there will be one right answer to ethical and political questions has to be superseded. That does not mean that "anything goes." But it does mean that we should expect regularly to encounter reasonable disagreement, even among well-informed and well-intentioned people, about the proper course of action, the right policy, the best program, and the like. If democratic legitimacy rests in the end on the informed and reasoned consent of the governed, reasonable disagreements of this sort call for modes of conflict resolution and decision making that do not rely on *substantive* consensus. If they involve, as they often do, differences in basic values, they will not always be susceptible to the sorts of compromise tailored to competing interests. In such cases, it seems, the *procedural* qualities of justice as fairness will be crucial, that is, some people will have to accept decisions arrived at as the outcomes of procedures that provided everyone involved a fair chance to be heard and to persuade others to their view. But I don't think that this can always be a matter of simple majority rule. Particularly in the case of permanent minorities, special accommodations may have to be made—as Kymlicka and others have argued. Accordingly, we have to think of practical political reason as striving for respectful accommodation as well as for rational consensus and fair compromise.

The Future of Critical Theory

We would now like to ask some questions regarding certain problems and prospects for the future development of critical theory. There seems to be a common perception, at least here in Europe, that Habermasian critical theory has become little more than a version of liberal constitutionalism. How does critical theory today differ from liberalism?

I think one has to read Habermas's work over the past two decades as one developing whole rather than reading his most recent work as a shift in position. That is to say, the version of constitutionalism developed in *Between Facts and Norms* has to be understood against the social-theoretical background painted in *The Theory of Communicative Action*. In fact, one might even say that from *The Structural Transformation of the Public Sphere* in 1962 to *Between Facts and Norms* in 1992, he was elaborating one and the same project: conceptualizing a genuinely democratic organization of society. But there is no doubt that he eventually came to believe—at the latest with *The Theory of Communicative Action*—that a direct democratization of *all* politically relevant social institutions, including economic ones, was not possible in large, complex societies. And this meant that we simply couldn't do away with markets and state administrations—as Marx sometimes suggested we could—but had to learn how to tame them, as Habermas put it. That shift brought him, it is true, closer to the traditional concerns of liberal constitutionalism. The question now becomes how best to secure a full schedule of basic rights for everyone, how to structure political institutions and processes so that individuals and groups have a say in the decisions that affect them, and how to design distributive and redistributive mechanisms to ensure that all have adequate resources to exercise their rights and pursue their life projects. This is, to be sure, less radical a project than the Marxian vision, but it provides a critical perspective on *all* actually existing forms of political liberalism. No existing societies come close to measuring up to these standards. So they still have critical bite.

Many of these concerns would be shared by liberals, like John Rawls, for example. How does Habermas differ from Rawls?

Well, Rawls's difference principle is a pretty strong redistributive principle, which could, as he says himself, countenance anything up to democratic socialism. The difference with Habermas is that Rawls does normative political theory in a contemporary Anglo-American style without a full social-theoretical background. That makes a huge difference in what they regard as the crucial issues. The second difference, which comes out in their recent exchange in the *Journal of Philosophy*, is that Habermas sees Rawls as privileging individual personal rights. I think this is true and we see it, for example, in "The Law of Peoples" where Rawls is willing to drop explicitly egalitarian or participatory concerns.[8] What Rawls wants to hold on to is a certain schedule of individual rights and this takes him in a very different direction to Habermas.

Given the perceived proximity of critical theory to contemporary liberalism do you think the tradition must now give up on its radical aspirations?

There is proximity in one sense but not in another. The ideas of the liberal tradition are certainly the raw material for this concept of social justice. But it is not the liberalism of the early modern period— not the liberalism of Locke, say—but liberalism informed by the democratic struggles since the eighteenth century and the struggle for social justice since the nineteenth century. The term liberalism has since come to cover everything from possessive individualism to social democracy and the distance between the poles, of course, makes a great deal of difference. Critical theorists should be careful not to talk as if it doesn't. As Habermas understands them, the ideas of personal, political, and social rights, their full legal institutionalization and procedural implementation could be used to conceptualize everything from social democracy to democratic socialism. And they place only the broadest formal constraints on individual and group experimentation with emancipated forms of life. I guess the question is—what's the alternative?

Habermas has characterized the task of philosophy in postmetaphysical terms. This rules out, some would say in a draconian manner, certain kinds of ontological speculation. Do you also see the need to defend this deflated conception of the tasks of philosophy?

In the late twentieth century, I think the burden of argument is on the other side; what specific forms of ontological speculation are we supposed to take seriously and why? So far as I can see, attempts to revive premodern forms, for instance in some versions of radical ecology, run immediately into the very problems to which metaphysical thought eventually succumbed in the modern period. That leaves, I suppose, the postmodern forms stemming largely from Heidegger. I do have considerable sympathy with efforts to raise the ontological presuppositions of thought and action to awareness—becoming more conscious of our embeddedness and embodiment as it were. But I think of that more as a radicalization of the critical project started by Kant than as a return to speculative metaphysics. It's not so much that I feel a need to defend myself against the latter—I don't. It's just that I haven't found any of the recent efforts in that vein very convincing. But perhaps you have something specific in mind?

Besides Heidegger, the German idealist tradition comes to mind. We can consider this tradition as engaged not so much in proposing specific validity claims, or in laying the foundations for scientific theories of nature, as in speculating on what it is to see nature "aright."

I am more sympathetic with the latter than with the specifically Heideggerian versions. There was a time when I was thoroughly enthused about the idea of redoing a Hegelian or Schellingian philosophy of nature in a contemporary context. The point would be to work back through the science of our age. This would mean a philosophy of nature that is not done by disregarding science, or claiming that there is a whole different way of talking about nature that is deeper and that can ignore science. It would be a rereading of science in philosophical terminology. But that is an enormous enterprise. When I was in Germany somebody was attempting to do that with Hegel. I found it tremendously exciting—a sort of top-down reading of nature. To be sure, dealing as it does with *Geist*, such a project is not likely to satisfy a concern for a nonanthropomorphic conception of the ethics of nature. In the Hegelian case you would have to read all the way down the different orders of nature to the inorganic level, in terms of a whole different vocabulary. That would be a very interesting project. I even tried to convince a few graduate students to do it. I don't think anyone has done it yet, though I don't have anything against people trying.

Habermas himself seems to suggest that his conceptual framework draws on the Judeo-Christian religious tradition.⁹ What do you take to be the relationship between critical theory and religion?

I agree with Habermas that the proper medium of theory is reasoned discourse. Of course, in Habermas's hermeneutic forms, it can be used to critically-reflectively work up and work over culturally transmitted ideas of truth, justice, freedom, emancipation, the good life, and so on, including those transmitted by different religious traditions and kept alive in various and diverse cultural formations. But once you appeal to such ideas *as* religious, for example, as vouchsafed by revelation or religious experience, or what have you, I think you leave the realm of theory, which I understand as addressed to a potentially universal audience. On the other hand, theory is not the whole of life and there is room in the latter for lots of things that don't belong to the former.

Critical theory has always understood itself to be more than just an academic discipline. How do you think that it can avoid the danger of academic isolation?

Critical social theory in the twentieth century *has*, in fact, been closely tied to academic work. Most of its practitioners—from Hork-heimer, Adorno, and Marcuse to Habermas, Wellmer, and Honneth have spent much of their working lives connected, in one way or another, with universities and research institutes. The only ways I can see for it to keep from being completely absorbed into the academic routine are the familiar ones, that is, on the one hand, to resist the enormous pressures of disciplinary specialization to which professionalization exposes academics—to keep our eyes on the problems that interest us and then let the disciplinary chips fall where they may—and, on the other hand, to maintain vital contact with the progressive social movements of the day. Feminist theory, race theory, gay and lesbian studies, postcolonial studies and the like have recently been better at this than critical social theory—though they too have had their problems with too much distance from the lived forms of oppression they theorize. The Marxian tradition has been tied primarily to class politics, and in many industrialized countries, that form of politics has waned. In any case, new forms of politics have arisen and there is a need constantly to develop critical theory so as to articulate the concerns of new social movements. That's in a way what Seyla Benhabib, Axel Honneth, and others have been trying to do recently.

What do you see as the main challenges facing critical theory today?

The main challenges, I think, come from the general sense of social and cultural exhaustion that pervades both theory and practice today, the general skepticism about theory in anything stronger than its ironic or deconstructive forms, and the general feeling of help-lessness in the face of impersonal forces and the fragmentation of life. These things militate against any kind of renewal of the enlightenment project, let alone one with the utopian impulses of critical theory. I don't think there's much one can do here as a theorist, except to try to understand and theorize these forces, and to relate them to the actual political concerns of the day.

Notes

This interview was conducted in Belfast, June 30, 1996.

1. *Knowledge and Human Interests*, trans. J. J. Shapiro (Boston: Beacon Press, 1971); *Toward a Rational Society*, trans. J. J. Shapiro (Boston: Beacon Press, 1970); *Theory and Practice*, trans. J. Viertel (Boston: Beacon Press, 1973); *The Structural Transformation of the Public Sphere*, trans. T. Burger (Cambridge: MIT Press, 1989).

2. Cambridge, Mass.: MIT Press, 1978.

3. "Reconciliation through the Public Use of Reason," and John Rawls, "Reply to Habermas," *Journal of Philosophy* 92 (1995): 109–131 and 132–180, respectively.

4. *Between Facts and Norms*, trans. W. Rehg (Cambridge: MIT Press, 1996).

5. David Couzens Hoy and Thomas McCarthy, *Critical Theory* (Oxford: Blackwell, 1994).

6. *Justification and Application*, trans. C. Cronin (Cambridge: Polity Press, 1993).

7. *Ideals and Illusions* (Cambridge: MIT Press, 1991).

8. John Rawls, "The Law of Peoples," in *On Human Rights*, ed. S. Shute and S. Hurley (New York: Basic, 1993), 41–82.

9. *Postmetaphysical Thinking*, trans. W. M. Hohengarten (Cambridge: Polity Press, 1992), 15.

Bibliography of the Works and Translations of Thomas McCarthy

Book-length Monographs

The Critical Theory of Jürgen Habermas. Cambridge: MIT Press; London: Hutchinson, 1978. Paperback edition, Cambridge: MIT Press, 1981; Cambridge, Engl.: Polity, 1984. German edition, *Kritik der Verständigungsverhältnisse.* Frankfurt am Main: Suhrkamp, 1980; expanded edition, 1989. Spanish edition, *La Teoria Critica de Jürgen Habermas.* Madrid: Tecnos, 1987.

Ideals and Illusions: On Reconstruction and Deconstruction in Contemporary Critical Theory. Cambridge: MIT Press, 1991. Spanish edition, *Ideales e Ilusiones.* Madrid: Tecnos, 1992. German edition, expanded, *Ideale und Illusionen.* Frankfurt am Main: Suhrkamp, 1993.

With David Hoy. *Critical Theory.* Oxford: Blackwell, 1994.

Edited Works

With F. Dallmayr. *Understanding and Social Inquiry.* Notre Dame: University of Notre Dame Press, 1977.

With K. Baynes and J. Bohman. *After Philosophy: End or Transformation?* Cambridge: MIT Press, 1986.

With A. Honneth, C. Offe, and A. Wellmer. *Zwischenbetrachtungen im Prozess der Aufklärung.* Frankfurt am Main: Suhrkamp, 1989. English edition in two volumes: *Philosophical Interventions in the Unfinished Project of Enlightenment* and *Cultural-Political Interventions in the Unfinished Project of Enlightenment.* Cambridge: MIT Press, 1992.

Translations of Books

Habermas, J. *Legitimation Crisis.* Boston: Beacon, 1975.

Habermas, J. *Communication and the Evolution of Society.* Boston: Beacon, 1979.

Habermas, J. *The Theory of Communicative Action*. Boston: Beacon Press. Vol. 1, *Reason and the Rationalization of Society* (1984). Vol. 2, *Lifeworld and System: A Critique of Functionalist Reason* (1987).

Articles, Book Chapters, and Introductions

"Logic, Mathematics, and Ontology in Husserl." *The Journal of the British Society for Phenomenology* 3 (1972): 158–164.

"Der Wissenschaftsbegriff im westlichen Denken." *Sowjetsystem und demokratische Gesellschaft*. Freiburg: Herder, 1972. English edition, "The Concept of Science in Western Thought." In *Marxism, Communism and Western Society*, 274–286. Freiburg: Herder, 1973.

With K. Ballestrem. "Thesen zur Begründung einer kritischen Theorie der Gesellschaft." *Zeitschrift für allgemeine Wissenschaftstheorie*, 3/1 (1972): 49–62.

"On Misunderstanding Understanding." *Theory and Decision* 3 (1973): 351–370.

"A Theory of Communicative Competence." *Philosophy of the Social Sciences* 3 (1973): 135–156. Reprinted in *Critical Sociology*, edited by P. Connerton, 470–497. Harmondsworth: Penguin, 1976, and in *Schools of Thought in Sociology: Critical Sociology*, edited by L. Ray, 221–242. Brookfield, Vt.: Edward Elgar, 1990.

"The Problem of Rationality in Social Anthropology." *Stony Brook Studies in Philosophy* 1 (1974): 1–21.

"The Operation Called *Verstehen*: Towards a Redefinition of the Problem," *Boston Studies in the Philosophy of Science* 20 (1974): 167–193. (Earlier version of "On Misunderstanding Understanding".)

"Introduction" to *Legitimation Crisis* by J. Habermas, vii–xxiv. Boston: Beacon, 1975.

"History and Evolution: On the Changing Relation of Theory to Practice in the Work of Jürgen Habermas." In *Proceedings of the 1978 Biennial Meeting of the Philosophy of Science Association, PSA 1978*, vol. 2, edited by P. Asquith and I. Hacking, 397–423. Spanish translation in *Rivista Mexicana de Sociología*, 45 (1983): 1179–1207.

"Introduction" to *Communication and the Evolution of Society*, by J. Habermas, vii–xxiv. Boston: Beacon, 1979.

"Rationality and Discourse." In *Rationality Today*, edited by T. F. Geraets, 441–447. Ottawa: University of Ottawa Press, 1979.

"Rationality and Relativism: Habermas' 'Overcoming' of Hermeneutics." In *Habermas: Critical Debates*, edited by J. Thompson and D. Held, 57–78. London: Macmillan; Cambridge: MIT Press, 1982.

"Introduction" to *The Theory of Communicative Action* by J. Habermas, vol. 1, v–xxxvii. Boston: Beacon, 1984.

"Legitimation Problems in Advanced Capitalism," in *Legitimacy and the State*, edited by W. Connelly, 156–179. New York: New York University Press, 1984. Reprint of chapter 5 of *The Critical Theory of Jürgen Habermas* (1978).

Bibliography of Thomas McCarthy

"Reflections on Rationalization in the Theory of Communicative Action." *Praxis International* 4 (1984): 177–191. Reprinted in *Habermas and Modernity*, edited by R. J. Bernstein, 176–191. Cambridge, Engl.: Polity; Cambridge: MIT, 1985, and in *The Frankfurt School: Critical Assessments*, edited by J. Bernstein. London: Routledge, 1994.

"Complexity and Democracy, or the Seducements of Systems Theory." *New German Critique* 35 (1985): 27–53. Reprinted in *Communicative Action*, edited by A. Honneth and H. Joas, 119–139. Cambridge: MIT Press; Cambridge, Engl.: Polity Press, 1991. Expanded German version in *Kommunikatives Handeln*, edited by A. Honneth and H. Joas, 177–215. Frankfurt am Main: Suhrkamp, 1986. French translation in *Reseaux* 34 (1989): 51–77.

"Philosophie und Wissenssoziologie: Zur Aktualität der kritischen Theorie." In *Die Frankfurter Schule und die Folgen*, edited by A. Honneth and A. Wellmer, 113–127. Berlin: de Gruyter, 1986. Serbo-Croatian translation in *Theoria* (1985): 99–112.

"Philosophical Foundations of Political Theology." In *Civil Religion and Political Theology*, edited by L. Rouner, 23–40. Notre Dame: University of Notre Dame Press, 1986. German translation in *Babylon* 6 (1989): 7–21.

"Introduction" to *The Philosophical Discourse of Modernity*, by J. Habermas, vii–xvii. Cambridge: MIT Press, 1987.

"Scientific Rationality and the 'Strong Program' in the Sociology of Knowledge." In *Construction and Constraint: The Shaping of Scientific Rationality*, edited by E. McMullin, 75–95. Notre Dame: University of Notre Dame Press, 1988.

"Contra Relativism: A Thought-Experiment." *Zeitschrift für Philosophische Forschung* 43 (1989): 318–330. Reprinted in *Relativism: Interpretation and Confrontation*, edited by M. Krausz, 256–271. Notre Dame: University of Notre Dame Press, 1989. Spanish translation in *Politica Y Sociedad* 2 (1989): 89–98.

"Philosophy and Social Practice: Avoiding the Ethnocentric Predicament." In *Zwischenbetrachtungen im Prozess der Aufklärung*, edited by A. Honneth, T. McCarthy, C. Offe, and A. Wellmer, 190–209. Frankfurt am Main: Suhrkamp, 1989.

"The Politics of the Ineffable: Derrida's Deconstructionism." *The Philosophical Forum* 21 (1989–1990): 146–168. Reprinted in *Hermeneutics and Critical Theory in Ethics and Politics*, edited by M. Kelly, 146–168. Cambridge: MIT Press, 1990. Spanish translation, *La Balsa de la Medusa* 12 (1989): 17–42.

"Private Irony and Public Decency: Richard Rorty's New Pragmatism." *Critical Inquiry* 16 (1990): 355–370. Spanish translation, *La Balsa de la Medusa* 8 (1988): 53–69. French translation in *Lire Rorty*, edited by J.-P. Cometti, 77–100. Combas, France: Editions de l'éclat, 1992.

"Ironist Theory as a Vocation: A Response to Rorty." *Critical Inquiry* 16 (1990): 644–655. French translation in *Lire Rorty*, edited by J.-P. Cometti, 195–212. Combas, France: Editions de l'éclat, 1992.

"The Critique of Impure Reason: Foucault and the Frankfurt School." *Political Theory* 18 (1990): 437–469. Reprinted in *Rethinking Power*, edited by T. Wartenberg, 121–148. Albany: SUNY Press, 1992, and in *Critique and Power*, edited by M. Kelly, 243–282. Cambridge: MIT Press, 1994. Spanish translation, *Isegoria* 1 (1990): 49–84. Japanese translation in *Iwanami Lectures on Modern Thought*, vol. 8, 155–213. Tokyo: Iwanami Shoten, 1994.

"After the Linguistic Turn: Critical Theory versus the New Pragmatism." In *Wirkungen Kritischer Theorie und Kritisches Denken*, edited by Ph.v. Engeldorp Gastelaars, Sl. Magala, and O. Preuss, 99–116. The Hague: Universitaire Pers Rotterdam, 1990; and in *Critical Theory Today*, edited by Ph.v. Engeldorp Gastelaars, Sl. Magala, and O. Preuss, 105–122. The Hague: University Press Rotterdam, 1990.

"Heidegger and Critical Theory: The First Encounter." In *Martin Heidegger: Politics, Art, and Technology*, edited by K. Harries and Ch. Jamme, 210–224. New York: Holmes & Meier, 1994. German translation in *Martin Heidegger: Kunst-Politik-Technik*, edited by Ch. Jamme and K. Harries , 279–293. Munich: Wilhelm Fink, 1992.

"Deconstruction and Reconstruction in Contemporary Critical Theory." *Canadian Journal of Philosophy*, supplementary vol. 19, *Reconstructing Philosophy? New Essays in Metaphilosophy*, edited by J. Couture and K. Nielsen, 247–264. Calgary, Alberta: University of Calgary Press, 1993. Earlier version in *Modernitet: Differensiering og Rasjonalisering*, edited by N. Gilje, 75–93. Bergen: Ariadne, 1992. Spanish translation in *La Balsa de la Medusa* 21 (1992): 19–33.

"Practical Discourse and the Relation between Morality and Politics." In *Habermas and the Public Sphere*, edited by C. Calhoun, 51–72. Cambridge: MIT Press, 1992. Reprinted in *Modernitet: Differensiering og Rasjonalisering*, edited by N. Gilje, 1–25. Bergen: Ariadne, 1992, and in *Revue Internationale de Philosophie* 49 (1995): 461–481. Spanish translation in *Jürgen Habermas: Moralidad, ética y politica*, edited by M. Herrera Lima, 147–171. Mexico: Alianza, 1992.

"Doing the Right Thing in Cross-Cultural Representation." *Ethics* 102 (1992): 635–649.

"The Idea of a Critical Theory and Its Relation to Philosophy." In *On Max Horkheimer: New Perspectives*, edited by S. Benhabib, W. Bonss, and J. McCole, 127–151. Cambridge: MIT Press, 1993.

"Multikultureller Universalismus: Variationen zu einigen Themen Kants." In *Zur Verteidigung der Vernunft*, edited by Ch. Menke and M. Seel, 26–45. Frankfurt am Main: Suhrkamp, 1993.

"On the Communicative Dimension of Social Practice." In *Artifacts, Representations, and Social Practice*, edited by C. Gould and R. Cohen, 83–102. Dordrecht: Kluwer, 1993. Reprinted in *El trabajo filosofico de hoy en el continente*, edited by C. Gutierrez, 131–145. Bogotás: ABC, 1995. Also in *Beyond Theory*, edited by S. Toulmin and B. Gustavsen, 159–177. Philadelphia: John Benjamin's Publishing, 1996. Spanish translation, *Isegoria* 8 (1993): 65–84.

"Kantian Constructivism and Reconstructivism: Rawls and Habermas in Dialogue." *Ethics* 105 (1994): 44–63. Reprinted in the following: *Chinese Social Sciences Quarterly* (Winter 1994): 141–158. *Public Reason*, edited by F. D'Agostino and G. Gans, Aldershot, Engl.: Ashgate, 1998. *The Philosophy of Rawls*. New York: Garland, 2000. Spanish translation in *La Filosofia Moral y Politica de Juergen Habermas*, edited by J. A. Gimbernat, 35–62. Madrid: Biblioteca Nueva, 1997.

Bibliography of Thomas McCarthy

"Legitimacy and Diversity: Dialectical Reflections on Analytical Distinctions." *Protosoziologie* 6 (1994): 199–228. Reprinted in the following: *Cardozo Law Review* 17 (1996): 1083–1125. *Rechtstheorie* 27 (1996): 329–365. *Habermas on Law and Democracy: Critical Exchanges,* edited by A. Arato and M. Rosenfeld, 115–153. Berkeley: University of California Press, 1998.

"Enlightenment and the Idea of Public Reason." *European Journal of Philosophy* 3 (1995): 242–256. Reprinted in the following: *Proceedings of the Eighth International Kant Congress,* vol. 1, part 3, 1049–1064. Milwaukee: Marquette University Press, 1995. *Theorie und Praxis,* edited by K. Ballestrem and H. Ottman, 59–76. Berlin: Duncker and Humblot, 1996. *Questioning Ethics: Contemporary Debates in Philosophy,* edited by R. Kearney and M. Dooley, 164–180. London: Routledge, 1999.

"The Philosophy of the Limit and Its Other." *Constellations* 2 (1995): 175–188.

"A Reply to Georgia Warnke and David Hoy." *Philosophy and Social Criticism* 22 (1996): 99–108.

"Philosophy and Critical Theory: A Reply to Richard Rorty and Seyla Benhabib." *Constellations* 3 (1996): 95–103.

"Critical Theory and Postmodernism: A Response to David Hoy." In *Handbook of Critical Theory,* edited by D. Rasmussen, 340–368. Oxford: Blackwell, 1996. Reprinted from *Critical Theory.*

"On The Idea of a Reasonable Law of Peoples." In *Perpetual Peace: Essays on Kant's Cosmopolitan Ideal,* edited by J. Bohman and M. Lutz-Bachmann, 201–217. Cambridge: MIT Press, 1997. German translation in *Frieden durch Recht: Kants Friedensidee und das Problem einer neuen Weltordnung,* 200–219. Frankfurt am Main: Surkamp, 1996.

"On the Pragmatics of Communicative Reason." Japanese translation of chapter 3 of *Critical Theory.* In *The Latest American Work on Critical Theory,* edited by M. Jay, 31–50. Tokyo: Kochi Shobo, 1997.

"Habermas." In *A Companion to Continental Philosophy,* edited by S. Critchley and W. R. Schroeder, 397–406. Malden, Mass.: Blackwell, 1998.

"Two Conceptions of Cosmopolitan Justice." In *Reconstituting Social Criticism,* edited by I. MacKenzie and S. O'Neill, 191–214. London: Macmillan; New York: St. Martin's, 1999. Spanish translation in *Isegoria* 16 (1997): 37–60.

"On Reconciling National Diversity and Cosmopolitan Unity." *Public Culture* 11 (1999): 175–208.

"Political Philosophy and the Problem of Race." In *Die Öffentlichkeit der Vernunft und die Vernunft der Öffentlichkeit,* edited by K. Günther and L. Wingert. Frankfurt am Main: Suhrkamp, 2001.

"Political Philosophy and Racial Injustice: From Normative to Critical Theory." Forthcoming in *Political Theory.*

Contributors

Joel Anderson is Assistant Professor of Philosophy at Washington University in St. Louis. He has published articles on Hegel, Charles Taylor, Harry Frankfurt, and Habermas, as well as, most recently, "The 'Third Generation' of the Frankfurt School," *Intellectual History Newsletter* (fall, 2000). He is the translator of *The Struggle for Recognition* by Axel Honneth (MIT Press, 1996) and is currently writing a book that develops a social conception of personal autonomy.

Kenneth Baynes is Associate Professor of Philosophy at the State University of New York at Stony Brook. He is the author of *The Normative Grounds of Social Criticism: Kant, Rawls, and Habermas* (SUNY Press, 1992) and co-editor with Rene von Schomberg of *Discourse and Democracy: Essays on Habermas's "Between Facts and Norms"* (SUNY Press, 2001). He also edits the SUNY Series in Social and Political Thought.

Seyla Benhabib is the Eugene Meyer Professor of Political Science and Philosophy at Yale University. Her publications include *Critique, Norm, and Utopia* (Columbia University Press, 1986), *Situating the Self* (Routledge, 1992), *The Reluctant Modernism of Hannah Arendt* (Sage, 1996), and *Democratic Equality and Cultural Diversity* (Princeton University Press, 2001; German edition, 1999). Currently she is working on the philosophical and constitutional issues that underlie the debates on citizenship and immigration.

James Bohman is Danforth Professor of Philosophy at Saint Louis University. He is author of *Public Deliberation: Pluralism, Complexity, and Democracy* (MIT Press, 1996) and *New Philosophy of Social Science: Problems of Indeterminacy* (MIT Press, 1991). He has recently edited *Deliberative Democracy* (with William Rehg, MIT Press, 1997) and *Perpetual Peace: Essays on Kant's Cosmopolitan Ideal* (with Matthias Lutz-Bachmann, MIT Press, 1997). He is currently writing a book on cosmopolitan democracy.

Andrew Buchwalter chairs the Department of Philosophy at the University of North Florida. He is the author of *Culture and Democracy: Social and Ethical Issues in Public Support for the Arts and Humanities* (Westview, 1992) and the translator of *Observations on the "Spiritual Situation of the Age,"* edited by Jürgen Habermas (MIT Press, 1985). Currently he is completing a book on the contemporary significance of Hegel's political thought.

Barbara Fultner is Associate Professor of Philosophy at Denison University. She has published in the areas of critical theory and the philosophy of language and is working on a book on social pragmatist theories of meaning. She has recently published a translation of Jürgen Habermas's *On the Pragmatics of Social Interaction* (MIT Press, 2001).

Jürgen Habermas is Professor Emeritus at the University of Frankfurt and Professor of Philosophy at Northwestern University. He has written extensively in the areas of critical theory, moral-political theory, and the pragmatic theory of language. His recent works include *Between Facts and Norms* (MIT Press, 1996), *The Inclusion of the Other* (MIT Press, 1998), *On the Pragmatics of Communication* (MIT Press, 1998), and *Wahrheit und Rechtfertigung* (Suhrkamp, 1999).

Joseph Heath holds a Canada Research Chair in Philosophy at the Université de Montréal. He is the author of *Communicative Action and Rational Choice* (MIT Press, 2001).

Axel Honneth is Professor of Philosophy at the University of Frankfurt and Director of the Institute for Social Research in Frankfurt am Main. His translated works include *The Critique of Power* (MIT Press, 1991), *The Struggle for Recognition* (Polity, 1995), and *The Fragmented World of the Social* (SUNY Press, 1995).

Johanna Meehan was a student of Thomas McCarthy in the early 1980s, and is now Associate Professor Philosophy at Grinnell College. She is the editor of *Feminists Read Habermas: Gendering the Subject of Discourse* (Routledge, 1997) and has written articles on critical theory, feminism, child development, and the work of Arendt. Currently she is working on a book with the tentative title of *Playing for Keeps: Essays on the Self.*

Shane O'Neill is a Reader in the School of Politics, Queen's University Belfast. He is the author of *Impartiality in Context: Grounding Justice in a Pluralist World* (SUNY Press, 1997) and co-editor of *Reconstituting Social Criticism: Political Morality in an Age of Scepticism* (Macmillan and St. Martin's Press, 1999).

David M. Rasmussen is Professor of Philosophy at Boston College. He is Founder and Editor-in-Chief of the *Philosophy and Social Criticism* journal and book series. He has authored several books, including *Mythic-Symbolic Language and Philosophical Anthropology: A Constructive Interpretation of the Thought of Paul Ricoeur* (Martinus Nijhoff, 1971), *The Narrative Path: The Later Works of Paul Ricoeur* (with Peter Kemp, MIT Press, 1989), and *Reading Habermas* (MIT Press, 1990);

he also is the editor of *The Handbook of Critical Theory* (Blackwell, 1996). He is currently writing a book entitled *Paradigms of Public Reason.*

William Rehg is Associate Professor of Philosophy at Saint Louis University. He is the author of *Insight and Solidarity: The Discourse Ethics of Jürgen Habermas* (University of California Press, 1994), the translator of Habermas's *Between Facts and Norms* (MIT Press, 1996), and coeditor, with James Bohman, of *Deliberative Democracy* (MIT Press, 1997). His current research interests include discourse ethics, science and technology studies, and argumentation theory.

Richard Rorty has taught philosophy at Wellesley College, Princeton University, and the University of Virginia, and is now Professor of Comparative Literature at Stanford University. His books include *Consequences of Pragmatism* (University of Minnesota Press, 1982), *Contingency, Irony and Solidarity* (Cambridge University Press, 1989), *Achieving Our Country* (Harvard University Press, 1998), and *Philosophy and Social Hope* (Penquin, 1999).

Nicholas H. Smith is senior lecturer in philosophy at Macquarie University in Sydney, Australia. He is the author of *Strong Hermeneutics: Contingency and Moral Identity* (Routledge, 1997) and *Charles Taylor* (Polity, forthcoming).

Georgia Warnke is Professor of Philosophy at University of California, Riverside. She has written on hermeneutics and critical theory; her latest book is *Legitimate Differences: Interpretation in the Abortion Controversy and Other Public Debates* (University of California Press, 1999).

Joel Whitebook is a practicing psychoanalyst in New York City and a member of the Faculty of the Columbia University Center for Psychoanalytic Training and Research. He is the author of *Perversion and Utopia: A Study in Psychoanalysis and Critical Theory* (MIT Press, 1995) and "Weighty Objects: Adorno's Kant-Freud Interpretation," which will appear in the *Cambridge Companion to Adorno.* His current research interests include the theory of the subject, the limits of the linguistic turn, and the "hermeneutics of suspicion" and critique, genealogy, and sublimation. He is currently completing a book on Freud and Foucault for MIT Press.

Index